ARIZONA CHARLIE

A Legendary Cowboy, Klondike Stampeder and Wild West Showman

Author—Mrs. Jean Beach King
Foreword—Mr. Don Dedera
Editor/Publisher—Dr. John L. Myers
Heritage Publishers
Phoenix, Arizona

A Heritage Publishers Book/April 1989

Dr. John L. Myers
Heritage Publishers
4633 N. 30th Place
Phoenix, Arizona 85016
(602) 468-9143

Printed in the
United States of America

Library of Congress Cataloging
88-83842

King, Jean Beach
Arizona Charlie
Includes index.
Cowboy, Alaska Gold Rush
Wild West Showman
ISBN 0-929690-04-4

Arizona Charlie carries the reader back in time to the era of Territorial Days and early Statehood. His worldwide travels and fame as a legendary cowboy give the reader a better appreciation of this period in the history of our state. This story, written by Jean Beach King, is a delightful tribute to Arizona Charlie.

Rose Mofford, Governor
State of Arizona

Arizona Charlie covers the period from 1860 to 1932. The research, manuscripts, and notes include words, names, and places which were often spelled differently. This publication has attempted to spell words exactly as they appeared. Little or no attempt was made to change the spelling unless the correct spelling appeared more appropriate. Reference credit was provided where and when known. All references are listed in the bibliography.

Other Books and Family Histories by Heritage Publishers, Inc.

Salt River Pima-Maricopa Indians
More Than Most
John Newton Norris
Darlene and Cecil King
The State of Arizona Governors
Nicole Bailey Maddux
The Wheelers
Robert Gryder: Reflections
The History of the University of Nevada Las Vegas—
Department of Intercollegiate Athletics: The First Thirty Years
Mildred and Elzie Myers
The Gerringers
The Cunninghams
Stephen John Demos
Risto and Dragich Masonich Vucichevich
The Bill Long Family

In Memory of

Maggie Meadows Beach

my grandmother who, at the tender age of 13, valiantly defended the family homestead against an attack by hostile Apache Indians;

and

Thomas Beach, Jr.

my father who, tried to interest me in this story. Then, when he was gone, it all became so precious. His voice still inspires me today.

TABLE OF CONTENTS

Chapter

ACKNOWLEDGMENTS

This book was published with the significant assistance and special interest shown by my first cousin, Mr. Ernest Becker, Sr., Las Vegas, Nevada. He and his family are the owners of the new casino, "Arizona Charlie's," opened in April, 1988 in Las Vegas in commemoration of Abraham Henson Meadows, "Arizona Charlie."

A special thanks to family members: Mr. Don Meadows for use of his notes, letters, and papers; Mrs. Lucille Greenblat for her mother's collection (Ida Gregory); Mrs. Thelma Findley for her mother's papers and documents (Sadie Connelly); Mrs. Marjorie Ormsby (deceased) for her mother's collection (Pearl Milam Lewis); Dr. Lee Fitzhugh and Mr. Ron Loving for pictures, letters, and genealogy; Meryal Woodsen for her recollections; Mr. Mobley Milam for a very rare program; Mr. George Meadows (deceased) for his memories; Mr. Mack O. Meadows, Helen Mills, Victor Meador, and Ray McCutchen, genealogy; and John Beach, photos.

Mrs. Alice Weeks, though now deceased, of Salem, Oregon, was a magnificent discovery. She filled in the loopholes regarding the very short marriage of her mother, Marion Mae Murray, and Charles Meadows. Thanks also go to her daughter, Mrs. Vivian Cady, for her recent help.

Special thanks go to Mr. John Carlock, of Washington, D. C., and Vernon, Arizona, for his continued interest and contributions, and for personally introducing me to the Arizona Historical Society personnel in Tucson. Thank you, Mrs. Mary Ellen Swietzer, of Payson, Arizona, for chauffeuring me to the Tonto Rim and to the location of the Meadows family ranch.

A very special thank you goes to Mr. David Kiefer, of the local Granada Hills Library, who with the help of the Metropolitan Cooperative Library System, and the Southern California Answering Service (SCAN), did so many searches for me over a long period of years. David's help was tremendous.

Sincere thanks go to Conrad and Bonny Boyce, of Victoria, B. C., for their help and their dedicated effort in bringing about the Arizona Charlie Memorial in Yuma, Arizona. I also want to thank Linda Bierlmeier, of Parks, Canada, Dawson City, Yukon, and Mike and Kathy Gates of Dawson City for their contributions; the Klondike and Yukon Visitor's Associations; and the Honorable Mayor of Dawson City, Peter Jenkins.

My thanks to Mr. James Rogers, for his letters concerning his father, Will, and Charles Meadows; to Thelma Bonney Towle, Don Russell, Dan Thrapp, Pierre Berton, Annie Mitchell, Robert Cunningham, Jr., author-historians; and to Dorothy Middleton and Melanie Mayer.

There were many from Yuma, Arizona who contributed their time and materials to my project. Mr. Harvey Johnson of the Yuma Historical Society so willingly opened the Century House Museum for me on a Sunday; Mrs. Lavena Coffeen, who donated material and a personal interview and recollections about her neighbor, Charles Meadows; Mr. Leo K. Murphy (deceased); Mr. Ernie Johannson; Mr. Cecil Huling; Joan Heida, of the Yuma Public Library; Elizabeth DeWitt of the Yuma Historical Society; Ruby Adair; Drusilla Hazelton of Tonopah, Arizona; and Mr. Ira Murphy and Mrs. Marguerite Noble, of Payson, Arizona; and Mr. Ray Lewis (deceased), Yuma.

Last, but not least, my sincere appreciation is extended to Mr. Sol Stember, an author, who shared a continued interest in my subject, and who gave my manuscript some critique.

TABLE OF PHOTOGRAPHS

Arizona Charlie

Foreword

The Grassroots Historian

All over America there are tens of millions of citizens who do nothing to preserve, interpret and publish the significant history of their times.

Packets of old letters are casually pitched into the fireplace. Photographic albums are sent off to the dump. The memories of aging grandparents are allowed to fade to finality.

But fortunately there are a faithful, relative few, the likes of Jean Beach King. Within her, an instinct insisted that she do her very best to conserve the adventures and images of her extraordinary great-uncle, Arizona Charlie.

"The switch turned on inside me in 1979," said Jean recently. "Something would not let me allow Arizona Charlie to vanish into the sunset. Primarily, I think, I wanted the future generations of my own family to know about their colorful forebear. And I wanted the greater world to have access to the record of Charlie's deeds."

So for most of her waking hours over a decade, Mrs. King propelled herself down Charlie's sometimes cold trail. She wrote hundreds of letters, and spun through 83 rolls of newspaper microfilm. She visited Charlie's scenes of bloody violence, high drama, devastating loss. She begged for help from strangers in foreign lands where Charlie's boots had trod. And she assembled a compelling portfolio of authentic pictures relating to Abraham Henson Meadows who lived in the American West from 1860 to 1932.

"Grassroots historians," is a term coined by Dr. C. L. Sonnichsen for people like Jean Beach King. Dr. Sonnichsen, the author of *Roy Bean, the Law West of the Pecos,* and dean of Southwestern historians, wrote: "The fact that we have a recorded past distinguishes us from the other animals and gives us something in common with the hosts in heaven, where St. Peter is said to keep careful records. With a past, we can profit from our mistakes and become civilized."

Grassroots historians generally have only a span of human memory of about 150 years with which to work. That is the period of oral history transferable over six generations. That was about all that was available to the world's first historian, Herodotus. In the Fifth Century B.C. he walked the battlefields and interviewed survivors and reported upon the Persian Wars.

Before Herodotus the human record was muddled by amusing tall tales, superstitious myths, and legendary interventions of numerous gods.

"What actually happened?" Herodotus demanded to know. And that's what he wrote down.

In that tradition today, there prospers a booming international, largely amateur revival of oral, family grassroots history. The Nashville, Tennessee-based American Association for State and Local history counts 6,000 member institutions. The authors of *Oral History: A Guide for Teachers,* state: "Historians, folklorists, and other educational and religious groups now recognize the importance of preserving the recollections of people about the past. The recorded memories of famous and common folk alike provide a vital complement to textbook history, bringing the past to life through the stories of those who lived it."

Arizona Charlie certainly was not "common folk." In a day when international travel was the luxury of the rich and royal, this Arizona pioneer cowboy travelled to Australia and New Zealand, Burma and India, the Philippines and Japan, England, France, and Scotland, Mexico and Alaska. He met Rudyard Kipling, Jack London, Buffalo Bill, Annie Oakley and Zane Grey. He was on hand for the birth of a genuine American sport: rodeo. Between the time he was born in a covered wagon in California and died in a snowstorm in Yuma, Arizona, Charlie Meadows saw the elephant.

His grand-niece has gathered up a variegated herd of facts, memories and documents. In becoming modesty she makes no claim to be a professional historian, rather: "I simply am the kind of person who cannot leave something undone. Charlie's life history was not done, and I had to do it."

Critics beware—if you can question a fact or challenge a conclusion in this work, keep your comment in perspective. I, myself, do not agree with every understanding of details of the Pleasant Valley War and the Indian uprisings of Tonto Basin.

But the overriding reality is that Jean Beach King has brought together in an interesting text a mass of material about an authentic Western character. Thanks to her, Arizona Charlie can belong to us all.

Don Dedera
Phoenix, Arizona

PROLOGUE

"Arizona Charlie" was a genuine Western idol of an age that has turned to legend. Born during the Civil War period when the cowboy first appeared on the dusty horizon, Charlie was true to America's boldest legend and actually "shot it out with the Indians," broke wild horses, lassoed wild bears, and lived his life with exuberance and passionate gusto.

This authentic cowboy basked in the blazing sun for a mere generation, but in that short interlude, Arizona Charlie, the "world's most persistent rainbow chaser," packed in enough thrills and adventure to "stagger a sober man's imagination."

Disdaining the commonplace of life, Charlie was the living type of dime-novel hero. Self confident and gregarious by nature, he was a born leader who led a life-long quest filled with excitement. Utterly without fear and thirsting for new frontiers, he was forever seeking fame, fortune, and fast action.

Charlie toiled as a rancher; scouted for the government; fought bravely against Indians; amazed the world's audiences as a master showman, broadswordsman, and bullfighter. Charlie lusted after gold in the Klondike stampede; he wrote with a gift and sometimes published. He was a rodeo great known as the "King of the Cowboys" and the "Winchester Wizard." Charlie became the champion lassoist of the world and later headed his own Wild West Show. Charlie was flamboyant, swashbuckling, six-foot-six and handsome enough to stir up the fillies in any corral. This goateed and moustached *vaquero* (cowboy) had rare moral courage and a gentle charisma.

An exhibitionist with a towering ego, Charlie preferred his many romantic adventures with a certain element of danger. At the end of his many rainbows there always seemed to be a beckoning pot of gold. Charlie relished the pomp and publicity he received from men and women and even royalty, all over the world.

Charlie's daily conduct and personal appearance were picturesque. He rode tall in the saddle as if he were leading a circus parade. He wore sparkling jewels, fancy spurs, and beaded gauntlets. In his big ten-gallon hat, fringed buckskins, and soft leather leggings, he sat royally upon his bearskin saddle blanket. He resembled a gentlemen rather than a crude cowboy.

Arizona Charlie, like others with tales to tell, could have written this book. Shortly before his death, he decided to talk to two people: The Arizona State Historian, Mrs. Effie Keen, and Mr. Zane Grey, the Western fiction writer, who characterized Charlie in his book, *Stairs of Sand*. Mr. Grey had earlier endeavored to procure Charlie's version of the "Tonto Vendetta," or the Pleasant Valley War, often referred to as the "Tewksbury-Graham Feud," for use in his book, *To The Last Man*.

Neither saint nor sinner, Charlie left his mark across the lands in a multitude of court cases; many diaries, newspaper headlines and articles, and treasured scrapbooks. His name is also sprinkled in many history books. With this wealth of information, along with letters, family notes and testimonies, my intention is to correct previously held but inaccurate accounts and misconceptions about his life—a story I have to tell before it is lost to dust with the passage of time.

What follows is my account of his adventurous life. Generally accepted as fact, it is a true and concise account of the principal characters and interesting events in his life; the enemies he fought, the contests he won and lost, the women he loved—and left, or lost; the fortunes he made and squandered; the fun and excitement he had; the bitter sorrows he endured; and the famous or not-so-famous people who shared it all with him.

When I was a young child I knew this legendary man. He was my great-uncle, "Arizona Charlie, one of the most colorful cowboy characters to ever gallop across Arizona's mountains and plains, he was a true Westerner who played the part."

Jean Beach King

INTRODUCTION

Captain John Smith and 100 cavaliers landed their three ships on May 13, 1607, in Virginia and founded the first permanent English settlement in the New World, calling it Jamestown after their King, James I. It was not until 1620 that the fateful voyages of the *Speedwell* and *Mayflower* left port at Plymouth, England, only to have the *Speedwell* return because of a leaking hull. The *Mayflower* thrown off course by fierce storms, landed on the coast of Massachusetts rather than the intended Virginia destination.

Pilgrims settling in Massachusetts, like their counterparts in Jamestown, suffered enormous hardships. Indian attacks in the South and severe winters in the North took many lives of the colonists. Disease and a shortage of food made the already difficult situation even worse. In Warrisquike County of Virginia alone, only 33 people were left alive. These hardships were a terrible blow to the nonconformist political and religious exiles, who, calling themselves Puritans and having travelled so far, had suffered already a repressive lack of religious freedom and the power of kings.

Ambrose Meador in the New World

During these dark years, between 1622 and 1632, a gentleman named Ambrose Meador arrived in the colony of Virginia. It is not clear whether he arrived from where many Puritans had fled, England or Holland; it is likely that his home was in Suffolk County, an area known as Agricultural East Anglia, a Puritan stronghold, located northeast of London. King James I of England, after hearing the Puritan's case in 1604, declared, "If this be all they have to say, I shall make them conform themselves, or I shall harry them out of the land...or worse." Ambrose Meador took the King at his word, no doubt, for he had been witness to the questionable behavior of the English monarchy. He arrived in the New World in search of freedom.

John Moberly Meadows, Father of Charles Meadows

CHAPTER 1

1860-1876
THE EARLY YEARS

More than 225 years after Ambrose Meador settled in Virginia, his direct descendant, Abraham Henson Meadows, was born on March 10, 1860, in a small immigrant settlement on Elbow Creek, a tributary of the Kaweah River near what is now Visalia, California. Abraham was the sixth child of John Moberly Meadows and his wife, Margaret. Of various spellings for the name *Meador,* including *Medor*, *Meads*, and *Medow, Meador* or *Meadows*; it was the name *Meadows* that the newborn Abraham inherited.

Young Abraham was born in the family's covered wagon, a Conestoga, also known as a "Prairie Schooner," which served as his cradle. It rested under a giant valley oak that spread its lofty branches like a huge umbrella, shielding it from a blanket of a late-falling snow. Years later he described himself as a "delicate baby, doomed to perish of malnutrition until, as a last resort, my parents fed me mare's milk on which I began to thrive."

Abraham's father, John Moberly Meadows, had completed his fourth trip; Abraham's mother, Margaret, crossed this rugged clod of land three times during the first frantic decade of immigration to the West. They crossed dry, desolate plains, treacherous mountain passes, and sandy sinks. They forded rivers, braved hostile Indians and wild beasts; they were often beset by plague, fever, and harsh weather conditions. Through all of these hardships, they had six children; some were born at one end of the trip and some at the other, and one on the plains of Kansas. They had come to California by the Old Spanish Trail, driving "blooded stock," and leading friends and kinfolk who had succumbed to the historic dream—the "Westerning urge," seeking a more suitable climate and a new life rich with California gold.

Life seemed to agree with the young Abraham. "I was as happy and healthy as my brothers and sisters," he said, "but when I refused to talk until I was so big, the family became alarmed and consulted a physician, who assured them my organs of speech were alright, and not to worry."

That same year (1860), when Abraham was born, Abraham Lincoln was elected (on November 6) President of the United States. Lincoln assumed his duties without the blessing of John Moberly Meadows, a resolute man known as the "Fighting Parson." John Meadows never kept slaves, but he was a staunch Confederate and a firm believer in State's Rights, self government, and the Southern cause. He was furious with the choice of Lincoln, due to his political differences, and filled with loathing that he was a Republican.

John Meadows was a tall, wise man who possessed unquestioned integrity. He was also a popular man, having been elected Sheriff of Tulare County, California by an overwhelming majority. Because of the perilous situations he might face, the position required a man of courage, sound judgment, and high-caliber enthusiasm. And so it was in 1861 that there was a stoic Republican in the White House, and a fiesty Democrat elected to the Tulare County Court House.

During the same year, the Overland Telegraph system replaced the Pony Express and opened up communication between the densely populated East and the rugged expanse of the West. As the telegraph wires were being strung across the nation, the Central Pacific Railroad in the East and the Union Pacific Railroad in the West began laying track for the first transcontinental railway made possible by a bill signed into law by President Abraham Lincoln.

The Civil War Period

As the bridge of communication and transportation began to unite the shores of the country, a fissure of discontent and hatred formed between the North and South. On

February 8, 1861, seven Southern states seceded from the Union, forming the Confederate States of America and choosing Jefferson Davis as President. On April 12, Confederate soldiers fired on Fort Sumter in South Carolina and the first shots of the Civil War rang out. As suddenly as the nation had been joined, it had been torn apart.

John Meadows' peaceful town of Visalia in the San Joaquin Valley—which in large part had been settled by Southerners, a good many of whom had been brought West by him—was, in the words of a pro-Union newspaper editor, "a veritable hotbed of sedition." California remained a sovereign state, but sentiment ran deep for its people. One was either pro-Union or pro-Confederate and the quick tempered were ready, at the slightest provocation, to fight for their particular cause. John Meadows, a rabid Southerner, unabashedly stated his opinion in this partisan battle by taking an active part in Confederate activities in the area.

One day John Meadows' youngest child, the mute Abraham, surprised his family by exclaiming in his first spoken words, "Hurrah for Jeff Davis!" From that point on, said the young Confederate, "I began to chatter so incessantly, to show off my new vocabulary, that soon my family wished for my previous silence."

The Union Army that commanded California sent two companies of volunteers, members of the Second Cavalry, to Visalia, where they established Camp Babbitt. The hotheaded Sheriff of Tulare County refused to recognize their authority. John Meadows loudly proclaimed that he would not carry out his duties as Sheriff—nor would he resign.

The *Equal Rights Expositor*, an "extremely radical" Visalia newspaper published by fervent Southerners, S. J. Garrison and L. P. Hall, publicly expressed the Confederate viewpoint of the Southern faction. Its columns were filled with inflammatory accusations against the North and its leaders, while heaping praise on Jefferson Davis and Stonewall Jackson. The *Expositor* was attempting to justify secession in the minds of the public and referred to President Lincoln as a "narrow-minded bigot," "a driveling, idiotic imbecile creature," and an "illiterate back-woodsman." But the harsh epithets were not used against Lincoln exclusively; his Cabinet also came under fire from the *Expositor* as being the "most tyrannical crew that ever polluted the earth."

While the *Equal Rights Expositor* screamed out in banner headlines their deep indignation of President Lincoln, similar ridicule was vented in the *Marysville E*xpress published in the Sacramento Valley; the *Argus Democrat* , in Stockton; the *San Jose Tribune*; and the *Mariposa Free Press*, each with the President as their prime target. Public contributions to finance the *Expositor* began to pour in. Women, active in the Confederate cause, raised $300 in support of the *Expositor*.

Half a year later, on April 15, 1861, President Lincoln called for 75,000 volunteers to form a stronger Union Army with which to repel the Confederate forces. Four days later he called for a blockade of Southern ports thereby cutting off vital exports and aid. Lincoln was resolute in his stand against the Rebels, as obstinate and determined as John Meadows was against Lincoln.

In Visalia, there was an uneasy mixture of "young blood" Rebels and Union men. Rot-gut whiskey flowed steadily in the noisy saloons, which helped fuel the fires of their respective predisposition. The situation was often dangerous; fights were not infrequent, with bottles flying through the air, chairs crashing down on the backs of unsuspecting victims; and thievery, even murder, was no stranger to this highly apprehensive group of men.

By May, eleven states had seceded from the Union. The Rebels gained their first major victory when they defeated the Union forces in the Battle of Bull Run on July 21, 1861.

For John Moberly Meadows, the proverbial "straw that broke the camel's back" occurred two years later, when, on March 5, 1863, a mob of Northern sympathizers descended on the offices of the *Expositor*, tied Editor Garrison to his chair, tossed the type into the street, and effectively destroyed the printing presses. John Meadows, in the clutches of his fiery temperament, reacted by stalwartly exclaiming, "No son of mine shall bear the name of the President who brought this shameful war upon us!" And so Abraham

Henson, the youngest son of John and Margaret Meadows, breathed his last breath. Abraham became known as "Charlie."

Almost four years to the day after the first shots of the United States Civil War, on April 9, 1865, at the Appomattox Court House in Virginia, General Robert E. Lee surrendered 27,800 Confederate troops to General Ulysses S. Grant thereby ending the bloodshed. With the defeat of the Rebel forces, John Meadows became a bitter and unhappy man. But he never lost his faith in the Lord, or energy as a religious leader in the community. He held camp meetings "preaching the comforting mercy of God"; and his "brush arbor" services, as they were called in the Old South, were held in forest glades and fields.

The Arizona Territory Beckons

John Meadows continued building his cattle and horse ranch with all his strength, working out his frustrations lingering from a lost cause. On one occasion he and his boys drove a herd of turkeys to market in San Francisco. They would often make the long trip to Sacramento for supplies. On one of these trips John Meadows met a man named Abe McGinnis, who owned the general store in Sacramento. Soon after their new friendship, a distraught miner entered Abe's store and stabbed another man to whom he had entrusted his money. Blood splattered all over Abe's stack of overalls. This prompted Abe to sell his store, and as luck would have it, he was asked to accompany John Meadows and his boys back to Visalia. Abe McGinnis and John Meadows became fast friends. They packed meat in the winter and mined in the summer. In 1870, Abe, at age 40, and Rhoda Meadows, age 14, were united in marriage with the blessing of the Meadows family. In the years to come, Rhoda was to bear twelve children to Abe, a man twenty-six years her senior.

As John Meadows herds flourished, so did his family over the years, eventually to embrace twelve children. In new communities early education was "catch as catch can." Charlie and his siblings received their early education at the Elbow School. In 1874, John Meadows was instrumental in establishing the Visalia Seminary, or "normal" school. He wanted to be sure his children's basic needs were met, and their minds and bodies developed equally as his lands.

Charlie Meadows seemed to come along at just the right time; his education appears to be the most complete in comparison with his siblings. Though his spelling was not letter-perfect, he showed signs of a remarkable journalistic ability. His quill-style had flamboyant dips and rises, like that of John Hancock, and he made few grammatical errors in his later writings, a testament to the fact that he had learned well at an early age.

Charlie was tall and lean as a "bean pole." He had penetrating eyes of liquid blue and dark auburn hair that contrasted with his extroverted nature. At an early age he became a young leader in the community, learning to ride, master the lariat, and rope wild mustangs on the Tulare plains. Little did Charlie realize that he would soon take up the ropes of an American Legacy—the Cowboy.

By the 1870's, California was undergoing a great "land rush" that, outstripping the Gold Rush of the 1840's, nearly doubled the state's population. In 1874, the California Legislature passed the so-called "no fence" law—which required ranchers to confine their herds to their own lands—rather than allowing them to pasture at large. As the new farmers settled, the vast landscape of the state improved with picturesque orchards and farms which, to John Meadows' temperament, was proof that the "no fence" law was a "no sense" law. He felt his freedom had been grossly infringed upon.

The law stirred up talk among the cattle and horse breeders about early reports from the Arizona Territory—of good mining opportunities, a wonderful climate, and lush grasses that reached "nigh unto the stirrups of a tall stallion."

Upon hearing the news of Arizona, John Meadows' thoughts turned back to 1848, when at the age of 20, he had been consumed with a pioneering spirit. At that young age he had sold his meager belongings, packed a small valise, said good-bye to his parents and, with a few eager young friends, made his first journey to California. They came from Arkansas, first by horseback, then ship, and finally across the Isthmus of Panama by way of the Chagres River in "dug-outs" or "bongóes." John Meadows and his friends were seeking a personal *El Dorado*, a new life rich in gold and magnificent climate.

For the time being, the scrupulous old pioneer, John Meadows, had to let his dream of Arizona wait for another day. Margaret had become pregnant with her twelfth child, Mobley, and her health was "poorly"; it was unlikely she could make the journey. Their staying seemed a stroke of good luck. A new gold strike had opened in Mineral King in the mountains east of Visalia and John was eager to commence digging. The area known as "Beulah Land of Promise" was a good prospect, and in 1874, John and his boys along with son-in-law, Abe McGinnis, entered Mineral King and established Silver City. They filed on four mines: the "Lady Alice", "Black Wolf," "Half Potato," and the "Young America."

John Valentine Meadows Travels to Arizona

The "White Man" had not ventured into the Tonto Basin region of the Arizona Territory to any extent until the 1860's. The California gold rush was booming and had captured a goodly portion of the Western pioneers. It was not until after the Civil War that the Army had finally set up a few poorly manned outposts. It was not long before a considerable number of lion hunters and prospectors followed. Prior to this period, Arizona's history had been a bloody one; the Apache Indians had committed many crimes against the "White Man."

After great devastation and many atrocities perpetrated at the hands of the Apache, the early settlers demanded protection from the Cavalry. When the Apaches were approached with the option of a peaceful treaty or a disastrous bloody siege, they realized the hopelessness of their situation and reluctantly agreed to settle on the San Carlos Reservation. But upon hearing of the plan, Geronimo, the fierce and unyielding leader of the Chiricahuas, the most unyielding tribe of all, fled to Mexico with his family and friends.

In 1876, Parson John Meadows sent his second son, John Valentine Meadows, to the Arizona Territory for a "look-see," and to map out a prospective ranch site. John Valentine drove fifty head of mixed red Durham cattle with him—because soon most of the family would follow. According to a report by forest ranger, Fred Croxen entitled *Grazing on Tonto* and presented to the Tonto Grazing Conference in 1926, John Valentine was the first man to bring cattle into the Tonto Basin.

"My brother, John Valentine, took a partner with him by the name of Charlie Siegel, and the two set up a small cow spread near Old Fort Reno," Charlie said to the *Arizona Republican* of April 13, 1927. "One day a young Irish-American by the name of Edward Doheny showed up in camp and offered to buy into their operation. Doheny was from New York and was rather well educated. He was quick and athletic, looking for fortune and adventure. He was taken into the partnership with John Valentine and Charlie Siegel and the trio moved their cattle to the border of the Apache Reservation in the White Mountains. Doheny was an apt pupil in taking up the ways of the "wild and woolie" West. He became a crack shot, a good horseman, and a tireless prospector. John Valentine and Charlie Siegel found him to be fair, honest, and a loyal friend. Their desire was to get rich quick and the best place to stumble onto a gold mine was to venture where no man dared—where no man made a track or stuck a stick into the ground.

Together they mined, raised cattle, and when the grubstake ran low they would drive their cattle near to a mining camp where each of them would take a job until they earned enough to load up on provisions. When they returned to camp, they would often have to play hide and seek with Victorio, the warring Apache Chief, and other Indian renegades who roamed the hills.

John Valentine sent word home to Visalia that the Apache appeared to be subdued, the land was unrestricted and open for settlement, there was a seemingly endless expanse of grass—unfenced and inviting—and that he had located the perfect place for his family to settle.

Winter had settled in Visalia, so Charlie and Abe McGinnis buried their tools at the foot of Sawtooth Pass in Mineral King, intending to come back in the spring to continue their "'diggin's'" at the "Young America" mine.

In the meantime, Margaret Meadows' continuous child-bearing and the ordinary hardships of a pioneer woman's life were seriously affecting her health. John Meadows felt that now was the time to seek a more salutary climate for her. If she improved in Arizona, John's plan was to return to Visalia, to dispose of some of his property there, and to divide the rest with his married daughters: Mary Angelina Arnold (their eldest), Sarah Dean and Rhoda McGinnis. These three would remain in California to rear their families.

Margaret Enlow Meadows, Mother of Charles Meadows

CHAPTER 2

1877-1880
THE MEADOWS MIGRATE TO ARIZONA

In the glorious spring of 1877, the astute old wagon master, John Meadows, gave a quick lash of his whip and bellowed, "Gidiyap," as they pulled out of Visalia one early morning, bound for green pastures in the Tonto Basin of Arizona. Sarah, Mary, and Rhoda could be seen waving their bonnets wildly as the long procession of wagons and livestock lurched into motion and lumbered away at a mere crawl. The caravan disappeared into the dawn carrying with it the hopes and dreams of great opportunities in a promised land.

"It was a banner year. California had just emerged from a long drought. The skies were clear and blue, the air was sweet with the nectar of wild flowers, and the country was lush and green," Charlie described the Meadows' family journey for the *Arizona Republican*. "From the Sacramento capitol to the Mojave Desert, California had become a virtual paradise of hay fields and flower gardens. When the caravan started off each morning, a man led the white bell mare, and three hundred horses followed. Following the horses were six wagons, attached to the last was a trailer carrying a half-dozen calves. Then came the milk cows, strung out for four or five miles. No one was in a hurry, there was food and water everywhere, the herd was fat, satisfied and playful, and everyone was good natured."

The Meadows family on the journey included fifteen-year-old Eva, who drove one of the wagons; Henry, 25, and Rose, 12, who helped herd the cattle and horses; and Maggie, 8, James, 7, Jacob, 5, and Mobley, 3, who rode in the wagon with their mother. At night when the chuck wagon was cleared, the wagons were circled around the animals—as was the custom, while coyotes made the evenings melodious. As the camp fire flickered gently beneath a blanket of stars, the children would gather around to hear their father read from the Bible. The rest of the evening was spent "spinning yarns" and singing old hymns from the South, or other nostalgic songs of the day.

The trip was a monumental adventure for the 16-year-old Charlie. As he rode alongside the *caballada*, it brought to mind the fascinating tales his father had told him of their earlier migration to California. Parson John told his son of the hardships and suffering they had endured, and of the driving force that pushed the pioneers Westward—a force they themselves did not really comprehend. He told Charlie about skirmishes with the "dreaded redskins" and of a particular incident when a renegade brave "dared to take up" (kidnap) Charlie's older sister, Rhoda. Margaret Meadows cried hysterically, wringing her hands, as the three-week-old infant was spirited from her arms. Just as the child was to disappear forever, John thrashed the warrior brave with his leather bull whip and retrieved the squalling babe, Rhoda Kansas Meadows, so named because she had been born on the plains of Kansas. The Indians retaliated by killing an ox from the team. John quickly hitched up a cow from the herd to replace the slain ox. Then, to avoid any further reprisals from the Indians, he flicked the "snapper" of his hickory-handled bull whip at the flanks of the team and the caravan hurried on its way. The travellers watched in horror as the "blood-and-gut eaters" devoured raw chunks of the dead beast.

These stories were equally devoured by the awestruck Charlie, as they sat around the camp fire evenings "tale spinning." His father told a story of a previous trip through Utah where his party "missed a ghastly date with death." On that day his caravan came across what remained of an earlier wagon train; it was the scene of the famous "Mountain Meadows Massacre" where bits of hair, flesh, and clothing were evidence of the pitiless butchery that had taken place. This gruesome scene caused great anxiety amongst the "overlanders" travelling in John Meadows' care, but they continued safely on their journey to California.

In comparison, the present trip to Arizona was without serious incident. "Along with us went our cousins, the Stephens family, our grandfather, William J. Meadows (all of whom settled in Kingman, Arizona) and my lifelong friend, Frank Prothero" and, Charlie added, "By inheritance and by choice, I took to the cactus trail like a rabbit to the bush. I was to learn in the years to come of the bitter hardships of the pioneer, but to me, this was a continuous picnic. We crossed the silvery Colorado River on Wooster Hardy's ferry, where John Valentine met and escorted us through Western Arizona."

The caravan traversed old wagon tracks, creaking and groaning over rocky countryside covered with curly *mesquite, yucca, manzanita*, and silk tassel bush, into Prescott and Old Yavapai. The wagons rumbled over the Camp Verde-Fort Apache Military Road through dense forests of ponderosa pine, scrub oak, alder and juniper; they slid cumbersomely over steep precipices with the assistance of giant logs, block and tackle down Strawberry Hill into the Tonto Basin.

Ahead of them lay beauty on the grandest scale—perhaps the most beautiful region of the Southwestern United States. A timber-lined meadow of luscious grasses flowed through the valley like an undulating wave of green velvet, sprinkled here and there with scrub oak and towering pines. This magnificent pastoral setting was surrounded by the overpowering Mogollon (pronounced Muggy-own) Mountains, which run from Northwest to Southeast—with extreme variations, onward into New Mexico. The Sierra Ancha and Mazatzal Mountain ranges come in from each side to butt their heads into the Mogollon Rim, or Tonto Rim. This rim was so named after the book written by Zane Grey, *Under the Tonto Rim*. It is here that viewers are afforded the best outlook of the world's largest, pure strand of ponderosa pine. As the gruelling trip that had taken three months neared its completion, they were tired, but very happy.

They pastured their herds in Green Valley (which later became their little hometown of Payson). The Meadows began exploring the surrounding countryside, and John Valentine led them to a small, isolated and tranquil valley nestled deep within the Mogollons. The valley had a span of six miles from its edge to its conclusion at Rim Rock. At the foundation of the valley, the East Verde River meandered through the thickly wooded, rocky hollow. Every rock and pebble was distinct in the cool transparent water that flowed from underground springs, nurturing thick masses of wild watercress along its banks. The valley floor was carpeted with juicy black gramma and pine bunch grasses that stood up to three feet high in great clusters; these were the very best grasses for grazing. Bare out-croppings of sculptured sedimentary stone, in glorious shades of red, buff, brown and vermilion, interrupted the terrain, the result of an upheaval during the Mesozoic Age. It was a beautiful setting beyond description with a climate both intoxicating and healthful.

The prudent, old pioneer father, John Meadows, could not have been happier. The spot could not have suited him better, and the decision was made to settle there. He named his new homestead "Diamond Valley" because of its shape. Weeks later he traveled the eighty-odd miles to Prescott, the Yavapai County seat, where he filed on his two brands—one was diamond-shaped with a "J" for the blooded stock, mares, and old stock; the other was diamond-shaped with a quarter circle, for the half-bred stock. Also, he laid claim to the land at Diamond Valley by possessor's right. According to the Homestead Act, title was given by the U.S. Land Office to those who took possession of unsurveyed land whereon they agreed to reside and pay taxes.

At that time, few squatters dotted the whole Tonto Basin, the former hunting grounds of the Apache Indian. But, little by little, others flocked to this paradise.

When the older brothers had settled the stock, John Meadows took Margaret and the younger children to Oaks & Willows, an early-day stage station on the Fort Mohave-Prescott Road. He hoped she could regain her health there. Once recuperated, they could return to Visalia to settle their affairs. Charlie, Frank Prothero, John Valentine, and Henry Meadows, the eldest son, cleared a section of their land between the third and fourth crossings of the Verde stream, cut pine logs and built corrals and two log cabins. The cabins were connected by a common roof, which made a hall in between. The cabins were built in this manner to provide the family with fortified protection. They were unchinked with tamped dirt floors. There was but one window facing east. There were no "glass lights" nor much of a door, just a make-shift one of crude shakes to ward off the wild animals and elements. But to the Meadows family it was "home sweet home."

When the cabins and corrals were completed, Henry and Frank Prothero stayed with the stock in Diamond Valley. Charlie accompanied John Valentine to his ranch in the wilderness of the White Mountains. Riding solidly in the stirrup, John told Charlie many hair-raising stories as they galloped across the rugged terrain of the Salt River Valley—now known as Phoenix, Arizona and the Valley of the Sun. Charlie recalled John's tales:

"It was here that John told me that many of the snakes and toads had horns, and there was a dry-land alligator called a Gila Monster (pronounced he-lah), the most dreaded of all reptiles. The Gila Monster of Arizona found its favorite habitat here and attained its greatest dimensions. John also told me there were wild, naked cannibals.

"For his own amusement and my special benefit, John rather enlarged on the story of the venomous desert alligator. He said that one had entered King Woolsey's corral and with a deadly wallop of its tail killed several work oxen. Another story was that one of Jack Swilling's pack mules had kicked a medium-sized one, about four feet long, and it exhaled a deadly fume that killed the whole pack train instantly!" Jack Swilling was an adventurer, Confederate officer, and later a Union scout. He was considered the father of irrigation in the Salt River Valley . . . and the Founder of Phoenix, Arizona. King Woolsey was a famous old Indian fighter.

"John thought the monster sluggish and hard-boiled against bullets, except just behind the front legs where a bullet could penetrate," said Charlie. Charlie swallowed the incredible tale in its entirety. This only fueled his curiosity further.

"I craved a contest with a Gila Monster," Charlie continued, "and laid out my plan of battle. I had a good pistol and a splendid horse who knew his onions, and so did I. My first move, I decided, would be to take advantage of the wind so as to avoid the poison breath. I would adopt the system of 'hit and run,' by first riding by at full speed and shooting, aiming just behind the front legs. Hit or miss, I would return, throw the full length of my rope, catch the monster and ride facing the wind until he was dragged to a pulp!

"We were riding light; our kitchen had hardtack, coffee and sugar, two tomato cans for making our coffee in, a large and small canteen, two light blankets, and an old cavalry coat of Civil War vintage. We filled our canteens at the famous Vulture Mine. The wind was blowing, so we camped in a dry wash 20 miles down the road, made a fire and went to bed.

"Under a Palo Verde tree I saw what looked like an outline of a five-foot Gila Monster. I was ever ready, don'cherknow, my pistol was in hand, full-cocked, and my eyes were riveted on the subject. There was no movement or sound. I fell asleep only to awaken soon, choking and coughing from the most deadly fume I had ever come in contact with!

"I covered my head with the old cavalry coat," Charlie said, "which was no improvement. In a kind of choking fit I pulled the trigger. The shot aroused John, who was also coughing." John sat straight up in bed and bellered, "What in the devil is all that noise for?" Charlie recovered sufficiently to whisper, "Gila Monster, he has got me, water." John slid down to the foot of the bed and got the big canteen. There was a hole straight through the center and not a drop of water in it. He then reached for the small canteen under the saddle at the head of the bed and found the smelly old cavalry coat and other things smouldering in the fire. The Gila conversation, that the boys had so generously fed themselves up on at the beginning of their trip, lagged considerably during the remainder of their journey.

When John and Charlie reached the ranch in the White Mountains, they found that Siegel and Doheny had finished their work during John's absence. The branding had been completed, the corrals repaired, and the two men had been out working their claims in the nearby hills. Charlie recounted:

"We sat into the evening spinning yarns," and the subject came up about Edward's ability to defend the trio in time of trouble. If in any of the camps a barroom bully encroached upon the rights of either of them, it was up to Edward to do the taming, which he usually did with neatness and dispatch, having developed a powerful punch before he ran away from Harvard to seek his fortune in the West.

"The camp was usually well divided while in the mountains. There was much hard joshing and chafing between the "Flying Dutchman," (Charlie Siegel); the "Wild Irishman," (Edward Doheny); and the "Hard-headed Scotchman," (John Valentine Meadows). When there was a mix-up or brush with the Indians or outlaws, they stuck together as one man. The three fortune hunters camped near the New Mexico and Arizona line—high up in the mountains—at one time. Victorio, they said, was operating farther south and east. The three partners left the cattle at this point while John took a roundabout route to look up some contact."

Fort Apache is situated in White Mountain country, resplendent with pines and cedars, near the rushing White River. An abundance of trout glistened there, like the shadows of quick silver, beneath the frosty surface; droves of deer and elk browsed the tender foliage; and wild daisies, sunflowers and Indian Paint Brush nodded their colorful heads in the highland meadows. Fort Apache, and its surrounding countryside, was truly a paradise.

"Doheny, the 'Wild Irishman,' rode ahead," Charlie continued, "where he saw the antlers of a bull elk visible among the foliage, and shot it for a specimen. Siegel was dissatisfied; they had plenty of venison, and the shot would only attract Indians—if any were about. Doheny insisted on going into the canyon for his trophy. They managed to get near enough to see the splendid animal lying in the deep, rocky ravine, but there were no horns on it, so they passed on. Siegel rubbed it in because Doheny did not know the difference between a cow and a bull. Doheny was sure he had killed a bull elk—he saw it fall and roll down the steep mountainside." A search, months later, revealed where the animal fell, and how the horns had broken off when the animal was slain because it was shedding season.

Siegel wouldn't let it lie. "He found a great joke in what he thought was the Irishman's mistake and continued to chafe until he aroused Doheny's fighting blood," Charlie reported. "Doheny was quick to get back at Siegel, and declared a very unwelcome visitor, one that he himself had used every precaution to part company with, the mining habituate that was to become known so well as 'cootie' during the World War. He declared that Siegel, 'The Flying Dutchman,' kept the camp stocked and he proposed a clean up—or duel. They could stand with their 'backs together,' he said, 'walk ten paces, turn and fire' their pistols.

"Siegel proposed a genuine 'wash-up' and bath in the cold waters of the White River. Doheny agreed. The blankets, even the saddle blankets, were weighed down with stones and allowed to float in the rippling water. Every stitch of their clothing was washed, the men bathed and the clothes were spread out on the branches of the willows. Then a large pitch pine tree was set afire and the drying process started.

"The two men had mountain trout for dinner. Following up a sluice-head tributary, they used willow branches in a series of dams to catch the squirming fish. After the sport and excitement they turned toward the camp to find the whole heavens ablaze. A huge fire was raging. Their hobbled horses had found a place of safety. From the debris of the camp they were able to retrieve the bridles, bits and cinch rings, and a handleless knife. It was more than a hundred miles to Fort Apache, which was the first habitation. But they had not a stitch of clothing, a match to light a fire, or any provisions.

"It was a long ride without nourishment of any kind, and a little cold on bareback horses in the fall of the year. On the second day as they neared Fort Apache, they had the problem of getting into town without clothes. Six or eight miles out from the fort, they saw a number of squaws and papooses gathering berries and grass seed. They felt this was their chance. They agreed to rob a squaw of her dress and buckskin trappings and garb themselves sufficiently to get to the store in town. They would return the clothes to the Indian agent with no harm done. But the question was, how to catch the squaw before robbing her?

"The 'Wild Irishman' was delegated to the task, while Siegel remained with the horses. Doheny selected the best dressed squaw, gave his horse the rein and the chase was on! The squaw ran for dear life, the Irishman's long, yellow hair streaming out behind, and 'fanning the breeze' on both sides of his neck. Just as Doheny reached out to catch the squaw by the hair, she reached a large juniper tree and round and round they went, the squaw having the best of it all. The horse was no match for her on such a short circle.

"Edward jumped off the horse. But the squaw had moccasins on; and, over sharp rocks and thorns, she had the advantage and soon out-distanced her pursuer. She ran into Fort Apache and hysterically reported to the commanding officer that a 'red devil' on a spotted horse threatened to kill her. The report was carried out over the fort and a scouting party was ordered out.

"My brother, John, had reached Fort Apache by this time; and, while standing in front of the store discussing the squaw's story with a number of officers, who should walk in—but the horse the 'Wild Irishman' had been riding! John knew then his partners were in trouble. He threw on his saddle and back-tracked to the others where he divided his clothing and got them into town for badly needed refreshments and clothing."

Many weeks passed and a long-overdue letter came through from the family in Visalia. Parson John Meadows had spread the good word to his friends and relatives of the stockman's paradise in Arizona, with fine grasses, well-watered ranges and ideal climate. His glowing tales influenced the Houston brothers: Sam, Andrew, and William, to leave Tulare County for the Tonto Basin. Mother Margaret was "holding her own," and Mineral King was experiencing a great "boom." They would not be coming with their friends, the Houstons, however; they stayed in Visalia through 1879, the year "Beulah" showed her greatest prosperity. John Moberly Meadows' claims reportedly were worth one million dollars.

About this time, Frank Prothero, Charlie's close friend who had come to the Tonto Basin with the family on the first trip, set out on his own. He purchased a few animals from Charlie's older brother, Henry Meadows, and three mares and a gelding from Emer Chilson, another early Tonto Basin settler. Frank set up his own stock spread several miles distant, and he later made a name for himself as a famous Arizona tracker and lawman.

At Diamond Valley Ranch, Henry and Charlie went about their routine tasks of "branding up," castrating and ranging the stock. Game was plentiful in those early days, and hunting was excellent. Considerable time was spent bagging bear, deer and wild turkey. The bear meat was dressed out and along with the oil was sold to the Indian agencies at Fort Apache and San Carlos. The venison made fine jerky for the larder. Each lion, a menace to young colts, fetched a $20 bounty from the territory. Occasionally, the boys got into Marysville, a small mining community three miles west of Payson, or Green Valley for supplies; Chilson store records show they traded in gold bullion or silver.

One early morning Doheny, "The Wild Irishman," galloped into the Diamond Valley ranch quite unexpectedly amid "dust and flurry," riding the fast horse John Valentine had provided him. Doheny told the two boys to "hide him out" because, through some misunderstanding, he had been accused of horse theft. Traditionally, horse thieves were shown no mercy. Doheny was not keen on the idea of swinging from the nearest cottonwood tree, and that had been a nerve-fraying possibility. These accusations were not uncommon, although a suspect often was not guilty. After the charges subsided, Doheny returned to the ranch in the White Mountains, where the partnership eventually broke up.

"Meantime," Charlie recounted to a reporter from the *Arizona Republican*, "my brother John moved into Mexico where, with Señor Coulter, they gave the first alarm that saved 50 families by getting them into a stockade before it was besieged by the wild Apache, Victorio, who finally withdrew when his cartridges and grub were depleted." A short time later Victorio was blown to pieces in a box canyon ambush. Charlie Siegel returned to the Salt River Valley, and Edward Doheny drifted into New Mexico, where he discovered the Black Range mining district in 1880.

Doheny soon sold out there, realizing a profit of $30,000. He took his money and went to Los Angeles. As luck would have it, he discovered a black tarry substance oozing out of the ground near downtown Los Angeles. He had taken in a partner, and the two men sunk a shaft 155 feet deep. They feared asphyxiation from noxious gasses that they would have hit at that level, so Doheny cut a long branch from a nearby eucalyptus tree and the two men worked it through the shaft. After they had reached a considerable depth, oil spewed out in great quantity—many barrels a day. The two prosperous partners took their profits from this discovery and went to Mexico, where they bought 400,000 acres of land near Tampico, and where Doheny was positive oil would be found. Eventually, their Cassiano property brought in one of the greatest oil discoveries of all time, producing 70,000 barrels a day for nine years.

"This wild pioneer friend of ours became a multi-millionaire oil magnate," Charlie reported. But Edward Doheny never forgot his old friends who had helped him in those early years, and later came back into John Valentine's life again.

John Valentine returned to the family ranch in Diamond Valley. In the fall of that same year, the brothers welcomed the family's return to Arizona with cries of joy. Mineral King had produced gold and silver—their father had been celebrated as being the "most enthusiastic and confident" of the early day locaters, and "withal a brave, honest and conscientious man." But these minerals became too expensive to extract and the isolated mining camp in Mineral King died. Parson John Meadows brought with him thirty mares and three fine stallions. The horses were traded in Visalia with the Halstead brothers in exchange for five houses and a band of the Meadows' sheep. Included in his possessions were apple and pear tree saplings propagated by him from some of the first apple and pear trees ever grown in the Tulare County, planted there by him in the 1850's. Traveling with the Meadows was the Lafayette Philander Nash family.

The Meadows family earnestly took to their work at Diamond Valley—the young trees were set out about the cabin area and are today reported to be the oldest apple and pear trees of their kind in Arizona. The family churned their own butter and packed their own meat. Leaf suet was rendered from the backs and kidneys, then the cut and seared steaks were layered in crocks and hot tallow poured between; the meat kept for two to three months at a time. Some of the meat was made into corned beef, for variety, and some made into jerky by Margaret Meadows. She used thin strips of beef or venison, salting them down in a large crock to "cure" or "ripen" for thirty-six hours before being hung to dry. Occasionally, hot peppers were pounded into the meat Indian style for a further assortment of taste. She also melted down the suet which, poured into milk pans to harden, was used for shortning in pies and biscuits. She added lye to the heavy fat to make soap for baths and laundry. Wild game graced the table—and the tender trout that filled the stream, cooked in home-churned butter over a wood stove, was most tempting to the palate.

The younger Meadows boys—James, Jake, and Mobley—"circumambulated" the ranch, crawling among the boulders and rocky crevices in little more than a "breech clout" or loin cloth. The girls—Eva Mae, Rose Anne, and Margaret Ellen (Maggie)—whiled their spare time wrapping each other's hair in rags or preparing their frocks and bonnets for the rather sparse social life that was available.

Charlie said of those years between 1880-1882, "Those early days in Diamond Valley were the happiest of my life." But little did any of them suspect the cruel, tragic events that were to follow.

Charles Henson Meadows, *Circa* Age 24

Henry William Meadows, John and Margaret's Eldest Son,
Brother of Charles Meadows

CHAPTER 3

1881-1883
UNREST AT FORT APACHE

The restricted life of the reservation was deeply oppressive to the Apache Indians. In the summer of 1881, at the Fort Apache Indian Reservation, these conditions led a young medicine man and religious fanatic, by the name of Nochaydelclinne (pronounced Noch-ay-del-clinne) to claim he could resurrect Apache Chiefs, Cochise and Mangus Colorados—prophesying that their spirits would drive all the "white squatters" from Apache lands.

Nochaydelclinne, or "Bobby," as he was known to the soldiers at Fort Apache, led his people in a ceremonial dance that lasted forty-five days and nights. They proceeded to get insanely drunk on "Tiswin," a powerfully intoxicating liquor made from barley. Tiswin roused all that was turbulent and vicious in those who imbibed. These Apaches, considered by the U.S. Cavalry to be prisoners of war, were neither disarmed nor dismounted because of their traditional need to hunt. Armed and mounted, the Apaches were formidable foes. The Indians became increasingly insolent, restless, and anxious to take to the warpath. This unrest was trouble for the military men stationed at Fort Apache to watch over them. Therefore, an order went out to "capture or kill Nochaydelclinne," who was in isolation in the Valley of the Cibicue. Eighty-five officers and men of the 6th Cavalry and twenty-three Indian scouts were assembled under General Carr to capture Bobby. Upon reaching the Cibicue, Carr and his men were met by "swarms of painted Indians . . .buzzing like rattlesnakes." The soldiers cautiously arrested Bobby and departed for their camp located in a meadow two and one half miles downstream from their present position. When the soldiers reached the camp, Carr's attention was called to Indians who were fording the river upstream. Captain Hentig and several of his men yelled for the Apache intruders to "Ukashe!" which meant to "Get out!" As Hentig raised his hand to motion to one of his scouts, a half-witted young buck fired and gave the war cry. Suddenly, more than a hundred Indians swept down upon the camp to free their beloved Bobby. Hentig fell with a bullet lodged in his body as General Carr gave the order to "Kill the medicine man!" Bobby was yelling and yammering when Lieutenant Carter's trumpeter thrust a pistol into the medicine man's mouth and pulled the trigger. The blast merely stunned the frenzied Bobby. The bloody shoot out finally ended, and Bobby, who was presumed dead, could be seen crawling on his hands and knees away from the camp. Sergeant John Smith took up an ax and delivered a fatal bone-crushing blow to the medicine man's head.

Seventy-five of Bobby's surviving braves fled to the mountains led by the warrior Nantiatish (pronounced Nan-tia-tish), who assumed the powers of leadership. Among the Indian band was the feared brother of Chief Cooley, Nantangotayz.

On September 2, 1881, Nantangotayz and six renegades plundered the Middleton Ranch on Cherry Creek. Old Man Middleton was wounded, but George Turner, Jr. and Henry Moody, who had come to warn the Middleton family, were killed. After this brutal attack, the Indian renegades escaped to higher country, where food and water were more plentiful, and remained there in hiding.

The unrest at Fort Apache, the bloodshed at the Cibicue, and the attack on the Middleton Ranch indirectly affected the Meadows family. Life went on at Diamond Valley Ranch. This relative tranquility was to be short lived.

Margaret "Maggie" Ellen Meadows-Beach, Sister of Charles Meadows

July of 1882

On July 7, 1882, two neighbors of the Meadows family, Jim Burchett and John Kerr, arrived at Diamond Valley Ranch, winded and gasping after a furious ride from the town of Globe. They brought with them terrifying news that a band of White Mountain Apaches had broken out of the San Carlos Agency, a reservation in eastern Arizona, and had formed a raiding jamboree in company with the "red fiend" Nantangotayz. They quit the reservation in rebellion of black market activities of a small group of corrupt men at San Carlos. There was a shortage of ration coupons and wanton speculation in military and Indian contracts, as well as forced labor. Central to these activities was Agent J. C. Tiffany who had used Indians on the reservation for various chores. The day after Burchett and Kerr had warned the Meadows—erroneously, it should be pointed out—believing the report that all personnel at San Carlos had been killed, and the raiders numbered upward of forty, Police Chief Charles Colvig and two of his aides were waylaid and murdered.

Upon hearing of the Indian raiders, settlers went scurrying from their homes fearing for their lives. Charlie Meadows could understand the Indians' complaints and dissatisfaction with the state of affairs at San Carlos. The agency was governed by a group of unscrupulous speculators who deserved to be brought to justice; however, he could not understand why these same Indians found it necessary to vent their grievances on innocent men, women, and children.

Charlie's father was reluctant to leave his land. He could not imagine turning his animals, and all he had worked for, over to a "murderous gang of redskins." On the other hand, he had his wife and children to consider first. John Meadows was a man of cast-iron innards, but he was no fool. Hurriedly, the family set about packing a few belongings, piling them in the spring wagon. They mounted their horses, with the hounds tagging alongside, and headed for the safety of Green Valley. When they arrived, they boarded up at Fort McDonald, a red stone structure on McDonald Hill a half mile west of Payson. Other settlers boarded up at August Pieper's Dance Hall inside town.

Three days later, supposedly on reliable authority, a lone rider brought news that it was safe for the settlers to return to their homes. John Meadows wasted no time in leaving, because of his concern for the well-being of his livestock and property. At this same time, Henry Meadows was wrangling horses for the Army at Fort Verde. Rose and Eva Meadows remained in town, presumably, at Grandma Obedience Hazelton's place with Ida and Laura Hazelton. Sarah Hazelton, a pretty 22 year-old school teacher who was "a mite sweet on Henry," it is believed, accompanied the Meadows family back to their ranch until Henry and her brother, Carter, returned.

Diamond Valley Ranch was much as they had left it, except for some damage caused by a marauding bear that had broken into their food supply. What wasn't known was that the gang of hostile Apaches were already nearby in Pleasant Valley performing their "dastardly deeds." The previous day the raiders had stolen every horse from the sparsely populated mining settlement of McMillanville, setting homes on fire on the outskirts of the little town. The men of McMillanville, well prepared and amply fortified to meet their foes, managed to drive the Apaches off after a fight that waxed hot for an hour or more. Couriers, making the long, hot trip by foot because of the lack of horses, were slow in getting word to the town of Globe about the attack on McMillanville. In the meantime, the Indian raiders had joined forces with another group of hostiles led by Nantiatish, who were believed to be some 200 strong and headed in the direction of the Pleasant and Salt River Valleys.

Not knowing where the "ruthless warriors" might strike next, the Army found it almost impossible to defend all the settlements. But now that the merciless Apache had made an attack, the Army was ready to move in force. From McMillanville, the "two-footed coyotes" swung by the Al Rose and Church ranches, set fires to the cabins, then ran off cattle at the Tewksbury and Stinson ranges. On July 12, the Indians, including squaws and papooses, committed their next depredations on the Pleasant Valley range of the Sigsby brothers.

In a letter to Arizona State Historian Effie Keene, Charlie wrote, "The following is just a horseback synopsis of my recollections of many years ago, happening in a series of tragedies that for years I have sought to dismiss from my memories."

"They killed Will Sigsby and Lou Houdon on the range and mutilated their bodies; then attacked Bob Sigsby as he was entering his cabin carrying a bucket of water. He was shot through the lungs but managed to bar the door and brace himself up against the gun holes in the cabin, and put up a desperate fight of resistance for thirty-six hours before the hostiles sensed the pursuit of the troops. Then they vanished over the ridges as swiftly as they had emerged. A hasty formation of townsfolk from Globe, some twenty in number, who had friends and relations in the Tonto Basin, formed a company whose purpose was to get in front of the Apaches and hold and harass them until the U.S. troops could overtake them. A few that I remember were Jim Burchett, John Robbins, Lindsey Lewis, and Wint House. Robbins was married to a sister of the late 'Pink' Cole, Tonto cow king.

"Frank Prothero had meantime joined the Zimmerman pack train on Pine Creek as a scrub scout. The Lieutenant in charge needed packers and guides who were familiar with the General Springs Pass of the Tonto Rim to escort the government commissary division. Frank suggested me, because I knew every trail and hiding place in the Tonto Basin and the surrounding countryside, and because he believed I had the courage.

"On the 14th," Charlie wrote, "Frank rode into the ranch looking for me. I was more than ready to help in this campaign against the deadly marauders, who had committed so many atrocities against my friends and neighbors. At that time 'the only good Apache was a dead Apache'."

Charlie's first concern, however, was for the safety and welfare of his family, and he hesitated in leaving. But his father, a fearless old sermonizer who had many earlier scrapes with Indians, assured him they would be able to care for themselves; and, in his southern twang, he remarked: "thar' ain't no bullet cast that kin kill me."

So late that same night on July 14, 1882, Charlie and Frank "skinned out" in feverish haste for Pine Creek under the command of Major Adna C. Chaffee of the 6th Division of the U.S. Cavalry; and Chief of Scouts Al Seiber, a man known to be braver than all his warriors and an expert in tracking and killing Apaches. From Pine Creek they were to rendezvous with the Army detachment from Fort McDowell, in Pleasant Valley.

Chaffee's company was known as the White Horse Company, as all were mounted on white or iron-grey steeds, except Chaffee, who rode a splendid black charger. Al Seiber's faithful, trusted Indian scouts came along as did famous scouts Tom Horn and Mickey Free. Horn came in as a scrub scout shortly before Charlie did, but didn't gain recognition until some years later.

Charlie and Frank had reached Pine Creek when Henry, alarmed to hear the Apaches were headed in the direction of Diamond Valley, returned home from Camp Verde the night of July 14th. He found everyone sleeping soundly and everything secure. He retired shortly afterward, intending to let the family know the Apaches could be nearby when he awoke the next morning. This, it turned out, was a grave mistake.

At 2:00 a.m., the morning of July 15th, the sleeping Meadows family was awakened by the loud barking of their dogs. Jake was sleeping at the time with his father and brother, Henry. At the first sign of dawn John Moberly Meadows got up to see why the dogs were barking. He thought it was the bear that had been invading the premises the previous two nights. Henry suspected Indians. As John Meadows got up, he took his long-tom fifty rifle off the shelf, placed his Remington 44 in its holster and started through the dense willows that lined the creek on the side of the house. He told Henry to cross the creek and they would meet where the dogs were barking. Jake, 10, got up with his mother at the same time and the two watched from the doorway as his father left the house. When his father got close to a brushy area, they heard a shot. He was about 70 yards from the house when they saw him throw up his hands and holler, "My God," and fall. Henry ran into the house and awakened John Valentine, and they both ran out with their guns toward where their father had fallen. John Valentine took one side of the creek, and Henry the opposite side. They called several times without an answer. When they came together, the Indians had surrounded them and commenced shooting before they had a chance to return fire themselves.

They were badly wounded, their clothing bright with blood, and both made a dash for the house. John hollered, "Get into the house before we are all killed!" Henry fell on the doorstep from where Jake and his mother dragged him into the house. "It was all excitement in the house," Jake testified later, "and once in a while the Indians would fire a volley at the cabins." Then, they commenced firing at the terrified milk cows in the pasture. About eight o'clock they quit firing and from that time on they could be seen gathering horses which they drove into the Meadows' fenced-in corn field, completely destroying the crop that had "just tasselled out." They gathered close to 200 horses, and could be seen "whistling down around the point. We were pretty bothered up, still there was always one of us that kept a look-out to see what they were doing." When last seen, they were driving a seething mass of frightened cattle and horses up the canyon, then the main horseback trail from Winslow to Flagstaff. Jake added: "Their dark, lean bodies were almost completely naked—their faces streaked with antelope blood, and their black, stringy unkempt hair adorned with feathered headdresses made a hideous, unbelievable sight." It was sometime after the hostiles left when Johnny Grey and Doc Massey, the first settlers of the Cold Springs Ranch, arrived. Mother Margaret told them what had happened. Johnny Grey left immediately to inform the people of the settlement and get word to Charlie at Pine Creek. Doc Massey stayed and cared for the wounded.

Grey rode hard and fast, and arrived in Green Valley at 4:30 p.m. with the frightening news. A courier wrongly informed Charlie soon afterward that "his father and brothers had been killed, the horses and cattle owned by Diamond Valley Ranch had been driven off, and the women and children were putting up a desperate fight of resistance."

"The Captain," Charlie said, "dispatched Frank Prothero, Marion Derrick, an old Indian fighter with King Woolsey way back in 1860, who knew the ways of the Indian, and a United States soldier to accompany me to the ranch." As the men arrived at the fork of "Hellgate" Trail, Marion Derrick said to them, "We will not pass here where the Indians might possibly slaughter us." He urged them to continue to the top of the mountain where they could get a better view of the Meadows' family cabins. Heeding the old soldier's advice, the party reconnoitered at the summit for a short time. They knew the Indians, if any were about, would be surprised by an air-chilling war-whoop, and the "bloody savages would take off for tall timber at the repeated sounds of our rifle fire."

Charlie burning with revenge, was heavy with remorse. He could have kicked himself into the next county for leaving his family at such a critical time. He also agonized for the condition of his mother and the little ones who were without the care and protection of the men in the family. His ride of uncertainty seemed an eternity to him.

"We reached the ranch at sundown," Charlie said. Other than the whimpering of the hounds and a bawling calf or two, they found everything ominously quiet. Thankfully, Charlie added, "The boys were still alive, thank the good Lord. They were suffering from their wounds but complained little."

The rest of the family was visibly shaken with grief and terror from their desperate experience, but all were bearing up well. Henry was unable to move from the waist down. John Valentine was bleeding badly and lay helplessly—his arms dangling uselessly. Their father was still missing.

In a letter to his sister, Rhoda McGinnis, in Visalia, Charlie wrote, "In the first volley, John's right arm had been shot through at the elbow, and a shot hit him over the heart. The bullet struck a clay pipe that was in his pocket, turning it to the left and saving his life. Henry was shot in the foot. The boys started to retreat when the Indians followed them closely and fired another volley. In this volley, John's other arm was broken at the wrist and a musket ball passed through the stock of Henry's gun. Another shot hit Henry's cartridge belt, exploding a cartridge into his groin that left a gaping hole."

Mother Margaret, Sarah Hazelton, and the children put up a miraculous defense. Henry loaded the extra guns with gun powder to make it look like the cabins were well defended. The younger boys, Jake and Mobley, were put under beds and covered with feathered mattresses. Maggie, 13, and James, 12, stood on tubs and flour sacks, tensely manning their smoking rifles and helping to repulse the whooping raiders like seasoned gunfighters.

The Meadows family was slack on the most important matter on which their lives depended. They kept very little water inside the cabins and built their cabins a good many yards from the river bed.

A letter to Charlie from his sister, Maggie Meadows Beach, survives in the Century House Museum in Yuma, Arizona. It reads:

> Pa did not have time to shoot. Only one shot rang out until the boys had gotten almost to him. We had rifles and pistols and Henry loaded everything with cartridges while he lay on his back. Mother ran out and got water and she and Sarah Hazelton were very busy trying to keep John from hemorrhaging to death. He was in a faint most of the time. Henry was unable to move from the waist down. He would not own up to being wounded until the Indians quit firing. I stood by his side while he showed me how to shoot, how to aim and how not to shoot until I could see the whites of their eyes. Jim had two guns and already knew how to shoot. He stood six feet from me on the same side of the house. We were very busy. Henry drank a lot of water and demanded a pair of scissors, which I got for him, so he could cut off the fat and flesh that was hanging from his groin. They did not shoot his cartridge belt off as some have said. He was carrying it in his hand and they shot his own cartridge into his groin. The surgeon cut it out the next day.
>
> Jake ran out and let the sixty head of dairy cows out that were making such a fuss, and Jim ran out and caught an old brood mare that had come up to the house from fright and tied her in the hall. I was to ride her out after night if help did not come.

But help did come with the arrival of Johnny Grey and Doc Massey, their neighbors.

Maggie would have been a very brave girl had she ridden out at night alone. But one refuge the helpless family had in their favor was that the cunning Apache, even if unpredictable, would never attack during darkness because of his superstitious belief that if he were killed, his spirit would wander there forever.

Charlie, Frank, and Marion Derrick found John Meadows lying on his back in the heavily wooded ravine, looking up at the sky with a bullet hole clear through his breast. "He was packed into the house that adjoined the fort and a close watch was kept," Charlie said. It was the most painful day of Charlie's life, bringing his father home to his Ma, who knew in her heart all along he was dead, as she courageously worked to stop the flow of blood from her desperately wounded boys.

News of the terrible tragedy spread swiftly. In Charlie's letter to his sister, Rhoda, he said, "At ten o'clock, Sam and William Houston, Bill Burch, Bill McDonald, and another man or two came. The soldier who had been dispatched for medical assistance was ambushed about a mile from the house, but escaped uninjured. A picket guard was put out and the boy's wounds were dressed, but there was no medicine to be had.

"Next morning, on July 16, 1882, at 8 a.m., Rose arrived home with an escort of four men, Sarah's brother Carter, who was anxious over his sister's safety, Monroe House, Charlie Bacon, and Ike Lowthian. Eva remained in town with friends. We wrapped Pa in blankets and with a sombre ceremony, buried him in the dirt floor of the hall between the two cabins. All traces of the grave were obliterated to prevent the Indians from coming back later and mutilating him. Pa was only a few feet from the one that killed him, while Henry and John were about fifteen feet away. It was truly a miraculous escape for the women and children, and we all rejoiced for that, but it was sad rejoicing.

"We placed feather beds in the wagons, and the wounded were made as comfortable as possible. Our belongings were placed in another, and at eleven on the morning of the 16th, we saddled up and started for Sidella under guard of fourteen well-armed men."

The grim column of settlers jolted down the winding, pot-holed and washer-board road, where only the dull creak of the wagons broke the disconcerting silence. "The road was rough, the heat intense," Charlie said, "and the last two miles Henry had to be carried on a litter to prevent re-opening of his wounds. At noon John's arm was swelling considerably, but Henry was resting easily. We left Sidella when the day cooled down and resumed our sorrowful journey in quest of a surgeon. One eventually met us in Green Valley and removed the cartridge from Henry's groin, then cleaned and sutured John's ghastly wounds." Henry's prognosis was grave. Wounds to the abdomen meant almost certain death. With medical technology as it was, most abdominal injuries were left to fester and putrefy.

On the following morning, July 17, after caring for his stunned and grieving family, Charlie sent his letter informing the kinfolk in Visalia of the tragedy. Then, with a heavy heart, he and Frank Prothero left "tolerably early" to return to Diamond Valley Ranch to check on John Moberly Meadows' grave and assess the damage.

In the grey light of dawn, on the morning of July 17, Charlie, torn with heartache and bitterness, rode into the ranch with Frank for the first time since the savage attack. He vowed he would never rest, swearing vengeance for the brutal attack the merciless Indians had made against his family. The awful smell of death was everywhere. The boys found the horses that had not been driven off had taken to tall timber from fright; sometimes frightened horses have been known to stampede for a distance of 40 miles without stopping. A few others gave a whinnied greeting that echoed across the ghostlike aura of the canyon. Other horses, along with a few remaining dairy herd, were swishing their tails and munching away in the demolished corn field. A few bloating carcasses, ravaged by varmints, crawling with flies and cattle grubs, lay strewn about the cabin area. Charlie and Frank shuddered at the sight but, fortunately, John Meadows' grave was left undisturbed.

Twenty-two year-old Charlie, pushed by the ravages of the Apache into manhood and the position of leadership within his family, looked upon the remains of Diamond Valley with a hard, cold eye. One cannot help but wonder, as surely Charlie did, what would have been the outcome had circumstances not placed him away from his family when they were attacked. It was then up to him to salvage what he could and scrap out an existence for those who were now solely dependent on him.

Prothero and Charlie traced the trail leading up the ravine, then followed it in a northerly direction out of the ranch and tallied the dead stock bearing the Diamond Valley brand. Nothing in Charlie's experience had prepared him for the slaughter he had just witnessed. Tears of pain sprung to his eyes, for there was a picture to be engraved in his memory forever. Shattered by the slow sobering of reality, Charlie finally broke down, bewailing the tragic loss of his father, and everything his father had worked for. Charlie Meadows cried honestly and unashamedly at one of the few times in his life.

"We found numerous animals between the ranch and the main trail, leading up to what is now the 'old tunnel road.' After we hit the main trail we came across horses and cattle from the Sigsby and Tewksbury ranges as well. It was a well-defined trail cut through the sand, and in many places only a foot or two wide," Charlie later testified in his Indian depredations claim, "In other places the tracks of horses and Indians spread from 20-30 feet on either side. Some of the carcasses were easily identified by flesh and brand marks. We had to dismount to identify others.

"We had seven stallions three Morgan, two Belmont, and two Blackwhip. Four we found dead on the trail. The others were never recovered and presumed dead. There were eleven American mules, sixty blooded brood mares, seventy-five half-breed mares, twenty-three saddle horses, and ninety-one colts (two- and three-year-olds) either missing or dead; some stabbed, speared or shot, and others had their throats slit . . . pot luck for the wheeling flight of vultures soaring overhead. We estimated our Diamond Valley Ranch losses based on the number of bands and the number of animals in each band."

Many years later, in a letter to the Arizona State Historian, Effie Keene, Charlie wrote, "The Indians had a well-directed plan to annihilate the White Horse Company, but unknown to them a part of the 3rd and 9th Cavalry, under the command of Major Evans, joined the fight. When we had gone ten miles, the footprints and hoof prints from Major Evans' troops completely obliterated the trail. We were met here by some flankers. I remember a Lieutenant Kingsbury and a Captain Wallace. Colonel Dodd, who made the famous long-distance march into Mexico during President Woodrow Wilson's administration, was a Lieutenant at the Chevelon Fork Battle. Most of these men were on the battlefield when we rode in that night." There were dead Indians scattered about the battle area and amongst the boulders. One, they told him, was the crumpled form of the warrior Nantiatish. Through the years, evidence proved several more Indians had crawled away and died in caves amongst the rocky mountainside.

Charlie saw a few squaws and papooses captured by the troops, and carcasses of horses and mules caught in the cross fire lying in the field. One squaw was found with a shattered leg, and, as a matter of course, the Army surgeon laid her across a large rock and amputated it on the spot. The story goes that she wanted them to take the other leg off as well, so she could walk on short stumps, which they refused to do. Later, when attempting to move her onto a litter, she began giving frantic gestures, which eventually led them to her papoose who was concealed amongst the rocks. Both were returned to the reservation.

Charlie testified that "Among the citizens there to claim their stock, were G. O. Sigsby, Bill Richards, and Sam and William Houston. We all stayed the night of the 17th, recovering our stock upon identification the next morning. Frank Prothero and I returned to the ranch that afternoon, recovering only thirteen live head of horses."

There were only a few Army casualties. One was buried where he fell, and the six wounded were removed by government ambulance cart to Fort Verde. So ended the fight the Army insists on calling "The Battle of the Big Dry Wash"—the last major action between the military and hostile Indians in Arizona.

The horrid butcheries exercised against defenseless fellow citizens did not fail to excite in every bosom a spirit of revenge. The public, in a strong wave of loud and angry protest, demanded an end to the Apache menace in Arizona. General Crook was ordered back on September 3, 1882, to take charge. Had the Indians been able to read or write, the criminal neglect at San Carlos might have been exposed earlier, and the Meadows family might have been spared from tragedy as a result of the Indians' discontent. When General Crook later counseled with the Apache leaders, it was then he learned of the crimes committed at San Carlos. Tiffany, and a few others, were relieved of authority.

A Return to Normalcy

Frank Prothero stayed on to help Charlie while John Valentine and Henry recovered from their wounds, since the burden of total responsibility was likely too much for Charlie to handle alone. He was surely grateful to have such a trusted and loyal friend as Frank Prothero to assist him through the ordeal. L. J. Horton, another family friend, helped him with the distressful task of exhuming his father's mortal remains and moving them to a grassy knoll below Fort McDonald, on the west side of town, where he had the distinguished honor of being the first person buried in what is now the Payson Pioneer Cemetery.

On September 17, 1882, two months to the day after the Battle of the Big Dry Wash and the demise of the "murderous fiend" Nantiatish, Henry lost his desperate fight for life. He succumbed to mortification of his wounds, which literally "ate his guts away." He died a painful death and was buried next to his father. One man in the prime of his life, the other with an entire life ahead of him, both now slept eternity away together.

Life in the Arizona wilderness proved to be a constant hazard—leaving little room for cowardice. With single-minded determination, Charlie polished his skills and acquired a deadly, unerring aim with his rifle and unbelievable expertise with the lasso. He was never without his Winchester and *reata* close at hand. The Winchester was a fine weapon, with more lethal capacity than the ordinary rifles of the American and Mexican Armies. As he naturally had a personal grudge against these particular Indians, he gathered a group of tough cowboys from the basin experienced in Indian fighting. They never closed their eyes without first putting out "pickets" to give the alarm in case of the slightest suspicion. They were a wild bunch, the cowboys of old Yavapai, trigger conscious and ready for any adventure. Danger made them callous, suspicious, and rudely realistic; the Indians had a deadly fear of them. "Because the government failed miserably in their efforts to keep them on the reservation," Charlie remarked to a reporter, "some of the boys and I taught them the reservation was a pretty healthy place to be. Fighting and running from naked Indians became my business and pastime, and from time to time we enjoyed a bit of sweet revenge."

Promiscuous shooting was going on in the crowded streets of the little frontier town of Phoenix. Saloons were filled with drunk and disorderly cowboy toughs, barroom brawlers and diverse types of individuals who "wore 'em low." Wandering in from places like Calabasa and Tombstone, they yelled and yipped and shot holes in the sky as they galloped. It was a wonder more were not hurt by their deviltries. All the hard cases and troublemakers were warned to leave town fast—or be jailed. Tombstone and Calabasa were told if they had any more to spare, to send them to Phoenix, where they would be well taken care of—perhaps like others, hung by lynch law.

Mother Margaret Meadows and the younger children did not return to Diamond Valley. There was too much heartache to live there anymore. After Henry's death, Charlie moved her and the younger children to Phoenix, where they could go to school and she would be near a doctor. Her condition worsened rapidly. Eva changed her name to Mrs. Edward Applestill, while Rose married Stephen Dole. Charlie's sister, Maggie, was the only one left at home to care for her mother and three younger brothers, James, Jake, and Mobley.

John's stiff and crippled arms mended slowly while he and Charlie resumed their routine tasks about the ranch, working hard to get it back on a paying basis. As executor of the estate of J. M. Meadows, Charlie rode over to Prescott, the Yavapai County Seat, on October 10, 1883 to re-register the Diamond Valley brands under the Meadows Brothers' names—the stock having been equally divided amongst the heirs—and hear the fiddles play on Whiskey Row. That same year John took title to the Augusta and Atlantic mining claims where the boys wanted to hit pay dirt.

On September 24, 1883, Sarah Jane Hazelton became the bride of Bill McDonald. Her courageous efforts on behalf of the family on that hellish day, and her grief over Henry's death just one year before, were never forgotten, and the Meadows family wished her happiness. Her brother, Carter, who helped move the Meadows to Green Valley after the brutal attack, established a ranch with George Felton on Rye Creek.

In two short years, their loving mother, broken-hearted and in ill health, gave up her will to live. Mr. and Mrs. Horton helped Charlie and John by staying at her side two weeks prior to her death. It was the final blow in a series of tragedies that had been their cross to bear. Her pine coffin was brought home over a long, rough wagon trail and placed beneath the sod next to the others. Maggie assumed all household tasks at their new home with John and Charlie at Buckhead Ranch on Sidella Creek, and was the guiding light for her three younger brothers. Little brother, Mobley, took to horses like a puppy to warm milk, and became Charlie's constant shadow.

John Valentine Meadows, Brother of Charles Meadows

James Harvey Meadows, Mobley Augustus Meadows, Jacob "Jake" David Meadows

CHAPTER 4

1884
CHARLIE'S FIRST WILD WEST RODEO

Charlie was a genial, handsome, cheerful, and reckless giant. He had the air of a gentleman, incapable of embarrassment or dismay, who early demonstrated that he was a born leader.

Having grown up on a horse with a lasso in his hands and a rifle in his saddle boot, Charlie entered his first Wild West roping contest in August of 1884. He competed against another early settler and fellow "Hassayamper," John Chilson, in Payson's mid-town cow pasture. (It is said those who drink from the Hassayampa River in Arizona never tell the truth.) This contest set a precedent—one that has been carried out each August since 1884. Two years later on July 4th, 1886, he entered his first publicly-announced exhibition in Prescott at the Independence Day celebration. It was here that Charlie won with a time of 59.5 seconds, after the steer was given a 100-yard start.

Organized rodeo is reputed to have originated in 1876, in Denver, Colorado. But, as early as 1869 at Deer Trail, Colorado, the title was given to the "Champion Bronco Buster of the Plains," and a suit of clothes awarded the winner, Emilne Gardenshire of the Miliron Ranch. Yet, the *Encyclopedia Americana* states, "Most authorities agree that the first public contest for prizes for bronco and steer roping was held near Pecos, Texas, on July 4, 1883." Nevertheless, another earlier event for prizes, where a wild steer was ridden at a *Fourth of July* celebration, was held in Cheyenne, Wyoming in 1872. The Rodeo Cowboy's Association Yearbook of some years back, sums it up well when it states, "Rodeo's beginning is hidden in the haze from countless cattle drives and camp fire smoke on the open ranges of the West for over a hundred years."

Jim Blackburn, who was Deputy Sheriff in Pine, Arizona some years ago, and a rodeo contestant in earlier years, said that Doc Pardee, who ramrodded rodeos and horse races in Prescott back in the 1930's, agreed, after many arguments, that Payson's claim to the world's oldest rodeo was valid. Prescott claims that the first contest for which an admission fee was charged and prizes awarded, was held at Prescott, Arizona, July 4, 1888. Yet, the *Encyclopedia Britannica* listed Denver, Colorado as the traditionally accepted birthplace of paid spectator rodeo, October, 1887.

The world's oldest rodeo will probably remain unknown, but Charlie's 1884 Payson rodeo is considered by many to have been the first genuine Wild West rodeo ever held.

Charlie entered every contest around, astride his favorite horse, "Snowstorm." He bedecked Snowstorm with a saddle blanket made from the fur-skin of an obliging bear.

Charlie exhibited his skills in every country carnival and side show in the whole territory. He became fair game for the journalists locally—as well as nationally. Their headlines reported him being a "crack shot," "a good sport," the "fastest man with a rope in the business," and "fast company for all comers."

Some of the sports that appealed to the settlers at these grass roots affairs, other than the lusty cowboy events, were: cock-fighting, chicken pulling, pole climbing, pig catching, foot, sack and squaw races—each for a purse—and, pitching dollars to the line, a gambling practice second only to horse racing.

The excitement afforded in cowboy tournaments is equally divided by the performer and the spectator. In Charlie's day the stockmen of the West perpetuated the custom of encouraging their men to become deserving riders and experts with the *reata*.

Bronc Busting

Now "bustin' a bronc" or "bronc stompin'" as the early day "waddies" called it, or "breaking a mustang," as the city dudes prefer, attracts all the men from the range to the corral. During tournament days, people in Texas, Arizona, and Colorado suspended their businesses and closed their doors to see the battle of the supremacy among the graduates of the plains. Money, cattle, and horses were regarded with reckless hands, and often interest in the contests became so intense that lively pool selling was carried on two to three weeks ahead of the contest.

The corral is full of broncos that have never known what it is to wear a halter or have a lasso around them since their branding, usually three years earlier. The cowboy enters the enclosure with the lasso in his hands; his entrance is a signal for the ponies to stampede. Soon, everything is wild confusion. The cowboy singles out a mustang, then whirls his lasso through the air; the pony is stopped and thrown heavily to the ground. The animal struggles for a moment, but his captor gives an extra turn to his lariat and the bronco is held fast by the rope. After this, the expeditious cowboy places a cloth or bandana over the eyes of the prostrate pony and he quickly slips the hackmore over his head. Then the lasso is loosened and the mustang springs to his feet. It stands as motionless as a statue, with the exception of its body quivers caused by the excitement of the conflict. Practically blind by the cloth before his eyes, the loss of vision is beyond comprehension. A forty-pound saddle is thrown on his back and the broad horsehair cinch is drawn tight with a firm hand. The cowboy then bounds lightly into the saddle and, leaning forward, removes the bandana from the animal's eyes.

The bronco takes in the situation like a flash. In a fraction of a second, the bronco and rider are in the air in wild confusion—while the ranch hands and spectators look on with delight. Horse and cowboy quickly return to earth—the mustang with its back arched, its head rigidly down to its knees, tail tightly tucked between its legs, and all four feet close together.

The impact is terrific. Off goes the cowboy's *sombrero*, his guns seem to fly from their holsters and his garments sometimes actually part at the seams. The mustang leaps again and again, but the rider holds on for all he is worth, burying the rowels of his big Mexican spurs into the cinch of the saddle. This skyward vaulting, interspersed with bolting and running, is kept up until the cowboy has shed the bulk of his clothing except for his shirt and spurs. Usually the rider remains on the "hurricane deck" of his "beast friend," while his cowboy friends lined along the fence railing on the outer edge of the enclosure shout words of encouragement. Either the mustang or cowboy must conquer; generally, it is the cowboy. Occasionally, the cinch gives way and the rider hits the corral dust. Sometimes he gets thrown over the mustang's head by the impetus given by the indescribable bucks, landing 6 to 10 feet away from the spirited brute he was astride only seconds before. In those olden days of bronc' stompin', the rider stayed on the beast until he fell, or was thrown off. Nowadays all the rider has to do is stay on for ten seconds and, if he does stay that long, the pick-up man takes him off for the ride is complete.

Steer Tying

Steer and bull tying were more challenging to Charlie because a good roper separated the real cowboy from the pretender, and Charlie was a serious contender. In those days, big, heavy, lanky, mean brutes were used, nothing like the small calves in some of today's roping events. Chutes were not used in those days either, and the beast was given up to a 100-yard start. Big, long, leather *reata*s, made from the finest parts of a young heifer's hide, were used instead of the grass ropes used today. Cowboys developed a special devotion for their equipment and spent days perfecting it in preparation for the rigors of the arena.

At the Territorial Fair held in Phoenix in 1888, Charlie accomplished this feat in 59 seconds, establishing a new record. These times compare favorably with the present-day professionals who use calves from a chute; whereas in Charlie's day, the steer was given a 100-yard start. Most of the rodeo cowboys nowadays are not working cowhands as they were in those earlier days.

The wild steers were brought upon the grounds in a herd before the spectators, rounded up and held by the *vaqueros* in a "snorting pen" near the judge's stand. Superiority in this contest is based on the time devoted to the accomplishment of the work. When all is in readiness, the cowboy singles out the steer of his choice and, with a hair-raising whoop and holler, rushes the animal down the line indicated by the flagman. The cowboy contestant straddled on a thoroughly trained mustang is stationed at a distance of 25 feet from the flagman. As the steer crosses the "deadline," the flagman drops the flag as a signal for the cowboy to begin. The cowboy digs his spurs into the horse's flanks and he is off with a bound that overtakes the swiftly fleeing steer. With a rapid swing of his lasso whirled through the air, the loop lands around the bovine. The contestant then draws the rope up along the right side of the animal and reins his horse to the left at right angles to the course of the steer. This brings the lariat across the hind legs of the beast. The lasso is quickly wrapped around the horn of the saddle and all slack taken up. The cowboy throws his weight with the lasso away from the steer. Its head is drawn to the right, its hind legs crowded forward and, before the steer can comprehend what has taken place, it has lost its footing and is lying in a heap on the ground. By a skillful turn, the lariat is slipped from the hind legs of the prostrate animal up to the forelegs, which are drawn forward to the steer's head.

The well-trained pony, which seems to take as much interest in and is no less an expert in the business than its master, sits back on the rope fast around the horn of the saddle, holds it tight, and stands as if anchored there. The cowboy then dismounts—taking a short rope or "piggin' string," from about his waist—and binds the steer's feet. After accomplishing this, he signals the judge. Time is counted from the drop of the flag to this signal. The skill and agility developed by these cowhands are beyond the comprehension of a tenderfoot.

Of course, this wild western sport is not without peril. The steers are frequently fierce brutes. Should the lariat break, or the mustang give it slack, the steer can regain his freedom and head for the cowboy who is endeavoring to tie him. The horse and cowboy must act in unison, with a perfect understanding; otherwise, the fierce and powerful brute they have sought to overcome may turn on them to their injury and possible death. Charlie witnessed these injuries—many of which were serious. Few contestants came out of contests without injury. "Doc" Goodwin, the most reckless and daring of all cowboy contestants known to Charlie, took many life-threatening spills.

In those early days, interference from humane groups was unknown. But, in later years, putting on a good rodeo brought bitter entanglements with the Humane Society. Concern was for the animal, but the "two legged" variety received the broken bones. Although frequently injured, the real cowboy suffered his pain silently.

There were few purses for the winners in those days. In the Arizona Territory, it has been said, "Gambling was the profession of many a man, the recreation of most of them, and the avocation of a considerable number." Charlie was a serious gambler, and the first order of business in his contests was to make up a purse to serve as prize money which was badly needed to help support his family.

The laws of the rodeo in those days were simple. The rules relating to rodeos, as they appear in the *Arizona Revised Statutes* during Charlie's time, are as follows:

> *Section 1.* Cattle owners living in the same general neighborhood can agree upon the time, manner, and place of holding rodeos, but such rodeos shall be held once each year. When the time of rodeos is agreed upon, notice of the same must be posted in three public places in the neighborhood, at least ten days prior to such rodeos.

> *Section 2.* Cattle owners after each rodeo shall drive all the cattle belonging to them back to the ranches in possession of the owners of such cattle respectively.
> *Section 3.* Whenever any person turns cattle loose on any range already occupied or in possession of another, he shall furnish water on such range in addition to that already thereon free, unfenced and on the surface sufficient to water all such cattle.
> *Section 4.* Any person violating the provisions of this act is guilty of a misdemeanor by the penal code. (*Hoofs and Horns*)

Charlie's roping exploits and Indian scrapes received considerable mention in the *National Police Gazette,* and other leading publications in the East, as well as journals in the West. One unidentified newspaper printed the following decorous verse:

> To the West! To The West! To the Land of the Free,
> Where Tall Charlie Meadows is Having a Spree,
> And the Mexican Bronco is Arching His Back,
> To the Shooting Iron's Frequent and Petulant Crack.

Charlie Meadows, with Horse, Snowstorm, and the Yavapai Cowboys

CHAPTER 5

1885-1886
GERONIMO

The next ten years were turbulent times for the Arizona pioneer. The turbulence was caused not only by the Apache but by warring factions of white men as well. The Tonto Basin had been cursed by a gang of cutthroats and robbers who hesitated at no crime. Down South, the days of the legendary Earps were numbered and they were soon run out of Tombstone. A new crowd of thugs and riffraff moved in, with fourteen murders in ten days. Shotgun rule was again the order of the day. Territories were expected to be self-governing before qualifying for statehood. President Chester A. Arthur threatened to declare marshal law in Arizona if the territory was not immediately cleaned up even though there was some measure of law and order.

Then the Chiricahua Warm Springs Apaches, under the leadership of Geronimo, Natchez, and their warriors, returned to the reservation from a bloody interlude in Mexico and resumed their grisly deeds, committing horrible outrages. Roving bands of Indians continued raiding white men's ranches and marking their line of travel with fire and blood. Reportedly, Charlie was involved in several of these skirmishes and in 1884 led a band of cowboys after them, "taking my first scalp in one of the altercations; my receipt for a 'good' Apache." He seemed to relish the danger.

Geronimo, Natchez, and others continued on the warpath, raiding and plundering in and out of Mexico, killing ranchers' wives and their children. General Crook captured Geronimo once, only to have him escape. Crook was disheartened and broken in spirit and asked to be relieved of his command. "Here is a job for someone," he announced, "Geronimo cannot be subdued in twenty years."

But General Miles was anxious to try, and asked to take over his dangerous position. After relieving General Crook of his command, he issued the following statement: "Arizona has been a graveyard of reputations, but I do not intend it be mine. A more turbulent and desperate, disreputable band of human beings I have never seen before and hope to never see again. Indian depredations and atrocities have been endured long enough, and must end in this territory."

In time, Geronimo surrendered. The Chiricahuas band had their fangs pulled and were safely incarcerated in Florida. The other tribes, 4,000 at San Carlos and 1,800 who were self-sustained at Fort Apache, became more industrious under the direction of General Miles—peaceable, happy and productive. At that time they had 1,000 acres of barley and wheat under cultivation, with nearly as much corn, pumpkins, and squash. Eager to learn the white man's inscrutable ways, they owned large numbers of cattle and horses in fine condition, and were fast falling into the "White Man's" way of handling them.

It is doubtful that Charlie was involved in the Geronimo campaign. With a family to support and a ranch to handle, he had more than enough to keep him occupied. There was a great deal of yarn swapping, and a good many outrageous tales were told when the cowboys got together. Charlie never stood in the way of a good story, especially those about himself, and it did not matter whether the yarn was true or not. He had an uncanny knack for mixing fact with fiction, and it amused him to play upon the tenderfoot's innocence. It is possible he told the following story for the benefit of the tenderfoot. Lieutenant R. L. Robinson, a historian and correspondent with the *San Francisco Chronicle,* either swallowed it whole, or was looking for a spectacular and apocryphal piece of reporting he hoped would satisfy his readers, when on February 6, 1893, he graphically described "A Terror To Apaches" for his newspaper.

In this article Robinson said, "The only wound Geronimo ever received in any campaign was in the Canyon Creek fight of September 3, 1886, and was inflicted by none other than Arizona Charlie, just before Geronimo's capture in the Mogollon Mountains.

The cowboys, nine in number, camped at Bear Springs on Canyon Creek. They hobbled their horses, spread out their bedrolls, and laid down to sleep."

This particular night, the Apaches, who never attacked at night, were on the cliff above getting water. They noticed the sleeping camp and planned an attack early the next morning.

Robinson continued by saying, "The frontier instinct of the cowboys saved their lives, for, instead of sleeping near the fire, they unrolled their blankets about 100 feet away, where the boulders protected them from the blowing sand." The Indians, "about fifty in number," he said, "who had swung themselves over the precipice with the aid of their *reatas*, fired into the saddles which they mistook for the sleeping whites. Before the Indians knew their danger, a sheet of flame burst from the crevices behind the *Palos Verdes,* and nine of the foremost bucks fell dead." Of course, they succeeded in killing a few of the whites.

Geronimo then took the remainder of his warriors, waiting on the cliff, and made an attempt to overrun the whites. When the frightened horses ran rapidly by in their hobbled condition, the cowboys lassoed them and quickly threw on their saddles, as they "dashed down the gorge in the face of 200 redskins!" A heated battle was supposed to have ensued and, "with the last shot in his Winchester, Charlie broke the chief's thigh!" Charlie then lost his hat, his hair was clotted with blood from a spear wound delivered by Geronimo himself, and his face was begrimed with dirt.

"Geronimo attempted to escape," explained Robinson, "but Charlie uncoiled his lasso, and caught the fleeing pony, throwing the Indian and his pony down a steep trail. Warriors were supposed to have picked him up, but the whole band made a hasty retreat over the *mesa*. They took the chief to one of their camps in the mountains, where he partially recovered. Even after he was captured and put on trial, he asked for a gun to kill Meadows."

Charlie Meadows' Saddle Medal

CHAPTER 6

1886-1887
BLOODY FEUD IN PLEASANT VALLEY

The tide of lawlessness was rising rapidly and troubles were compounding for the settlers. John Valentine Meadows was sworn in as first Coroner and Justice of the Peace in Payson about this time. The exact date is unknown. These records, according to Earl Forrest, author of *Arizona's Dark and Bloody Ground*, were lost in a fire at Payson.

Next door in Pleasant Valley, the place with a "harmonious name," the largest, most gruesome of all white man's blood, feuds "erupted with a vengeance" between the Tewksbury and Graham families.

The Tewksburys were the first settlers in Pleasant Valley in 1880, building their cabin at the junction of Cherry and Rock Creeks. After the death of his Indian wife in California, James Dunning Tewksbury and his three sons, Edwin, John, and James, first moved to Globe, Arizona, where James D. married another woman before settling in the Tonto Basin.

The Grahams, Thomas and John, came from Iowa by way of California, and settled two miles northwest of the Tewksbury ranch in 1882.

In the beginning the two families were friends, both in the employ of a cattleman named Stinson. One report states that the Grahams and Tewksburys were stealing from their boss and putting their own brands on his stock. A quarrel resulted and a "smouldering enmity" burst into flame with the two accusing each other of taking more than their share. Stinson supported this account by stating his cattle were disappearing. First the Grahams and then the Tewksburys were charged in court with this crime, but both cases were dismissed for lack of evidence. Then in 1886, Ed Tewksbury shot and wounded James Stinson's ranch foreman for accusing him of stealing cattle. The Tewksburys began losing cattle as well, and like many other cattlemen who had been robbed, decided to raise sheep, an animal not easily stolen. But the sheepmen were the enemy of cattlemen; the entrance of sheep represented a theft of the juicy grasslands which the cattlemen regarded as rightfully theirs. The "woolies" nibbled the grasses down to the bare roots and then their cloven hooves cut the tender roots to pieces.

Charlie wrote, "Though cattlemen themselves had no love for the 'woolie stinkers,' I, myself, do not believe it was solely a contention between cattle and sheepmen for mastery of the range, but caused by a band of organized rustlers who made their headquarters at the Graham stronghold in Pleasant Valley."

Another account describes the Graham compound as the "most revengeful and thoroughly organized bunch of criminals, just waiting for the settlers to clean out the Indians—when by 'hook or crook,' they could take possession." Records taken by Judge Hicks in Prescott show the Grahams were criminals before entering the Tonto Basin. Warrants were issued for their arrest.

The feud between the two families continued to deepen, with other settlers joining in sympathy with one side or the other until more than three score "had died with their boots on."

In August of 1887, J. D. Houck, a Tewksbury partisan, rode in to Pleasant Valley with a warrant for the arrest of James Stott for horse theft, when Billy Graham confronted him on the trail. Both men drew their guns simultaneously—with Houck a mite quicker on the trigger, leaving Billy Graham dead by the wayside. Soon after, John Paine, considered by some to be a "bad man" and member of the Hashknife gang, along with Hampton Blevins, Tom Tucker, and Bob Gillespie, rode into Pleasant Valley armed with enough ammunition to wage war. John Paine's main job was to watch for sheep that might water at the springs and forage on the adjacent range. Paine had learned of the trouble in Pleasant Valley, and the disappearance of Hampton Blevin's father, and was anxious to "even" the score. The four men stopped at the Flying V Ranch, owned by two "neutral" and prominent citizens named J. J. Vosberg and George Newton, and asked for some food.

The two owners apparently were out, but in those days locked cabins were considered an inhospitable act. So that day someone took advantage of this hospitality and sat waiting behind the dark doors. Being denied by a rude reply of "no food for the likes of you," the men wheeled their horses and started to leave when a volley of shots burst from the gun holes in the cabin. Now John Paine and Hampton Blevins lay dead. No one knew who had done the shooting, but the Grahams maintained that Ed Tewksbury and his brother, Jim, were inside the house, and it was believed James Roberts was with them. Roberts was equally bitter over the loss of a valuable stallion at his ranch on Tonto Creek just below the Mogollon Rim, which is the present Zane Grey place. He blamed this on the Graham band of rustlers, and joined with the Tewksbury forces. Thus, the feud began in earnest.

Coroner and Justice of the Peace John V. Meadows, along with the help of storekeeper Charles Perkins, buried the two cowboys, Paine and Blevins, who, in the words of an old frontier ballad, "got shot in the body." One book states that the burial was "without service of any kind, for Perkins and Meadows were not familiar with such rites and did the best they could."

John's father was a Minister of the Lord, who believed in heaven, the Bible, Holy Trinity, blessed spirits, and hell. He made sure his children were all knowledgeable of the Almighty and words of the Good Book.

A dedicated exponent of frontier law and order, Justice John Meadows' courage and valor during this critical period has been told in many books and articles. One stated that "no braver or more daring man ever lived in Arizona than Judge John V. Meadows."

Charlie said, "Why such prominent citizens as George Newton and J. J. Vosberg, owners of the Flying V Ranch, were involved in this terrible vendetta will always be a mystery to me."

The Pleasant Valley troubles were of such magnitude that the Yavapai County Government was powerless to interfere. The lawless polecats took advantage of this laxity and acted as their passions and prejudices desired, hunting each other like wild animals and leaving a stench in the nostrils of decent folk. Every ranch in Pleasant Valley was deserted as no one felt safe in carrying out his own business. The women and children were bunched together and placed where they could better be protected from the death-dealing rifles of the "free-booters" and "brand wranglers" who acted upon the "bushwhacking" plan, shooting from concealment and making away with their plunder. It was not the intention of the bushwhackers to confine their murderous assaults to the two parties entirely, but to stage an open fight between the scores of friends and sympathizers on both sides.

The smouldering fire of vengeance continued to spread with fury. It was much healthier to take an impartial attitude in this bloody conflict. Trouble was always as close as the next bend in the road. Even though the Tewksbury boys were their friends, the Meadows brothers acted prudently and wisely to secure their own self-preservation. "Why walk into death when life could be so free and sweet," was their philosophy. With John as Justice of the Peace they enjoyed a certain amount of immunity, but Charlie always looked straight ahead, never over his shoulder, slept with one eye open and stayed as alert as the weasel. "Innocent settlers were drawn into the fracas and the report that so-and-so had joined up with the Tewksburys, or vice versa, often made disinterested parties a poor insurance risk," Charlie said.

But the Meadows family was not completely immune from the lawlessness going on in those parts. In March of 1887, Charlie and Frank drove two men from the Meadows family ranch, employees of a Mr. Hoy, they said, who claimed the ranch was his. The following day Charlie and Frank encountered Hoy on the public road, stuck a shining revolver in his face and took him into Payson at gunpoint. Charlie felt he had a "right to defend" his property, and Hoy was a trespasser with hostile intentions. Though such was the case, Charlie was informed that the "law should have been invoked to dispossess him and the right of legal ownership established." It is not hard to imagine what Charlie thought of that. It was surely enough to pucker his chin whiskers, rankle his spurs, and exasperate him more than a den of provoked Arizona rattlers.

Then, because of his suspected friendship with the Tewksburys, it was the intention of Graham's band of rustlers to turn Charlie into food for worms, by accusing him of killing a calf belonging to the Waters Cattle Company. In August of 1887, Charlie and Frank Prothero were in Flagstaff with a couple of the "boys," enjoying a bit of the "horse's neck" at the Blue Grass Exchange Saloon—a favorite hangout, when they received the following note which read,

> C. Meadows and Prothero
> Flagstaff.
>
> Bissig and John Meadows got back last evening from the Gordon country, and say they learned from reliable parties that the Waters Cattle Company men were waiting for you—to take you in had you passed that way to Flag. They also say from information, it was that outfit that shot up the house. Be careful in what road you take in coming back.
>
> Yours in haste,
> Wentworth.
> (Judge John W.)

The feud reached a climatic level in 1887 when John Valentine Meadows became deeply involved in his legal capacity as Justice of the Peace. On September 21, 1887, "with gravel in his gizzard," he rode over to Pleasant Valley alone. It was some twenty-odd miles he had to go—on his favorite horse, "Old Dunn," and in his shirt sleeves to show he carried no concealed weapons—into the thick of the battle at the Tewksbury ranch, which one report maintained had been held under siege by the Graham band for 11 days. It was an extremely "ticklish" situation for John to be in, and he had second thoughts of why he even went there alone. No one else wanted to take the chance and go with him. John ordered the attackers away and, with respect for the Justice, the men sullenly withdrew. However, had Justice John Meadows not arrived when he did to restore order, it was generally believed the invaders would have torched the Tewksbury's cabin that night.

Then John's grisly task was to perform inquests on the decomposed bodies of feud victims, John Tewksbury and Bill Jacobs, who had lain for days in the yard of the Tewksbury's home unburied. While Mrs. John Tewksbury watched the wild hogs root and devour parts of her dead husband, the Graham rustlers stood guard so no one could leave the cabin to bury them. With the help of the storekeeper, Charles Perkins, John dug a shallow pit and the two men rolled the foul-smelling and badly mutilated bodies into it with their shovels. The effect of this atrocity on the Tewksbury family was told by Jim Tewksbury, who said, "No damned man can kill a brother of mine, and then stand by while the hogs eat him, and live within a mile of me!"

The Graham terrorists intended to ambush John Meadows at Hellgate Trail so the news of their brutal atrocities would never reach the people. But John decided to cut across to the upper trail and stay the night at the Horton ranch. This sudden change of plans saved his life.

The stirring feud continued to rage, and Judge John Meadows tried many of the murderous culprits in his court. Many of the verdicts were for dismissal, for "lack of evidence," but the two unfortunate factions failed to see the futility of it all until it was too late. In the end all but two had been "wounded to death." Some to this day still lay in unknown graves in the Arizona wilderness. John's official count of the dead was 34, a large percentage when you consider there were only 400 souls in all of Gila County at that time. Payson became part of Gila County in 1890.

There are some records of feud expenses. On October 6, 1887, John Meadows collected expenses totaling $72, and on January 3, 1888, his expenses in line of duty netted him another $175. Charlie served some bench warrants for Sheriff Mulvenon and received a modest fee for his efforts.

Tom Graham and Ed Tewksbury, the two survivors of the feuding families, seemed ready to forget the dreadful feud that had claimed so many members of their families and friends. But some of their partisans continued to wax trigger-happy.

First, George Newton, a Tewksbury sympathizer and operator of the Flying V Ranch, disappeared as he rode the 65 miles from his jewelry shop in Globe to his ranch in Pleasant Valley. Then, Tom Graham took his family and moved to Tempe, Arizona, where he lived "peacefully" until August 2, 1892. As he drove a wagon load of grain from his farm to Tempe, two horsemen waiting in a thicket shot him in the back. Ed Tewksbury and John Rhodes were arrested for his murder and sent to trial. This left Ed Tewksbury the sole survivor of the two feuding families involved in the Pleasant Valley War.

Hashknife Cowboy Comes to Payson

While this heated affair was at its zenith, a personable young cowboy named Tom Beach rode into the Tonto Basin. Tom had been orphaned at a tender age, and struck out on his own at age 13. This was when young Tom saw both sides of life. He worked his way down the Mississippi River, living for a spell with a grizzled old buffalo hunter and his squaw wife. Tom was given a Buffalo rifle. Soon the big buffalo guns were booming, and 17 year-old Tom was kept busy with a sharp skinning knife. Tom helped haul the green hides back to camp and pegged them out—hair side down, to stink and lay stiff like big boards. But Tom could not stand the stink and squalor of the maggot-filled carcasses long. He made his way to Texas.

Tom joined a group of cowboys who were driving a herd of long-horned steers from Texas to Holbrook, Arizona, for the Aztec Land and Cattle Company, one of the largest outfits in all the Southwest that ranged their herds as far as the Tonto Basin. Most of these cowboys were sons of Confederate soldiers—trying to get lost in the West. They became known as the "Hashknife" cowboys because of the shape of their brand—which resembled a crude tool used for cooking. Some were first-hand cowhands, and some were wild, lawless, bragging, whiskey-drinking bums, naturally looking for a good gunfight. Some of these "punchers" left Texas to seek greener pastures because they were not wanted in Texas, while others left for the opposite reason—because they *were* wanted in Texas. The Old West had its fools of pointless courage and senseless killing, who joined the Graham band of rustlers and were known as the "Hashknife Renegades."

Tom needed his job, but he did not fit in well with this lot, so he left to work for the Waters Cattle Company. One day he and two other drovers were sent down into the Basin to seek new grazing lands. They slept that night at a horse camp in the mountains. Early the next morning the three cowboys were roused out of bed by a group of men who took them over to show them three men hanging by their necks from a tree. They were told—if they cared to stay healthy—they best go back from whence they came. The three unfortunate victims were suspected horse thieves, James Stott, James Scott, and Jeff Wilson.

Tom definitely wanted no part of this trouble, and he was not looking to be a guest at his own "string party." He quickly put the spurs to his horse and returned to the Waters Cattle Company to pull down his pay; then he moved down into the Tonto Basin to seek work. Tom punched cows for a time for Ed Tewksbury. He met Maggie Meadows at a barn dance in the little mountain hamlet of Pine, and lost his heart. This is borne out in Maggie's memory book when Tom wrote,

> I love thee morning, noon and night,
> with clouds and sun and stars,
> I love thee when the moon lets light
> break through its silvery bars.
> I love thee when the skies let fall,

their loving drops of dew,
But I think I love you most of all,
When I am nearest you.

Thomas Beach.

Forthwith, Maggie became Tom's promised bride.

CHAPTER 7

1887-1890
INTERLUDE

From time to time Charlie kept a diary or journal of his life, perhaps with the intention of someday writing his life story, but, above all, he never wanted the world to forget him. In one of his diaries he wrote: "When I went into the stock business on my own five years ago, my only capital consisted of nothing more than an old, worn-out saddle and a long, cow-hide *reata*. I had accumulated two small houses and lots in the little town of Payson, taken cattle on share, contracted with the government for what I could get, and gradually worked up to a good sized band of cattle and horses. Cattle was worth much less than when I started and the range was over-stocked by new settlers coming in from Texas. The sheepmen were burning the grasses in belief they would come up stronger in the spring, but they were disappearing and not coming up as before, and times were bad."

Charlie had found another way to fatten his impoverished purse. Recent laws had been enacted by Congress to reimburse those persons who had suffered losses from Indian depredations, and these persons were advised to communicate with an attorney. This was great news, as their losses were heavy and they certainly needed the money. By August of 1890, 10,000 Indian depredations claims totaling $50,000,000 had been filed.

It was in December of 1887 when, as was their habit, Charlie and Frank Prothero saddled up and left—to spend the winter months in the rugged and lively little frontier town of Phoenix, to renew acquaintances with the fairer sex, hang out with the sports and stock dealers, partake of a little Arizona "snake juice" and good-natured buffoonery mingled with a little rough humor, sarcastic wit, and laughter. But above all they came to gamble. They were inveterate gamblers who gambled like the pros at such famous games as seven-up, faro and poker—in which money, saddles, horses, six-shooters, spurs and various other paraphernalia changed hands. Charlie was a born gambler who seldom lost.

This particular year they were glad to leave the bloody turmoil of the Pleasant Valley War behind, and the very heavy snowfall that blanketed the basin. They drove a small herd of dairy cows with them, hoping to make a trade that would keep them in grub, give them a little for gambling, tobacco and cigarette papers, and have enough left to send the folks back home.

Charlie and Frank arrived in town on the 15th, with cows in tow, dirty, tired and weary. They tethered their horses and went straight to Schumaker's Bath Room and Barber Shop for a first-class cleanup to remove the rank odor of horse and sweat. Then the two cowboys splurged on a haircut and some new clothes before locating a room. The following day Charlie made contact with an attorney by the name of Frank Cox, and filed the first papers in connection with his Indian depredations claim, in the Phoenix Court of Claims.

By the 1880's, the railroad had eased the difficulties of transportation, and the circus came into its own as the "Greatest Show in the West," offering one breathtaking sight after another. The two friends were enthusiastic to learn that Forepaugh and Samwell's new railroad show was announced to hit Phoenix on December 17, 1887. They were anxious to be in town by that time. Whatever may be said or written about the uniform character and family resemblance of circuses, the fact remained that the gay trappings, gaudy tinsel and prancing steeds, the sawdust-scented ring, and the oft-times mournfully funny clowns which made up the joys of the circus, were popular.

The circus was bigger and better than any they had seen before. The streets were bustling with throngs of excited people from outlying communities; a mixture of ranchmen and their ladies and children, bronze-faced "waddies" and petticoat rustlers, spurred and armed, a few liquored-up cowhands, and some bewhiskered prospectors who came to witness the grand street parade. Monstrous bands and the enthusiasm displayed by the crowds were stimulating to Charlie, and brought to mind the times he had thoroughly captivated the populace with his cowboy skills.

The thoroughbred horses were trained beautifully, and there were cages full of rare wild animals representing all species of the brute creation. Bicycle experts performed feats that would astound the world. The gymnasts, acrobats, and monarch of the upper air were the greatest artists ever seen. They were simply astounding. Show business was in Charlie's blood, and he developes a nagging desire to fulfill those dreams someday. Frank's tastes and likings tended to run along the line of the law, chasing criminals back home in the Tonto Basin.

John Valentine completed his hectic term as Coroner and Justice of the Peace in 1888, and his friend, Bill Burch, former deputy under Sheriff Mulvenon, took over in his place. Diamond Valley Ranch was sold to the pioneer Haught family, who, in turn, sold it to a nephew named Hendershot. The balance of the Meadows Brothers' stock was moved to their new location at Sidella.

A year later, John, returning from a business trip, alighted his train in Phoenix. Alongside the tracks lay a knot of half-naked Indian idlers. One recognized him, came forward and boasted as having been in the band that swept through Diamond Valley Ranch that nightmarish day, killing their Pa and mortally wounding Henry. John, who suffered crippling wounds, now reeling with blinding rage and bitter memories flashing through his brain, whipped out his revolver, and without hesitation, blasted his foe dead as yesterday. It was certainly smart for him to be hard to find, and for this none of the family blamed him. He caught the next train out of Phoenix for San Jose, California, notifying the family later of his hasty departure.

The younger Meadows Brothers were growing up fast. James was 18, Jake, 16, and Mobley, 14. With their help Charlie worked the ranch, desperately trying to make a living. He took in cattle from Mr. E. F. Kellner of Globe, and ran it on his range. Mobley became his shadow and, like Charlie, knew his "cow sense" and "horse flesh." Together they practiced their cowboy skills and Mobley became as expert a horseman as his older brother.

King of Cowboys vs. Tom Horn

When Tom Horn finished as Chief of Scouts under General Miles during the Geronimo campaign, he was quick to volunteer as deputy under Sheriff Mulvenon during the Pleasant Valley War. Charlie and Tom often crossed paths and they became friends. Tom was one of the best cowhands around, next to Charlie, of course, and Charlie never wanted anyone to forget it. Even though there was a special camaraderie amongst the cowboys, there was always much rivalry around the territory as to who was the "quickest man in the business," and Tom was always good at "tooting his own horn," loud and long. Some have implied that the two cowboys were bitter rivals, but there is not a whit of evidence to substantiate this rumor.

After hostilities ceased in Pleasant Valley, due to the fact that hardly anyone lived to tell the tale, Charlie entered the following card in Prescott's *Hoofs and Horns,* (April 1888):

> "Charlie Meadows of Payson, this territory, challenges any man in the world to an all-round cowboy contest for $500 or $1000 a side. He also wagers either of the above amounts with any man in the steer-tying contest, either three or five steers to be tied. Expert cowpunchers make a note of this." (Re-printed in the *Phoenix Arizonian.*)

A braggadocio of the worst kind, Tom spread the word around that he could whip Charlie in any type of contest, for any amount of money he could muster, and leave him like so much manure in a cloud of corral dust.

In April, Charlie gave Horn his chance and made him eat his words, taking the first prize with a time of 1 minute and 24 seconds. Tom's time: 1 minute, 47 seconds. Charlie compounded Horn's pain by roping and tying three steers in 4 minutes and 28 seconds; the steers were given a 100-yard start.

From all indications, Horn's tongue hung out a foot and forty inches. Charlie didn't hear from him for quite some time.

Another important event took place in Prescott during their Frontier Days celebration on the Fourth of July that same year. This celebration is now known to last for four days, complete with rodeo events and a gigantic street parade.

On that particular Fourth of July in 1888, everything started out well for Charlie. His animal was roped and tied in quick time, and it looked like he had the contest all wrapped up. But then his steer kicked loose and no time was given; he felt a keen disappointment. Juan de Livias, a fine roper, took first prize for the quickest time of 1 minute and 17 seconds. Juan received a beautiful cowboy outfit valued at $125. He and Charlie shared the $50 prize for bronco riding. There were eight entries. (*Globe Silver Belt,* July 14, 1888.)

Two months later, in September, Charlie went on to achieve the cherished distinction of being the "King of the Cowboys" at the Territorial Fair in Phoenix. He won the roping and tying contest in 59 seconds, setting a new record which gained for him an excellent tooled saddle and a great deal of acclaim. (*National Police Gazette*, N.Y. October 20, 1888; *Arizona Champion*, October 27, 1888; *Arizona Historical Review*, date unknown; *Tucson Star,* October 27, 1888.)

The Territorial Fair was for the exhibition of agricultural, horticultural, livestock and mineral production of the Territory.

With new found assurance, Charlie again challenged a similar contest to anyone living. Tom Horn came forward again. The following month the *Tucson Star* (November 25, 1888) and the *Apache Review* (December 12, 1888) reported the contest as follows:

"The result of the racing-riding and steer-tying contest at Payson, Crowder beat Hungry John in the horse race by 45 feet. The roping and tying was won by Charles Meadows in 1 minute and 24 seconds;.Tom Horn of Pleasant Valley secured second place with a time of 1 minute and 47 seconds; and John Gilliland of Payson, third. His time was 2 minutes and 23 seconds. In the contest for the best lady rider, Miss Mollie Birchette proved the victor, the prize being $25; Mrs. William Boardman, second; and Mrs. John Gilliland, third. For the best bronco riding after a spirited contest between George Felton and Charles Meadows, the former was awarded the prize of $25, Meadows second, for $15. In a roping and tying contest between Charles Meadows and Tom Horn the prize was $50 a side, each man to tie three steers. Meadows won in 4 minutes and 28 seconds, against Horn's time of 6 minutes and 24 seconds."

There was a continual round of pleasure that lasted three days, and Charlie's hat took on a new size.

Charlie's reputation soon turned from the "fastest man with a rope," to "World's Champion Cowboy." He was beginning to hear from others, each believing they could take the glory away from him.

One such customer was Charles McGary, who challenged Charlie to a contest for $500. The *Prescott Journal Miner* of December 12, 1888, reported: "Both gentlemen are experts and some good work in this line is expected should Meadows accept."

Of course, Charlie accepted. By this time his self-confidence was fairly bursting through his hat. The event took place in April of 1889. Both fellows ran into bad luck; Charlie's horse got away and his *reata* broke. Some were unkind enough to hint that it was all prearranged that the rope should break on the last steer. The steer-tying contest was the first on the program. It was won by McGary with three steers roped in the aggregate time of 4 minutes and 34 seconds. McGary roped and tied his last steer in one minute and "won the right to be classed amongst the best." The crowd stampeded his horse, after he dismounted and was tying his steer; and on his second steer, his horse got away and ran himself down, thereby incapacitating him in the subsequent trials. Charlie's aggregate time was 5 minutes, 9 and three-quarters seconds. Charlie won the 250-yard flag race, five flags 50 yards apart. He got three and McGary got one, with a time of 15 seconds. Then Charlie repeated his luck by winning the bronco riding. Having won two out of three contests, Charlie was declared the winner of the $500. (*Arizona Champion*, April 27, 1889.)

That fall, Tom Horn and Charlie met again in Phoenix. This time Tom Horn had worked hard sharpening his skills—and carried away the honors. It was a tough blow to handsome Charlie's ego. Horn tied his steer in 1 minute and 19 seconds, and Charlie came in second with 1 minute and 26 seconds. Mr. W. D. Sears came in with a time of 1 minute and 28 seconds and Mr. J. T. Gibson, in 1 minute and 40 seconds. (*St. Johns Herald*, October 31, 1889.)

Tom Horn said, "Charlie Meadows was making a big talk that he could beat me tying at the Territorial Fair in Phoenix. Our boys concluded I must go to the fair and make a trial for the territorial prize, and take it out on Meadows. I had known Meadows for years and thought I could beat him, and so did my friends."

Charlie hated to admit defeat, but Horn made good his boast, came in first again and walked off with the coveted prize. This was a second bitter blow to Charlie's pride, as Horn broke Charlie's record of 59 seconds, with a new one of 49. Now when Horn's name comes up, mention is always made of how Horn beat Charlie Meadows; but what is never mentioned are the times Charlie whipped him. Because Charlie was hard to beat, the news was bigger when he lost. The other contestants that day were Bill McCann, Charles Iago, and Ramon Barca.

Later in 1894, in San Jose, California, Charlie came through with a new record of 41 seconds (*San Jose Mercury,* May 4, 1884.) All in all, Charlie had won sixteen contests and many prizes including a beautiful diamond ring which he always wore. Before long his exploits gained him honor and fame. He was recognized as the champion of all cowboy skills in America, and was determined to prove that claim at every performance.

Things were looking up. Charlie's idol, Buffalo Bill, and his entourage, were in the audience that day at the fair witnessing the thrilling contest between Charlie and Tom Horn. Cody was most impressed with the two cowboys. After the show, he invited them to have dinner with him, offering both top spots in his show soon headed for Europe. Tom wasn't interested in being a show cowboy, and quickly declined the offer, which later proved to be a bad move as Tom's life sadly ended on the business end of a hangman's noose, while Charlie was being applauded the world over.

Cody knew Charlie had everything it took to be a good showman, and, of course, the thought of fame and fortune put Charlie in a state of euphoria. Cody suggested, "Why don't you come to my ranch in Wyoming to discuss the business?" Charlie arriving jubilantly at the specified time, soon discovered that Cody was a terrible businessman who never kept accurate records. Cody had forgotten their appointment. He was in Chicago. Charlie vexed with disappointment and with his heart slid into his boots, practically collapsed. He was not about to give up the idea of show business—a challenge which he passionately vowed to pursue.

It was reported that the first thing Charlie did was to let his hair grow. Next, he sent out letters to circuses. Once this tale was written, it was passed on as the gospel truth. The following is the true story from Charlie's journal, in his own words, as it occurred and as he reflected:

"It was July of 1890, that I was returning from the annual beef drive from the Tonto Basin with about $2,000 in my pocket. I had sold about 100 head of three-and four-year-old steers, and after figuring up my indebtedness, I found myself with a cash balance of less than $1,000. Beef was a better price than it had been for a long time and at the present figure it was a close hand game for a small stock man. When I went into the stock business eight years before upon the death of my father, my sole ambition was to own a good ranch or two, a small band of good horses and five or six hundred head of cattle. Cattle was worth $25 per head all-round when I went into business, and now they were less than one-third that price.

"I had the cattle, had worked hard and earnest, took cattle on share, cared for other people's cattle for what I could get and gradually worked up until my books showed I must have had about 1,000 head of cattle and horses. I had two ranches, as good as any in this beautiful country, and a good prospect of a gold mine. Now that I had what I had worked so long for, it at last dawned on me that they were not worth as much to me as a salary of $75 per month. The range was over-stocked, the grass was gone almost completely and failed to come again as yore. Steers were poor, cows failed to breed, my houses didn't bring any rent and my gold mine was a draw from $200 to $500 per year, and had at last 'pinched out,' as the old prospectors say.

"It looked like a clear case of freeze-out at the present prices. I could not stand the stock business the way it was and there was little hope of it getting better. This fact looked fair in the face as I rode over the Mogollon Mountains into the Tonto Basin, the place I had spent the best part of my life from the age of seventeen to twenty-nine years of age.

"The ground I was riding over was bare, and now and then I could see a small bunch of Texas cattle, some half-blind with ticks in their ears. Texas had suffered from drought and the country was flooded with Texas ponies and longhorn cattle. Their owners had hoped of finding a place where they could escape from the bitter blizzards and 'northwesters'. Every little valley was taken up, and as the Texas people had come short-handed, very little money was circulated and times were dull.

"Only a few years before, the country I was riding over was unsettled and wild; full of deer, bear, antelope and wild turkeys, with now and then a small band of renegade Indians. The grass was belly-high to a horse and a perfect sea of verdant beauty the year round. Little did I believe it would ever come to this state of condition when I had ridden over it before, driving beef to Fort Apache. I was now compelled to subsist on meat alone for three or four days at a time, unable to find a settler or a camp.

"Eventually all the live boys had gone from the basin, save a few that had married, to hunt for pastures anew in South America, Washington Territory, or other places. Some were elected to county offices or had gone off to live in the towns, so the country was dead. I began to look for a loophole where I could get out. To sell out was impossible; of all the money in the Tonto Basin, there was not enough loose change to take me out of the country. I had been very lucky, occasionally being able to put in some time in Phoenix with the cattlemen and the sports, returning in the spring to the Tonto. I began to look on Phoenix as a kind of "headquarters" and, when all the spring work was done, I again would go down to the Great Salt River Valley and kill time gambling with the card sharks and stock dealers until October."

Charlie Meadows, *Circa* Age 32

CHAPTER 8

1890—1892
INTRODUCTION INTO SHOW BUSINESS

About this same time the weeklies and monthly magazines were full of Buffalo Bill's famous Wild West tour of Europe—at the Paris Expo, and in London, where the Queen of England honored him with her presence during his special performance at Windsor Castle. It was the talk of the World and America. Australia had never seen a real American Indian or cowboy, but many people had read the highly romantic novels by James Fenimore Cooper who spoke so eloquently about the American West. There was so much "big talk" in their newspapers, that the Wirth Brothers' Circus, one of the largest in Australia, intended to capitalize on it by adding a wild west show of their own.

Harry Wirth was delegated to come to America and obtain top men of wild west fame. He engaged Captain "Happy Jack" Sutton, and asked him to gather a group of number one, hand-picked cowboys and some of his Indian friends, squaws and papooses.

Charlie recorded in his journal his own version of the events:

"When I rode into Payson that day, amongst my mail was a postal card asking me if I would like to join a Wild West Show, soon leaving for Australia. It was signed, H. J. Sutton" Charlie knew who Sutton was, as everyone did. Unknown to Charlie, Sutton had heard about Charlie's accomplishments. Sutton supposedly was the first genuine cowboy ever placed on exhibition, and the first to introduce Wild West into show business. He was under contract at the time with the great P. T. Barnum, when he took the first party of genuine Sioux Indians to Europe. He was married to "Prairie Pearl," the champion lady rough rider from Colorado, who was the subject of many western books of that period.

"I paid no attention to the card," Charlie wrote, "not believing I could go." Then with a restlessness as big as a barfly's thirst, Charlie started at once for Phoenix. "All my saddle horses were in poor condition so I threw my lasso over one of the first mares that I found—and charged off. I rode as far as the E. K. Ranch on Tonto Creek, and put up with my friend, Jack Brown. Jack had the driest wit of any man I ever knew. He was a young man from the same town I was born in and the son of the leading attorney of that place. For some reason, Jack sought the wilds of Arizona, and by his thorough knowledge of stock, attentiveness and business dispatch, was soon made foreman of the Shadeland Ranch."

Like Charlie, Brown had the saddle itch. So it wasn't long before Charlie persuaded him to go to Phoenix with him, to take in a little fun and frolic for a week or so and to "palliate their primal hungers." "We had a seventy mile ride to go, so we took an early start. We reached the Sugar Loaf Mountains when my mare began to limp. She had wrenched her foot in some way, and with every step she seemed to get worse. I walked her for a while. It was getting dark and we were still forty miles from Phoenix.

"About nine o'clock that night we were going down a long sand wash and saw a large bunch of horses coming in to water. I took Brown's horse and waited until all their heads were down and drinking. Then I made a dash and the little horse was on them in a flash. When they raised their heads I got my lasso over the big horse, and around his neck and one foreleg. We were a long time getting up to him and had a hard time saddling him. When I finally got on he took me over boulders, through cactus and catclaws, and through flume and hollow. He did not stop until we reached Fort McDowell. Brown led the little mare and we travelled all night once the burden was off her back.

"The next morning Brown was up telling all the fort that I had ridden a Mormon's horse almost to death, hoping to see some fun between the Mormons and me."

The two cowboys shook the wrinkles out of their socks and rolled a cigarette. You either snuffed, "chawed," or rolled your own in those days for "real Cowmen" never smoked "ready-mades." They slid into their saddles and left for Phoenix.

"Reaching Phoenix I found another postal card there from Sutton, and in a few days a friend came to Phoenix and brought me another. Sutton's insistence put me to thinking, and I immediately sat down and wrote him a letter asking to hear his terms. In due time an answer came stating that the contract would be for a season of six months. The route would extend through the leading towns and cities of the Australian Colonies. My salary would be $200 a month, and all expenses both ways, while there, and to bring along another good all-round man or two and be ready to sail August 23rd.

"The family started to scatter, forced out to find other ways to make their living. Jake had gone to the rowdy silver mining town of Tombstone to act as a peace officer, and James took off to seek his luck in the Salt River Valley. My sister, Maggie, was the only sister left at home, but from every indication she would be married soon.

"I did not take kindly to the proposition at first, owing to the fact it was of too short notice to do up my business. I showed the letter to some of my friends, and the very next morning the Phoenix papers came out with the story. That day when I walked into town everyone asked me when I was going to leave for Australia. Brown had already returned to the Shadeland Ranch, and I thought I would give up the notion of going, but the more I found out about the country the more I wanted to see it. So I wired Sutton and accepted his proposition. So little did I think of the postal cards while Brown was in Phoenix that I did not even mention them to him. I knew, however, I could get him if at all possible. I had been authorized to pay $100 a month for a good man, and Brown was certainly that." The more Charlie thought about the proposition, the "sweeter" it looked.

Excited as a den of teased snakes, Charlie forked his horse and headed out of Phoenix—through foothills of giant Saguaro, crimson-flowered Barrel and Beavertail cactus, and through the Sugarloaf Mountains, he dashed—destined for the Shadeland Ranch.

"I rode hard and fast and reached the Shadeland Ranch shortly after midnight. I rode up on the porch and into the hall, gave a war whoop that would scare off an Apache, and shot my pistol into the ceiling. Brown heard me coming and knew it was me, but I got the worst of the scare when he rolled over and emptied his pistol and yelled like a wild man. As soon as I had unsaddled my horse I told him I was off for Australia with a Wild West Show, and made him an offer.

"We read Sutton's letter over and concluded it was some kind of a picnic party gotten up by the aristocracy, or an amateur Buffalo Bill affair. Brown was just one minute in making up his mind to go. He had a very good idea of the country and spoke in glowing terms of its qualities as a stock country. We sat up the rest of the night talking the matter over. Brown said, 'life is hardly worth living if I have to live alone and do my own cooking. It's a dull place and I'm tortured by the anguish of loneliness, boredom and isolation. Besides, I can come back anytime I want and get my place back—for it is a good one.

"Early the next morning Brown swung onto his saddle and headed for Globe to settle up and put his resignation before Mr. Kellner. I was off for Payson, and on the road I met the Honorable O. C. Felton, who told me about George, his son who was going to leave the country. 'Having read the papers,' he said, 'I would like for you to arrange a place for him. George will go to Australia anyway, but if he can find a place like yours it will fall right into his hand. George promised to come to Payson the next day and I promised to see him through if they wanted any more help."

A Wedding on Horseback

"After spending a few hours in Payson, I went home and broke the news to my folks. My sister, Maggie, wanted me to wait until after the wedding. That was impossible, so with little persuasion she agreed to make the date suit my departure. I wrote Brown to come to Payson, there would be a big thing in the way of a ball and wedding."

Charlie vowed the event would be noteworthy. It was at this time he began to display the *savoir faire* that makes a successful showman and promoter.

"I went to see about the best man and bridesmaid, and they told me they were also going to be married, and would just as soon make it four-handed. I sent out invitations in red ink in my flourishing handwriting. The arrangements were quickly completed and all hands agreed to be married on horseback on the main street of town. I promised to make both couples a present of as many stock as they could rope and brand between noon and sundown the day of the wedding. I drove my saddle horses off to a brushy canyon, and on my way found a bunch of blooded mares and colts, and carefully stole those away, determined to confine the young married couples to cattle as much as possible.

"All the morning of the wedding day guests were arriving from a distance, so that by the appointed hour there were fully 200 present. Emer Cole, the other groom, was on hand—mounted on a young horse with blinds on, and with a quick, nervous movement that told me he was a bronco. His girl, Julia Hall, was dressed in a bottle green riding habit and the wide brimmed, regulation white Stetson hat. We all got together and had a glass of wine, and then went out to meet the other couple, my sister Maggie and Tom Beach. About one mile out of town we met and all hands joined in a go-as-you-please race to Payson. Miss Hall had not gotten the consent of her parents for her wedding and there were a few of us who knew she was really too young.

"As the couples lined up on their horses and faced the justice, those who had an inkling of the truth began whooping that Cole was to be married to Julia Hall. The Justice, Bill Burch, was an old Hassayamper who enjoyed the novelty of the wedding on horseback. Mounted on his big stallion, he drew a small book out of his hip pocket and asked, 'Are you now ready?' Then he proceeded to splice the first couple, Tom and Maggie, and immediately after the last word was over, Emer Cole who by now had turned white, raised his broad hat and took the hand of Julia. In a few minutes, in the briefest of ceremony, they were made man and wife. As soon as congratulations commenced, Cole's horse began to buck. As he shook hands with some of his friends and relatives, the horse began to buck again. The horse would stop his bucking only long enough for his rider to get straight and to outstretch his hand to some friend, when the horse would commence his contortions once again.

"Tom Beach rode down to the saloon to buy seven cases of wine and, armed with glasses and cork screws, several of the guests commenced to distribute the wine to those on horseback. I announced my present of the cattle and, among other things, I gave Tom and Maggie some silver vases, a house and lot, two baby cradles and a sack of flour.

"The bridegrooms were both presented with long lassoes and I expected them to go out to Burch Mesa at once and commence rounding up my cattle. To my surprise they went directly to a dairy where a family had a number of our cows milking and commenced branding. The wine started to tell on the cowboys and everybody was anxious to get a rope on and give a hand. The young married ladies kept the fire going and carried branding irons. They were joined by the ladies amongst the guests and, the way they branded with their own irons, it did not take long to brand all eighteen cows in the dairy. Then they turned to the *mesa*. Emer Cole was acquainted with the range and acted as Judge of the Plains. All the people assembled for a cattle drive and, in less than an hour, there were a thousand head of cattle rounded up on Burch Mesa that day. Everyone was feeling the effects of the wine and each cowboy was trying to see how reckless he could be as bunches of cattle were driven in. One cowboy would lasso a steer, throw him, and another would ride him into the herd. Every horse that could be was spurred into giving a buck or jumping exhibition.

"Of all the Wild West shows, I never expected to see one to equal this. The riding on Burch Mesa that day, beyond question or doubt in my mind, was the most reckless and daring ever displayed at one place in so short a time.

"Some of the boys thrown from steers came in riding behind comrades. Some would come to the round-up on a run, reach down on the opposite side of their horse a la Comanche, and pick up stones at the same time. Brown rode along at full speed by the side of a steer, threw his left foot out of the stirrup, swung himself onto the steer facing the steer's tail and rode the bucking steer into the herd despite his bucking.

"Everyone wanted to lasso something until no one was left to help the newlyweds tail down and brand. They branded thirty or forty head, then gave up saying they had all they wanted. But we did not return to town until every steer in the herd had been ridden by the cowboys. That night a big, breezy ball and banquet followed. I enjoyed myself immensely. Brown, though, got fairly drunk."

Interestingly, that evening Lil' Nina Nash, who was just a little girl at that time, attended the wedding with her parents, who accompanied the Meadows to Arizona from Visalia. A short time before Maggie's wedding, Layfayette Philander Nash, the teacher at the little log cabin schoolhouse in Strawberry Valley, and his wife, Mary, had given little Nina a baby brother. Since she already had a brother, Herbert, and wanted so much to have a sister; she was naturally disappointed and heart-broken. One day while sitting on her porch lamenting her plight, along came Charlie—her dashing idol. Galloping up to the porch with one of his marks of distinction—his red kerchief around his neck—Charlie dismounted, swished Lil' Nina up in his arms and listened intently to her tale of woe. He promised her one of his young fillies, which he delivered a few days later. Also, he explained, "with my sister's coming marriage, I promise you that if Maggie's first child is a girl, I know Maggie will share the baby with you!"

A Double Wedding in Arizona

When Charlie saw her at the wedding, he swooped her up in his arms. He walked her across the dance floor high on his shoulders and presented her to the bride and groom. Nina was delighted to have the deal cinched, too young, of course, to realize the embarrassment to Maggie. Nina, later recalling her visit to Tom and Maggie at their log cabin nestled in the willows along the Verde River, remembered accompanying Maggie to the stream where she kept butter and milk cold by setting them on a rock just above stream level. Nina eventually had three more brothers—not...one...sister, and to make the situation worse, Maggie's first three children were all boys.

Meanwhile, Charlie continued his preparations: "I made out a bill of sale for everything—except for my fine stallion, 'Governor,' a small band of horses, and a few cattle which I held in partnership with a friend, Bill Brodie—to my youngest brother, Mobley."

With his mark of identification—a bright red kerchief knotted around his neck, slipped through a spherical wild boar's tusk he always wore—he donned his wide-brimmed *sombrero,* and said good-bye to his friends and loved ones. With George Felton's help, he stashed Jack Brown's belly gun, so as not to shoot his toes off; heaved Brown's wobbly bulk topside his horse, securely propping him up behind the horn of his saddle; tightened the cinches and drew the harness firm, and off. "The three of us skipped out that morning at 3 o'clock," said Charlie, who was about to start the second great adventure of his life.

A two-day holdover in Phoenix gave them time to refurbish in elegant, store-bought show duds, and assorted gallimaufry; and time to get "barbered up." Charlie then visited Hartwell's Photo Shop for a generous supply of publicity photos for distribution in the Antipodes.

Interlude in San Francisco

In his journal, Charlie wrote, "A big farewell banquet was planned for us by some lovely lady friends, and only the boys going to Australia were to be there. Besides the lady of the house and two beautiful young widows, there was only one servant. 'Me thinks' the ladies planned it that way. After supper each of us ordered a buggy and drove up and down lover's lane until almost morning.

"I bade farewell to black coffee, beef jerky, a wet saddle blanket for my bed, and when the train was ready to leave that morning, we were all there on time.

"Twenty-four hours brought us to the Tulare Plains, the place where Brown and I had spent our boyhood. A wonderful change had taken place in the surrounding country. Only ten or twelve years before it was a treeless plain, covered only with alfilorie grass and an occasional small herd of sheep, yet, it was the wealthiest part of California. Often, while hunting wild horses over this rugged country, we suffered for something to eat for it was so scarcely settled. Now fine gum-bud ornamental trees and hundreds of windmills could be seen from the train—every ten or twelve miles we could see a beautiful village or city.

"Along the San Joaquin Valley, the country seemed one continuous vineyard or orchard, watered by artesian wells and large canals. I had chased wild mustang over the site fourteen years before, when there was not a mark of the hand of man for miles around. Now there was a beautiful and thriving city of 5,000 inhabitants.

"A few hours ride brought us to San Francisco where we were met by Jackson 'Happy Jack' Sutton, a grand specimen of a cowboy. He wore the regulation Stetson hat, a low neck shirt, and a watch chain of Indian beads. His hair, long and inclined to curl or wave, made him the first long-haired cowboy I had ever seen, and when I asked him if he had bet his scalp on a Presidential election long ago, he seemed not to understand. I had seen one stockman who, vowing never to cut his hair until another Democrat was elected President, had worn long hair from the inauguration of Grant to that of Cleveland."

It was at this time the Arizona boys let their hair grow long, with Sutton wearing only a moustache, and Charlie wearing both the moustache and goatee—perhaps in imitation of his idol, Buffalo Bill.

"We were taken by Sutton to a place up on Pacific Street where the ranch smelled strongly of Swiss cheese. There we met the other cowboys. The three fellows had long hair, wore unbuttoned shirts, big hats and belts made of beads, and used poker chips for buttoned vests and coats. *Chaparreras* (leather leggings) adorned the cowboys who were definitely from Butchertown, and I'm sure they had never been out of the city. From all indications they couldn't tell the difference between cow dung and wild honey.

"We were as clean and comfortable as we could be, but we didn't like our quarters there much, so we moved to the Hackmeyer Hotel. As we went out of the place, Brown said, 'I think we have joined a patent-medicine fake. I am sure none of those fellows have ever seen a cow's track, much less a stock range.'

"I made an appointment next day to see the proprietor of the circus we would be working for at the Crystal Palace Saloon. I had a fondness for spectacular uniform of theatrical appearance, so I dug out my white Prince Albert coat, high silk hat and gold-headed cane. I had never in all my life worked for another man, and I was anxious to see the man that was to be my new boss. I walked into the saloon but couldn't see anyone who looked like a show proprietor. I treated the bartender to a drink, looked over the paper, and watched everyone that passed by hoping to see Mr. Wirth. After a short period of time I looked over the top of the paper and saw a small, pugnacious-looking man walk up to the counter where he asked his companions if he might buy them a drink. He then pulled out his watch that hung from a huge double chain with a half dollar piece for a charm, and said, 'I can't understand why that bloody cowboy don't come on. He can go to *baggora* if he is not here in the next ten minutes!'

"I waited for him to finish his drink, then walked over and asked him if he was looking for any more cowboys to go to Australia. 'No,' he said, 'I'm not looking for any more. I have got the best bloody troupe in the world, just in from Arizona last night.' "I asked, "Who have you got?"

'I've got Charlie Meadows, the best bloody man in the world, Cruel Jack Brown, and two more from the same place. Then I have 'the Arkansas Kid,' 'Bronco' George, and Jim Keogh,' he said, meaning the three San Francisco hoodlums.

'Well,' I said, 'my name is Meadows, and if you are Mr. Wirth, it is you I have come to see.'

"Wirth was loathe to think I was Meadows, and, if I was, he could not believe I was a cowboy. I telephoned Brown and Felton and they were down in a few minutes. They were nicely dressed in the latest San Francisco style, but wore their big regulation Stetson hats. The Stetson was as much a part of the old West as Bull Durham. We had the contracts signed right away before the British Consular, and then we were off to see the town. I did not pay attention to where we were going, as Brown had been to the city before and I relied on him to act as our guide.

"My sister, Mary, lived in San Francisco, so the next day we located her and moved over to her place. The following day all the cowboys were together and our new acquaintances sold us a dozen bottles of Pawnee Indian medicine. Neither of us had ever had a day's sickness, but the way they brought out the virtues of that medicine was a caution. We had all drunk considerably that day. I did not pay any attention to any of the streets and was lost all the time, only following Brown.

"When we got up the next morning after our day with the San Francisco boys, my sister asked what we were doing with all that medicine. We told her how we got it and she nearly laughed herself into a fit! She told us we had joined a patent-medicine faking outfit. When we described our friends to her she said she had seen them selling the Pawnee medicine on a corner for the last two months. Neither of us said too much, but our interest in the Wild West Show could have been bought cheap. It looked very different from the aristocratic amateur outfit we thought we were going to join.

"We had only one more day until time of sailing. Brown and I promised to spend the day at the residence of a friend we had met. He was a dudish kind of man, but very nice and polite, whose wife would be glad to have us come and have dinner with them before we left. Then I met up with a gambler from Los Angeles who I had seen down in the territories, and who told me the gentlemanly fellow was a "knocker" and would drug and rob us for sure if we had anything to do with him. He was kind of a boss amongst the dog and prize fight business, he said. His name was Harry Maynard, and he had smoked many a glass and taken the last cent from many country people who had gotten into his spider web."

They were just two typical cowboys fresh from the herd, but were very cautious when they met Maynard that day. As Charlie explained it, "The first drink out of the regulation smoked glass didn't affect either of us much, for we had been used to drinking the Arizona whiskey, and this was mild compared to the snake juice we were accustomed to.

"Maynard treated us again and the glasses were smoked once more. I tried to get Brown to drink lemonade with me, but he insisted on the whiskey. I leaned around him and winked trying to get him to understand he was being doped. He appeared to pay no attention, to speak of, but gave me a kind of cunning look. I thought for sure he was gone and began to feel gone myself. When Maynard took his eyes off the drinks, I saw Brown change glasses with him. Then Brown said, 'Let us have one more.' The glasses were filled, and I had my lemonade as usual and was ready to help Brown make the change. I got Maynard's attention by showing him my press card. Then Brown switched the glasses once more.

"We were all getting sleepy, but Maynard had two doses to our one and, almost limp, staggered into a chair. Brown roused him and said we would see him home. He protested and said he didn't want to go. The bartender understood that the wrong man got the dose and protested us taking him. Brown showed him the card with Maynard's number on it and we started for his place.

"At the door of the saloon was an Italian banana peddler with a two-wheeled cart pulled by a decrepit horse. Brown laid Maynard upon the oranges. The Italian protested loudly but Brown insisted and took out his loaded pistol, scaring the Italian off in search of a policeman. Then Brown ordered me to drive and follow him. He put his cowboy hat on Maynard with the string under his nose. Brown staggered across the street with pistol in hand when he saw a streetcar approaching. It looked to me like two cars separating at times and converging again. As I neared them they seemed to separate once more. I threw a banana at the old horse hoping that, by taking advantage of the opening, I could make a hurricane jump, which I did—only to hit the car. There was a terrible screech. One wheel broke off the axle. Maynard, all the fruit and myself, landed by the side of the streetcar track! The horse broke loose from one shaft and commenced to waltz around in a circle. Brown pulled me loose from the untidy mess, but by that time a very large crowd had gathered. Through the mob a policeman of giant stature made his way and arrested Maynard, as I heard him say, 'You cowboys cannot run San Francisco!' Two other policemen caught the horse. Brown quickly jerked my hat off tucking it under his arm where it could not be seen, and ushered me quietly away toward some of our acquaintances on Taylor Street. He wanted to send for a small black hat for me, and went to ring for a messenger. Ringing the bell several different ways, the lady of the house soon appeared on the scene all ruffled and agitated. I was pretty well gone from the booze and do not remember much, but I do know that in short notice a very large crowd of people had gathered outside—the whole fire brigade and any amount of police. I was sure our time had come. He had rung the fire alarm, the police call, and messenger all at once on that peculiar little contrivance.

"The lady of the house tried to explain that it was all a false alarm. The whole thing sobered me up considerably. As soon as it was dark, we sneaked down to the boat; and, as quiet as a graveyard after midnight, we got into our berths and stayed there until the steamer sailed for Australia."

All the time this was taking place, Wirth's agent, William Alexander took the steamer, *Mariposa*, home to get chariots, wagons, hunter's cabin, et cetera, ready for the Wild West portion of the circus. Meantime, Harry Wirth toured the United States visiting other circuses. He was astounded over the size of Barnum and Bailey's Three-ring Circus, Hippodrome, and Wild West Show. He insisted that they also incorporate three-rings to their operation and run it on the same principle.

One problem after the other plagued Sutton. The acquisition of the cowboys had not been a serious problem, but the Indians were another matter. He first went to Red Gulch and obtained several Sioux Indians who had accompanied him on his first venture in 1882. There were several fine-looking bucks, their squaws and papooses, who were sent to San Francisco. While waiting for the sailing date, one of the squaws gave birth, but the infant died. The whole tribe took this as a "bad omen" and demanded to return to the reservation.

Sutton then hurried to another reservation at Lakeport where he secured another batch of Indians, and, as before, purchased them new trappings so that they too seemed satisfied and happy. Then their Chief paid them a visit from the reservation, told them they would be crossing a great water to the other side of the earth where they would never see their friends and relatives again, and persuaded them to go home with him.

Sutton was at his wit's end. The ship was about to sail. A Wild West show without Indians would not be considered an attraction at all. It was just hours before sailing when his luck changed for the better. He had met up with a medicine show that had several Sioux, a Cognagwagga Indian buck and his squaw wife and papoose, and one Pawnee Indian. This time Sutton took them straight to the boat and installed a guard to watch over them.

"The Honorable Sam Purdy of Yuma gave me my own personal Indian," Charlie continued, "one that had been in his family as a servant. He was a big Yuma, with long hair clear down to his waist. His name was Juan Catoto (pronounced Ca-to-to), and Purdy held me personally responsible for his safe return to America. The total Wild West company then was composed of twelve Indians, fifteen cowboys, two Mexicans and three American women."

The Wild West Floats Across the Pacific

"Purdy was there with the Indian, my sister Mary was there with our baggage, and my brother John came from San Jose to see us off. We kept very quiet for fear of the police, but managed to get off for several drinks. We said good-bye—to all, but John. We could not find him. The engine gave one prolonged whistle, the gangplank was pulled up, and, with a big sigh, I waved good-bye to my friends and relations and the country I knew as home."

On August 23, 1890, when the mail steamer, *Zealandia*, sailed out of Golden Gate Park, with Captain K. Van Oterndorp at the helm and G. McLane as the purser, "Brown and I took out our guns and fired a half dozen shots into the water as a kind of farewell and defiance to the police. I was 30 years old and about to begin a new life, but I regretted I had been unable to find my brother to bid him good-bye. He had come a long way to see me off, and we had been together only one night before we got separated.

"Strolling up on the hurricane deck, I never was more surprised in my life when I saw John sitting there asleep! I woke him up and said, 'Where do you think you're going?'

'To Australia,' he said. "Well, why didn't you say so?" 'Okay, I'm sorry. Now go away! I'm sick and don't want to be bothered.'

"On the high lope, Australia probably looked pretty good to John," Charlie said, "but he was too cross to be very good company, so I left to find the other boys. Then there seemed to be a kind of goneness about my own stomach, as though I had eaten something that I should not have eaten. When I located the rest of the boys, they were lined up against the railing all hollering, 'New York,' as they polluted the water with their stomachs' contents."

The first two days out, strong winds and heavy swell prevailed, after which moderate northeast trade winds prevailed until they reached Honolulu. Of these two days, Charlie wrote:

"I laid in my stateroom two whole days, while Brown was laid up the same length of time. He and I were the only two of the Wild West group who went first class. Many thoughts—how we suffered those two days, how I wished I was back on the ranch, how the wise old adage, 'stay at home is best'—made me feel that much more miserable!

"The steamboat life was simply marvelous for ye cowpunchers and we enjoyed the luxury immensely—once we recuperated from our sea sickness. There were 180 passengers on board, mostly aristocratic English on a world tour. Their ways were very strange to us. We put in several hours a day answering questions and spinning frontier yarns. There was a soap and perfume drummer on board by the name of Gregg He was the biggest talker that I had ever seen in my life. Not a hair had he upon his head—he who wore horn-rimmed glasses. I allowed him about an hour a day to lecture me on the Australian laws and tell me many funny stories.

"There was a great amount of gambling on the run of the ship. I was induced to buy a pool in a sweepstakes and, as luck would have it, won $62.50. At a crap and poker game, where I took a seat and soon found I had the best of the game, I won several hundred dollars and broke most of the players of their gambling money in half a day. Then Mr. William Gregg, who was so terribly near sighted he could not have seen a white elephant if it had run across the table, built a faro bank. Brown fixed up some hair coppers, putting hair to the corks we were using for coppers, and we went against Mr. William Red-eyes and busted his bank. He also over-played himself to the tune of $200, and failed altogether to liquidate.

"The wonderful voyage seemed more like a dream than a reality," Charlie said of his seven-day, magnificent Pacific adventure. His letter reporting on the steamer which reached Honolulu on August 30, 1890, was published by the *Tulare Valley Times* practically a year later, March 26, 1891: "The days spent steaming over the trackless water of the grand Pacific, the beautiful tropical islands with their strange trees, magnificent ferns, and luscious fruits; the full-breasted, Adam-clad islanders coming on board, swimming and diving for pennies; the strange vehicles with never more than one horse attached, all tend to recall, for one who has read the Good Book, the old biblical days."

After an eight-hour stay in Honolulu, the steamer pushed on. On September 7th she touched off Tutuila, when moderate easterly winds set in, but on the 9th and 10th these winds increased into a gale with heavy seas. Thence, light westerly winds with heavy swells prevailed until their arrival in New Zealand.

"Between these islands and New Zealand," Charlie wrote, "a terrible storm came upon us. It is impossible for me to describe the feeling of complete goneness that took possession of me during the 24 hours we were shut out from the light. The monster boat creaked and cracked under the mountains of sea that rolled over her, leaving only the smoke stack and masts uncovered. The Captain himself said, 'had she shipped another sea at a different time, all would have perished.' "

Charlie's letter to his brother-in-law, Tom Beach, told the story about exercising his horse on deck one morning near the Sandwich Islands, when lo! to his surprise, he was suddenly thrust over the hurricane deck into the Pacific Ocean astride his devoted friend! His alert cowboy pards—with their *reata*s pitched full length—pulled both out of the briny deep, very wet indeed.

Just out of these islands a gloom settled over the company with the sudden death of Sutton's wife, "Prairie Pearl." She was buried at sea. A famous woman sharp-shooter who assisted her husband in the program called, "The Chase for a Bride," her skill as a crack shot enabled her to cut the rope—from which a horse thief was hanging in mid-air—with a rifle bullet. A replacement would always be hard to find. This presented another problem for the Wild West, another "Prairie Pearl."

Reaching Auckland, New Zealand, on September 13, 1890, a great throng of people on the wharf awaited their arrival. The romantic mystique of the cowboy and the Wild West craze were sweeping the country. For the fashion of the day the men and boys wore cowboy hats. Charlie's first impression was that there were more cowboys in New Zealand, than in Texas and Arizona combined.

Shortly after docking, the work of discharging 18 passengers—the Wild West Show's members and their impedimenta—plus 84 tons of general cargo began. The steamer, after taking in a supply of coal on September 14, sailed for Australia with new passengers from Auckland, as well as the original 60 from San Francisco. Parting company at this time, however, were the two brothers, John and Charlie. John continued on to Australia, where they planned to meet at a later date.

The Wild West in New Zealand

"Auckland, New Zealand was a rich and beautiful country," Charlie wrote. "The scenery was simply grand. The climate is something like that on the coast of middle California."

One of Charlie's first activities was to accompany Captain Sutton to the *Auckland News* for a little advance press coverage. Quoting from their very fine article the following flattering words were reported:

"Two finer-looking men it would be hard to find than Captain Sutton and Charlie Meadows, champion roper, who are here in Auckland now with Wirth's Wild West Show. They called at our offices yesterday for a chat, and talked in such an amiable light-hearted way—of warring with Indians, riding buck-jumpers, hunting wild bear, and other strange things—that it is like listening to a chapter out of one of Mayne Reid's novels, excepting, as usual, fact is stranger than fiction. During the chat which resulted in this story, Mr. Meadows sat with his legs on the table lazily smoking. He, too, is a big fine-looking fellow to look at, and a most amusing talker. He is the champion roper in the world, and has issued a challenge of one thousand dollars for anyone to beat him. His time for roping is 59 seconds."

The cowboys had a week of practice before opening day. Much of Charlie's time was spent in preparation for a butcher-knife duel, the most blood-chillingest of all weapons to face, with Juan Catoto, who played a leading part in all the dramas.

From sketchy notes in Charlie's diary, it appears the cowboys were high-spirited and prankish, bursting with virility. Charlie, Catoto, Brown, Felton and some of the others, took in the city evenings, "mashing on the girls," he said, visiting the "publicans," or hotels, indulging in a lot of "conversation fluid," each place sporting at least three bars. The fun-loving cowboys were astounded to see so many young women working as bartenders, and the girls were equally surprised to see real American cowboys. Soon each of them had a girl on his lap. Life for them was a continual round of boisterous gaiety and indulgence in sensual pleasures. They drew a crowd wherever they went.

Their first entertainment was given at Wellesly Street on Monday night, September 22, 1890. It was projected to be on a scale to rival Barnum's great show, the main feature was the Wild West Show. Wirth's advertised Charlie as the "Great Cow King" "Greatest Horseman," and "Champion Lasso Twirler of the Century." "Seven thousand people came out in the rain and mud to see our performance," which, Charlie reported, "is said to be the largest audience ever congregated under one roof in New Zealand."

Newspaper articles, along with Wirth's Auckland programme, featured the three-ring circus and hippodrome races which started the show off, but, as they had seen circuses many times before, the public grew impatient to get on with the Wild West portion of the program. The cowboys led off—with the *Virginia Reel* done on horseback—accompanied by other members of the company in the parts of western ranchmen and cowgirls. The second act—*Indian War Dance*—was a dance common amongst the aboriginal races, whereas the Indians were especially noticed for their ferocious expressions while performing.

The *Bucking Horses Exhibition* done by cowgirls and Mexicans, was followed by the *Immigrant Train*, showing the dangers and hardships the hearty pioneers had to contend with, which crossed the prairies long before the railways were built. *The Hanging of a Horse Thief*, a self-explanatory illusion of lynch law in the West, showed how the Westerners saved the government many a dollar by dispensing with a trial in this manner. *The Daring Race of Minnehaha* came next. The cowboys then gave a lassoing exhibition, showing how cattle were handled without the aid of stockyards or enclosures. *The Attack on the Famous Deadwood Stagecoach,* an exciting, dashing and daring fight between the Indians and stagecoach passengers, brought the cowboys to the rescue, thoroughly routing the dusky warriors.

Cowboy sports followed. The exciting act of picking up ground objects from a speeding horse, showed how the cowboy retrieves his lasso or other equipment dropped from his horse while on a dead run. Riding one horse, Charlie and Jack Brown were the champions of this double, picking-up act. Advertised by others, but never done, the double pickup was performed here for the first time in the world, thanks to Charlie and Jack.

The *Chase for the Bride*, the act originated by Captain Sutton for his wife, "Prairie Pearl," was undertaken by the Wirth Brothers' sister, Madeline. She had to learn to shoot and master the lasso. The danger precluded the use of a loaded rifle, so the cartridges taken from her gun were replaced with wads, and the rope was faked with a "dog-slip." The act, adopted from the Indians, showed their mode of matrimony in the early days of the Northwestern Indian tribes.

The method of transporting the mail—in early days across the prairies, before construction of the railroads—was illustrated by the *Pony Express*. Next came the exciting *Congress of Nations*, a race between the Mexicans, cowboys and Indians, and a race won by Charlie. Then, "Last but not least," Charlie said, "our thrilling *Attack on the Hunter's Cabin* and a few other scenes that would have brought out the 'bad-egg' brigade in America."

Describing Wirth's show as the "most unique" that ever visited the New Zealand shores, the Auckland audience enthusiastically praised and applauded the splendid performance by the Wild West.

Also describing the Arizona boys in his book, *Round the World with a Circus* , George Wirth said:

"Charlie Meadows was 'boomed' as the boss cowboy, as he was a very tall, fine-looking fellow with plenty of assurance and of cultured manner. He was six-foot-seven inches tall. Another tall man and a good looker, was George Felton. Then Jack Brown was six-foot-six inches tall. These men were exceedingly well-built, supple and muscular. Sutton himself was over six feet tall, and was the most picturesque of the crowd. With his long black wavy hair hanging down over his broad shoulders, the Maoris christened him 'Jesus,' because of his resemblance to our Lord's pictures. The other tall men were Jim Keogh, and the Arkansas Kid. Ralph, the Mexican, was of short stature with a handsome face. He was a splendid roper, buck-jump rider, and rider of steers, and would fight a bull as well as any Spanish *toreador* I have ever seen. "

By now all the native boys and half of New Zealand's young men could be seen practicing the new craze, the art of roping. "Though a great stock country, never before had they seen a lasso thrown, they themselves using only a stock whip," Charlie wrote.

An open air exhibition was given at Potter's Paddock the following Saturday. The Indians were a continual problem, being regularly truant, getting drunk and raising all kinds of hell. Sutton would have to make a search and round them up before each performance. The old adage, "You can take the cowboy out of the country, but you can't take the country out of the cowboy," rang true with the Arizona "bronco busters." Full of "balloon juice," they engaged in their share of deviltries, raising a little hell now and then, and generally "blowin' 'er in," so to speak. Because they carried revolvers, everyone, including the police, feared them. It took some time for most people to find that, on closer acquaintance, they were by no means bad fellows.

John Omohundra, Jr., also known as "Texas Jack, Jr."

Juan Catoto

"It was a bad day," Charlie said, "but 3,500 people came out in a drenching rain to see our exhibition. Under a wager of 50 guineas, we were to catch and tie down a notorious seven-year-old bullock. In one minute and a-half, we had the bullock down and tied. Brown was soon on him, careening around the paddock. Ralph, the Mexican, could not suppress himself with a cry of 'Viva America' and the enraged stock dealer who lost the wager set a howling mob of one hundred larrikins upon us in short notice! The cowboys were soon to the rescue, and with lasso and pistols loaded with blanks, put the rascals to flight for good."

Then at the conclusion of the performance, two cowboys, Antonio Esquivel and Thomas Ross, had a dispute over the ownership of a rope. Hot words passed between them, and before Charlie and Captain Sutton could intervene, Esquivel was pulled from his saddle and a brief scuffle ensued. Neither man was hurt, but Charlie and Sutton managed to break it up and remove the cowboy.

"Several well-dressed, apparently respectable people who were watching the fracas, made a disgraceful exhibition by hooting and inciting the men to fight," reported the local press.

The paddock show, being their best, was given in every town where a race course could be obtained. The cowboys recognized how popular an exhibition it was, and it suddenly dawned on them that they did not need a manager. They could put this show on by themselves. One day, on the way back to their quarters by horse, Charlie remarked, "Say fellows, we gave this afternoon's show all on our own. Why not quit these suckers?"

George Wirth, riding along in the group, but unaware that Charlie knew he was there, rode alongside Charlie to tell him there was such a thing as a legal contract by which he and the others were bound. With this, Charlie cantered off, but the whole idea got the others to thinking. Things had not been going well between them and the management over money matters so, if the problem was not resolved immediately, the boys had already made plans to abscond with their services.

"On October 5, we sailed for Gisborne on the *S.S. St. Nichol*," Charlie wrote. "Business was good there, but the season was early with considerable rain. It was October 10, 1890, in Palmerston, on the North Island of New Zealand that we finally decided to make the break. The cowboys suddenly became inoculated with 'strike fever,' and a general bust-up was the result."

The trip to Palmerston had not gone well. Usually three trains were used to convey the company from one town to another. The company comprised 120 persons, including the cowboys and Indians. As the railway had not been cut through the Manawatu Gorge between Woodville and Palmerston, wagons, lorries and drays were hired to move one hundred horses, tents, and other paraphernalia, while coaches transported all that did not ride their horses through. The gorge was very narrow and one wagon had the misfortune of breaking down in the middle, holding up the *Hunter's Cabin* behind.

A great crowd was waiting in Palmerston in compliance with Wirth's advertisement. Many came from a long distance. A large number had come from the Foxton area, some 200 in number, on a special train with their families, and arrived to witness the "celebrated Circus and Wild West Show." The crowd found the tent had not been erected. With the help of these people, the tent finally went up and at 9:30 the crowd was allowed to roll in. But they still had another hour to wait as the first entry did not take place until 10:30, when all but the *Hunter's Cabin* had arrived.

The crowd was restless and noisy, for some had been drinking during the long wait letting it be known that they really came to see the Wild West and that they would be satisfied to see that portion only, since they were all-too-familiar with the circus. The hippodrome races were given first, much to the antagonism of the crowd. The Wild West followed with their regular program. The *Hunter's Cabin*—a scene where the Indians shoot the hunter, scalp him, and burn his cabin—was usually the last act, but, because there was no cabin, the cowboys were instructed to do their lassoing when they finished the show. The bandmaster, uninformed of the change, misinterpretingly considered the show over and, to the astonishment of the audience, played, "God Save the Queen!" It might have suited the occasion better had it been altered to "God Save the Manager!" because Charlie, to be advertised as the "Greatest Lassoist in the World" is exactly just what the people demanded.

The unruly throng let out a loud, prolonged cacophony of shrieks and howls. Then, a man identified as Colonel Gorton, said to be "ever ready to face an enemy," immediately jumped into the ring and declared Wirth's show a swindle. The ring became a seething mass of hysterical victims, and loud demands were made for the manager to show himself. An attorney by the name of Southy Baker followed to address the crowd about their rights, whereupon Colonel Gorton publicly announced that he would wire ahead to Wangunui to advertise the shabby manner in which the Wirths treated their Palmerston visitors. Three-quarters of an hour spent on the circus part of the show, as a means to justify the manager's retention of the admission money, brought forth hoots and hissing, then cries of "give us back our money," all of which rang loud and clear! The disgruntled audience began to break up the seats and destroy other property. The ropes were cut and the tents came down over the huge oil lights, causing a severe threat of fire. Luckily no blaze occurred. The band players, fearing blows other than those from their horns, tucked their instruments between their legs and calmly pulled themselves down under the tent flaps. The Wild West portion of the entertainment was never completed.

The Wirths ordered the cowboys to line up like the cavalry, to charge the crowd on their horses, and to fire with their revolvers which, though loaded with wads, nevertheless could do considerable damage if they struck anyone. The cowboys refused to do this and left the grounds. George Wirth, meanwhile, gathered together the other artists and ordered them to run amongst the crowd. While some were hurt, they formed a body and charged, driving the unruly people from the premises. Charlie now was convinced the time had come to sever relations with the Wirths.

The next morning as the Wirths packed their gear to leave Palmerston, they discovered the cowboys had taken their baggage and left. Charlie could not find Jim Keogh, who had fallen asleep in a railway car. He was left behind. The public sympathized with them in their difficulty; but, unfortunately, that did not end the matter.

In an attempt to hush the whole matter, the press was muzzled and the highly controversial telegram, dispatched in connection with the rumpus at the Wild West Show, was withdrawn the next day. Charlie, Bronco George, the Arkansas Kid, George Felton, Jack Brown, Ralph Felz, the Mexican, and Catoto, the Indian, remained in Palmerston North. They gave a private exhibition for the lawyer, Southy Baker , who "was suffering from an attack of the cowboy fever."

An open air performance was given at the A & P Show Grounds the following Wednesday afternoon. The cowboys invited the public to bring them any unbroken horses or wild cattle so they could show their way of dealing with them. The show thrilled and delighted the crowd who, generous in their praise, considered it a huge success.

The Wirth Show, now somewhat crippled, retaliated by dragging the Mexican and Indian to court, arresting them shortly after the show was over that day. They were compelled to leave for court in Wellington. It was apparent that Charlie's cowboys were out of business for the time being. Then Sutton paid them a visit to induce Felton, Kid, and Bronco George to turn tail and return to the Wirth Show.

First, Mexican Ralph was accused of stealing a show saddle; then, the Indian was charged with larceny of an Indian dress. The case for the prosecution was that the accused, Ralph Felz, had left the company at Palmerston North but kept in his possession a saddle, which belonged to the Wirth Brothers, and the cost of which had been applied to him for the purpose of performing his feats in the show. Witnesses, in cross examination, admitted that Mexican Ralph picked out the saddle when it was bought in San Francisco, but money was taken from his wages for the purchase price. Charlie, who heard Mexican Ralph's plan to leave with the Wirths enough money to cover the value of the whole saddle, testified accordingly; whereas George Cooper, another witness, acknowledged that he heard Wirth's manager, Mr. Alexander, state that the only complaint he had was that

Felz had not come to him to say something about the saddle. Sutton and Cooper also testified. The Magistrate, intimating that the case was exceedingly weak insofar as any criminal intent was concerned, could not see how he could commit Felz. No further evidence was offered, his Worship dismissed the case and did not make a decision on the ownership of the saddle.

Catoto also was found not guilty of the charges against him. The prosecution alleged that Catoto kept the dress in his possession when he left the company at Palmerston. Catoto's counsel, Mr. Baker, opened the defense by characterizing the case as "an impudent attempt of Mr. Alexander to wrest the criminal law to his own business purposes." The Indian understood he was charged with the value of the outfit, as all the cowboys were, but, he had left enough in accrued wages to cover the value of the suit. His Worship interrupted Mr. Baker stating that he did not think there was any "felonious intent," though Catoto may have erred in keeping the garments. This case was also dismissed, and his Worship directed the police to use their own discretion for disposing of the property which was still in Catoto's possession. Everything turned out in Catoto's favor. They were all exceedingly jubilant, and "after the acquittal," Charlie said, "we all entered Wirth's Circus in disguise, just for the lark of it, and were not discovered.

"The following day," as accounted for by Charlie, "we shipped to Christchurch, where we opened our show on the cricket grounds of Lancaster Park, much to the wrathful indignation of the cricketers. During our parade, behind a blasting band through the principal streets, bad weather again plagued us, and a blustery northwester nearly blew us away. I had succeeded in obtaining several good steers, some of which showed good sport in the lassoing trials, and our exhibition in handling those wild bullocks in the ring received general admiration. After the performance we were mobbed by a crowd, and Brown and Felton were 'copped' by some pretty admirers of the female persuasion."

Their humorous production, *The Arizona Kicker,* was met with wild and delightful enthusiasm. The result of their visit is best told by the *Christchurch Press,* dated October 22, 1890:

"The members of the company, headed by Mr. Meadows, are exceedingly expert in their use of the lasso. In this part of the show Mr. Meadows himself is very expert, and fully sustained the reputation he claims as the champion of this kind of work, and was ably seconded by his confreres. Some excellent riding, particularly in picking up objects from the ground at full speed and vaulting on and off their horses, was shown."

Charlie's journal additionally cited: "On October 25, the Wirth Company arrived in Christchurch. Sutton again paid us a surprise visit, offering higher salaries. Brown was induced to return at a leadership position and a salary of $150 per week, which he could not refuse. During their stay of about three months throughout these islands, he was received by the elite and nobility with outstretched arms, and the name of Captain Jack Brown, Arizona buccaroo, became a household word. As an Indian Dramatist he was a success, and in that country he was regarded as a wonder!"

Onward to Australia

Texas Jack, Jr., who had previously been an outstanding attraction in New Zealand and Australia on his own, and well-known there, expressed a desire to join "Wild America" as a partner, uniting with Charlie at Palmerston. Jack was a noted American scout, and the namesake of his benefactor, John Burwell "Texas Jack" Omohundra, a well-known Texas Ranger. In 1872, Jack Senior co-starred with Buffalo Bill and Wild Bill Hickok in Chicago in *Scouts of the Prairie.* This was one of the original Wild West shows. Jack Senior was a noted Confederate scout with a physically impressive and magnetic personality. He was married to the beautiful *Premier Danseuse*, Guisippini Morlacchi, a noted dancer and actress of Italian parentage. The couple were never fortunate to have children of their own.

The small, whimpering boy was rescued by Jack after his own mother and father, who had hidden him under the floorboards of their pioneer cabin home, were savagely murdered by marauding Indians. Not knowing his real name, the boy took his guardian's name. Jack placed him in good hands in Fort Worth, Texas, and provided for his care and schooling while his "adoptive parents" were on the road.

About this time (January 13, 1891), Thomas Alva Edison's phonograph was giving its first performance in New Zealand.

"During the time Brown was raising a sensation in New Zealand," Charlie wrote, "Texas Jack Jr., the Mexican, the Indian, and I, completely circumnavigated the little islands on the *S.S. Monawai*, and landed in Melbourne, Australia, the 'fastest sporting town in the world.' When the ship docked I came up missing my fine Arizona show saddle and some other valuable artifacts and belongings.

"All kinds of outdoor sports were wonderfully popular and patronized by all classes from the nobleman to the peasant. Horse racing was their passion, and the Melbourne Cup is by law a National Holiday. The Australian boasts that it is the 'greatest horse fete' day in all the world, way ahead of the English Derby. The day after my arrival I secured a seat in the grandstand on the Flemington race course. The two-mile race was won by 'Carbine.' The price of admission to this department was $10. Sixty thousand people were jam-packed in this place, and, of course, with all the participants, there were almost double that many souls.

"After my name appeared on the hotel register, I was raided by a number of reporters. I did not deny I was the one Wirth's had advertised as the 'Arizona Cow King,' 'Boss Indian Fighter,' and 'Champion Lasso Twirler of the Century.' I immediately bought up all the leading billboards and had painted in very large letters, only ARIZONA and WILD AMERICA. In one week all of Melbourne was curious to know, 'What is it?' and 'Where is it?' After three weeks, WILD AMERICA added a circus variety of twenty artists, and today the largest canvas in all of Australia bears the name WILD AMERICA, with 'Arizona,' the Visalia-born cowboy, sole proprietor.

"We gave a private exhibition for Lord and Lady Carrington, a few members of Parliament, and the Press. Through the influence of Lord Carrington, I secured the magnificent exhibition buildings and grounds for our show, and the gates were thrown open on November 15, 1890. Thirteen thousand people paid admission to see 'Wild America,' and wild it was, for three members of our support team were badly crippled, and in the Indian attack on the *Deadwood Stage Coach*, one of the horses was accidently killed. We dragged him from the arena by the horn of the saddle. It was a unanimous voice that he was a wonderfully trained horse. It would have been a different story had the Society for the Prevention of Cruelty to Animals known he was really dead."

Texas Jack and his drama was received overwhelmingly. The play itself was a highly vivid and melodramatic presentation of life on the frontier, renegade Indians, beautiful maidens and, of course, scouts. Also, the play somewhat dramatized events in Jack's own life, and every performance found enthusiastic crowds bestowing lavish applause and filling the amphitheatre for the unusual entertainment.

Charlie was a physical specimen worth noticing. The Melbourne reporters, speaking of a Royal fox hunt where Charlie was a guest of Lord Carrington, responded with the following flattering flow of superlatives:

"All the picturesque horsemanship of the famous bedouin, sinks into child's play before this Mameluke of the Plains. No one that we have ever seen, so adequately fulfills the eye, or all the conditions of picturesque beauty, absolute grace and perfect identity with his animal. If an artist or a riding master had wanted to mold a living idol of romantic equestrianship, containing in outline the action of Harry of Navarre, the Americanism of Custer, the automatic majesty of the Indian and the untutored crudeness of the cowboy, he would have measured Charlie Meadows in the saddle; he is the only man we have ever seen who rides as if he could not help it, as if the sculpture and the soldier had come together in his act. Raised on the plains, he has surpassed through every grade and won fame in each line. Thus it is he who holds the supremacy, in fact, receives from his associates an adoration surpassing popularity.

"Never was a finer picture of American Manhood presented, than when Charlie Meadows rode out to show the capabilities of the cowboy, with lasso—head and shoulders above the lot of ordinary mortals—straight as an arrow, not an ounce of useless flesh upon his limbs, but every muscle firm and hard as sinnows of a stag with the frank, kindly eye of a devoted friend; and a natural grace of manner which would become a Marshal of France. Charlie Meadows is from spur to *sombrero* one of the finest types of manhood the continent of America ever produced. Those who had expected a different class of men, must have been pleasantly surprised in these genuine sons of the plains, every one of whom was stamped with the natural easy grace and courtesy of manner, which marks the man who is born a gentleman."

In a letter home, the Arizona cowboy said, "I do not intend to express myself on the subject of the Australian girl, whose life is sadly handicapped by the watchful eye of the ever-present chaperone. I often found myself wondering what some of those pretty, pleasure-loving and good-natured young ladies would have done if the hand of adversity was to lay its icy grip upon them and they were thrown upon their own resources. The eagle-eye of Mother Grundy was upon her, and the machinery of the Old Dame's unsavory tongue was set in motion if an innocent girl saw fit to take a friendly walk with the respectable member of the opposite species, 'He.'

"Catoto, like the rest of us, had a weakness for the gentler sex, and it almost wrecked my show in Melbourne. One morning I was almost thunderstruck to meet this reckless specimen of humankind with his hair shingled, a Prince Albert coat on with dude trousers, and a cane to complete the outfit, walking down the street with a well-dressed and handsome lady. I had to run him down and after some delay, had him fitted with a wig so he was able to resume his role."

The show on its own did exceptionally well in Melbourne. Their performances attended by what seemed like thoroughly spontaneous applause from the *Gallery Gods,* but then WILD AMERICA got an exceptional offer they could not refuse, and joined *Harmston's Great American and Continental Cirque* on the road. W. G. Harmston, the proprietor, had arrived the previous March direct from San Francisco via Auckland, New Zealand. It was said in Australia that Harmston was "second only to Cooper and Bailey's." This publicity did not set well with the Wirths.

Harmston's regular troupe consisted of Mlle. LeBlonde, P. H. Montgomery, who was a well-known Australian, George Harmston, and Gilberto, who were all fantastic bareback riders. Mr. Montgomery sprung from the ground to the back of his horse, and his riding was extremely skillful. Mr. Harmston performed with a specially trained stallion named *Black Eagle.* There were twelve tumblers, including a Japanese family who were exceedingly good, exhibiting the ease with which the human body could be twisted into contorted positions and postures. A trained donkey was an amusing attraction, delighting the children. Mlle. Minetta, an iron-jawed woman whose strength was incredible, "could have been a leading legislator if ever the franchise was extended to the fair sex," said the press. With ease she could lift a twelve-stone man in her teeth and hold a trapeze in her jaws while a man performed on it, which simply astounded the audience.

In a short time Harmston had engaged practically all of the Wirth Brothers' artists, much to the displeasure of that company, because their pay was much better. Word spread swiftly of their super-unique enterprise, and the original Wild West boys still in Wirth's employ were anxious once again to make their exit. The Wirths had learned a hard lesson, however, and had them securely bound by legal contract.

Harmston acquired several of Australia's finest riders; among them the Champion Lady *Equestrienne* of Australia, a young woman known only as Miss Millie, and another young lady of exceedingly attractive appearance with a sylph-like figure, Miss Marion Mae Murray, who had run away from home to join the circus. Charlie and Texas Jack became completely dazzled over these two beautiful and talented young women. Warm, passionate glows passed between Charlie and Miss Murray, he being drawn by a force outside of himself, stronger than gravitation, while the ladies were equally enthralled with the two handsome cowboys. It was not long before they became lively twosomes, Charlie and Miss Murray, Jack and Miss Millie.

The realization that Charlie and his partner, Texas Jack, "the two best darn showmen in the world," and the other turn-coat artists were drawing great crowds and playing ahead of Wirth's dates, with an opposition show, embittered the Wirths who, in turn, planned an ugly attack of retribution. Approaching Harmston, the Wirths told him he was hurting the name of "Wild West," and had the audacity to offer to buy out Harmston's printing if he would cut out that portion of his show. If Harmston chose to do this, the Wirths promised not to give him any opposition at all, and would play opposite towns. Harmston's reaction was scarcely ecstatic but he was not to be intimidated, saying, "I don't even want to know the Wirths!" But say there, Charlie, hadn't the Wirth brothers already said you were the "best bloody cowboy in the world"?

Meantime Brown and Felton were performing well, holding up the Wild West portion of Wirth's enterprise. In a contest with the Australian champion rider, Mick Fenton, George Felton chased, lassoed and branded a steer in an amazing time of 12 seconds!

But poor Felton's luck did not hold. Later, he was severely injured in a peculiar accident. The cowboys bantered him into riding a wild stallion which had never been saddled, and as described in a Phoenix paper, "He threw the animal, cinched on his heavy saddle, then pulled up the blinders and hung to the cantle. But the animal was mad, as well as untamed, and it ran across the plain and jumped into the yawning crater of a volcanic spring. Though badly hurt, George escaped with his life, while the horse was cooked alive in the boiling mud below." He was a very lucky fellow, though he had to spend eighteen months in an Australian hospital, and his fine Arizona stock saddle was lost.

Harmston played in the principal towns and cities in and around Melbourne, Maryborough, Dunnelly and Ballarat. He gloried in the limelight. "Dunnelly was Miss Murray's home town, and Texas Jack and I had good times with the girls there, exchanging humorous pleasantries, and laughing and talking exhaustively. Jack's girl even had a frightening experience on a runaway horse that caused us all great anxiety," Charlie's notes say. He also briefly mentions a horseback dance in the streets. Because of her age, Miss Murray was compelled to leave the show here and return to her home; she rejoined them later.

"Doc" Carver, known as the *Evil Spirit of the Plains*, had completed a most successful tour of Europe with Buffalo Bill Cody, and arrived in Melbourne on WILD AMERICA'S coat-tails. Cody had returned to America, and in January of 1891, having an honorable commission as Brigadier General of the Nebraska National Guard, joined General Miles at Pine Ridge during the trouble with the Indians that culminated with the killing of Sitting Bull.

Doc Carver put on a few performances in Melbourne, then sent the greater part of his show home to America. He remained in Melbourne and produced a few Wild West dramas in the Alexandria Theatre. Charlie and Jack were great admirers of Carver, and spent their leisure time attending his productions. One dramatization was *The Scout,* a scene in which the horse and rider fall through a broken bridge to the water below. Carver found it to be a problem getting a horse that would cross more than once.

Carver was acknowledged as the champion sharp shooter of the world. He was handsome, much taller than Cody, and a better shot. He taught Charlie the trick of using bird shot for knocking out targets thrown into the air. This act was impossible to detect with the naked eye and made an exciting show.

Many show contestants used shot shells while pretending otherwise. Buffalo Bill's own arms crew admitted the fact that he also shattered glass balls in mid-air in this manner, by using rifles "that had been bored smooth to accept .44 calibre shells loaded with a quarter ounce of number 7-1/2 chilled shot, while claiming his rifles and cartridges to be normal solid bullet rounds."

The Wirths figured the next possible way to vent their spleen would be to knock Harmston's cowboys out of his show. Without cowboys, Harmston would not have a Wild West Show. So at Ballarat, a warrant was issued for Catoto and Charlie to answer charges for absconding from their hired service with the Wirth Company. They shrugged it off and sent their counsel, Baker, to stay the date, and played on to Albury, Wagga Wagga, and Goulburn in New South Wales. Charlie's notes mention the cowboys were all suffering the stupors of overindulgence in the flowering bowl as "three blasting bands" escorted them to the depot for their destination to Burwood. It was at Burwood that Mssrs. Wirth had them arrested immediately after their last act. They were to answer charges at the Newtown Police Court. Harry Wirth was there, and it appears that he and Charlie were heatedly involved in a war of words that led to a little hard-knuckle fisticuffs. Then he charged Charlie with assault on top of it all and had him locked up.

William Alexander, Wirth's representative, gave evidence to the effect that they had signed a contract before the British Consul in San Francisco, and after leaving there, performed for them in Auckland, New Zealand. He stated that the agreement explained to them that it embraced the whole of the Australian Colonies. Charlie and Catoto were defended by a Mr. Gannon, who pointed out to the Bench that the agreement was not made in the Colonies as it should have been when they arrived, and contended it had not infringed on the Fugitive Defender's Act. The Magistrate was of the same opinion and discharged the two men. "We came clear the court kissing the Bible," Charlie said, but the Mssrs. Wirth were staggered by the decision and set out on a bitter smear campaign.

Piqued and surprised at the rude and discourteous actions of his rival competitor, Harmston entered the following card in the *Newcastle Chronicle* of January 12, 1891, which read:

"MR. HARMSTON and Son desire to call attention to the fact that never since their arrival in this country from America have they ever found it necessary to descend to malicious and ill-mannered attacks upon anyone in the same business as themselves. They rely solely upon the general excellence of their entertainment and the exceptional ability of the lady and gentlemen artists in their employ for support, and feel confident that any exhibition of bad taste and want of managerial tact such as recently published by others, will readily be recognized and depreciated by those best of judges and lovers of fair play, the public."

On Wednesday, January 14, 1891, Mr. Harmston announced in the *Newcastle Chronicle* his opening on the vacant allotment opposite the Honeysuckle Post Office, with Charlie and Texas Jack as featured attractions: Charlie as the "*Champion Lasso Twirler of the World,*" and Texas Jack as the "*Reckless Spirit of the Plains*," an all-round marksman and cowboy. Unlike the usual circus tent, Harmston's tent had no top, so on the first day they were sadly rained out by a real "gully-washer," and to top it off, Charlie lost his voice.

Below Harmston's ad, Wirth Brothers bought the space and entered the following retaliation:

"WIRTH'S ORIGINAL WILD WEST SHOWS
Do Not Be Deceived by False Advertisements
We Are The Genuine People
Wait for Us and Judge for Yourselves

TONIGHT AT 8:45
We Send Up a BALLOON
from BRENT'S PADDOCK
Darby Street."

The Wirths let it be known to Harmston, "you will be sorry you ever heard of us," and sent a man named Frost ahead of their show with a hot-air balloon, and another man to make an ascent and parachute from the clouds, releasing thousands of handbills from the sky that came floating down over the town like snowflakes. Printed on the handbills was, "WAIT FOR WIRTH'S ORIGINAL WILD WEST SHOW," which announced there would be a night ascension with an illuminated parachute dive and fireworks. But Charlie and his boys were tired of Wirth's dirty tricks, so they banded together and "completely routed the balloon man."

Mr. Harmston put out the following announcement in the *Chronicle* regarding the continued agitation from the opposition:

"About this time Mssrs. Harmston and Son experienced a petty annoyance in the shape of a company of sideshow people hailing from Sydney Market, or some other catch-penny showmen. Like the snarling cur that ever barks at the heels of his superior, so did these mushroom entertainers have the audacity and effrontery to pose in opposition to a troupe of admittedly the cleverest people that ever came to this country. To such an extent did their impudence go, that they have ever since followed in the wake of the Harmston Co., styling themselves the original and only Wild West Show in the Colonies, and advertising many false and insulting statements. This, however, instead of proving beneficial to them, only resulted in their direct failure, for so inferior was their exhibition to the entertainment preceding it, that in every instance have they been compelled to bring their season to an abrupt and speedy termination. Readers of this journal have probably noticed, from advertisements lately inserted, that this blight or pest, or petty irritation, or whatever you are pleased to term it, is still skulking behind; and, notwithstanding the snarling and convulsive upheavals from its very weak stomach, it keeps a respectable distance in the rear. Not yet have these people had the temerity to come within sufficient range—to try conclusions with a company composed entirely of champions and performers, or where each is an artist in the first rank—doubtless realizing the fact that such an effort would only result in ignominious and disgraceful defeat in themselves. And it is quite probable the attempt will be made in a town where no anxiety exists, except possibly on the part of certain trades people who have good reason to remember their visit."

The old saying, "if you've seen one circus you've seen the lot," did not apply to Harmston's show because of its unique and original composition. *The Newcastle Chronicle* of January 16, 1891, reported on the WILD FRONTIER LIFE Company as follows:

"TEXAS JACK, a typical cowboy, CHARLES MEADOWS, an Arizona lad, who is without a doubt one of the most expert horsemen and lasso throwers of the world and three others, including a red Indian, took part. In Arizona and the southwest, Meadows is well-known as a fearless horseman and champion lasso thrower. Last evening he gave some wonderful exhibitions of his skill with the rope, catching a horse around the neck, the foreleg, hindleg, and a man by the body as many times as he liked without a miss while going at full speed round the track. Once, his animal fell on him. But in a second he rose along with his animal. Then with Texas Jack he showed that while riding at full swing a cowboy can pick up even a piece of straw from the ground. Texas Jack, who is well-known here, gave a speech on cowboy life, and showed that he was both quick and certain with his six-shooter. He rode a buck-jumper during the evening well. The show was a good one, and the best part of it was keenly appreciated by the thousands who were present."

Mexican Bill joined them in Newcastle, and acting as advance agents for Harmston, to negotiate terms and arrange accommodations, he and Charlie arrived in Sydney a day ahead of the company resolved to kill a portion of their intervening time by looking over the city. To this end they jumped into a hack and commanded the *jehu* to "get a Wild West move on." The driver's seat was out of view, but the speedy manner in which the horses started down the street satisfied them that he was attending strictly to the matter of "getting a Wild West move on."

The team fairly flew over the cobbles, and the carriage was yanked from one side of the street to the other, in a manner which threatened at any minute to wreck the whole outfit. The fast and furious gait just suited the Arizona gentleman, who called out from time to time to the invisible driver to "let 'er go." Astonished crowds flocked to the curb to see their rig go by, and the Arizona man was in his element. Reclining against the cushions he assumed an indifference to the whole proceeding, which was clearly a bluff.

Finally, between thumps, he came aware of the presence of a half dozen mounted police galloping by the side of their cab with wild gesticulations and admonitions to "keep cool." At a sharp turn in the road one of the bluecoats swung a lariat over the head of the team, caught one of them about the neck and brought the outfit to a standstill. It was only then that Charlie and his friend discovered that they had been without a driver all the time. The team had started up before the hackman had time to mount his seat, and had galloped through the principal streets of Sydney at their own sweet will.

"Oh, yes, to be sure," Charlie remarked, "I will not conceal the fact that we had a cocktail or two, and that was one occasion I got all the excitement I wanted."

Harmston's foes, the Wirth Company, continued to have problems. When they opened their show on the 24th of January, 1891, in Sydney, the paddock gates were rushed and the back fence of the grounds was torn down by many wild larrikins who entered the show without paying the admission, and not being content with this, they rushed the enclosure where Jack Brown and the other cowboys were working. Two of the cowboys tied a lasso from one saddle to the other and galloped through the crowd, virtually mowing down the bellicose bummers. Some were hurt, but it turned the trick.

From Newcastle and Sydney, Harmston moved on to Maitland, where they opened a two-night season. Their parade down the principal streets, with the band playing in full blast, created a sensation. Their press coverage was excellent. The *Maitland Mercury* of January 22, 1891, reported:

"Texas Jack, Jr., who already has shown in Maitland, a very clever rider and sharp shot, and all-round disciple of Buffalo Bill; Charlie Meadows, a gigantic specimen of humanity, with a romantic history, and two or three others, including a real, unadulterated Indian. Meadows is proficient in the use of the lasso, and many scenes of cowboy life which are common enough on the wide and rolling plains, were very entertaining to the large audience."

They toured the towns and cities of Musswellbrook, Tamworth, Armidale, Quinindi, and Tenterfield. In his letter home to the editor of the *Tulare County Times,* Charlie wrote, "During the three months of constant travel through South Australia, Victoria, New South Wales and Queensland, I have enjoyed an unprecedented success. There is nothing left but Brisbane, and a short route through North Queensland to China and India, where I hope to be in two months. We will meet Brown and the opposition show day after tomorrow. If we fail to wake Brisbane up, Barnum and Buffalo Bill need not try!"

The editor of the *Tulare Times* appears to have been one of Charlie's teachers, as Charlie continued to say, "It is my intention to travel around this huge clod ye editor used to teach me so much about. Often when I become entangled in latitudes and longitudes, I think what a pity that you did not apply the rod more frequently."

The circus arrived in Brisbane, Queensland, February 10, 1891. The Wirths preceded them and obtained the spacious Breakfast Creek grounds. The Wirths again advertised themselves to be the "genuine show," and had in their employ the "champion cowboys of the world, bar none." In this advertisement, they also had the audacity to say, "Our imitators advertise to appear, but never have the temerity to play their dates when we appear in any city."

Harmston's operation was scheduled to open on Wednesday, February 18, at the Town Hall Reserve. Mr. Harmston, in a gentlemanly manner, responded to Wirth's final, discourteous outburst. In the *Brisbane Courier* of February 16, 1891, he put out the following answer:

Interesting Memo

> The public has no doubt been concerned as to why our original date, February 14, has not been adhered to. The extraordinary success that has attended our overland tour, during which time we have been compelled night after night to refuse money at the doors, and have performed to larger business than any combination that has previously traveled the same route,

has compelled me to give additional representations in several towns visited. We regret exceedingly that the public has been misled during our journey hither as to what a Wild West Show should be; which has resulted, not only in dire financial failure to the instigators, but has spoilt us from giving our representations of Wild Frontier Life the same grand scale of completeness and detail originally intended. However, the commodius reserve above mentioned has been secured, where we shall open our American and Continental Palace Cirque, composed of lady and gentlemen artists, who have graduated in the business from infancy, and have attained their exceptional ability after long years of hard training. Our representations of American Wild Life will still be given, and although not having the required space at our command, yet we confidently assure the public that we shall be enabled to present them with scenes from WILD FRONTIER LIFE correctly represented by:

TEXAS JACK
Champion Rifle Shot and Rough Rider of the World
&
CHARLIE MEADOWS
Champion Lassoist of the World, (Bar None)

Admission to this great Exhibition
will be 3s, 2s and One Shilling.
Watch For Our Great Street Parade.
An Entertainment in Itself.

Harmston closed a most successful five-week season, their performances bordering on the spectacular. Charlie said, "We rang down the curtain in the last act by landing in jail, all hands, proprietors, and performers, sued for $25,000, with bond fixed at the same amount pending the action. This was for the accidental shooting of a small boy in the audience during the sharp-shooting performance. A compromise was arranged in short order, the small boy quickly recovered, and he and his mother took a three thousand dollar trip home to England."

During the same performance a little excitement was also caused when an Australian youth accepted Texas Jack's offer to give a sovereign to the person who could, for a half minute, "ride pretty" on an unbroken horse. A rider mounted the animal but was shortly forced to relinquish his seat. It appeared to be a moot point whether he had ridden the horse for the stipulated time, but the occupants in the pit demanded payment of the sovereign by hooting and yelling, and at length the management handed the venturesome horseman his money. Texas Jack then mounted the beast and rode him while bucking 'round the circle' with the greatest of ease and confidence.

Charlie wrote in his journal, "The Arizona Company then pulled out for the stock and mining districts of Queensland, in Northern Australia. We were well received by the Queenslanders, whose kindness and hospitality were unflagging. Our show attracted attention from squatters for miles around, and many of them followed us several hundred miles up the coast. After having surpassed their English cousins in feats of horsemanship, they are loathe to acknowledge that anyone but an Australian can ride a bit better. They are daring and fearless riders, but have little knowledge of controlling a horse. A few of them will remember the merry string they were led by the cowboys at their favorite sport, fox hunting and stag chasing, wherein the Australian invariably came out second best. The young lady feels herself equal to her ambitious male companion in the wild ride of the steeplechase, and complains less over a 'fall or nawsty cropper,' don'cherknow, than an American lady would over a slight shaking-up in a buggy!

"One of the leading characteristics of the Australians was their sporting qualities. The average member of Parliament knows more about the prize ring and race horse pedigrees than he does of the laws of the land. Queensland was by far the richest colony in Australia, the soil fertile, the timber good and the climate similar to that of the Salt River Valley in Arizona, with winters probably a bit milder. Droughts occurred occasionally and were very destructive to stock, and disease was common.

"This was the land ye cowpunchers had looked forward to for pastures anew, and where we had hoped to chase fat, long-horned steers as of yore on the fast fading ranges of Arizona. After giving the grazing question a thorough investigation, I came to the conclusion that to stay home was the best."

Texas Jack and Miss Millie surrendered to cupid's arrow, and entered the blissful state of matrimony. From that time on, Harmston billed her as "Mrs. Texas," or "Millie Omohundra, Champion Lady *Equestrienne.*"

"We scored successes up the coast of Queensland to Maryborough and Rockhampton," Charlie wrote. Miss Murray rejoined the company at Rockhampton, and once again Charlie was drawn to her abilities, feminine charm and captivating personality. Charlie's brief notes mention a fight with a big Queenslander about this same time.

At Rockhampton, a new play was introduced: *Dick Turpin's Ride to York,* which vividly portrayed the various incidents in the career of the desperate highwayman, and portrayed with realistic skill the events leading up to the death of Bonny Black Bess. A comedy of four acts was also presented, *The Strategist.* "Each player was applauded to the echo, for a ripple of merriment to a tornado of approbation," reported the *Rockhampton News* of April 1, 1891.

From Rockhampton they took in the cities of Townsville and Charters Towers, arriving May 10, at Cooktown, in the northern part of the continent. The next port o'call was Java. By this time, Charlie's relationship with Miss Murray blossomed into a flame that began to glow and smoulder; and before long, their romance burst into a torment of delicious madness. The glory of his success, the love of a beautiful woman, and the excitability of the whole adventure was overwhelming to the Arizona cowboy "fresh from the range."

Fearing news of a possible cholera epidemic, Charlie and Texas Jack wisely persuaded the two ladies to stay in Australia and rejoin them after their Java tour.

Charlie Meadows, *Circa* Age 32

CHAPTER 9

1891-1892
SURABAJAII, THE GRAVEYARD OF THE PROFESSIONAL

"On May 13, 1891, we boarded the British-India boat, the B.I.S.S. *Bundero*, that was to steam us away from the Antipodes; our destination was Java, via Thursday Island and the Gulf of Carpenteria. A great crowd and two bands followed us to the wharf," Charlie wrote. "When the steamer gave out one long prolonged whistle, the band tootled, "The Girl I Left Behind Me," and 'me thinks' there were several cowpunchers that did not soon forget their feelings as we pulled out and waved a long farewell to those we left behind."

Charlie's brother, John, was among those left behind, and neither was sure they would ever see each other again.

"The voyage was an uneventful one," Charlie said, "other than the experience of being caught on a coral reef for 12 hours, which resulted in more of a scare than otherwise actual damage. In and around the famous fisheries of Thursday Island we could see the boats that had fallen victims to the coral reefs that were constantly forming and had so retarded transit and navigation.

"There was a great amount of gambling for high stakes amongst the cowboys and ship officers. Drinking was heavy enough to make a hummingbird spit in a rattlesnake's eye. As we moved closer to the equator, the heat became very oppressive, and fever prevalent. After fourteen days of sail, we reached Java and sailed into the Harbor of Surabajaii with the Yankee flag flying on our main mast. Java was not larger than the territory of Arizona. Surabajaii was the cholera bed of the East, and the dreadful disease was raging at the time. Before we anchored, several sampans and canoes came to meet us. We wasted no time getting ashore.

"Standing on the wharf and looking up at a gradual slope, we were facing a city of more than a half-million inhabitants surrounded by beautiful mountain scenery with all its original loveliness of the tropical land. What a vision of glory and what a revelation for ye cowpuncher. We walked under acacias, palmettos, and breadfruit trees, and innumerable shrubs in all the glowing blossom of spring. Palms grew up thickly, covered with coconuts, and full of beautiful plumed birds, flying squirrels and monkeys. There were houses of strange architectural structure, covered with vines, and a surging throng of people moved about in the narrow streets in gaudy, varied costume. Our little party of four consisted of Texas Jack, Mexican Bill, the Indian and myself.

"With difficulty we got permission from the resident who acted as a kind of Governor, Chief Magistrate, and Justice. Our cargo, 52 tons altogether, was carried three-quarters of a mile by coolies. Some of the pieces weighed more than a ton and were transferred cheaper than could be done by dray. It was amusing to see them work; a perfect string of human carriers for three-quarters of a mile long. We found the hotels to be perfect palaces of marble, arranged of the best plan for comfort. Each guest was provided with a servant that shadowed by day, fanned us with great fronds, and attended to our every want.

"Java was governed by the Dutch, and the Dutch men and women sat around in the gardens in easy chairs and in dresses that for brevity would shame a Yuma Indian. All interest in opposition shows was lost, and the saw-dust gladiators—Sleeping Beauty and Romeo and Juliet, became insignificant when we opened our show. Neither entertainment survived a second night. For ten nights after our opening, there was not a vacant seat in the large tent, and thousands were turned away. Cholera broke out amongst the company, and in a few days five were stricken. One survived and bore the distinction of being the only European to overcome this dreadful disease. He told a woeful tale of the scenes in the Cholera ward of the hospital where many died with agonizing cramps. Once affected with the disease, the patient was taken to the hospital and not allowed to see anyone except the physicians and assistants.

"Europeans seldom survived more than two hours and were buried one hour after death. There was no one, he said, in the hospital that spoke English, and their rules of admittance were strictly adhered to. In many of the large towns and cities of Java, India, and Burma, there was no burying ground for those that could not produce the money required. These people were thrown into a bone yard of a large paddock enclosed with high stone walls, and swarming with half-starved dogs and vultures that shrieked and barked and fought over the ghastly remains of the unfortunate. In Java the bone yard was about done away with, but in Bangkok and Bombay it could be seen anytime.

"In Surabajaii we were unable to agree with the Harmston heads, and Texas Jack, Mexican Bill, Juan Catoto and I pulled out for Batavia at the other end of the island. On June 9, 1891, we joined up with Frank Fillis, GREAT CIRCUS AND MENAGERIE for the rest of the Java season, opening our first show with them on the 25th in Buitenzorg. We showed all through the leading towns and cities of Java, including Bandung, Semerang, and the native stronghold of Solo, where we witnessed the Four Princes' procession. We played here under the patronage of the Governor and Sultan and the Crown Prince and their wives, the former with 60 and the latter with 48. Together they had 700 servants. From the humble servant to the Sultan himself, they were covered with an effusion of diamonds that fairly set the tent ablaze with splendor! We gave them an outstanding performance, and the Sultan, in appreciation, presented me with his prized possession: a kris. The ugly weapon was the identical one with which he had killed six of his wives who had offended him in some manner known only to Sultanic Majesties, and was presented to me by the Sultan himself—in the presence of his 60 remaining wives, and surrounded by all his court retinue, servants, etc., during the exhibition of our company."

Notes say that Texas Jack took quite an interest in a small boy, a member of the Royal family, who was lavishly adorned with diamonds. The boy, it appears, took an idealistic liking to Jack and his drama. A serious accident occurred during their performance when the lion tamer was badly torn up during his act and had to be hospitalized.

It was in Batavia, Charlie wrote, that he contrived to learn the art of the broadsword, and graduated from the butcher-knife duels previously enacted. He mastered the technique so well that he met and defeated the master, Von Llicise, in a mounted sword contest.

"Being persuaded the sickly season was over," Charlie said, "we returned to Surabajaii, the graveyard of the professional. Every company had left several of their number there. Within the first three days, four of our company had died; Fischer, the boss canvassman, Peacock and Trent. On the sixth night, when the tent was packed to suffocation, and just before the curtain went up, news came that one of the leading performers had died in the hotel after a few minutes' illness, and that another had been taken to the hospital.

"Panic broke out amongst the artists. The company fled in fear and excitement to the mountains on special trains, trams and bullock carts. But the Wild West stayed, along with the lion tamer who was still recovering from his wounds. After a few days, Texas Jack and I left Java on August 28, 1891, with the Mexican and Indian on board the S.S. *Davenhurst*. Shortly after sailing we were boarded at sea in the Straits of Surabajaii by quarantine officials, turned back, ejected, and placed under quarantine. But these cowboys were not to be fenced in, and the following day we escaped on the *Cleydra*, disguised as wealthy Englishmen and their servants, arriving in Singapore, the melting pot of nations, on September 1st. By the 4th we reached Penang and Harmston's Company, swallowed our pride and rejoined him five minutes before the bell rang."

Charlie and Texas Jack sent for the girls, and after a separation of nearly four months, they were a welcome sight to see. Charlie missed his girl more than he was prepared to admit. He could not deny there had been other amorous interludes—females threw themselves at handsome Charlie's feet. He had his lusts and faults as well as his ideals and virtues. Penang was no exception, for his notes say "my romantic pursuits included both light and dusky maidens." But he never was known to boast of his sexual exploits where a good woman's name was concerned.

His power to command was magnificent. The *Straits Independent and Penang Chronicle*, in their very fine description of Charlie, said, "Charlie is a finely set-up man, standing six-foot-six in his stocking feet, and muscular in proportion, His shoulder-of-mutton fist being calculated to hold elephants as well as bucking broncos. Handsome and intelligent in appearance, he is a popular favorite all-round, and if we should ever abandon the press and start a matrimonial agency, we would like to get him as a secretary."

Besides clearing the cobwebs from their brains, the cowboys did not have to be told whisky was a great deterrent for disease. The artists all took their share, since drink was prevalent throughout the company, and regarded it strong enough to peel the hide off a Gila Monster. Their over-indulgence at the Shrine of Bacchas once again proved their downfall, and responsible for an unfortunate accident involving a rickshaw. Charlie's very brief notes do not go into detail, other than they "squared everything for $1,000"; and left Penang with its glorious waterfalls, botanic gardens and unusual wealth of jungle-clad hills and flowers, for India, via the Straits of Malocca and the Bay of Bengal.

Charlie Meets Rudyard Kipling

"Remarkable luck accompanied our expedition," Charlie said. "While traveling between Morsoe and Hederbad, an express train crashed into our coach, killing twelve natives and wounding several others, while not a single member of our troupe received a scratch, although we were sandwiched in between unfortunate victims in every direction."

Their company arrived in Delhi on the 17th of September, opening their show to a great crowd on the local racecourse that abounded in tigers. A native jockey had the tragic misfortune of being torn limb from limb and eaten by a tiger before the shocked and horrified audience.

"We were under the patronage of the Sultan, an obnoxious individual, who had a flock of secluded concubines as well as numerous wives behind the scenes," said Charlie. "After our usual performances, and half a night in a hell-hole, we said, "To hell with the Sultan," and departed from Bombay, journeying on to Calcutta, enjoying spontaneous applause and welcome receptions. The whole country was suffering from the McKinley Bill, a stiff tariff imposed during the administration of President McKinley, that ruined India's tobacco industry, and almost bankrupt their economy."

In Calcutta, Charlie and Texas Jack had the good fortune to meet a remarkable young author by the name of Rudyard Kipling, whose father was curator of the Lahore Museum in Calcutta. Magnetized by the American West, Kipling had "cowboy fever," and admired the two cowboys' skills and dexterity. Kipling had not yet gained prominence as a writer, but was becoming famous for possessing the spell of the storyteller and the "magic of atmosphere" that soon made his works remarkable. The two cowboys enjoyed a close relationship with him as he followed them through several countries they went on to visit.

It was in Calcutta that Charlie was again drawn to the broadsword when he had the occasion to match blades with Colonel Fred Watson of the British Army, finishing in a draw after an exciting match that lasted two hours.

From Charlie's brief notes, he wrote, "We returned to Penang and arranged our next show, opening it on the 15th of October in the nearby city of Taipeng. We fairly wallowed in the mud, with the early season drenching with rain and the show a disappointment as the result." There Texas Jack tried his hand at Texas Cowboy Tea Planting.

On to Burma, the Philippines, China and Japan

On October 25, they departed Penang, loaded with curios, native dress and weapons, and set out on their voyage to Rangoon, Burma, via the Andaman Sea and the Gulf of Martaban. Their first exhibition was given on November 2, under the curious eye of thousands of native on-lookers. "The Burmese are a very independent people, and a spectacle in their gaudy dress," Charlie wrote.

The usual long list of attractions was viewed by a full house. The jockey quadrilles, followed by two clowns boxing, caused considerable laughter. The Risling ladders by the Komo Japanese Company was a particularly good performance, which was more than maintained by one in the company with an umbrella and a tub. The Roman two-horse race in the hippodrome was brought to an end by a rather heavy fall by one rider, but fortunately with no serious injury. Some clever juggling was performed by Madame Rosina, while Walhalla and Mathews were clever with the fiddles and bells. Johnny Sharman and his dogs were great fun, but the Wild West received the greatest bursts of applause. The *Rangoon Gazette* chronicling the event, reported, "After a Virginia Reel, which was well done, Charlie Meadows showed his great skill with the lasso. While at a gallop, he lassoed an Indian, first around the neck; then pinioned his arms, thus preventing him from using any firearms he might have, then lassoed a horse at a gallop, first by the neck and finally by the feet. A buck-jumper, which must have shaken his rider considerably, was introduced but could not unhorse him. Finally, a scene of real life, the *Immigrant Train,* the *Attack by the Indians on the Camp*, and the *Repulse* closed the entertainment. "

At their leisure, Charlie's notes imply, he and Jack practiced riding Burmese ponies over difficult hurdles. They visited the pagoda working elephants in the countryside. Their final performance in Burma was given in the city of Moulmein.

The Sultan of Java

Indonesian Princess

On November 5, 1891, they set sail for Singapore, opening their show on December 14 for a week's entertainment. Business was disappointing. On Christmas Day, the company boarded the S. S. *Salvadore,* and set out for the Philippine Islands.

They swept across the fathomless deep blue of the South China Seas. During the five-day sentimental voyage, Charlie, a handsome young cowboy, and Miss Murray, an irresistible young woman—under a canopy of one starlit night—felt the pangs of love and desire and fell helpless victims to the emotions of the heart. They made plans for an elopement, but many of those memories were too private for him to share. These memories were not detailed in his diaries.

Anchor was dropped on New Year's Day, 1892, in Manilla Harbor, with their initial performance being given six days later. "The band escorting our most impressive procession was superb, the weather excellent, and the natives noticeably clean," he continued. "The laws of the land were very strict, however, and forgiveness never heard of, the punishment being the screw press. The Priest was a mighty high individual, with gambling and virgins a daily indulgence.

"On January 23, we had an excellent performance for the Governor; however, the troublesome experience of a pony that invaded his box during the lassoing scene had to be dealt with. There were the cockfighting pits, and special bullfights to excite the stouthearted for our leisure entertainment.

"We toured overland to the city of Mauben; the natives here appeared ignorant of the circus. Our final exhibition was at Mallolos, where, by now, most of the company suffered the torments of dysentery. I, myself, suffered with high fever and loss of blood."

On shipboard in Mallolos, Miss Marion Mae Murray roped and tied Charlie with the Holy Bonds, and it was then ye cowpuncher gave up 32 years of bachelorhood and cast his little bark upon the mysterious waters of wedlock for the first time.

Their three-month season ended in April, 1892. The company steamed out of Manilla Harbor on a romantic honeymoon cruise for the two happy newlyweds who were destined for the next port-o'call, the exciting city of Hong Kong. As they crossed the troubled South China Seas, darkness soon concealed the heavens with a chill of uncertainty. Suddenly, they were in a storm that had greatly augmented, the ship swayed with a sickening rhythm, and the whole company "suffered the effect of monsoon sickness," Charlie reported.

"Hong Kong was a beautiful city of startling contrasts, busy with inhabitants and luxuriant with vegetation. We opened on the 4th of April to a very large audience. Between performances, Texas Jack and I, along with the ladies, visited the gambling "hells" of Kowloon, across the bay, and the four of us on every possible occasion satisfied our longing for Chinese dumplings."

Charlie's Christmas Card from Burma

Charlie, and Mr. Armstrong, Harmston's business manager, on the particular juncture, had business that kept them at the show site all day. So Marion Mae and Mrs. Armstrong who was wearing her usual elegant and valuable jewelry, decided to return to their hotel and wait for the men. The men put the two ladies in a rickshaw and sent them on their merry way. The driver started off at a very fast gait. The two ladies became suddenly alarmed, realizing the driver was taking the wrong route. They should have reached the hotel sooner. The streets were unfamiliar to the frightened Marion Mae and Mrs. Armstrong, the area becoming more and more squalid as they passed each subsequent darkened alley littered with rough-looking Chinese, beggars, and cripples. Some had their faces partially eaten away from leprosy, pressing in close to the rickshaw as they passed.

Fearing great harm, Marion Mae and Mrs. Armstrong became thoroughly terrified. They believed the rickshaw driver intended to rob them and take Mrs. Armstrong's diamonds. They began to shout for him to stop, but he only went faster, drawing the little carriage into ever-darkening side streets. Then over the heads of the rough-looking crowd, Marion Mae sighted a uniformed Bobby, stood up in the rickshaw and screamed at the top of her lungs. At this point, the rickshaw man dropped the shaves and ran off. They later learned that if a person stands up in a rickshaw, it cannot be pulled. The English Bobby, who was a most welcome sight, came to their rescue and called another rickshaw to escort them safely to their hotel. The actual intention of the driver was never known, but when Charlie and Armstrong returned home that evening, they welcomed their wives with quiet relief.

On the 22nd of April they boarded the S.S. *Shanghai,* and steamed out of Hong Kong through the Straits of Formosa and the East China Seas, bound for Shanghai, China. "We suffered through a typhoon in the Yellow Sea," Charlie said, "and encountered pirates off the coast of China. I was robbed as before of many of my curios and jewelry on board." They reached Shanghai Harbor April 26, and gave their first performance two days later. The weather was excellent and business was good. Their plan was to set up inside the Great Wall, but on advice of the Emperor they "should do so at their own risk." So they set up just outside the wall, but a visit was made later through this proud marvel of man's ambition, which was a "grand revelation for ye cowpuncher."

About this same time Marion Mae began to complain of illness and had a desperate desire for Chinese dumplings. It was confirmed that she was in a "delicate" condition. Their hearts were filled with joy. But the circus was "not a place to rear a family," she told Charlie, and they would have to "quit show business," and settle down to domestic tranquility.

Charlie knew deep down in his gut that he could never give up show business and would always follow a band as a wanderlust showman. But to pacify his new bride, he agreed that "someday" they would settle down.

An amusing incident occurred, as they packed up their gear to depart Shanghai— the mainspring pole for a large tent swung out of control, flattening a string of vending carts, sending the equipment and wares splattering in all directions.

The two cowboys, Charlie and Texas Jack, left the Harmston Company at this point and joined Woodyear's troupe for a tour of Japan. Charlie was advance agent for the company. They sailed from Shanghai on the *Saiku Maru*, and suffered through a raging typhoon in the Yellow Sea, docking in Nagasaki harbor on June 13, 1892. A city of shipbuilding and thriving fisheries, Nagasaki sat in a deep-cut bay surrounded with mountains—giving the effect of a large amphitheatre. Outstanding exhibitions were greeted with glorious tribute and special courtesy wherever they went. Other stops were made at Yokohama, and Kobe, the major seaport of Japan. Charlie created a tremendous audience when he challenged the Japanese broadsword champion to a match. He won.

"Between performances we took in the Japanese high-life, the Sing-Song girls, serpentine dancers in all their glorious colors, acrobatic dancers of unique and original style, and a romantic place called the Fish Pond, where we glanced endlessly into the embers dying in the ashes. Some of the ladies and gentlemen were startled by the appearance of a cowboy, but the average globe-trotter was regarded as an ordinary human being," Charlie wrote.

A Tip of the Hat from Buffalo Bill

After the frontier war with the Indians at Pine Ridge was over, Buffalo Bill put together another company for one last grand exhibition in Europe. He gathered his Indians from the Chiefs amongst the "friendlies" at Pine Ridge, including Lone Wolf, No Neck, Yangton Charlie, and Black Heart. The others included some of the hostages taken at Fort Sheridan: Short Bull, Kicking Bear, Scatter, and Revenge.

When Doc Carver returned to America, he reported the grand reception and the many laurels Charlie had won on his tour of the Far East. Even though Cody and Carver had not spoken since their feuding partnership the year before, Charlie's name and fame had spread fast in the circus world.

Cody expressed a keen desire to obtain Charlie's services in his forthcoming show. Charlie was all fire and excitement. Performing with the master showman had been his life's goal, but he had to complete his Japanese tour first. When he informed his bride of the great offer, the resulting steam almost took the crease out of the old lasso wrangler's *sombrero*. He agreed they would leave for Vancouver, Canada, and then decide their next move. It is not known why Charlie and Marion Mae went to Vancouver, unless it was possibly the only ship available at the time.

Then, there was the heart-wrenching task of bidding their old friends good-bye. It was especially difficult for Charlie to leave his old pard, Texas Jack, and his wife, Millie. Jack and Charlie had often discussed reuniting in South Africa. Meantime, Charlie wished Jack "good luck."

Ten years later, in 1902, Jack hired a young trick rider and lassoist, a cowboy who had come to Ladysmith, South Africa where Jack was showing, chaperoning a ship load of livestock. Jack, as he did in all his shows, was awarding a medal to the contestant who could throw a rope the best at his afternoon performances, and this young man was Jack's ideal. The boy's deft fingers could make the loop of his lasso "writhe and jump as though it were alive." Jack billed him as the "Cherokee Kid," a name the young man concocted for himself. The talented young lassoist was none other than the man we all know as Will Rogers.

Will stayed on with Jack until 1903, at which time Jack intended to come home. He gave Will a letter of recommendation and, on Will's way home by way of Australia, who should pick him but Wirth Brothers Circus, who billed him as the "Champion Trick Roper and Lassoist of the World" Circus people enjoy a certain kind of kinship to one another; and, of course, Jack had told Will all about Charlie and their close association. When Will returned home to America a few years later, he immediately looked up Charlie. Will and his wife, Betty, often tramped the desert near Charlie's ranch in Yuma, and, on several occasions were guests at Charlie's Yuma headquarters.

Will looked up to Charlie as being the master of the lasso, but Charlie, in turn, said Will was the best "trick" lassoist he had ever seen. Neither Charlie nor Will were ever to see Jack again, he never made it home—and Charlie did not go to South Africa as he had intended. Texas Jack, still a young man, died in Kroonstadt, South Africa in 1905, and was buried far away from his home. The cause of his death was unknown. Charlie never forgot him. The same is probably true for Will Rogers, who wrote and spoke fondly of Texas Jack many times.

Charlie, Marion Mae, and Catoto sailed for Vancouver on July 1, 1892, aboard the *City of Peking*, loaded with curios, native dress of every kind, and miscellaneous weapons, war clubs, and artifacts from each country visited. "A lavish Fourth of July celebration was enjoyed by all on board, the smoking tariff a little high, I remember, for the likes of a cowboy," Charlie said of his trip. They were leaving a strange and wondrous land, a land called the *Orient,* which has a history and people that sink back into eternity. Charlie had left a bachelor cowboy who had seen little but the confines of the Western

United States—and was returning as a husband, a father-to-be, an experienced traveler, and very much more worldly wise.

Marion Mae Murray Meadows (Charlie's First Wife)

NEW YORK, SATURDAY, DECEMBER 10, 189

ARIZONA CHARLIE, HERO.

A Cowboy Who Can Fight and Ride Well.

EXPERT WITH THE LASSO.

Has Defeated All Comers in Cowboy Tournaments.

ADVENTURES WITH INDIANS.

When Arizona Charlie, the champion cowboy, walked into the POLICE GAZETTE office the other morning every man on the staff put his hand on his watch and pocketbook. The sporting editor threw up both hands and was ready to begin opening the safe at the word of command. But a moment's conversation with the tall, long-haired, diamond-studded giant, with his rakish sombrero and free, honest manners, soon showed that Charlie Meadows, which is his proper name, is by no means the rough and wild individual his appearance might lead the "tenderfoot" observer imagine. His fathom and five inches of linear dimensions is supported by over two hundred weight avoirdupois, and if this is a cowboy we have a great curiosity to see a cowman.

Charlie has been a champion in all the cowboy exercises of skill for the last six years, and has a thousand dollar challenge in the POLICE GAZETTE and all the leading stock journals of the West, to meet any man in an all round contest or any mark of horsemanship in cowboy exercise. He has met and defeated in matches Chilson, Johnson, Horne and McGarrey, and won twenty-six tournaments, defeating in all over one hundred men.

At the Territorial Fair in Phœnix, Arizona, Oct. 20, 1888, he eclipsed all previous records in the steer-

CHARLIE WITH HIS LASSO.

monkey and hangs on to the trappings of his saddle while a horse is bucking, would stand a poor show in a tournament where each contestant is supposed to sit upright, with as much grace and ease as if he were in a comfortable armchair.

Mr. Meadows dropped in to let us know that there had been one cowboy around the world. During his two years tour he has exhibited his skill and given representations of wild America through New Zealand, Australia, India, China and Japan. He says he has had some thrilling adventures with the mobs of Australia, the coral reefs of Thursday Islands, escaped the cholera of Java, was in a railway disaster in Myrsoe, India, had an experience with a typhoon in the Yellow sea, and encountered the Chinese pirates off the Coast of China. He is glad to return to the safety of his native heath.

Charlie Meadows was born March 10, 1863, at Visalia, California, belonging to an old frontier family that made for the borders of civilization in the early

Article from *New York National Police Gazette* , 1892

CHAPTER 10

1892
CHARLIE JOINS THE "MASTER," BUFFALO BILL

With the worldly wisdom he had accumulated, along with a downright zest for living and a consuming desire for the limelight, Charlie still lusted for the sound of applause that was ringing in his ears. He had a feverish desire to have his own Wild West Show. He had learned the business by sheer grit and perseverance, savored the sweet smell of success, and felt a man should have the liberty of choosing his own means of making a livelihood. The weight of his thoughts was unbearable; he knew he must pursue his destiny. He also wanted the experience of performing with the world's most reknown Wild West exhibition. So, he informed his young wife he could not forego his life's dream, and he would go to England to perform for a few weeks with the Congress of Rough Riders of the World—with her or without. For him it was hardly a decision—it was inevitable.

Of course, they quarreled; and if he went, she said, their "marriage was over." Charlie figured that to be so much *burro* milk. With the drive of a wild mustang, and a violent stirring for the "yeasty" life, he was confident that, after an absence of only two months, all would be forgiven. Providing well for her, he and Catoto left immediately, but her parting remark stunned his soul. He was then less than certain she would ever change her mind.

The farewell was soon forgotten, as they stretched their necks from a thundering train, all interest taken up in the surrounding countryside and the ecstatic anticipation of the thrilling and romantic adventure that awaited them.

A stopover in New York and a visit to Niagara Falls offered another "grand revelation" for ye cowpuncher. During Charlie's stay, he learned that his old admirer, Kipling, had married a New York belle, Miss Caroline Starr Ballastier, and was living in America.

Buffalo Bill had arrived in Glasgow, Scotland the previous March 5; he went to London on April 28, opening at Earl's Court on May 7. Charlie and Catoto reached London to join him on August 10, 1892. A grand reception awaited them as honored guests at the great showman's sumptuous festal table. Of course, there was considerable wine-bibbing. Cody never drank unless he was alone or with someone, and he was especially generous with his liquor when he'd already "been to the barrel" himself. His favorite drink was a "Stone Fence," which consisted of a shot of Rye and a twist of lemon in a glass of cider.

As the jolly festivities unfolded, there seemed no better time to select a show name for Charlie. Charlie never had sat around a table with such noted people including "Pony Bob" Haslam, "Arizona John" Burke, and star performer, Johnny "Cowboy Kid" Baker. So Cody suggested, "Why not 'Arizona Charlie'?" Many already referred to him as "Arizona," and that is how Charlie officially became "Arizona Charlie."

Buffalo Bill was a showman in the best and broadest sense of the word. Now labeled as "Buffalo Bill's Wild West and Congress of Rough Riders of the World," the Grand Entrance scene was a thrill Charlie never forgot. The furious dash of the Indian braves in war paint, galloping at break-neck speed; cossacks of the Russian Cavalry led by Prince Rostonov Macherdase; Arabs on thoroughbreds; members of the Queen's own Lancers; South American *Gauchos*; detachments of the U. S. Cavalry, artillery, cowboys and others, brought out huge crowds. All of this was followed by Buffalo Bill's grand entrance: dressed in big hat and his usual leather breeches, riding with great ease and stately grace to take his place under the limelight. With one grand, sweeping gesture, he announced to the huge audience, "Ladies and Gentlemen, permit me to introduce to you the Congress of Rough Riders of the World!"

Annie Oakley, given the name of Watanya Cicilia which means "Little Sure Shot," by famous Sioux Chief, Sitting Bull, always appeared first on the program. She had 35 different costumes.

Charlie was introduced by Cody as the "best all-round man the West has ever produced," and he drew tremendous applause. This was a thrill Charlie never forgot, and his friends became lasting friendships. Following his exhibitions there, his brief diary notes mention the Crystal Palace, Picadilly Square, and the Royal Olympian Aquarium. Samuel Franklin Cody was performing in a family Wild West shooting act at the Aquarium, and it is a good assumption that the "Winchester Wizard" gave some performances there.

Charlie and Catoto toured Glasgow Scotland, Paris, France, and the Isle of Man on their own. Paris, a city given up to pleasure, was an exciting experience for the Arizona gentleman; the streets were packed with all classes of humanity. Charlie was particularly impressed with the Paris Hippodrome, located on le Boulevard de Clinchy, one of the finest amusement palaces of the world. Sightseeing included Le Tour Eiffel. It was a thrilling sensation for the Arizona man and his Indian to experience the different feelings as they made their ascension up the 991-foot, architecturally perfect structure, that covered almost seven acres.

Charlie had agreed to be responsible for the return to America of his Indian, Juan Catoto, but Catoto elected to stay and tour throughout Glasgow in partnership with Mexican Joe—Jose Barrera of Buffalo Bill's company—an expert with the *reata*. Charlie knew one week's pay would bring the Indian home when he desired to return. Catoto was a very intelligent Indian who spoke several languages. But at some point during this period Catoto met an aristocratic English lady, married her, and settled down in England. Charlie never saw him again. Mexican Joe went to India, and between there and Sumatra he slipped into obscurity for a few years, but reappeared in Pawnee Bill's Wild West in 1899.

Buffalo Bill's Wild West sailed for home on the S. S. *Mohawk* on October 15, 1892, and arrived in New York on the 26th. Buffalo Bill sent his company on to winter quarters in Cincinnati; he and Charlie went to pay Cody's old friend and colleague, Colonel Ingraham, a visit to extend him an invitation.

Ingraham was a playwright, author, and soldier of fortune. His accomplishments were many; he fought in the Confederate army and was wounded twice; he joined Juarez' troops in Mexico, then fought in Europe and Prussia. Still he made time to write over 120 dime novels and several plays about Cody, his favorite subject. After meeting Charlie, Prentiss Ingraham chronicled him in several fictionalized, "yellowback" episodes.

Jose Barrera

Annie Oakley

Buffalo Bill's Wild West Setting—World Columbian Exposition

Buffalo Bill's Stagecoach, "The Deadwood"

Colonel Prentiss Ingraham

A Return to Paradise

Army officers of rank and title of all countries admired the commanding personality of Charlie's compatriot, Buffalo Bill. While Cody was in London, top men of the Mormon Church called upon him to interest the English aristocracy in the *Kaibab*, or "Grand Canyon," as a hunting mecca. They asked him to head a hunting expedition there. The Mormons in Utah, much to the antagonism of the Arizonans, had great visions of annexing the North Rim into Utah before the Arizona territory had gained its statehood. Before the advent of the automobile the canyon was too great a distance from the nearest railroad. It was extremely difficult to open the canyon to tourism, but it could be reached by horse and wagon.

Colonel Cody obliged, and extended an invitation to several prominent European dignitaries to join him in a bit of the wild west with its marvelous landscape and abundance of wild game. Charlie was eager to return to this awe-inspiring country that had thrilled him as a young cowboy, and he helped stage the event.

Charlie saw Doc Carver's drama in the East, then stopped at the *New York Police Gazette* and let them know "there had been one cowboy around the world." Charlie thought there was no time like the present to make his name known through the New York press.

He put his hand on his watch, and the"sporting editor threw up both hands and was ready to begin opening the safe at his command," reported the *Gazette*. "But a moment's conversation with the long-haired, diamond-studded giant, with his big *sombrero* and free, honest manners, soon told the editor it was Charlie Meadows, and by no means the rough and wild individual; and, if this is a cowboy, we have yet to see a cowman!" said the editor.

Charlie's thoughts then turned to his wife, the woman whose image he carried in his heart. He hurried to Vancouver, expecting her to throw herself into his arms. But he had another thought coming, because she had vanished without a trace. A thousand disorganized thoughts raced through his mind, and he wondered if the loss of the loving warmth of a good woman had really been worth it. He solicited the services of a detective who made a diligent search to locate his wife, but his efforts were in vain. The price he paid was enormous. He had lost a wife—as well as a child yet to be born—so he headed home to Arizona in a dazed state of mind. Twenty-three years passed before he learned whether he had a son or a daughter.

There had been a great change at home. Jake had married Martha Roberts, sister of the celebrated Jim Roberts, lawman, and hero of the Pleasant Valley War. Jim was considered "the last man" to survive the bitter feud, and was called the "coolest and deadliest fighter of them all." Tom and Maggie had added two sons, Jess and Tom Jr., to their family, and moved their expanding herd to the old Roberts ranch, presently the Zane Grey Place. Charlie's little brother, Mobley, whom he lovingly had called "Dink," had grown into a man; the telephone was on trial in Phoenix; the merchants, Goldwater Brothers, had returned to Phoenix to test their luck for the second time; and Frank Prothero, daring deputy sheriff, had tracked, trailed and successfully captured King Ussary for robbery of the Globe-Florence stage, recovering the loot of two silver bars.

Meantime the distinguished gentlemen from Europe had arrived, along with some American dignitaries, Army officers of rank and title, and members of Buffalo Bill's own company; John M. "Arizona John" Burke; Robert "Pony Bob" Haslam; and, of course, Colonel Prentiss Ingraham. All these men joined Cody in Chicago where General Miles provided him with a special train and military escort from Chicago to Nebraska, and a two-day visit at Buffalo Bill's Scout's Rest Ranch. From there they proceeded to Denver, where they took in needed supplies, and arrived at a rendezvous point in Flagstaff soon after. Charlie, along with Daniel Seigmiller and President Wooley of the Kanab Stake, and their contingent of Mormon guides and scouts, had a group of twenty cowboys, fifty horses, three wagons and two buckboards ready for them as they disembarked their train. These cowboys, guides and scouts set out immediately to escort them as body guards until the larger Indian settlements were safely passed. Cody's party hunted the *Kaibab* on an adventurous 1,000 mile trip in the saddle—with an arsenal of the latest hunting weapons, and explored the magnificent Grand Canyon Rim and the serenity of its stone layer-cake inner gorge.

The hunting was outstanding, with mountain sheep, elk, deer, bear, antelope, turkey, ducks and fish taken, plus all the other luxuries the country afforded. Buffalo Bill always liked to "put on a little style," even in the wilderness. So to be sure the game was well prepared, Cody, a *bon vivant* gourmandizer, brought along his own French chef.

A few panic-stricken moments were experienced when Major A. John Mildmay of the Grenadier Guards of England was saved, by the quick action of Buffalo Bill's lasso, when he lost his footing and nearly plunged to his death over a 1,000 foot precipice. All in all, the trip was a good one. They slept like cowmen just off a cattle drive, and everyone seemed in high spirits considering how horribly sore they were after so many miles in the saddle.

In awe of the splendor and magnificence of the Grand Canyon, the visitors declared that such a trip had never been paralleled, but declined to make the Grand Canyon their hunting "mecca," saying it was just too far away from home to enjoy.

Buffalo Bill and his party returned to Denver and civilization. A news dispatch reported Charlie had returned to Phoenix on the same day. After Cody bid his distinguished guests farewell, he returned to his winter headquarters in Cincinnati to prepare for his upcoming exhibition at the World's Columbian Exposition in Chicago the following month. Charlie hated to "talk like a Texan" by patting himself on the back, but Cody asked him to take the lead in his show. Buffalo Bill had previously commented to the press that "Meadows is the best all-round man the West has ever produced."

Emboldened by his successes, Charlie had the insatiable desire to get started on his own if he could arrange the finances, and he was confident he could; he still had $30,000 burning a hole in his buckskins, collected on his Australian-Asian tour. He had learned from the best—had gained a hell of a lot of experience, and earned an excellent reputation.

Charlie Leads Posse After the Apache Kid

Meantime, Governor Hunt of Arizona pushed through a bill in the House making $5,000 immediately available for the apprehension of the Apache Kid. As was to be expected, publicity-loving Charlie would gallop off with his own posse. He concluded that it would be a good way to gain prestige for either road he intended to travel—his own show or Buffalo Bill's, if he went to Chicago. After all, he reasoned, wasn't it good publicity and the press that got Buffalo Bill where he was? So, Charlie led a posse after the Kid, making stiff wagers on his immediate capture. But that was one of the few times in his life Charlie lost by gambling. It is a fair guess that the Kid made "like greased lightning" when he learned Charlie was on his trail—being a crack shot and all. But Charlie did get a good bit of notoriety, and he figured that was what the game was all about.

Charlie wrote to Frank Butler, husband of Miss Annie Oakley, both of Buffalo Bill's company, informing him of his plans and his need for a good agent. If things went as planned, Charlie's intentions were to take his own show on the road—ending up in Chicago and bringing some new acts. A new idea had entered his mind involving a jackass rabbit shoot complete with Indians.

Mata Gente; "Killer Horse"

While Charlie waited for all this to develop, he and several of his cowboy pards put on "one hell of a rodeo" in Phoenix. Doc Goodwin, George, Tom and Perry Sears, Tom Wills, Stewart Knight, H. Martin, Charles Hollingshead, and Jimmie Gibson were the contestants, along with Charlie and his brother, Mobley. For show purposes, Mobley took the name of "Kid" Meadows. Kid Meadows was well on his way to becoming one of the most adept trick riders ever seen.

The rodeo management had acquired the notorious "killer" horse, *Mata Gente*, that Charlie agreed to ride—because of his reputation of being "World Champion Cowboy," and the "most famous horseman known to four continents"—and offered anyone $100 who could produce a horse that could unseat him. *Mata Gente* had killed Dolores Figaro at the Lavino Ranch only six years before, and later bucked Ramon Reyes until he died of his injuries—and had long been a terror to the *vaqueros*, who knew the Spanish meaning of *Mata Gente*—people killer.

Well, Charlie rode that outlaw horse alright—but only for a quick swish of a mustang's tail—then he was thrown off just like all the others. It can be said that the old saying, "there ain't no horse that can't be rode, and there ain't no cowboy that can't be throwed," fits in well here. But for Charlie, the attempt was one heck of a thrill.

Arizona Charlie—Tonto Basin, *Circa* 1892-93

CHAPTER 11

1893-1894
ARIZONA CHARLIE'S HISTORICAL WILD WEST

About this time Charlie began to organize his troupe and to gather exciting scenes for his acts. He hired 16 Maricopa Indians from an Indian village—including their chiefs. He made sure that they all had long hair, and were the most ferocious-looking Indians who not only provided good atmosphere but also could be used as handy-hands in between. There were five regular cowboys in his troupe, and one stage driver, Bill Zent. Good luck came his way when he was able to acquire the old dilapidated Tombstone Stage Coach, "Grand Central"; which was famous as the one in which Bud Philpot was killed during one of the many robberies between Bisbee and Tombstone. Earlier the stage had once belonged to the Earp gang, but Charlie purchased it from a man named Linnear. Charlie bought a big railroad car, outfitted it with bunks in case it was too cold to sleep in the open fields, and used the car for his headquarters.

A reporter from *The Phoenix Gazette* reported the unusual goings on: "Charlie Meadows' Wild West Cowboys clattering down Center Street for a practice spurt, agitates even the pellucid flow of a *Gazette* reporter's arterial circulation."

Considerable interest was shown by Charlie's Phoenix friends who wanted a description of his world tour. While he was in town, he entertained a group of men in his rooms to view his splendid collection of Oriental oddities, clothing from many countries, curios and pictures, and a large arsenal of war clubs and hideous weapons collected throughout his tour of the Antipodes and Southeast Asia. Much fun was exhibited when a Colonel Egan suggested to Charlie, "Now you are prepared to go on the warpath in any language you choose."

Plans for Arizona Charlie's Historical Wild West were taking shape. Three more railroad cars were added, along with camp outfits and other paraphernalia. Two were for the stock, broncos, and steers, and the other two were for the cowboys and Indians. There were twenty Indians, seventeen bucks and three squaws. Also Charlie contracted for a herd of Gila monsters from the Irvine Company to go along with the menagerie.

When his itinerary was in place, quick arithmetic told the handsome cowboy that more running capital was necessary. Advertising and the cost of show sites would be expensive. He did not have time to earn money gambling, but he had his prized thoroughbred stallion, "Governor." Charlie knew Governor would bring him the needed cash. It pained him to think of parting with Governor who had been a present from Colonel Head, and had sired a number of high flyers in Yavapai County. At one time, he had been a pet in Senator Hearst's stables. During his palmy days, he had been a great favorite among bookmakers and sports in long distance racing. Charlie still had some of his issue—but it appeared that it would be sometime before he returned to ranching again. So he put out a card in the leading daily to stock dealers concerning his intentions to sell Governor. He waited.

When the show reached perfection, the Wild West opened to a cheering and enthusiastic crowd of 2,500 spectators in Phoenix at the race track on March 25, 1893. Charlie had the finest printing made, flashy billboards posted, and handbills flying in the streets. The Fourth of July never saw such a celebration. It was the first Wild West Show in Phoenix; it was a gala day. Charlie led the parade, mounted on his prancing white horse, "Snowstorm," outfitted in an elegant costume and his largest *sombrero*. He was no quibbler either, when it came to fine and showy silver-trimmed bridles made of rawhide and braided horsehair; his saddle with high horn, sweeping stirrups and wide expanse of tooled leather. These were the requirements of his profession. Charlie didn't mind saying he looked exceptionally good. Following him came the lively Pioneer Band, followed by a score or more of Pima Indian braves, marching to the inspiration of drum and bugle and painted in all the glorious shades of the rainbow. A mob of Arizona's best cowboys came after them, attired for the work of the range, and mounted on the most vicious brutes possible to find in the vicinity. These cowboys were the most expert manipulators of balky broncos to be found in the West. To conquer these brutes was not easy; however, Charlie's boys did this with apparent ease. A special train was arranged to bring visitors from Tempe, and he provided a dozen hacks for their convenience. Charlie did not leave out one single thing. By three o'clock the grandstand and fairgrounds were fairly packed. Auctioneer McAfee, great in that capacity, acted as master of ceremonies.

The cowboys in Charlie's show were some of the greatest cowhands of that day. They are still being talked about by historians and rodeo buffs. Tom Wills acted as Charlie's Chief of Cowboys, and the first act was put on by four of the West's most skillful riders: Jimmie Gibson, Doc Goodwin, Charles Hollingshead, and a man from Texas by the name of John Moore. Each gave an exhibition of bronco riding, and the ponies were said to be bad buckers with the true Arizona spirit. Jimmie Gibson won first prize for riding an "oily" bronc called "Dynamite." He was well named and he failed to dump Jimmie, who was considered by the judges to be the best rider. Doc Goodwin and Charles Hollingshead were close seconds.

Later, all cowboys performed a series of feats of dexterity and skill: picking up objects from the ground while leaning from speeding horses, and throwing the *reata*. Charlie astounded the audience in this last act, and the sounds of applause on his own turf were the sweetest music to him.

The most interesting feature was the steer-roping contest that followed. The animals were large and fully grown cattle brought in from nearby ranges where they had been developed into vigorous brutes just for this purpose. H. Martin, of Tonto Basin, was after one that the boys termed "rollicky," and after chasing it around the track several times, it charged its tormentor and upset both the horse and rider, then proceeded to gore the poor devil until the other cowboys swarmed to his rescue and roped and tied the rebellious critter. Perry Sears then jumped on his back and rode him around the track for awhile, as the crowd roared with delight. In this feature, Doc Goodwin finished with the phenomenal record of 48 seconds, lower than the best on record at that time. However, that time did not include George Felton's record, which was made outside the United States. George Sears came in second with a time of 2:01, while Stewart Knight had his steer roped in 15 seconds, but was unable to hold him. Despite this, he made the good time of 2:16.

Bud McClintock, a celebrity from Texas, was on deck next. He had a spunky steer to catch, but was mounted on a good horse. He dropped the steer a number of times but each time as he was running to tie him down, the wily brute would rise only to be held fast by the horse. Bud got tired of fooling around like that and tackled the seven year-old steer on foot, got a good tail hold, threw the animal and tied him up. The grandstand was delirious with joy by this time. These were the real men of the

Phoenix Rodeo, February 5, 1893

There was bull riding, trick bicycle racing, and throwing of the *bolas*, where three balls on a string were used instead of the usual *lasso*, and done by the South American *Gaucheros*. The last act was always the *Attack on the Deadwood Stagecoach*. Bill Zent acted as driver, and Marshall Blankenship and Huse Ward acted as guards. This act never failed to stir the audience into a fever pitch of excitement.

The coach was driven around the mile stretch of track, and on the third stretch a band of mounted, feathered and painted Indians would burst from ambush in the canebrake and give chase. The horses were pushed to their utmost speed, then rifles and revolvers "spoke in deadly earnest" from the coach top and from the throng of pursuing savages. Suddenly, the cowboys would break in from concealment by the roadside and, in a fusillade of pistol shots, wipe out the enemy. There would be a great deal of shooting of blanks, from guns that made such a terrifying noise that it frightened even the toughest of men, and forced women to scream, because the action was real to them.

Variations of this act were made. One scene consisted of a trapper living in the woods in a cabin with his pretty daughter. The Indians would come down and attack the cabin, driving the poor trapper and his daughter out with firebrands. The trapper would be captured, tied to a stake and burned as the braves danced around him. Or, sometimes the trapper would be killed in the fight and the daughter burned at the stake. Or, in order to save her from "a fate even worse than death," Prince Charming would come to her rescue. Did the girl fall into the arms of the chief cowboy? "It was all in the act, don'cherknow, all in the act. It was a great show," Charlie said. Of course, he was Prince Charming some of those times.

The sympathetic and admiring reporters were excellent in their coverage, and noted that "Arizona beats the world for dexterous and skillful men with the lasso," and said ye Arizona man's show "was worth miles of travel to see." "Arizona Charlie," *The Arizona Republican* reported, "who has but lately returned to this city, his home, from a tour embracing a belt around the world, was manager of the enterprise, and gave his friends a taste of excitement now most popular of all. The first act consisted of a parade through the principal streets; Charlie in the lead on his white horse, clothed in a fashion that surely must have been most effective in the Antipodes. He was everywhere present at the proper time and showed himself to be a good general." Good press coverage was highly important for success, and Charlie knew then he had succeeded. His chest was full-blown; he had really shown the townsfolk.

Charlie began to put his affairs in order, in preparation for taking his show on the road. Realizing his Indian depredations claim had not been filed properly, he executed a new claim on April 1, 1893.

As the month of April, 1893, wore on, Charlie received a reply to his letter to Mr. Frank Butler, of Buffalo Bill's Company:

> Mr. Charles Meadows,
>
> My dear Meadows, your clipper office reached me here today. I am indeed glad to hear from you and that you are doing well. But for the feat of Indians killing rabbits, that would never go or even be permitted in the East. We opened here yesterday in a terrible rain. Of course we did not have a big crowd but I think we will do well. Our company is about as big as when you seen *(sic)* it. We will not be at liberty until October, then if you are coming drop me a line. Might arrange a trip south. As for a long hand or a foot agent I don't know of any, but if you will take my advice you will look for one with brains. Never mind long hair and size. Your friend, Carver, is here playing in a theatre this week. He has been doing a good business I should think.
> Write me often.

Best wishes from Miss Oakley.

I am yours truly,

Frank E. Butler,
Wild West Company
Woodlawn,
Chicago, Illinois

A few days later a man named Thompkins purchased Charlie's stallion, Governor. Charlie quietly wept inside. He loved that horse.

Arizona Charlie

Arizona Charlie and His Indian Friend

Arizona Charlie's Wild West Indians

Charlie's First American Tour

Finally, the great day dawned. On May 4, 1893, Arizona Charlie's Historical Wild West left Phoenix on its first tour amid a joyful demonstration from well-wishers. *The Arizona Republican* of May 5, 1893, reported the departure to be "one of the finest equipages ever selected in that line, who are able to lasso anything from a Missouri mosquito to an elephant from the wilds of the Congo. . . ." Charlie was the happiest cowboy on God's dusty earth.

In those days, the territory was a rough land and a natural geographical haven for the lawless. The roughest, toughest, meanest, most wretched of these unsavory devils were incarcerated within the nightmarish walls of the Yuma Territorial Prison, "a place," it was said, "that could really try a man's soul." Arizona Charlie's Historical Wild West made their first stop there and gave a complete performance inside the penitentiary stockade. After that, they went to San Bernardino, California. The town was covered with handbills that flew in the streets, and the people thronged by the wayside to see the impressive parade go by. "California is where the people are," Charlie remarked to a reporter, "Arizona's two main towns are just grown-up villages."

"The show was doing good, and we dared enter Los Angeles," said Tom Wills, Charlie's Chief of Cowboys. *The Los Angeles Times* of May 24th, reporting:

> Arizona Charlie Ahoy!
>
> Los Angeles has been favored since Wednesday with a coterie of representatives of the plains who have given the public the most interesting entertainments ever witnessed in Southern California. The realistic scenes characteristic of early days are vividly and excitingly portrayed and the performances hold those that attend them fairly spellbound from the beginning to the close. Athletic Park, where the performances are taking place has been transformed temporarily into a cowboy and Indian reservation, Charles Meadows, better known as "Arizona Charlie," having taken charge. . .

Charlie was the master of ceremonies and barker. They opened with the Concord Stage Coach racing up in front of the show as Charlie would announce to the crowd in a roaring voice that the stage was about to leave. The people got into the show by paying the fare on the stagecoach. They climbed into the coach as Tom Wills jumped in front and acted as an armed escort. As they rode around, a band of masked men held them up with six-guns. This usually had the women screaming. It was such a flamboyant, boisterous kind of melodrama, and with the wild barrage of gunfire, some people even thought it was a real hold-up. They shot blanks, but they made just as much noise. The act was a big attraction, then they followed with the usual feat exhibitions.

During the parade one day, some little excitement developed into a life-threatening episode, that is described herewith by an unidentified Los Angeles newspaper:

> Arizona Charlie, otherwise known as Charles Meadows, gave an unrehearsed performance on South Spring Street yesterday, which for excitement equalled anything to be seen in his regular show.
>
> It was about one o'clock in the afternoon, and Arizona Charlie and his band of Indians and cowboys were parading along Spring Street to the inspiration sounds of drums and trumpet. Suddenly, a horse attached to a buggy belonging to the Llewellyn Brothers, took alarm to the noise, and dashed away at breakneck rate down the street. The road was crowded with men and women watching the parade, and as soon as the frightened animal tore along the crowd on all sides, several people escaped only just in time to prevent being trampled on. Just as the runaway reached Fourth Street, an old

> woman started to cross the street. She got half way over when she heard shouts, and looking around, the terrified woman saw the maddened animal within a few feet of her. Too scared to think of getting out of the way, the woman stood where she was, while those at hand held their breath and waited for the inevitable. Just at that moment, Arizona Charlie, who had seen the runaway horse and noted the woman's danger, came along on his mustang like a lightening flash, his long hair streaming in the wind and his lasso loose in his hand. Sitting firm as a rock with his eyes fixed on the frightened animal in front of him, he waited until he got within a few feet of his mark, when out went his noose, and before the excited spectators had time to realize what had happened, the runaway steed was lying on his back on the sidewalk, wondering what had struck him, and Arizona Charlie had rejoined his troupe and was nonchalantly coiling his lasso.

Officer Singleton, who saw that the horse was within six feet of the old woman when Arizona Charlie threw his rope, said, "There is no doubt the veteran cowboy saved her life by his quick actions."

This was the kind of publicity Charlie relished. This unidentified article was found in his scrapbook.

Before Charlie left Los Angeles for northern cities, he gave one last, free entertainment in Redondo Beach, with round-trip railway fares offered from Union Station at a minimal cost for those who cared to attend. Los Angeles was a huge success for the Arizona cowboy, and the city benefited as well, clearing some $15,000 from his appearances. Then Charlie was off for Bakersfield, Tulare, and his childhood town of Visalia, and on to Hanford, Stockton, and San Francisco.

Then Trouble Started

In Stockton, Tom Wills had the misfortune to suffer a serious accident. The Wild West had camped in a field of high grass where there was a great deal of water. Tom was roping steers when his horse slipped into an unseen pothole in the deep grass and was catapulted into the air, turning into a somersault that was not on the program. As he landed, the horse fell on top of him, landing hard between his legs—and it darn near curled him up. Tom was out for a good while. Later, they carried him to a hotel where he stayed for several days. The rest of the troupe went on to San Francisco without him and put on a good show, but the accident shook all of them up a bit. Bob Lee had been good to Tom, so Tom started him off in his place while he recuperated. Bob Lee did not get along with the others, nor they with him. Jealousy developed and the boys began to quarrel. They moved on to Oakland. During one performance, somebody put a real bullet in a gun and got off a wild shot—nearly hitting Bob. The show got a bad name; attendance fell off drastically. Charlie swallowed about as much as he could—his bristles were up, and he let loose with a running fire of trenchant rhetoric—spouting words eight to the pound.

"The strife in the tent took the enthusiasm out of the rest of the boys," said Charlie's head cowboy, Tom Wills, "and Charlie quit in high dudgeon and disgust." Charlie left with a bad taste of bile on his tongue, and took Tom Wills, Doc Goodwin, Bob Lee, and a few others with him. He left the troublemakers to carry on by themselves, but failure was the result in their attempt to fill the places with some local talent who were more accustomed to shooting the necks off *cognac* bottles in congenial saloons.

One undersized constable single-handedly captured four desperate and heavily-armed cowboys, a U.S. Marshal, and a band of unkempt and rather rough-looking Indians who were left behind. "This would never have happened if Arizona Charlie had not left the show," said the local press. The sheriff took over and sold at auction, steers, broncos, and teepees to cover some assigned claims totalling $230.65.

Until this ruckus occurred, a combination of luck and superb management made Charlie's show a profitable success, and he was able to leave with enough of the good old "mazuma" to compensate for his losses. His hopes—for taking his show to Chicago and other points east, then to South Africa to hook up with Texas Jack—were dashed for the moment, but for Charlie there would be another day.

Charlie Joins Buffalo Bill in Chicago

Charlie decided to go to Chicago alone, take in the fair, exhibit his vast collection of artifacts and weapons collected from around the world, and make a guest appearance or two with Buffalo Bill and the Congress of Rough Riders of the World at the World's Columbian Exposition.

Buffalo Bill's Wild West occupied 50 acres just outside the entrance to Jackson Park, scene of the exposition. His production outshone all previous successes with the addition of *Bedouins, Gauchos* from South America, Indians from the Far West, *Cossacks* from darkest Africa, combined with cowboys from western America. His grandstand, in the large amphitheatre, had a seating capacity of 18,000. Charlie rode in the Grand Review, as before, with the celebrated Rough Riders of the World, along with the soldiers of the Armies of America, Germany, France, and Russia; and as before, he participated in such acts as the *Illustration of a Prairie Immigrant Train,* the *Capture of the Deadwood Stage*, and the *Attack on the Settler's Cabin.* The military part of the show was a representative company from each of the four powers, and twenty-five men formed a company. There were military evolutions by a company of the Sixth Cavalry of the United States Army; a company of the First Guard Uhlan Regiment of His Majesty King William II; German Emperor, popularly known as the *Potsdamer* Reds a company of *French Chasseurs;* and a company of the 12th Lancers of the British Army. Each was officered and equipped as for active service in its own country. The Congress of Rough Riders of the World, where there were Arabs, Syrians, Mexicans, cowboys and Indians, and the *Cossacks* in their long coats of red and purple with curved sabers banging against their soft black leather boots, performed feats cowboys never heard of. The nobility were all in gold braid, crimson sashes and jeweled medals.

A huge mural painting measuring 44 x 306, consisting of California mountain scenery, Weber's Cannon, Pulpit Rock, the Devil's Slide, and other western scenes concealed the stables. A picture in Charlie's scrapbook shows Buffalo Bill, John Nelson, John Burke and Johnnie Baker, posed in the Old Deadwood Stagecoach, in front of this huge backdrop. The stagecoach was also referred to as the "Mail Coach," and was famous as having carried a great number of people who lost their lives on the road between Deadwood and Cheyenne, 18 years before.

Charlie returned to Chicago that fall and made more guest appearances. At the exhibits, Arizona took the best mineral awards, including the one for silver, zinc, gold, copper, and lead ores. When Cody's show closed in November, he had cleared upward of one million dollars. Charlie made a raise of $20,000—but it is not known how. He left with another *troupe* of his own.

The Tombstone Stage Coach, "The Grand Central"

CHAPTER 12

1894-1895
EQUESTRIAN CARNIVAL AND *FIESTA*

San Francisco was preparing for its Mid-Winter Fair of 1894. By now, Arizona Charlie's name and fame had spread from New York to San Francisco like a prairie fire. He was invited to head the equestrian part of the fair, and planned a genuine Spanish *fiesta*, complete with wild bullfights.

A grand idea entered Charlie's mind. As long as he was going to be in the bay district, he decided he could incorporate a *fiesta* in neighboring San Jose, and a show in Santa Cruz. So Charlie left for the north to arrange the necessary schedule and committees for these events. When a reporter from a San Francisco newspaper called attention to Charlie's long hair, which he always kept pinned up under his giant *sombrero* when he was on the street, Charlie responded that show business demanded that his "hirsute appendage be untrimmed."

He explained, "The cowpuncher has the reputation of being 'wild and woolie,' with long hair and a dirty face," he said. "I'm taking the occasion of redeeming the cowboy from the stigma popularly cast upon him. That long-haired, dirty-faced individual who goes around masquerading as a cowpuncher is a 'fake.' He never existed inside and never will exist outside the covers of a dime novel. The cowboy who really exists and lives to punch cows and fight Indians is quite a different sort. He is a gentleman, and has a habit of washing his face and getting his hair cut.

"The cowboy who should appear down in Arizona with his hair long would arouse the indignation of the populace, and they would see to it his locks were immediately shorn, and perhaps they wouldn't be as solicitous for his personal comfort as a San Francisco barber. Every dime novel and every stage hero, since Buffalo Bill first appeared before the public, has worn long hair; but it is a serious mistake and needs correcting. Buffalo Bill is not a real cowboy, but got his reputation on the plains solely as a buffalo hunter. Outside of myself and one or two others that I might name, I don't know of anyone running a Wild West Show who can honestly lay claim to the title, 'cowpuncher.'

"Let anyone who doubts that the real cowboy is a well-educated gentleman, go down into the Territory and see the lawyers, speakers and politicians, and he will find the best of them are proficient in the use of the lariat—and most all of them used to herd steers for a living."

Charlie's old Tonto pard, George Felton, left his Australian hospital bed and returned home to Phoenix. By then everyone in the Territory had heard of the miraculous escape George made from his terrifying experience of being dunked into a boiling spring. His amazing roping time of 12 seconds, made in Adelaide, Australia, earned him the handle, "Knight of the *Reata*." Phoenix gave him a tremendous homecoming celebration.

Felton had made a big name for himself, and Charlie figured a few fellows like him along in his next show wouldn't hurt one bit. But Felton was slow getting back into show business and didn't join up this trip. Brown, by then, was married and in charge of a large cattle station. Charlie was still able to gather a strong force of lariat men, which included his brother, "Kid" Meadows; rodeo "greats," Lew "Shorty" Compher, "Doc" Goodwin; and a few other saddle worthy Arizona bronc busters. The show hit the road in early April, 1894, for San Francisco and points north. No Indians accompanied them this trip—and Charlie vowed no mistakes would occur.

A Bitter Match

Charlie, a man of the world and full of confidence, developed an extravagant taste for fine clothes and life's worldly goods; quite unlike the exhilarated cowboy fresh from the herd who hit San Francisco only a few scant years before on his way to New Zealand. At this time, Charlie joined the prestigious Olympic Club, and became an expert with the rapiers and broadsword. Captain Jennings, the World's Champion from England was an instructor at the Olympic Club. For the purpose of gaining the championship, Charlie challenged Jennings, a wiry, slightly built, balding man, to a match. Charlie loved admiring crowds—and the press, and this match would bring both of them out. The *San Francisco Olympian* of April, 1894, made the following mention of the coming attraction:

"Charlie Meadows, the dashing king of Cowboys, who recently astonished European audiences with his daring performances, and who is now matched against Captain Jennings in a broadsword contest, is in town. He is well known all over the world as "Arizona Charlie," and is recognized as a most skillful horseman. Mr. Meadows has been a winner in sixteen cowboy tournaments and has successfully crossed swords with a number of expert swordsmen in Australia, India, and Japan."

Jennings had a worldwide reputation as a broadswordsman, and in one match he suffered a serious blow to the head, fracturing his skull and leaving a hideous scar across his forehead. Charlie was well aware of the dangers he must subject himself to. The match was devoid of faking; it was for $500 a side, the gate receipts, and the world championship. Over 300 people of a sporting turn of mind assembled to witness the scientific event. Charlie knew that permanent success depended on satisfying the people, and he felt he could beat Jennings.

It was just three o'clock when Charlie rode out in front of the grandstand with the pomp of a real showman, and announced to the audience, "Ladies and gentlemen! This announcement is to inform you the contest will be governed by military rule, and my sincere desire is that the best man win, and the first man to receive 15 points will be declared the winner."

A few minutes later the contestants appeared—mounted with swords and helmets, and accompanied by the referee, Lieutenant Schaffer of the Army of Holland. The usual formal introductions and salutes were made, and then the serious work began. Charlie took his position on first base at the ball grounds, and Jennings took his place on third base. The word "start" was given, and the two men spurred their horses; and, in almost an instant, they were together. The quick slashes of the swords kept the spectators on the edge of their seats, and the clever way in which they controlled their horses and placed them in advantageous positions amazed the audience. One minute their actions were still, and in the next they chased each other around in a circle in rapid revolutions. Jennings gained the first point, but neither man seemed to get into a good fighting mood until they had each scored 8 points. At that juncture, they stopped a few minutes to rest.

In the next round Charlie made quick work of his point, but was followed as quickly in the next by Jennings. When they came together again, Charlie had the opportunity to show the spectators his superior horsemanship. With a good feeling of accomplishment, Charlie was not ready for the well-directed blow from Jennings' sword. Jennings struck the foil from Charlie's hand, and it went flying across the grounds. This was quite an embarrassing position for Charlie because his sword was on the ground and his opponent followed quickly for a point. But Charlie surprised him by swiftly making a keen jump clean across the diamond, and as he passed his sword, he used his old retrieving act of dropping down to the side and grabbing it. Most of the spectators had never seen this done, and handsome Charlie was the recipient of tremendous applause. By uneventful exchanges, the score was brought up to 12-12. Charlie felt Jennings was worried, for he gave Charlie several sharp blows across the abdomen—below the belt, and the Arizona man considered them fouls. They were "real stingers" too, and his cowboy blood began to boil. The idea that a cowboy was after his championship didn't set well with Jennings. He appeared to be using every trick to prevent it.

Charlie quickly gave Jennings a swift tap on the thumb with his sword, which incited Jennings' ire further. Neither of them was in a good mood. Jennings threw his glove to one side, then he rode at a furious gait—and after striking a few blows as though to kill, he gained a point. By then the audience was thoroughly awakened to the fact that somebody was after blood, and watched the final rounds with mounting excitement and yells of, "Chop off his head, Charlie," or "Down the big man, Captain," as frequent exclamations.

Strange as it might seem, in the next round the two men clinched, but it wasn't because they loved each other. Charlie struck a vigorous blow, and after brief fencing, as they rode together, Jennings grabbed Charlie's arm. Had not the referee jumped in and broken up the *melee*, Charlie probably would have picked the little man from his horse and carried him off the field. Jennings' arm was hurt in the entanglement, and a short delay was caused in order to bandage it. The score at this point stood 13-13, and both men were angry.

In the following round, Jennings gave Charlie a blow across his bridle wrist which made him utterly helpless to control his horse. He had to dismount. Jennings did not win any friends by this action which was claimed a foul. The audience expressed disgust emphatically with howls of protest. It was thought at first Charlie's wrist was broken, and Doctors Gwin and Lewis were called. They assured Charlie that no bones were broken; they were just badly bruised. These incidents were reported to be the most exciting scenes ever witnessed on the ball grounds.

Charlie made the next point; no love pats were given. Then, Jennings struck Charlie across the abdomen below the belt again in an effort to draw his guard away from his head, and secured another point. The score stood 14—14, and the next man to gain a point would become the winner. After having his bridle arm injured and placed in a bandage, Charlie wrapped the reins of his hackamore about his elbow so he might finish the fight. The closing round was a furious one, and Jennings did not spare the injured Charlie in any way. Had he been able, Charlie probably would have taken satisfaction out on Jennings' head, but the latter gained the point. Then, the two men were surrounded by a crowd.

Charlie's ire had been thoroughly aroused because of the stinging blows which had been administered in places he claimed by rules were not allowed, and he told Jennings in no uncertain terms what he thought of him. As they sat on their horses passing out cutting words—Charlie was an expert—he touched the match of fire by saying, "Well, maybe you want to fight it out without helmets?" That remark was sufficient enough to set Jennings off, and they both dismounted as quick as a flash and threw their helmets aside. In an instant Jennings' bald head was glistening in the bright sunlight, and Charlie's long locks were disheveled and floating in the breeze. As their swords clashed together, the crowd scattered to protect themselves as the two men hacked away at each other, both determined not to give in. Lieutenant Schaffer had been in many such events and showed himself to be fearless by grabbing Charlie's arm and stopping the altercation. Neither man was hurt, but it was not because they did not try.

Jennings was pronounced the winner, but the crowd hung around for a while expecting a tilt. The heat of passion had cooled, and a swarm of eager reporters and fans—knowing, had Charlie used the same tactics, he could have easily beaten Jennings—followed him off the field.

San Jose *Fiesta*

It was Charlie's show that brought back the days of the old Spanish *fiestas* to San Jose. The city blossomed with bright yellow, red, and green banners that flung from the streets in mad profusion. Even the City Hall and engine house fronts were loudly bannered in colors for the occasion. The celebration assumed monstrous proportions, and so many people took such an interest that the concessionaires at the Mid-Winter Fair in San Francisco became interested. Twenty-two of them were booked to join Charlie's show in San Jose and Santa Cruz. They included the Samoan Islanders; Hindoo Mysteries; Monsieur Natalie and his trained pigs; Fred Musselman and his Turkish Bazaar; the Dancing Girls from the Streets of Cairo; and even Harry Maynard, the "knocker" Charlie met up with on his first trip to San Francisco on his way to New Zealand. Maynard was in charge of the boxing artists.

Charlie spent a day on the ranges near Gilroy and engaged a herd of wild steers, and a band of mustangs which had never had a rope on them since the days of their branding during the week preceding the San Jose *fiesta*. The cowboy tournament was the most popular and exciting event of the whole *fiesta*, and the winner of the steer-tying contest was crowned "King of Cowboys."

The gates in San Jose were thrown open on Thursday, May 24, 1894. Although the skies were overcast with occasional showers, approximately 8,000 people assembled at Agricultural Park that afternoon. At the head of the procession was a squad of San Jose policemen, all conveyed in patrol wagons, except for two who were mounted. A group of prominent citizens, gaudily bedecked in the prismatic colors of the *fiesta* management, followed.

As Marshall of the first division, Arizona Charlie wore an elegant costume with bright bead and *concha* decoration. Charlie was flanked by all of his aides, all mounted, and wearing holiday regalia. Schubert's band marked step for his division, and at his heels came the chariots driven by the lovely Mrs. Jennie Prather, and the equally beauteous Miss Rosalie Higgens. Miss Higgens, a very attractive semi-blonde from Ukiah, California, was Champion *Equestrienne* of all California. She was a noted hurdle rider, and one of the few ladies in the United States accustomed to hurdle riding. She had been awarded the first premium twice in Mendocino County, and once each in Monterey and Lake Counties. "Kid" had already looked her over—quickly made her acquaintance, and was thoroughly smitten.

The second and third divisions consisted of the *burro* brigade, and crowded with novelties including the Fandango Dancers, *equestriennes*, and performers from the various attractions along the Midway Plaisance, all headed by Parkman's band. Stockmen of Santa Clara Valley and beautifully decorated wagons from the various businesses followed.

After marching through the principal streets of San Jose, the procession proceeded directly to the fair grounds where a vast crowd waited. Every seat in the big grandstand was occupied and hundreds crowded the fences and inner grounds of the field to see the Arizona man's greatest achievement.

M. E. McAfee, Charlie's master of ceremonies, came dashing up the track on a snow-white steed and came to a halt in front of the grandstand amid a roar of applause. He removed his big hat and the "eloquent cowboy's voice sounded out the words of welcome and appreciation" for the grand reception and great interest in the *fiesta*.

On signal from McAfee—waving bright colors—the response was quick, and in a moment contestants dashed by the grandstand, all mounted on horses which were at a gallop. The "buccaneer of the pampas," Arizona Charlie, headed the cowboys, followed by the Algerian Lancers, chariots, and *equestriennes*. As they passed, the crowds cheered again and again. This was beautiful music to the old cowpuncher's ears. Then, each performer passed back and awaited his or her turn to perform.

The lassoing of the cowboys—catching the cowboys around the neck—was the real thrill of the day. Six of them came tearing down the track in one, two, three order, swinging their lariats with such rapidity that they made a loud buzzing sound as they whipped through the air. The second roped the first, the third the second, in that order, and all but the last man ended up with a noose around his neck. It was as thrilling to the cowboys as it was to the crowd.

The usual cowboy events followed. Stars of the exhibition were Doc Goodwin, Lou Compher, both Arizona men, and Dave Stansfield of Bakersfield. Applause followed their every movement.

The chariot races were extremely thrilling. Mrs. Prather's team almost ran away and had to be stopped by a band of cowboys. If this coordination went awry, instantaneous calamity could follow—animals tangling and falling, the chariot crashing and overturning. Professor Ordway, the champion bicycle rider of the world, was complete master of the wheel, whether it be riding forward or backward, standing or sitting, or one wheel or two. He was in complete control.

Doc Goodwin was a "strapping young fellow," could rejoice only when on a wild mustang's back. When he took the blinds off his horse, he let out an Apache war whoop that could knock your socks off. He didn't go straight ahead, but up in the air, and when he struck the ground his legs were like stiff bars. It was said they had "enough spring in them to make a streak of air about the same as greased lightning."

Lou "Shorty" Compher rode an animal with enough ginger to prompt him to the most effectual bucking procedures—the horse was known as "Skyscratchen." Charlie yearned to get back on the hurricane deck of a wild mustang, but an earlier hernia prevented his riding the "buckers."

Charlie gave an exhibition of his firearm skills. Running at full speed in front of the grandstand, he drew out two revolvers, six-shooters, and as fast as Dave Stansfield could throw glass balls into the air, Charlie broke them with as much ease as shooting at a parlor target, then shattered the pieces before they struck the ground. He broke 5 in succession, and 13 out of 16. "He is decidedly the best all-round cowboy living, whether it be as a horseman, marksman, or any other department of life on the plains," was the fine tribute paid to him by the *San Jose Mercury* of May 25, 1894.

There were always hair-breadth escapes. The hurdle race—with both cowboy and lady riders—was extremely exciting. The horses with lightning speed raced down the quarter mile stretch with three hurdles to be jumped. Dave Stansfield had an accident on the second hurdle when his horse stumbled and plunged headlong almost in front of the grandstand causing the crowd to shudder. But when the dust cleared, the horse was seen struggling to his feet. Dave was still in the saddle; he suffered few bruises.

The main feature of the day followed—the steer-tying contest, with only Arizona cowboys participating. Doc was first. He chased his steer down the track and downed it according to rules, but before he could get a small rope tied to its feet, the steer rose and ran down the track dragging the lariat behind him.

Shorty Compher downed his steer in 1 minute and 27 seconds, but met with trouble and had to throw the steer twice. Then the King of Cowboys, Arizona Charlie, beat the record. Charlie's steer darted down the line at a good rate and he downed him in front of the grandstand. Casting all modesty aside, he tied him with little effort as if he had all day. He was as happy as an old hound dog getting his belly scratched. His hands went up in 41 seconds; he retained the title of the "King of Cowboys." The steers had 25-yard starts and the cowboy exhibitions followed with a five-round sparring match between Jim Ryan and Billy Armstrong.

The afternoon program concluded with the Battle of the Plumed Knights, six cowboys wearing plumes of red and yellow. Each carried a light stick used to knock the plumes from the helmets of the riders.

Darkness did not interfere with the evening's entertainment. Schubert's band rendered a meritorious musical program for the merry-making crowd, who were there for a good time. A grand illumination of fireworks gained the approbation of the thousands of spectators. Eighteen prismatic fires, which were constantly changing colors, illuminated the grounds. Many other impressive fireworks were featured.

The rest of the evening was spent dancing—or at the gala Midway Plaisance, where there were cards and tables for the votaries of Whist, or the option to visit the apartments of the muscle dancers, which were filled to capacity with enthusiastic bug-eyed gentlemen, as well as other concessions to delight the happy crowd.

A grand bullfight was featured the following day. Charlie assured the public that no torture or cruelty would occur. Charlie contracted for two Mexican bullfighters, Alejandro Bueina, a robust native of Mexico, and Francisco Higuera, a native of California. These two men were gorgeously costumed in bright colors, and as a means of offense carried a cloth—yellow on one side and red on the other.

Señor Bueina made a big boast that he could, by grasping the bull's horns, pass a noose around his lower jaw and handle the beast with ease. He advanced into the ring with the "air of a conquering general," flaunting his bright colors at the bull, which gave a loud snort and rushed pell-mell at the *matador*. Bueina skipped from side to side to escape the rushes of the maddened animal. The crowd screamed and yelled, *"Toro, Toro!"* as the enraged bull went after the *matador* time after time, but each time he was too quick for the bull. Finally, Bueina, thinking the bull was getting tired, let down his guard and came near getting a horn run straight through him. Bueina lost most of his confidence, and part of his short trousers, but escaped into the retreat. Then Higuera gave the bull a turn or two and finished the fight. No bull was killed; this was against the law.

Somebody shouted for Compher and Goodwin to ride the wild bull. This resulted in a number of dangerously exciting turns that were not on the program and it appeared that someone might get hurt. Reckless Doc downed the bull and Compher jumped on. Then Charlie, along with Dave Stansfield and Goodwin, jumped into the ring to show the audience how bulls should be fought. They got so close that their only chance for defense was to grab the beast by the tail. Doc, like Charlie, was a big show-off; he was the most daring of all cowboy contestants that Charlie ever knew.

Then, the bull took out after Doc; all the retreats were full and he had to make a fast decision. Compher was still on the bull's back. A stroke of lightning struck Doc, and with one great leap he sprung on behind Shorty Compher. However, the bull dumped them both at the gate. Doc was quicker and got away, but Compher fell and the bull charged him. As the bull turned, Shorty grabbed his tail, and the bull swung him around at a fast clip. Just as he succeeded in getting away, one section of the fence, heavily laden with cowboys and spectators, collapsed, and the people quickly scattered. The bull dashed out of the opening; he'd had all he wanted. Thus, the excitement ended. The crowd roared with delight. This was the first show of its kind ever put on in the San Jose district.

The following day more of the same program was presented. On this day reckless Doc was thrown during the bull-teasing event which led to a horrifying moment. The bull got tangled in the *reata*s and Doc and Shorty had hold of his tail. The bull bellowed, charged, turned, and twisted, endeavoring to get his tormentors, but the cowboys were having the best of it—so they thought, until Shorty slipped on the damp, slick grass, throwing Doc Goodwin.

The bull turned and made a vicious lunge at the prostrate Doc. A chill washed through Charlie. As quick as the bull was, Charlie was quicker. He leaped into the ring, and grasping the bull by the horns, turned his head aside and held him in that position until the men had jumped to their feet. The crowd was ecstatic, and Charlie was the recipient of a loud roar of applause.

The following day, because of the threats by the Society for the Prevention of Cruelty to Animals, and considerable babble about the exhibition of nude muscle dancers, the lassoing of steers and bull-teasing were cancelled to give the cowboys a rest before their final big show the next day. Also, it was decided the exhibition of the muscle dancers, costumed like "nymphs in saloon pictures," should be given during the grand finale at the midnight performance on the last night.

Because there was no regular Society for the Suppression of Vice in San Jose, the Humane Society usually took its place, but in the matter of the nude dance the Humane Society did nothing. The sheriff did not know anything of the sort was planned, and the *fiesta* grounds were out of the jurisdiction of the city police. The secret was kept pretty well, but the Mayor did learn of the proposed dance and he also did nothing.

The Great Sandow, a semi-nude muscle man, then performing in San Francisco, prompted the muscle dance. Sandow attracted a large crowd of ladies, and if it was proper for the "perfect man" to pose before the ladies undraped, the gentlemen felt there should be no objection to the dancing girls performing before them in the same state.

There was a debate as to whether the cause of "art" would be best served by admitting only 100 interested gentlemen at $5 each, or opening it to all for the price of $3, though limited to the capacity of the place.

At midnight of the last night, vivid illustrations were supposed to have come off with the nude, wriggling, writhing girls from Cairo demonstrating—without as much as a fan or silken scarf, and with the draperies omitted, but opposition was enough to postpone the highly controversial display. A great deal of disappointment was felt by the audience.

Not a moment lacked exciting incidents, and Charlie was elated. All in all, the festival had been a good one, which satisfied and delighted the audience who participated.

An attendance of 8,000 people during the day, and 3,000 at night, was testimony that the performers' efforts were appreciated.

The last days of the Midwinter Fair over in San Francisco were generating into what some feared would leave a bad stain on the State of California, and cover San Francisco with a disgrace "not easily whitewashed." Charlie was a bit apprehensive as to what to expect when he arrived.

Con artists and shady characters were operating gambling dens, skin games, and games of chance along the Midway, such as "notorious" Dick Creighton's Gambling Hell, the Royal Pavilion, and Count Cornely's Sure-Fire Den, where "young women and greenhorns" were lured by barrel games, wheels of fortune, and by top and bottom men who quickly relieved the players of their money.

The operation was condemned by Secretary Holbrook of the Society for the Prevention of Cruelty to Animals, who also proposed to stop the *fiesta* and cowboy sports that were to arrive for the final days of the fair, because of the "torture" and "tormenting" of dumb animals. To Holbrook, roping and tying a steer and throwing the animal—an art practiced by all who work the range—could cause pain. Charlie would have agreed—if the roper was a greenhorn and did not know his business.

Secretary Holbrook was sent to the brink of his patience with the games of chance running openly and bull-baiting and chicken-combing promised. Holbrook's remark to a reporter from the *San Francisco Examiner* was: "I'll be glad when this fair is over. I wonder why the Society for the Suppression of Vice, and the Chief of Police have not put a stop to gambling and robbing games out here. But you can rest assured I will put a stop to cruelty to animals!"

The Director-General of the Exposition announced that Holbrook could stop the *fiesta* if he chose, but such sports were permitted all over the state—in San Diego, Los Angeles, Santa Barbara, and San Jose. Why not San Francisco?

Public opinion prompted the *fiesta* to continue, and Charlie promised Holbrook that there would be no cruelty—that possibly the matadors would be the ones to suffer the pain. Also, he made an agreement that the bulls would wear a leather yoke to prevent the darts thrown by the picadors from penetrating their necks. Furthermore, he promised to avoid any feature that might offend the "most refined tastes." Only then did Holbrook agree. Concern for the matadors apparently did not bother him.

Still fearing the worst might happen, but hoping it would not because of the contracts he had executed, Charlie moved his flock of human and animal talent into San Francisco, along with noted *equestrienne* performers from all over the State of California. The Southern Pacific Railroad provided free transportation both ways for horses and vehicles. First-class accommodations were provided for over 1,000 horses on the fair grounds, and horses and riders kept up their daily exercises at the Bay District Track, where Kid Meadows and the lovely Miss Rosalie Higgens were enjoying a lively romance.

Charlie and his committee assured a superior *fiesta* to anything ever seen in the state. The demand for private boxes and reserved seats was unprecedented. The *San Francisco Chronicle* of June 26, 1894, reported: "Society people are displaying great interest in this magnificent and unusual entertainment, the demand for reserved seats heavy by some of the best people of the city, and cities and towns within easy reach." An English stag hunt with hounds was arranged. "These hunts are in great favor with the 'swell set' in New York," said the *Chronicle,* "and their occurrence there is a signal for all 'swagger people' to turn out in *en masse* and don the colors of their clubs."

The San Francisco *fiesta* was brilliantly carried out—with a complete Wild West Show presented—"the ponies as wild as mountain birds, and vicious as venomous reptiles," said the *Chronicle.* There were contests and games, medieval combats and modern sword contests, and exhibitions of fancy riding by the regular Army men from the Presidio, and many private equipages to meet the demands of the most exciting tastes of all peoples of all nations. But the greatest fun for Charlie was yet to come at his Santa Cruz *fiesta*

On to the Santa Cruz with *La Fiesta's* Moving Spirit

Charlie and his entourage arrived in Santa Cruz during the first week in July, and within three hours after his breakfast at the Pacific Ocean House, he had a strong force of men working to erect an enclosure on the beach as large as that which enclosed the entire Midwinter Fair in San Francisco. Like the San Jose *Fiesta*, Charlie was entirely responsible for this show. Charlie posted billboards in *fiesta* colors all around the city, and gaudy badges and souvenirs were distributed by his *fiesta* committee. A number of Arizona bronc busters, who had never seen the ocean before, strolled the sands of the beach and took the first dip of their lives in the rolling surf.

Charlie sent his man, Sanchez, Chief over all his cowboys, to the mountains to select fresh bulls with the proper fighting spirit. Sanchez brought back some of the most vicious and wiry bulls Charlie had ever seen. They were just the kind he wanted.

The *fiesta* carriage, a creation of artistic beauty, rich and regal in every sense, was gaily bedecked with bright colors of King Carnival and carried the stunning Queen, Miss Ida Mae McKamish, a deeply bosomed and shapely young miss from Santa Cruz, selected by Charlie for her beauty and because of her *equestrienne* talent. She did not escape Charlie's roving eye. A San Francisco establishment furnished an elaborate line of grotesque costumes and gay attire for the merri-makers, if they so wished. A railroad strike developed, so ye cowpuncher chartered cruise boats for excursions to and from San Francisco. No element to ensure success was lacking.

"*La Fiesta's* Moving Spirit", (ye cowpuncher), was on the grounds daily," said the *Santa Cruz Sentinel* of July 19, 1894, "to see that no detail escaped his practiced eye." His manager, Dr. Charles Gore, busied himself arranging contracts at the Midway, with such exhibits as Millie Christine, the famous two-headed Nightingale; Zingara, the Gypsy Queen; and the Shaki-DeRosa Company, of the Oriental Concession; dancing girls, donkeys, and camels. Some new acts included a water carnival at the Dolphin Baths, with pretty girls and handsome men participating. "Bad and vicious horses are in demand at *La Fiesta* Grounds. If you have one—bring him to the grounds and let the cowboys ride him," said the *Sentinel*.

Miss McKamish was an accomplished *equestrienne* and for her featured performance, Charlie billed her as Mae Melbourne. Her name had a theatrical ring, and perhaps his glowing memories and fond experience—in Melbourne, Australia with Marion Mae, prompted his decision. But it can be safely said that Miss Melbourne knew nothing of that. After two years had passed, Charlie was beginning to realize his wife and child were gone from his life—perhaps, forever.

As time passed, Kid Meadows and Miss Higgens were inseparable. During a daring chariot race one day, she had a terrifying accident. As her horses careened around the track at a record speed, the chariot struck a hillock, causing her team to lunge into their collars and her to be thrown over the dashboard of the chariot—as the wheels passed over her body. Pluckily she retained the reins, the grand performer that she was, and as the horses were going at breakneck speed, she was dragged a considerable distance in a tangle of harness. She managed to make an appearance in another riding race, after which a deeply concerned Kid Meadows took her to her hotel in a carriage to rest. In a short time, she made a complete recovery.

Things were going well for Charlie; the coffers were bulging from the huge attendance, so he planned a grand free entertainment for the little folk the next day. Charlie loved children, and it was just as big a delight for him to see their happy faces as it was for the kids. Can you imagine that he wondered if perhaps his own son was somewhere in that audience? The children shouted and yelled themselves hoarse as each new event was announced. They bestowed unlimited applause on the performers. Their little faces projected such happiness that Charlie had the official *fiesta* photographers—McKean and Ort—take several shots of them.

But the older folk were not left out. In his flamboyant way, he shared his good fortune with them the following day, by chartering the steam yacht, the *Capitola*, and sent her on a cruise up the California coast 100 miles to gather thirty sacks of the biggest, juiciest, fattest clams—the size of your head—for a genuine old-fashioned Rhode Island clambake for those who paid just 25 cents admission to see the show. The fun started at twelve o'clock sharp, when he declared the clams "ripe and ready" to be picked, and he served them while they lasted. Everyone had a feast.

Charlie, a shrewd businessman on the one hand, and a free spender on the other, was no novice when it came to throwing money around.

The following day a stellar attraction was a sumptuous barbecue—free again with the price of admission. Four thousand pounds of mutton and beef were roasted over sizzling coals, provided by the *fiesta* management and the stockmen of Santa Cruz County. Charlie guaranteed every man, woman and child who visited the *fiesta* grounds all the barbecued beef and mutton they could eat. "Come early and bring your appetite," he announced. Feasts of this size had never before been attempted in Santa Cruz.

Then, to wind up the week in a blaze of glory, along with the fresh bulls, Charlie introduced two new *matadores*. He set the stage for some lively action. Ramon Chavarilla, a noted bullfighter from the Coast, announced that he was "56 years old and had not fought a bull for 15 years." He acknowledged that he "had not the old-time agility, but thought he still retained the nerve," said the *Sentinel*. His partner was Cethro Herman. Charlie said, "How the plucky *matadores* and the cowboys escaped with their lives will always be a mystery to me."

From the time the bull was dragged into the arena, the bull's eyes bulged and he stomped and dug up the earth as if to dare anyone to show his face over the strong board fence. The two *matadores* flaunted their red cloth at the bull—who was "boiling over with wrath," and the beast made ferocious lunges at his tormentors. Ramon's actions were not quick enough to equal the quick turns of the desperate animal, and the bull caught the old-time *matador* on his sharp horn and tossed him high into the air. The crowd was stunned. When the old-timer struck the ground, the brute was on him in an instant and Ramon's chances for life were 100 to 1 against him.

Every effort Ramon made to recover was met by a murderous attack. He was soon helpless; his clothes literally torn from his body—and he was bleeding like a stuck pig. Terror mounted in his eyes as Cethro ran to his aid, but the bull failed to follow the red cloth. By then the crowd was paralyzed. A thrill of fear overcame Charlie, women gasped and men held their breath. Something had to be done—and quickly.

Then Kid, seeing the grave danger, threw his *reata* clean over the high-board fence and lassoed the bull by the hind leg—and with a mighty jerk, his strong horse pulled the bull to the ground. Kid was the recipient of tremendous applause. Ramon was carried from the ring and his wounds dressed by Charlie's manager, Dr. Charles Gore.

The Arizona cowboys moved in on the bull. The gate was thrown open again and the bull passed out, and ye Arizona rope wrangler, Arizona Charlie, lassoed him. In a minute Shorty Compher was on his back screaming like an Apache, and whipping the bull with his hat. As the bull raced across the ground, one of Compher's spurs broke and he lost his hold. Soon, he was in a desperate encounter with the bull. One of the ropes tripped him up and the bull was on top once more. Shorty fought like a demon, paying no attention to the sharp thrusts he was receiving. Ye lariat wrestler, Charlie, grew nervous—it was only for a quick swish of a mustang's tail, however, when he ran to Shorty's rescue. Dismounting, and in a state of panic, Charlie grabbed the bull by the tail, and with super-human strength, swung the bull from the prostrate cowboy. Just then the bull turned on Charlie, and Sheriff Cope unmuzzled a bull dog who swiftly grabbed the bull by the neck. The crowd was ecstatic, and Charlie who by this time had developed a pretty healthy ego reveled in the spotlight of the public eye.

Then Charlie proceeded to cut Shorty's rope. "He must have been dragged 50 yards," it was reported, before Charlie overtook him and cut the rope. The most common form of death among cowboys is to be dragged by a horse, and a bull no doubt comes under the same rule. The bull was captured in a jiffy and the bulldog choked free. Compher, whom everyone thought was dead, jumped on Charlie's charger and dashed up to the grandstand where he received roaring applause. This exhibition proved exciting beyond all description, and prompted Charlie to plan a future genuine bullfight, one that would compare with a true Spanish *corrida*. There seemed to be no stopping Charlie now.

After that performance a great deal of excitement was caused by a wager of a steer-tying contest between Arizona Charlie and James Taylor. Taylor thought he could topple Charlie from his throne. The articles of agreement were signed by both parties. A number of Taylor's friends who knew him to be an experienced *reata* twirler offered to make stiff wagers on their favorite. Charlie and his friends bet the local man to a standstill, knowing his past record as a *reata* twirler. Other men of a sporting mind took quite an interest. Several hundred dollars were put up at the Pacific Ocean Club that night. The event was scheduled to take place the day after the bull fight.

This *fiesta* attracted the attention of Nick Roberts, a wide-awake show manager, late of the Cooke and Barnum Show who was on his way to Santa Cruz to book Charlie and his company of 70 cowboys and lady riders for appearances in Cincinnati, St. Louis, and Memphis. Charlie did not need to be in Phoenix until October 13 for the annual *fiesta*, and a short stint with Roberts fit his schedule. After this tour he intended to add twenty-five Indians and a company of El Paso bullfighters to his entourage; his plan was to leave for South Africa with Roberts as his manager. Once again, he planned to hook up with Texas Jack.

On the final day of the *fiesta* in Santa Cruz, a gentlemen's saddle race occupied the featured spot which was dedicated to the stockmen of Santa Cruz County. A large purse was collected for the event, which delighted the old Hassayamper and other men of sporting mind who cared to bet on the bangtails.

The bull fight was the last act of the day. But all good things have to come to an end—and they did. The Society for the Prevention of Cruelty to Animals, and the Constable of Santa Cruz County stepped in and stopped the bullfight and the steer-tying contest with Taylor. The authorities threw the lasso of justice and drug Charlie with his manager, Dr. Charles Gore, into Justice Gardner's court. This was a complication Charlie did not need in his already complicated life.

That Monday, when the gong sounded for court to begin, there was a fairly good-sized audience. Some of the jurors admitted they had seen the *fiesta* sports from Dead Head Hill and were excused. The court was also a free performance, and those who did not have the privilege of seeing the *fiesta* learned all about bull fights without the danger of being gored, when the Arizona cowpuncher, along with Dr. Charles Gore, made their entry into the "Arena of Justice." After a three-day hearing, they were pronounced "not guilty," and were free to go—but not for long. Like all men who achieve success, Charlie became the object of envy and suspicion.

On August 2, 1894, the Constable of Santa Cruz Township, and the people of the State of California, issued a warrant for Charlie's arrest for the crime of felony—to wit, embezzlement, brought on by the Shaki-DeRosa Company and the Oriental Concession. By this time, Charlie's temper was not his best. His show was due to leave town with Roberts, and this problem put a decided crimp in his schedule.

Charlie had signed an agreement with the company—giving them the exclusive right to exhibit at Santa Cruz the following attractions and shows: Oriental Girls, the Mysterious Execution of the Orient and the Turkish Bazaar and Creole Girls, on the condition they deposit with him $200 as a guarantee that they would bring the aforementioned attractions to *La Fiesta*, and further give him 20% of their gross receipts. The $200 was to apply on these commissions. Nothing in the agreement specified that the $200 would be returned.

Now came their claim that their gross receipts did not exceed $50 which appeared ridiculous to Charlie. They sought the return of $150 entrusted to him. Further, they claimed he admitted using their money for his own "personal satisfaction," and that he willfully and feloniously refused to return it. Charlie knew their claim was not valid, and told the court he had no money. Court records show, that among his final words were: "You can't get blood out of a stone." Charlie had so much fun entertaining the spectators with clam bakes and barbecues, he hardly earned expenses.

The case dragged on, and one by one Charlie's cowboys left for home to seek their living. And, of course, the brief circuit with Roberts was off. But more than anything, he was anxious to return to Phoenix where his sister, Eva Applestill, lay dangerously ill with typhoid fever.

The opposition had no witness—nor evidence to support their claim, and after weeks of filings, receipts, information, arraignments, demurrers, plus affidavits and motions for continuances, the time came for Shaki to appear on the stand. His name was called, but Shaki was nowhere to be found. His people announced that he was too ill to appear. On September 22, after a reasonable delay, an attempt was made by the sheriff to serve a subpoena on Shaki, only to learn he had gone East.

To say the least, Charlie was a bit upset. After seven weeks, the order came to discharge the defendant. Charlie began to realize just how completely he had been taken. Emotionally exhausted, he felt like a clumsy-fingered, amateur pick-pocket who had just discovered his own wallet missing.

However, all time was not lost because he indulged in a good bit of gentle liquid fortification to steady his nerves and soothe his tired brain. A warm relationship was also established with Mae Melbourne, and many long hours were spent in her company. Mae did not succeed in putting her brand on him, however; Charlie resisted the loop of love—he still had a wife and child somewhere.

Rosalie Higgens kept his brother Kid well entertained and amused. By the time the show was ready to leave town—what was left of it—the two had fallen hopelessly in love. When they pulled out, both Miss Higgens and Miss Melbourne, blushing with happiness, went along with them.

Upon reaching Phoenix, Charlie learned about the passing of his sister, Eva Applestill. Her death was reported to be from a difficult childbirth, possibly complicated by typhoid fever. Deeply distraught over the loss of a second sibling, the disquieting news palled the coming events for Charlie.

Phoenix Equestrian Festival

Charlie had two weeks to put another troupe together. Some top-notch cowboys from Prescott joined, along with some more from Tonto Basin, and other nearby areas. Charlie managed to gather 20 fiesty long-horned steers and a number of spirited unbroken horses. George Felton and his brother, Oscar, joined the trip. Other talented men included all Arizonans: Juan Fernando, Jack Gibson, Charlie Edwards, R. Henderson, and the lovely lady *equestrienne*, Miss Alice Hamilton. Brother James went along and added his numerous talents. He was a past master of juggling cards and games of chance; he threw a mean pair of dice, and had charge of a side show featuring a petrified man. James preferred gambling to eating and made his way with this skill.

Charlie and his manager, Dr. Charles Gore, worked incessantly to make the Phoenix *fiesta* a huge success. It was 25 days into October when he opened his show with all the glory of the Olympic Games. Festivities of the day began with the usual street parade and the entire Meadows combination, along with painted Indians, all led amid a wild blaring of bugles and the steady martial thump of drums. A little papoose strapped to its mama's back was in the parade and bounced around in a manner most heart-rending to tenderhearted mamas who lined the parade route. Phoenix was again in gay attire; Charlie was a "splendid figure" as Grand Marshal, and was ably assisted by Mayor Monohan. Colonel Poston, Orator of the Day, delivered an impressive speech, followed by this glowing tribute to Arizona Charlie: "We have in front of the procession today an equestrian hero native to the manner born, who has carried the fame of American horsemanship to the Antipodes and brought it home untarnished, Arizona Charlie."

There was tremendous applause at this point, and Charlie was in his glory, as the orator went on to say, "This illustrious cowboy began his career in Arizona when the wild Apache contended with the frontiersmen for the mastery of the plains and the ownership of the herds, and bore himself bravely in the long struggle between barbarism and civilization.

The transformation scene since then has equalled any of the stories of the fabled *Arabian Nights*. In the mountain passes, where the deadly ambush awaited the family of the pioneer, the whistle of the locomotive shrieks defiance as a warning signal of commerce and civilization.

"In honoring a fellow citizen who by his own prowess has become the most distinguished horseman known on four continents, we honor Arizona in her gifted son. In his honor and for the future glory of Arizona it affords me the pleasure to declare the Equestrian Festival of Arizona now open, and to hope that it may be perpetuated annually for 1,000 years."

The usual cowboy exercises began the day, followed by some expert target practice by painted and feathered Indians on horseback. Charlie gave an excellent exhibition of his dexterity with a colt revolver, and casting all modesty aside, he missed but 7 out of 50 balls. Charlie Edwards gave a fine demonstration of bronco busting, and showed himself to be a complete master of the horse as he sat as if glued to his animal. Perhaps the most exciting feature of the day was the thrilling chariot race by Miss Rosalie Higgens and Miss Mae Melbourne. Both of these ladies told of hairbreadth escapes in this swift race, and from one minute to the next did not know when they might be hurled into eternity. The race was won by Miss Higgens.

Kid and George Felton entered an exciting pony express race, illustrating how the mails were carried in the early days. Both were excellent riders and showed great agility in mounting, losing only a few seconds in changing horses at each station as the wiry little mustangs tore up the earth. The race was won by Felton.

Charlie then took front position and showed his acquaintance with the Winchester. While on horseback—going at full speed, he broke glass balls, missing 9 out of 67. This showed Charlie to be a rival—if not a superior—to any crack-shot in the world.

The grounds were hung profusely with Chinese and Japanese lanterns for the evening's performance. Then the famous *Midnight Attack on the Settler's Cabin* was enacted. Steer-tying on the second day was very creditable, with Kid Meadows making a good time of 1 minute and 38 seconds; Oscar Felton, 2 minutes and 20 seconds; and R. Henderson, 1 minute and 28 seconds. George Felton was also in the contest, but was handicapped by a steer which was there for other business, when a broken rope set him free, causing an improvised bullfight in which Felton narrowly escaped connection with the infuriated brute's sharp horns. He was awarded no time.

"The skill shown in the lassoing of wild horses was the most skillful exhibition of its kind ever witnessed in the valley, and Juan Fernando displayed a superiority in handling, riding, and the ultimate subjection of the most unregenerate bronco of the lot," said the *Gazette*. The second day the Wild West illicited as much enthusiasm as ever, the *Gazette* of October 27 reporting: "The cowboy exercise with Kid Meadows, George Felton, and Arizona Charlie was particularly excellent."

Charlie had a tremendous compassion for children, and his greatest happiness was making them happy. A special performance was given for them; their response was magnificent—and their little faces "pink with excitement."

Mounted sword combats and throwing of the *bolas*—iron balls on rawhide thongs, which were swung over their heads and hurled from a distance of 60 feet with fierce accuracy—finished the day.

Arizona Charlie

CHAPTER 13

1895
FRANK'S DESPERATE BATTLE

While Charlie was making headlines from New York to San Francisco, Deputy Frank Prothero, who could track bees in a blizzard, was again making headline news in the paper published in Phoenix. Frank had captured two desperate outlaws in Tule Canyon, near Gila Bend: William Price, a murderer who was due to hang, and Jim Young, a counterfeiter. Both men had escaped from jail. This was the final incident that developed from a saloon tragedy which began on the night of October 1, 1894. Price and Young were heavily armed, having been provided with a Winchester rifle and a revolver by an outside accomplice. Price died from wounds inflicted by Frank during his capture. Frank gave the *Phoenix Gazette* the following account of the desperate fight:

"We were satisfied that Price and Young were holed up in Tule Canyon. We left Gila Bend with a young guide named Billy Childs. When we entered the canyon, which is a wash about 15 feet deep, whose side on the south slopes off gradually, Childs and I were within 25 yards of the convicts' camp, and my assistants, Billy Kellogg and Billy Moore, were about 100 yards distant.

"The fight commenced at once and lasted only about a minute, but it was a hot one. We overtook to climb the southern side, when Young fell with a broken leg. Almost at the same time I shot Price in the shoulder, and right away afterwards he received the fatal wound in the abdomen. He still continued firing and it was his next-to-last shot that broke my arm.

"Finally, when he realized he was mortally wounded, he came to us and laid down. I was trying to bandage my arm, but I stopped long enough to say, 'Price, why did you keep shooting at me after you knew you 'was' killed?' 'Oh,' he said, 'I've done just what anyone in my fix would do.'

"The fight was over and I left with Moore for Gila Bend, leaving Kellogg and Childs with the prisoners."

From the night Frank left Phoenix, those who knew him predicted with confidence the capture or killing of the fugitives, so the result was not unexpected. Judge Baker was so pleased with the result that he sent Frank the following telegram:

> Frank Prothero, Deputy Sheriff, Gila Bend.
>
> "I congratulate you as a brave and faithful officer."
>
> A.C. Baker
> January 6, 1895
> Phoenix, Az.

Right after the Christmas holidays, Arizona Charlie's Historical Wild West left Phoenix for El Paso, Texas, the next point of adventure and excitement. Cupid threw his arrow, and Kid and Miss Higgens, both 21, fulfilled their love and married. As for Miss Melbourne, the pleasure she and Charlie shared in each other's company grew—but show business was Charlie's way of life, and nothing again would ever interfere with it.

A Tragic Accident

The El Paso exhibition was excellent; the riding, roping, and shooting most creditable, but a tragic accident interfered that overshadowed the performances. One of the highlights was to have been a steer-roping contest between two star performers, Pomp James and Joe Lawson. Considerable money was wagered on the results, but Lawson's friends "had the call on odds" and continued to offer money on their man even after no takers could be found.

Lawson was given his choice of a start and decided to make the first run. The flag was dropped, and Lawson shot down the track after the fleeing steer, but as he raised up in his stirrup to make his throw, a dog ran across the track and stopped the fleeing steer. Lawson rode up and tried to drive the dog away but he refused to go until he was whipped. Lawson finally lassoed the steer and had him down, but his pony failed to hold him, and the steer and rider were off in a dead heat. His next throw landed around the animal's body, and when Lawson dashed past the steer for a fall, the steer started back in the opposite direction, jerking the cowboy from his horse and into the dust. Lawson fell beneath his horse and was seriously injured, which put an abrupt end to the contest. Unconscious, he was put in a carriage and rushed to the city.

Joe Lawson never regained consciousness. The next day, in a strange land and under a foreign flag, Lawson died. Only 10 years earlier, Lawson left his native Scotland to seek his fortune under the *Stars and Stripes*. His fortune was his wealth of friendships. It was said "no braver heart ever beat under the cuirass of a Roman Gladiator." The Wild West troupe was deeply saddened with his loss, and the following day's activities were clouded from this terrible tragedy.

Shortly thereafter, Rosalie was forced to quit her strenuous and dangerous acts to await the birth of her first baby. The Old Hassayamper, Charlie, was as excited over the coming baby as his brother, Kid.

CHAPTER 14

1895
THE FEARLESS *GRINGO*

Charlie found that the most exciting of all his Wild West demonstrations involved bull wrestling. The crowds were the largest and spirits were the highest of all his exhibitions. His only desire was to bring to the public what appealed most to them, and bull fighting tempted both his ambitions and his adventuresome nature.

Situated on the border of Chihuahua, Mexico, El Paso lay just across the Rio Grande from the famous bullfight city of Juarez. Mexicans loved their *fiestas*; bull fighting was a part of their way of life, and gambling their chief occupation. They favored a potent potable concoction called *pulque*—another important part of their life—made by fermenting the milky fluid of the *Maguey* plant; a mixture "strong enough to grow horns on a mule."

Mexico beckoned. Arizona Charlie's Wild West spent the next seven months in that country delighting the masses—from pauper to politician. Their performances were given in conjunction with the bullfights. The feeling of pageantry was magnificent; the Wild West lent variety to their *Corridas de Toros*. The Wild West shows were performed in such rapid succession that the audience was kept in a perfect roar of excitement from start to finish. The performers gave a splendid performance to each crowded house.

From Juarez, Charlie made his way to Mexico City. On the way he learned about the U.S. Government Attorney DeWitt's visit to Phoenix regarding Indian Depredation Claims. Charlie's thoughts turned back to his family—his brothers and sisters—and the hard times which had befallen them since the loss of life, property and money at the hands of the Apaches. He wanted nothing more than to relieve them of their burden. Upon arriving in Mexico City, he sent a letter to DeWitt inquiring whether it was necessary for him to return to make his claim, or if perhaps Frank Prothero, Deputy Sheriff of Maricopa County, could provide all the needed information. With the letter posted, Charlie set about the business of making a living, and he would have to keep the welfare of his family in his prayers.

Bullfights are the national sport and principal amusement of Mexico, and the government takes a strong hand in it. In order to fight in the Federal arena, the bulls must come from one of the four *haciendas* that breed just for that purpose. This was the rule in Charlie's time. The government took 21% of the receipts and the Secretary of the Republic was the judge of the show. The bulls, fresh from Chihuahua, were said to be "as bad as they grow." At one fight, three horses were sacrificed to the enraged bulls, and Charlie was heard to say, "How the *picadores* escaped was always a mystery to the audience."

Along the way, Charlie challenged the ex-broadsword champion of Mexico to a mounted sword contest. But his agility was no match for Charlie's expert horsemanship—and Charlie won the match. Ponciano Diaz, the President's nephew and the most famous of all *toreadores* in Mexico at that time, delighted in what he had witnessed; he requested that Charlie join him and Carlos Garcia—as a *toreador* in their next bullfight in Juarez. Charlie, a man of many talents, was deeply caught up in the bravery of the pageant and was honored with his invitation, so he gladly accepted. He made his *entrada* (entrance) into the *macho* world of bull fighting—and the sweat and stink of the bullring.

The Buccarelli Bullring had a seating capacity of 20,000 persons with an arena about 150 feet in diameter. The seats were divided into *palcos* (theatre boxes); the *sombra*, or "shade side"; and the *sol*, the cheap or sun side. The amphitheatre quickly filled as it was Carlos Garcia's benefit, who was the pet of the Mexican public. According to the programme, five beautiful *Cazadera* bulls were to be run to their death.

At half past three, a loud applause seemed to burst from the grandstand and everyone looked in the direction of the judge's box that was brightly decorated in Mexican colors. The judge had arrived. The bugler sounded the trumpet, a door under the front seats on the opposite side of the ring sprung open, a horseman appeared, mounted on a beautiful and spirited white horse. He was dressed in a long flowing robe, knee breeches, and wore a cocked hat with a gaudy plume. The horse pranced within fifteen feet of the judge's stand, then with one bound he slid upon his haunches in front of the judge. The judge threw the rider the key—to the bullpen—which he gracefully caught. He would have been hissed out of the ring had he missed the key.

Arizona Charlie's Wild West Show in Camp, 1893

Another bugle call and the company of bullfighters entered: "Ye famous horseman of four continents," Arizona Charlie, up middle front, with Ponciano Diaz on one side and Carlos Garcia on the other. Behind them followed four *banderilleros*; and next, four *capaderos*, then four *picadores* on horseback and four white mules driven abreast. There was "not a costume but that was worth $1,000."

At another bugle call a small door opened up—and the bull, with a wide bound, sprang into the ring. No doubt someone had aggravated him on the other side of the barrier. Then, as he passed through the small door a man stuck a rosette into the bull's shoulder. Aggravated that much more, it kicked at its tormentor and went straight for Ponciano, who was standing in the center of the ring with the red cloth over his arm. Charlie's heart fairly flew up into his throat. He would not have given a "barmaid's smile" for Ponciano's life. The bull lowered its head—gave one snort, raised and shook its head, but Ponciano was not there. He had gracefully sprung aside and the bull only lifted the red cloth. Shouts of *"Ole!" "Ole!"* filled the air. By this time the bull was "boiling with wrath." It was a handsome black four-year old, with long, sharp horns, as sleek and active as a panther, with hair as fine as silk. In one second it seemed to take in the whole situation and, singling out a horseman, with a low bellow made a straight line for the trembling equine.

The *picador*, the horseman armed with a goad, took his position and as the bull made the last bound, he speared him in the shoulder, but the bull was too strong and determined. Catching the horse between its forelegs, it tossed the horse and rider into the air amid shouts of *"Toro!" "Toro!"* and, as the horse came down—with another thrust—he severed his jugular vein. The bull then gave its attention to the prostrate rider. It was in the act of making a lunge that would have sent the poor *picador* into another world, when Charlie glided between them; and, flaunting his cape in the bull's face, he started across the arena. It was a close call to save the *picador,* but Charlie left an opening for the bull. He had no time to position for a dodge, so he sped away across the ring by waving his cape in a circle behind—with the bull close at his heels. It was a ride for life, but only the "good" go to heaven, and that left Charlie out, so everything turned out all right. Events have proved that Charlie seemed to possess a charmed life.

But the wildest excitement prevailed. Men, women, and children "screamed" with bursts of *"Ole!" "Ole!"* and tequila bottles flew through the air from the sun side of the amphitheatre. Charlie glided back and forth in front of the bull. The band played a *dianna* (Reveilli), as hats, parasols, capes, shawls, and Mexican dollars went flying into the ring. Charlie had won their hearts; this was the greatest tribute they could give him. The next horseman turned the bull with his lance as Carlos Garcia got into the middle of the ring, and not moving more than 3 or 4 feet at a time, he remained until the animal made several passes. The bugle sounded again, the horses were taken and the *banderilleros*, "who thrust *banderillas* (small darts) into the bull, were next. Standing in the open ring, the men would wait; when the bull was fairly on them, the *banderilleros* then would spring to one side to place the darts in the ferocious animal's neck.

Seven pairs of *banderillas* were placed, and again the bugle sounded. This was the final act. Garcia handed the sword to Ponciano Diaz, the President's nephew, who gracefully surrendered it to Arizona Charlie. The audience was delighted and anxious to see what the handsome *gringo* could do—Mexican bullfighters are trained from childhood. Charlie was both fearless and active, but they had no idea of his expertise with the sword. They waited in eager anticipation.

The American part of the audience seemed fearful—yet they were proud of their representative. Charlie was resplendent in a handsome suit of blue and silver; his long hair neatly piled atop his head under his hat. An extract from an unidentified newspaper of that day paid tribute to ye bullfighter: "Never was a finer specimen of American manhood presented than when Arizona Charlie stepped out to show his capabilities with a sword. Tall, beyond the ordinary, with every muscle hard and firm, he was as fine a type of manhood as the continent of America has ever produced."

Not more than twenty seconds from the time he threw his cap to the judge, the bull came full-tilt across the ring—straight for ye plainsman who stood with drawn blade. Several fast movements were made, then everything went still as death. Then, in only a moment, wild bursts of *"Ole!" "Ole!"* filled the air, and the crowd yelled itself hoarse. The bull gave one mighty heave and fell in a heap with Charlie's sword planted deep in its heart. It was a scientifically precise blow and a great piece of *machismo*. It was Charlie's moment of glory. *Señoritas* blew kisses and threw flowers, and the victorious *matador,* the bullfighter who kills the bull with the sword, could hardly walk out of the arena for hats, cloaks, and bottles that were thrown into the arena. The white mules entered, "glittering with flags and tinkling with bells," to drag off the slain bull at a gallop, and the four other bulls which were killed in the same manner.

Mae Melbourne always had a hero worship toward Charlie, and dimpled with pleasure in his presence. Some said Charlie was an incredible egotist, but after the bullfight—to Mae he was the reincarnation of the gallant knights of old. He had the feeling Mae wanted him to ride up on his white charger, sweep her into his arms and gallop off into the sunset. He found her praise comforting, her attention flattering. Charlie was extremely fond of Mae—but not enough to marry her. There were too many worlds left for him to conquer before he could settle down. But if he ever did—he would place Mae's name on top of his list.

After the proper time, Rosalie was due to give birth. Events followed their natural course and Charlie was just as "jittery" as his brother, Kid. Mae helped prepare the tent for the arrival, and Charlie—always a showman, hung the *Stars and Stripes* over the tent flaps so the little one would be born an "American." Suddenly everything was abustle, and a fine boy emerged. They named him *Carlos* after Charlie.

Charlie, no doubt, found his mind spinning in wonderment for the son he possibly had somewhere in the world, and probably fell prey to conflicting thoughts and emotions. No doubt he herded his thoughts back into their corral and found solace with the riotous *pulque* drinkers behind the doors of the *Cantina del Toro*. Life in the tent took on a new meaning with the little one along, and Rosalie retired from the show to care for her child.

Carlos Garcia

CHAPTER 15

1895
EPISODE AT CRIPPLE CREEK

The Juarez bullfights were a decided improvement on the previous efforts of the season, but Charlie had finished what he had come to do in Mexico. The bullfight had greatly impressed a beady-eyed man of diminutive stature with a black mustache named Joe Wolfe, a spectator at the thrilling event, and proprietor of the Continental and Palace Hotels in Cripple Creek. He had come to Old Mexico—after travelling through Texas—in search of Charlie. He told Charlie his performance was the "most exciting spectacle" he had ever witnessed. Charlie had never heard of Mr. Wolfe before that time, even though he had a wide reputation as a tourist gypper, and a cultivated taste for various skin games, a vast number of bunkos, and other shady operations or get-rich-quick schemes. Nor did Charlie know some referred to Wolfe as a "red-faced bumpkin who ought to be back in the Missouri flats pulling cockleburrs out of a corn field."

Joe learned that the Secretary of Agriculture Morton was trying to force down the price of beef in the U.S. by allowing free entry of Mexican cattle. Also, he had read in the newspaper that ten fighting bulls had been shipped to the Atlanta Exposition for the purpose of giving exhibitions of bullfights. Joe informed Charlie that there had never been a true Mexican bullfight in the United States, and that he had the bright idea that the town of Cripple Creek, Colorado, "the greatest gold camp on earth," was the spot for one. Charlie was the man he had been looking for and he wanted to form a partnership with him.

Charlie could not deny that the thrill of pageantry was infectious, and being a man to always reach out for the spectacular, he liked the idea. "If you could import Mexican bulls and bullfighters," Joe said, "you could put on a genuine Spanish *corrida*." It was illegal to kill bulls in the United States, but Joe assured Charlie that Colorado laws were "lax," that he could find no mention of bullfights at all, and nothing could come of it until after the fights were over. Charlie made his living by "work or by wager," and was willing to take that chance. Everything was settled in a satisfactory manner, and the "Joe Wolfe Grand National Spanish Bullfight Company" was formed, with Joe as President and Charlie as Director.

Joe hurried back to Cripple Creek on August 5, to arrange financing and to make the arrangements for grounds at the race track in nearby West Beaver Park, Gillett. Charlie's job was to round up Mexican fighting bulls and the services of the noted *matadores*, Carlos Garcia, Jose *"Chi-Chi"* Morrero, Antonio Sentrea, and Morrero's stunning wife, "*la Charrita*" (Miss Randoricus), famous lady bullfighter. *La Charrita* was a beauty of the rarest description—a real pulse accelerator—who never failed to stir the flame of passion in every red-blooded male.

Arizona Charlie Shooting Glass Balls at Cripple Creek Bull Fight, 1895

la Charrita—Mexican Lady Bull Fighter

With his part taken care of, Charlie hurried back to Colorado to help Joe plaster the surrounding areas with posters announcing the coming *corrida*, then went to Colorado Springs and Denver to a press conference where he announced the bullfights would occur at Gillett on August 24-26, 1895. Then the two partners led a crew of carpenters out to Beaver Park and began construction of the arena. They built a ring to hold 5,000 persons, with twelve tiers of seats and seventy boxes for the *elite* and a raised throne for Joe and his party. Joe, who by then had assumed the role of *don Jose* Wolfe, was parading around town in a flowing black cape three sizes too big for him, and with a black beaver *sombrero* he had borrowed from *Chi-Chi Morrero*.

The bullfight announcements set off an explosive protest in Colorado Springs, where the Secretary of the Colorado Human Society, Francis B. Hill, learned of the proposed *corrida*. He informed Joe that there would be no barbaric killing of innocent bulls. *Don Jose* informed Hill that he "wasn't wanted in Cripple Creek," and to go back to the Springs.

About this time Mr. William Ballou, Vice President of the American Humane Society, wrote a letter to the Secretary of the Treasury Carlisle, stating that the tariff law did not apply to importation of fighting bulls for immoral purposes, that the bulls destined for the Atlanta Exposition should be held at the port of entry until a decision could be made by President Grover Cleveland. This prompted Francis Hill to send a similar plea to the Secretary of the Treasury informing him of their proposed fight, and to invoke the aid of his Department to keep bullfighting out of El Paso County.

Meantime, Joe was receiving continuous warnings from Francis Hill to call off the fights—or face jail. *Don Jose* ignored all warnings. After all, he had the backing of Constables Sherman Bell and Lou Lambert. Sherman Bell, who later became a Brigadier General, led Roosevelt's Rough Riders up San Juan Hill, Cuba. Meanwhile, the Cheyenne Mountain Club fellows who couldn't stand the sight of Francis Hill since he put the "screws" on pigeon shooting at their country club range, were all on Joe's side. He also deputized several of his friends to act as "marshals."

The Annual Flower Carnival was getting ready for its parade in Colorado Springs. Joe thought it would be good publicity if they joined the Flower Carnival in their colorful procession. So he approached the city "fathers"—who all eagerly looked forward to the bullfights and were about to honor Joe's request—when word got around, and Colorado Springs became a scene of mass meetings with hysterical opposition. The *Colorado Springs Gazette* received the following anonymous letter from a woman:

"It will be nothing else but a blot upon the reputation of our State and El Paso County if this monstrous troupe is allowed to disport itself in public. We of Colorado Springs pride ourselves upon our interest in education, culture and advancement. Then let us protest against this retrograde movement toward the dark ages. May we redeem ourselves by keeping bull fights from our borders and may we keep our Flower Carnival within the bounds of refinement and beauty."

Joe dropped his request, but he was happy with the publicity they received. Charlie wasn't so sure they needed that kind of publicity.

About this time, Charlie was feeling a little bit apprehensive but a big investment had been made and they had to make enough to repay Joe's loans. He learned that Joe had been run out of Cripple Creek by his creditors, and Charlie did not want all this to fall back on him. A man named Barth of Denver, held the mortgage, and a Cripple Creek merchant by the name of Wienberg, and Town Constable, Sherman Bell, helped back the enterprise financially. Both Charlie and Wolfe knew they had to "produce" or leave town—fast.

Hill consistently made every effort to stop the bullfights; he confronted Sheriff Bowers of El Paso County, but the sheriff seemed more concerned with votes than with bullfights—yet, reluctantly, said he "would look into it." Hill then telegraphed the head of the Humane Society, Thompson, in Denver. Thompson consulted with Governor McIntyre, who, in turn, consulted with Adjutant General Moses, Commander of the State Militia.

Nothing fazed *don Jose* Wolfe, who went right ahead as planned. Charlie learned about the quality of Wolfe's friends at that time. Joe had put one, a con-artist named Jefferson Randolph "Soapy" Smith, "manipulator of vast and shady skill," as a concessionaire. Soapy had made quite an unsavory reputation for himself, sporting the title "Denver Bunco King." He had been run out of Creede, Leadville, Denver and New Orleans, and banished from St. Louis, where his mother, wife and children lived, because of his "sure-thing" games. Joe made his first big mistake—Soapy trimmed the "suckers" so thoroughly, many had no money left to buy tickets for the bullfights. Even so, 3,000 ebullient persons passed through the gates.

Meantime all the authorities were passing the buck. General Moses came, looked, and did not do anything but reserve seats. The whole district was "talking bullfights, and dreaming bullfights," but no one could come up with a plan to stop them.

"*El Presidente*" Wolfe and "*el Director*" Meadows insisted that there would be no cruelty, so no interference was necessary. No one could agree on what constituted cruelty. With threats by the Militia, it looked extremely doubtful to some if a fight would indeed take place. Others felt the famous bullfighters were "really there for business," and it would be a genuine bullfight. To add confidence to the affair, the managers offered a $50 prize to the butcher who could skin and dress his animal in the quickest time.

Joe planned on having just as complete and just as cruel a fight as his bulls and *toreadores* could put on, but at the same time he tried to calm the suspicions of the Humane Society and the State officers by the most "preposterous" series of cock-and-bull stories. He told the Attorney General that the darts would be "blunted and tipped with wax," so that when they struck the animal, instead of penetrating his hide, they would only "adhere through the cohesive powers" of the waxy preparation. Then, he promised that the horns would "be removed and rubber tips substituted" and would contain a preparation of arnica and Vaseline, which would "spurt out" when the horn touched either *matador* or horse. He also claimed he was training the bulls to come to a complete standstill at the word "stop". He even had the unmitigated gall to send Governor McIntyre two complimentary tickets—offering him a place in the arena where he could, on the word "stop," bring the whole fight to an end. In the next breath, however, he declared he would "go to the penitentiary for ten years" before he would disappoint the people after the promises he had made.

On the morning of August 23, the bullfighters arrived amid wild excitement on a special train, complete with *banderillas*, swords, spears, "red rags and rich garments"—but there were no bulls. The Secretary of the Treasury, hearing of their plan, denied the ten *Cazadera* bulls entry at the Texas border. They had hit a devastating snag. There had been a tremendous outlay of money and the stakes to be played the next day were high. A complete fluke would have meant a heavy loss, and an up-and-up bullfight meant a Sunday crowd of 10,000 persons paying from $2 to $5 each. The two partners escorted the bullfighters to Cripple Creek without bulls, and ensconced them in *don Jose's* Palace Hotel. *Jose Chi-Chi* Morrero brought his valet with him and a magnificent wardrobe that filled the bill for the ideal bullfighting cavalier.

Charlie then sent a group of his cowboys off to locate some wild and spirited "local brutes," while he and Joe went ahead with their planned parade down Bennett Avenue, Cripple Creek. Joe was dressed in his green gaudy suit, heavy with silver buttons, black cape, black beaver sombrero borrowed from Morrero, and high-patent leather boots. Meadows was in fringed buckskins, soft leather leggings, and his large cream-colored *sombrero*. The band escorting the famous *matadores* enthroned in carriages, along with the whole Meadows' Wild West combination, followed in the rear. During the parade a serious accident occurred when the horses became frightened by the playing of the brass band, and tried to run away. In their struggle, they overturned the carriage which contained Mae Melbourne and the lovely *la Charrita*. *La Charrita* was not injured, but Mae suffered severe back injuries and badly bruised legs that prevented her from performing—for the first time—along with the Mexican lady as a *banderillera*. Charlie was deeply concerned over Mae's welfare. It was at this time he realized how much Mae meant to him.

Secretary Thompson arrived in Gillett expecting to be met by a representative sent by Governor McIntyre. No one came. Thompson became quite upset when he could not even reach Governor McIntyre by wire. The two partners, Wolfe and Meadows, planned for a Justice of the Peace to sit in Joe's box, so if Thompson was successful in stopping the fight, they promised it would only be long enough for them to post bond. Charlie made the remark that he was "inclined to hoot at the Humane Society," and expressed doubt that "Thompson could distinguish between a mule and a de-horned steer." In fact, he offered a small wager to the contrary. It seemed that Thompson was only "respectfully tolerated" by others. The press even demanded his immediate dismissal.

The arena and amphitheatre were finally completed and decorated during the afternoon, which presented a unique scene without a crowd. As Charlie looked around he could fairly hear shouts—and wave after wave of wild cheers. The ring, 150 feet in diameter and enclosed by a solid stockade of cedar posts rising eight feet above the ground, was almost level as a floor. The ground had been plowed and rolled, then scraped with a heavy railroad tie, leaving the soil packed and firm. The top of the stockade was draped with colorful bunting in *fiesta* shades. On a three-foot platform circling the arena, spaces had been partitioned off by scantling, making seventy-nine boxes, each containing five chairs. A few boxes had six, totaling 395 seats. Occupants could look directly down into the arena. At the south side was *don Jose's* elevated stand, holding six chairs for *el Presidente* and other officials of law and order—including the deputy marshals and Justice of the Peace to serve a bond, should that be necessary.

The Wild West entrance to the arena was on the west side. The bandstand was draped with *fiesta* colors. The same colors, red, green, yellow and white were raised, above the highest seats on the west side in the form of rosettes. The spectators' entrance was at the south side where steps led upward to the level stockade about the arena. The narrow entrance for the bulls was at the north side behind the private boxes. Then rose tiers of very pitched seats, where at the back of the top tier a protective railing was placed to prevent the "gallery Gods" from falling backward to the ground some 20 feet below. There were colorful streamers and flags draped over the entrance presenting a very gaudy scene that could be seen from hills and valleys for miles around.

At intervals inside the ring a heavy planked barrier was built, behind which the matador could dodge for safety, but too narrow of an opening to admit the bull. Inside the fair grounds leading up to the entrance to the bull ring, were saloons and places of refreshment—gorgeously arrayed "to beguile" the festive visitors; the wheel of fortune, impromptu restaurants—and various games of chance, operated by "Soapy" Smith, that made up the Midway.

Gillett, 4,000 feet below the shadow of Pike's Peak, had undergone a wondrous transformation. Its frame buildings had tripled in size; pines were brought down from the mountains to be planted along the Midway, to make shaded beer gardens for the visitors. Refreshment stands sprung up on every corner in town, and business fronts were gaudily decorated with *fiesta* colors. Bunting was hung from every building, and a huge banner flung across the main street pointed to the headquarters of the *fiesta* committee.

Joe's special train brought visitors from all over the state—as well as from the nearby gold camps of Victor, Altman, Anaconda, Elkton, and Goldfield. The great tangle of horses and vehicles on the fairgrounds reminded one of a big old-fashioned "down East picnic." Venders moved through the crowd peddling snacks, magazines, and cigars.

The local *Monte Carlo* on the hill prepared for a great influx of visitors, and the *parlour* houses in town—such as the beautiful and enterprising, henna-haired Pearl DeVere's elegant establishment, *Old Homestead*—made preparations for a brisk business with prices ranging from $50 to $100.

The bullfighters were ready, but somewhat disgusted about having to fight untrained Hereford and Durham bulls. About 32 years old, *Chi-Chi* the *espada*, or bullfighter who kills the bull with a sword, and great favorite, was a tall, powerful looking, smooth-faced man who attracted great notice. All of Cripple Creek looked on in amazement the next day at two swarthy-looking young men—who arrived secretly by stage during the night, blossoming out the next morning in gilt-buttoned regimentals of the National Guard; prancing with importance through the streets, darting in and out of hotels and business establishments; and generally cutting a "wide swath." They turned out to be Adjutant General Moses and Assistant General Klee of the State Militia who had come from the Flower Festival in Colorado Springs. Their street clothes had failed to arrive.

One local yokel dashed across Bennett Avenue, loudly exclaiming: "Holly gee! There's a band in town. Say Mister, what band are you with?" This was the last straw. The two men made a dash for the nearest clothing house, purchased corduroy coats and vests, and natty woolen caps, and threw their uniforms under the counter.

Attendance was tremendous. The first day the weather could not have been more magnificent. A few fleecy clouds hung across the scene—tempering at times the blazing sun. Many prominent businessmen, as well as mayors and officials from surrounding areas, were in attendance. Adjutant General Moses and Assistant General Klee were escorted to their box by Deputy Bob Mullins. They were joined by Deputy District Attorney Wilcox and Senator Kennedy.

Charlie was to receive 25% of the gate receipts, but knowing Joe's past record, he made certain his percentage came off the top—by putting two hands in his employ at the gate. Out of every $100, he put $25 down into his pockets. Shrewd Charlie "couldn't see any reason to wait for drawing up of balance sheets." The plan was simple, and as far as Charlie was concerned, it worked to perfection.

The last-minute spikes were being driven in when Constable Sherman Bell introduced Marshall McClure, Editor of the *Gillett Forum*. Mr. McClure prepared a flowery welcoming speech, but the crowd came to see a bullfight. They were not in the mood for his speech. The boozed-up throng let out loud shouts of "Bring on the bull!" "Where is the bull?" and "Let's trot out the bull!" Mr. McClure did not have a chance to speak through the loud shouts, so he made a hasty exit before trouble started. Even at that, the scene turned into a wild spectacle with a few bottles thrown. The bugle sounded and "ye buccaneer of the bull pen," Charlie, in bright costume, rode swiftly into the arena and brought his horse to his haunches right in front of *el Presidente's* box. *Don Jose* threw Charlie the key to the bull pen—just like they do in Mexico—which he missed catching. The American audience wasn't "awake" to the fact—but he would have been hissed out of the arena had this been Mexico. He turned his prancing horse, and leaned from his saddle—like he did for his acts—picked up the key, and dashed swiftly out of the arena. Then the grand entry of bullfighters and the Wild West Show, with three bulls leading, made their appearance. The participants saluted *el Presidente*, then rode out of the arena leaving the Americans on horseback and in chariots, followed by gaily-decorated teams of mules circling the field. . .which was a very impressive sight. Some clever work was done by the Wild West in their exhibition; the crowd shuddered when Charlie shot three glass balls from atop Mae's head from 25 yards.

The band played. Liquor and cigars were distributed to the crowd; wheels of fortune spun outside; and the mood was indeed festive. Then came the first real bullfight on American soil, which was carried out to the death and to the hauling away of the bulls.

The introduction of the bullfight, which was a big show of bulls being trotted in and out of the area, thoroughly excited the crowd. Charlie, and his brother, Kid, dashed into the arena armed with *picas*—the eight foot long, slender hickory poles with a sharp brad point set in the end. As they reined in their horses before the narrow entrance where the bull was to come, "ye victorious plainsmen" flung their *picas* into a barrier of logs—where they hung—held by the steel brad. This action told the crowd there would be no mercy for the bull. They backed their horses away and the bugle sounded.

The three bullfighters came in abreast: Jose *Chi-Chi* Morrero, the *espada*, or Captain, fighter of great skill, in the center. His shirt, jacket and knee breeches were of black satin, heavily embroidered in gold. He wore silk stockings of light salmon, a sash of the same color about his waist, and a tie of a lighter hue over an immaculate shirt front. He was a slow-moving man, yet graceful, and none were quicker or more daring than he. His dark green mantle, lined with salmon-colored silk, hung in heavy folds over his left arm.

"Carlos Garcia, a splendid specimen of humankind, a study in muscles, a tall, slender, sharp-faced Spaniard, wore a suit of green velvet, his jacket and breeches profusely embroidered in gold and silver," said Charlie. He wore a pink sash around his waist and his stockings and mantle were a gaudy yellow, lined with red, which, it was said, "could arouse the tamest of bulls." These two men wore close-cropped hair, with round black caps upon their heads and a little rosette attached to the back, reaching up to the middle of the head from which suspended a short queue—something of the sort a Chinaman might wear.

The third fighter, another Spaniard, Antonio Sentrea, had an immense bush of hair. His suit was dark maroon, which appeared almost black. His sash and stockings were lavender, his mantle a vivid green, edged with red. With great formality the three proudly saluted the occupants of *el Presidente's* box, then parted and stood near the wall of the arena. *Ye picadores* Meadows were to the left and right. The narrow gate swung open and the bull rushed out, infuriated with the gay *banderilla* that had just been thrust into his side as he left the pen.

Brigadier General Sherman S. Bell, A Roosevelt Rough Rider

A black Hereford breed animal, with a white face, charged to the right; and ye plainsman, Charlie, put the spurs to his horse, its flanks barely escaping the lowered horns of the beast, from which fluttered a bunch of bright ribbons. In an instant, *espada* Morrero was across the ring, and the bull turned to the bright mantle shaken before his face.

The bull charged but Morrero quickly stepped aside; then, the bull turned and chased him behind the barrier. Ye *picadores* Meadows gave the bull some wicked jabs, their mantles shaking "tantalizingly close," the bull fairly aroused, but shortly losing all interest. In Mexico with a savage bull, the *picador* needs all his skill in acting on the defensive; and, should their wicked jabs be ineffectual in rousing the animal to the requisite fury, the beast is hooted by the crowd.

Then, Carlos Garcia took up two of the darts, and posing one in each hand, stood proud in the center of the arena trying to attract the bull from guarding the barrier where Sentrea also had been compelled to jump for safety. Morrero came forward, and the bull charged him; but Sentrea nimbly stepped aside, and his mantle was caught and carried away on the horns of the bull. Before the bull could charge again, Carlos Garcia leaped forward and planted both *banderillas* in the animal's shoulder. A minute later two more *banderillas* had been buried in the beast's flesh.

Sheriff Bowers arrived from Colorado Springs after the fight was well underway, and went straight to *el Presidente's* box. He could see this was the real thing. "You are under arrest," Bowers said to Wolfe. Of course, "*don Jose*" expected this, and already had his friend and backer, Constable Lou Lambert, confine him to his custody. "I'm already under arrest," *don Jose* smugly informed the sheriff. A few sharp words were exchanged. Then, the bullfighters finished their deviling of the beast and everything was ready for the grand final scene.

"They've got him full of barbs," *el Director* Meadows explained. "He ought to be killed." Adjutant Moses jumped up from his box and went to meet the sheriff, who was moving toward him. They exchanged a few words. At the same moment the bugle sounded and the great *Chi-Chi* advanced slowly into the arena, an imposing figure in his magnificent costume. In his right hand he held a long, shiny sword, and in his left hand a heavy flag of red.

Then the loud voice of Sheriff Bowers boomed, "This has gone on long enough. The bull must be shot." "I'm sorry, but we are not going to shoot the bull," *el Presidente* informed him. While the talk got louder between the two, the daring *matador* made a savage thrust at the bull's heart—but missed the crucial point. Then after further maneuvering, the strong arm of the brave bullfighter sent the sword home to the proper spot—and the fight ended.

Morrero came across the ring with the "magnificent air" of a conquering general, and saluted Manager Wolfe with a broad smile of satisfaction. Sheriff Bowers, followed by Deputy Sterling and other deputies, left the building and grounds to form a newer strategy. More of the Wild West Show was presented.

Two lank, long-horned steers were chased into the ring. One of them had two great brass knobs attached to his horns. Ye Meadows Brothers worked with red cloaks and got quite a little fight out of "his knobs." Then ye plainsman roped and threw him, a surcingle was put about his body, then Kid rode him. After the bulls had the same exercise, Charlie and Kid gave some good roping and riding work, but it was too tame for the crowd.

Then, *don Jose* blew his little silver whistle and the bugle sounded for the second bull. He was in for the fight from the moment the door opened and the little torturing barbs were pinned into the base of his horns. He pranced around, then chased ye *picadores* behind the shields, lifting Charlie's horse off the ground with his blunt horns—and having a good time in general.

La Charrita, who took no part in the first killing, was the feature of the second fight. She was a magnificent horsewoman, as well as an exquisite beauty, and an eyeful to behold in her sequined jacket and tight-fitting *charro* pants. In spite of the cruel work she was engaged in, it was almost forgotten by seeing her face ablaze with enthusiasm and her mild, graceful riding, daring everything and fearing nothing. She had pinned the little barbs, and now it was Garcia's turn to put in the *banderillas*—and the bull went wild. Just then, a horrible commotion arose in the judge's box.

Sheriff Bowers had returned to order the fight stopped, and to tell *don Jose* that he was under arrest. There was intense excitement about the box area, and over the bullfight below. Constable Griffith insisted that *el Presidente* go with him, which was a dangerous situation. Wolfe had enough friends present with enough guns to resist arrest, but he did not want to call them. When the Sheriff stepped into the box this time, he was backed by several deputies, with Deputy Sterling brandishing a Winchester. At the drop of a hat, the situation could have turned into a riot.

"Stop this fight," roared Bowers.

"It's not going to stop," shouted Wolfe.

"Call off those men and I'll shoot him," Sterling said to Wolfe, as he raised his Winchester.

"You can't shoot him," cried Wolfe, foaming with passion. All the time down in the arena, the bullfight continued.

"I can't call off the fight," declared Wolfe. "It means $10,000 and double that for me. I'll submit to arrest but you and your deputies cannot take me out of here!"

Finally, Wolfe consented to go with the sheriff, but insisted that he be allowed to follow rather than precede the officials. This would not have looked good for *Macho don Jose* Wolfe. Then, Joe yelled down into the arena from his lofty perch, and ordered the *matadores* and ye *picadores* busy with the maddened bull to "go right ahead with the fight."

There was no reason why the fight could not go on, but Charlie thought "discretion the thing," and ordered the fight stopped after another five minutes, without the death of the second bull. With the *banderillas* swaying from the bull, making him a dangerous beast, the sheriff quickly stepped in and shot the bull.

But *el Presidente* had his own little "justice court" all ready for operation. He was taken before Justice Keith of Gillett as prisoner of the Constable, since Sheriff Bowers decided he must be turned over to the officer who first "arrested" him. A farcical trial followed in which *don Jose* Wolfe was acquitted, and the three Mexicans and ye Meadows Brothers were fined $5 each, plus costs. They paid their fines promptly, the money going to the City of Gillett.

That afternoon Deputy Constable Hathaway of Cripple Creek appeared on the grounds and ordered the flimflam games to shut down. He was at once "hustled" off the grounds and "arrested" for disturbing the peace.

Parade down Bennett Avenue in Cripple Creek, Colorado, August, 1895

Arizona Charlie, 1895

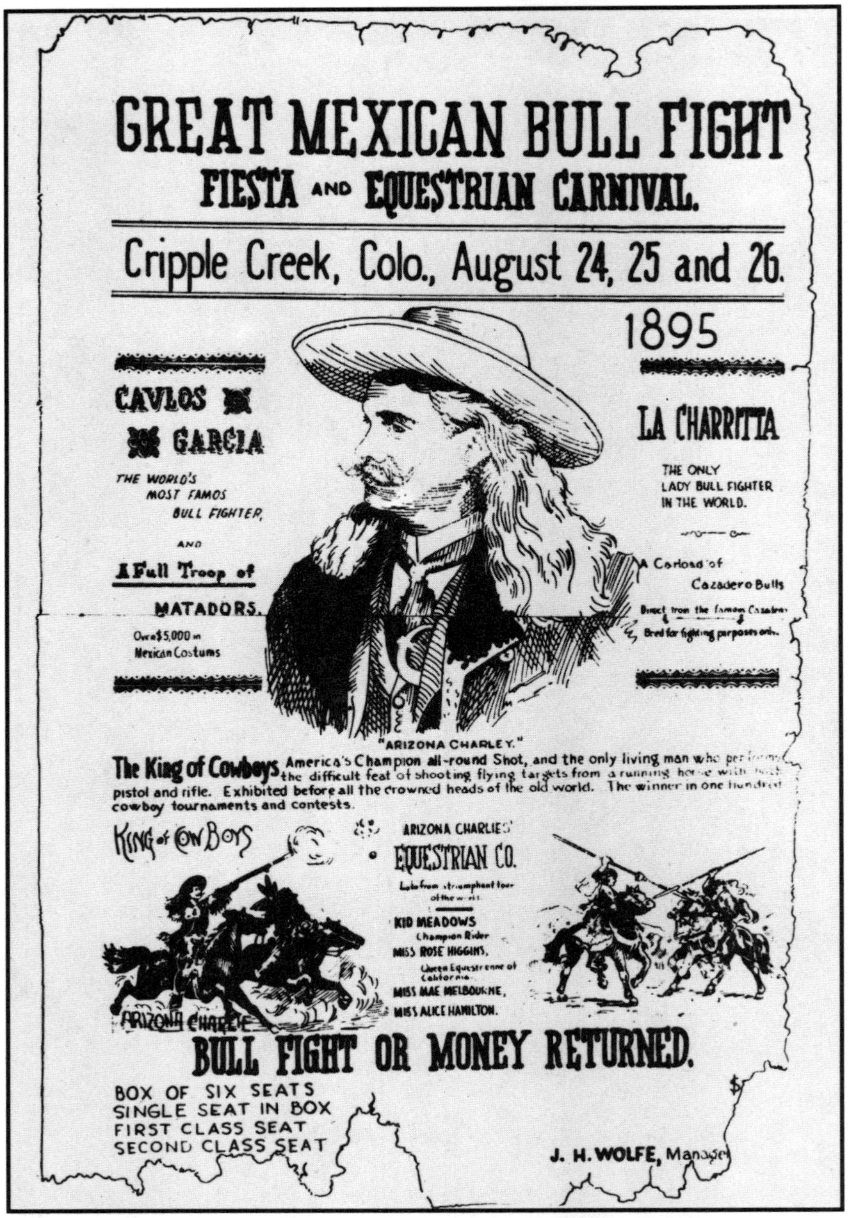

Poster from Bull Fight at Cripple Creek

Wolfe continued to "wave the red flag" in the face of his opponents, and announced he would kill five bulls on Sunday. He proved the Sheriff powerless, saying he would give his show and pay his fines. Then he added insult to injury by announcing a fight to the finish between two burly barroom brawlers, Frenchy Osborne and Georgie Hall. The general impression was that Wolfe had the best of it.

Secretary Hill was condemning the Governor in Colorado Springs, Secretary Thompson was condemning Sheriff Bowers in Denver; and Governor McIntyre, upon learning of the Sheriff's tactics, said, "If I had the power, I would remove Sheriff Bowers. I don't believe it would be hard to find a man who would take his place and stop that fight." Then, the local press spoke very plainly about Agent Thompson: "In the bullfight he made the public believe that there was to be a fight, thus advertised what was considered in advance a fake, and then he lacked courage to act at the proper time."

Sunday morning had not been uneventful. Sheriff Brisbin arrived from the Springs at the Terminal Hotel to see what he could do. Manager "*don Jose*" Wolfe was there seemingly unattended, and Brisbin told him he was under arrest on a warrant sworn out by order of the Governor. But Joe said he was already under arrest and in the custody of Constable Sherman Bell, who suddenly showed up on the scene and proclaimed, "This is my prisoner, don't let anyone interfere." The two walked out of the hotel without any protests from Brisbin. Joe's bodyguards fell in around him, and they all ambled across the street to the headquarters of the reception committee. The news hit the streets and caused intense excitement.

Charlie was busy with his duties at the bull ring, but warrants were also issued for the arrest of the Meadows Brothers, as well as for the Mexicans. Joe put a constable in charge of each of them with instructions to "let no sheriff or deputy take them under any circumstances." And to show the constables he meant business, each carried a six-shooter in case of determined interference.

"We have the whole town and the whole district with us," Mayor King announced. "This fight must go on today and nobody must interfere." His sentiments were echoed unanimously.

Deputy Sheriff Brisbin, surrounded by a huge crowd, stood outside the headquarters tent while all this was taking place. He had temporarily given up taking *el Presidente* into his custody. Then he declared to a man wearing a constable badge, "I tell you this is not going on today, and nobody is going to set foot on those grounds. I am acting under the direction of the Governor and will have a force here to stop it. I don't propose to be bluffed by a lot of fake constables. I mean what I say."

Joe did not want any more interruptions, so he and Brisbin and some of his backers met in the parlor of the hotel across the street for a conference. Rumors quickly spread that everything was settled, with "*don Jose*" submitting to arrest on conspiracy, and with the understanding that bond would be accepted for his appearance at Colorado Springs. This was given and ended the pitifully weak attempt of the El Paso County authorities to put a stop to the Sunday fights scheduled the next day.

This summer Sunday scene presented in Beaver Park was unparalleled in America. Gillett was fairly run over with people. Even the Gold Coach, which had taken part in the Flower Festival, pulled into Gillett with a big load of people. Some pretty bonnets and gay parasols were on display. Men, women and children were out for a holiday.

Once his legal entanglements and precautionary measures were settled, Joe went ahead superintending arrangements at the bull ring with his partner, Charlie. The day was beautiful as usual and the gates were thrown open. The band began a concert and the crowd started to arrive. Still fearing trickery of some sort, the constables kept watching developments very closely. On the elevated seats in back of Joe's box was row after row of men wearing salmon-colored badges, bearing the words, "Deputy Marshal." "You are going to have good sport this afternoon and need fear no trouble," Joe announced to them.

It was almost 3:30 p.m. when Charlie rode into the ring on his white charger. Doffing his *sombrero,* he made a little speech, which ended with a statement that was received with prolonged cheers: "I have promised the county officials that we will kill one bull this afternoon and will fight three or four more. The authorities will allow this and I am going to fulfill my promise to them and propose to see that they shall do the same for me."

Charlie had heard that the officers of the Humane Society were present and, if so, he "wished them to make themselves known." He also called upon Deputy Sterling, who responded and came up in front of the manager's box. There were groans and cries from all over the ring at his appearance, and during his opening words, yells and cries filled the air; but, as he finished, yells changed to cheers. "If the members of the Colorado Humane Society are here," he queried, "let them come and represent themselves. If Mr. Hill is here, let him come and represent himself, as I am not a Humane Society officer." Hill was conspicuously absent, and no other representative was present. Sheriff Bowers notified Governor McIntyre that morning that he was ill and confined to his bed. Neither Hill nor Bowers wanted to be in Gillett where the work was to be done. Besides, an election was to be held in El Paso County that fall and Bowers was a candidate.

At once Sterling crossed over to the east side of the bull ring, and at the same instant, *el Presidente's* solid phalanx of 100 men in back of his throne arose. They were immediately sworn in by Justice Burton as deputy marshals of the town of Gillett to preserve order in the bull ring. Guns were "thick as blackberries." The next moment Marshal Ricken served a warrant on "*don Jose*" Wolfe, charging him with "beating, wounding and maltreating" dumb animals.

"I'm your prisoner," Wolfe said, without looking around. This cleared everything so the fight could proceed, and the crowd settled back to await the most promised Mexican sport. It was not interrupted in any way, nor was the Sheriff nor Deputy heard from at any time during the afternoon. They were too busy watching the show.

The first three bulls were so docile they could not get any fight out of them. The fourth bull fought very little before being killed. In no way had they taken the place of real Mexican fighting bulls. The fight between Frenchy Osborne and Georgie Hall did not happen. Everyone had paid to see both entertainments, since Joe was losing money, he announced a special admission of $2.50 would be charged to see the fight. The audience was disgusted at the change of program—and walked out. "The few that were left were not enough to pay for one black eye, much less a finished fight," it was reported.

With Wolfe taken care of, Sheriff Brisbin turned his attention to the rest of them. He arrested Charlie and Kid, the Mexicans, and the backers, Weinberg and Sherman Bell. A heated conflict of authority almost caused bloodshed, when Deputy Hawkins arrested Charlie earlier in the day.

Cripple Creek Bull Fight, 1895

Photo #42
Cripple Creek Bull Fight, 1895

Cripple Creek Bull Fight, 1895

Charlie compromised the matter by agreeing to appear before the Justice of the Peace in Colorado Springs for a trial. *La Charrita* was in no way accused. In fact, she was pampered and coddled by the officers of the law.

Monday's fights did not happen. When the time came, only 200 people were in attendance and there was not enough fight in the bulls to maintain interest. Those who came were curious and wanted to see what the ruckus was all about. The probability of interference was the greatest drawing card—as most came to see a good brawl.

District Attorney Blackmer was determined that Joe should be severely punished and not escape from justice. He also wanted to "make it warm" for the gang of "toughs" whom Joe had made deputy marshals and who prevented him and the sheriff from doing their duty. He charged all of them with conspiracy.

Things were going rough for Joe, for he was some $3,000-$5,000 behind in the show, nevertheless, he had the satisfaction of staging a successful, authentic Spanish bullfight—where three bulls were killed strictly according to Spanish bullfight rules, and against the wishes of the Secretaries of Agriculture and Treasury, the American Humane Society, and the Churchmen of Colorado Springs.

The people at that end of the county were mad for having their "fun" stopped, and promised to get even. Their idea was that under the laws of the State, the spectators in an affair of that kind "were just as guilty" as the principals. There were quite a few officials who "went up to camp on business" while the bullfights were going on, and who showed up inside the arena while the killing of the bulls was in progress. Their names were all put on a list and warrants served on them.

Wolfe agreed on Saturday to settle his $1,200 bond in Justice Saxton's Court. Then Francis Hill managed to prosecute all of them. District Attorney Blackmer filed a complaint that charged Joe Wolfe, Jose Morrero, Antonio Sentrea, Sherman Bell, F. W. Weinberg, and ye Meadows Brothers, on the 24th day of August, 1895, in El Paso County, for unlawfully tormenting and killing "one" bull. They all spent Wednesday, August 28th in jail in Colorado Springs. They were a melancholy looking bunch. Charlie's hair was bunched up and held with pins, as he stalked impatiently about his cell--in the black cape which Joe had surrendered to him, rakishly draped over his shoulders. He thought it looked and fit him much better. With crest fallen expression, Kid's head sank like a rock into his hands as he sat morose and silent in a chair, hardly looking up. Charlie was unflappable, and always seemed to "roll with the punches," but Kid's nature was more reserved.

The three Mexicans sat alone talking to their manager. Mae, *la Charrita* and Rosalie came to console them with a basket of fruit, and a beautiful array of dark-eyed *Señoritas*, who admired the dash, charm and bravery of the American and Mexican bullfighters, peered longingly at the men as they sat squirming in their cells. Senator Casimiro Barela, the Mexican Counsel, arrived from Trinidad and held a consultation with the Mexicans before their cases came up that afternoon. Charlie and Constable Sherman Bell, both under bond, were interested spectators in the courtroom. Their best wishes were for the poor devils. Only Sentrea spoke English. Only he, if any of them, knew what he was getting himself into.

When the interpreter asked them if they were guilty, they replied, "*Si, Señor*," with the exception of Sentrea, who said in good English, "Guilty." The judge asked them if they would plead guilty, knowing the maximum fine was $250, and a year in the county jail—if he desired to inflict it. They replied they did. The Senator then addressed the court stating that he thought the men were more "sinned against" than "sinning," ignorant of the laws of this country, and unfamiliar with American customs. In their country, he said, it "was a creditable matter, rather than a disgrace," to engage in such sport. He went on to explain that when a contract is signed for a fight in their country, it is executed through the official who corresponds with the mayor in that country. It has been represented to these men that Joe Wolfe was that "great man" who had the authority to go ahead with the fight.

Mr. Blackmer stated that when he looked into the two partners' cases, he was convinced that they were the ones who had indeed done the sinning. He did not condone the offense committed by the Mexicans, "but punishment should not be harsh," and the defendants must pay the cost of the case which amounted to $97 against Morrero, and $105 against the others. The men had to remain in the county jail until all fines had been paid. Morrero was able to pay his; *la Charrita* was there with the money. Morrero then bid "*hasta la vista* " and quickly departed for Chihuahua, where he was scheduled to fight on Sunday. He was a hero there, where his pockets were full of money and his queer-looking hat full of presents. The bullfights were a grand symphony.

Charlie, Kid, Weinberg, and Bell, paid their fines, but Joe fought his because he wanted to show that there was no law against bullfights in Colorado. "He went around as chipper and hopeful as though he had not just scored a monumental failure," reported the local press. "I'll give another bullfight," he boasted, "as soon as people quiet down a little from this one." Charlie did not share his sentiments. He would have been off his mental reservation, and the Mexicans probably felt the same. But Joe's boast never materialized. He still had the twenty-year lease on the land, but his improvements—amphitheatre, fences, cattle sheds, judge's stand and ticket office—were all torn down by his creditors to satisfy their claims. This action made the land valueless for his intended use. Joe left Cripple Creek ahead of other creditors, winding up later in New York where he opened a steak house.

Secretary Thompson Has His Day

Garcia and Sentrea were still behind bars, and Charlie felt somewhat responsible for their predicament. He vowed he would help them by giving a Wild West performance at the Cheyenne Mountain Country Club, much to the consternation of the Humane Society. He paid the two fines, and the Mexicans were released. The performance was a monumental success; so he repeated the performance at the Denver Wheel Club Park, where vainglorious Charlie billed himself as "straight from the bush, and a grand specimen of the real cowboy."

To show his regard for the American cowboy, Garcia remained in town for the last exhibition and performed with Charlie in his bull-teasing acts. When it came time for the performance to begin, unexpected excitement and furor was demonstrated when Secretary Thompson of the Humane Society considered it his duty to follow Charlie's trail, to be on the grounds during the thrilling cowboy's show—even though Charlie assured him there would be no cruelty. However, he was there and in a position where he could "hop" into the arena at the slightest call for his services. Unabashed, Charlie was ready for him.

As advertised, Charlie's show consisted of exhibitions of rifle marksmanship, bucking bronco riding, chariot races, feats in the saddle and other similar acts, along with lassoing and tying bulls. He felt none of these exhibitions should offend anyone—nor be of any concern to Thompson.

At about four o'clock, six savage-looking bulls were driven into the arena in the center of the park; the bulls created considerable devastation to the bicycle track by pawing the ground before being induced to enter the field. The crowd thought this hilarious, and settled back to see the famous cowboy's greatest achievement. After skirmishing around the bulls several times, Charlie selected a vicious-looking animal from the herd, and dashing toward it, swung his lasso high over the animal's head. The other bulls, in a mad frenzy, scattered in all directions; the one selected making straight for the fence. Charlie spurred his horse and nearly caught up to him; with a loud hurrah, he threw his lasso. His first effort was fruitless, but he quickly gathered in his rope and made another throw which succeeded in catching the angry bull. After allowing the bull to run around the field awhile, Charlie, with a few dexterous movements of his horse, finally landed the bull heavily to the ground while the crowd yelled itself hoarse. Descending, Charlie approached the kicking beast and tied his legs fast together amid a roar of applause. Leaving the bull on the ground, he hastily mounted his horse and rode again for the herd. When he got about half way across the field, he noticed a commotion in front of the grandstand. It was Secretary Thompson of the Humane Society. Cane in hand, and with a determined look on his face, he made rapid strides toward the Arizona cowboy. At Thompson's call, Charlie reined in his animal and dismounted. In a calm manner Thompson informed Charlie, "You have violated the rules of the Humane Society, and must consider yourself under arrest."

Charlie was not so calm. In fact he was hotter than the hubs of hell. "I haven't violated your rules," he said in a loud voice, "and I want to proceed with my performance, let go of me."

But Thompson held on to Charlie's arm "with a grasp that would have done credit to Sandow." "You're under arrest, show or no show," Thompson demanded. Charlie gave him a vicious look and Thompson raised his trusty cane at the cowboy in a threatening manner—and sneered. Ye "buccaneer of the bull pen" finally let himself be led to the grandstand, followed by at least 100 admirers who rushed pell mell over the benches to see the scuffle. When they got outside the gate, Charlie stopped and announced to the spectators that "Although I am temporarily out of the show, the performance will continue, so everyone keep your seats." Then he turned to Thompson and said, "Let me go over to the office, and if you say you have me under arrest, I'll make matters smooth again."

Reluctantly, Thompson allowed him to go, but he stayed close to his side and carried his trusty cane with a firm grasp. Charlie, who had gotten used to this sort of treatment, displayed exceptional foresight when he took steps to have everything in readiness—a bondsman present with paper and ink. He never missed a trick. Actually, the bond was signed long before the performance began. That the paper, ink, and bondsman were on the spot when Charlie needed them was a cause for much comment among the bystanders, as well as a big surprise for Thompson. Charlie proceeded with his show after a few moments' delay.

Walking into the arena, he was met with prolonged applause. Bowing and doffing his *sombrero* in an elegant manner, he said to the audience, "Ladies and gentlemen! You notice I have been put to a little inconvenience, but I assure you it will not be repeated. I have secured a bondsman and have $100,000 at my back for all the bonds that they can bring me! I can, if necessary, give a bond for every bull, but that would be too much trouble, besides causing you considerable delay."

Thompson looked on as Charlie spoke—and even smiled at the last remark. Charlie elected not to proceed with the bull-catching part of the program. Instead, he told the crowd, he would water a vicious bull snorting in his pen close to the grandstand. The Secretary also was against this act and moved to the edge of the corral—while the spectators all rose and cheered Charlie on. Charlie looked for a water pail, while Thompson became the center of a crowd—some hissing, and others praising him for his pluck. Thompson had come under severe criticism for his lack of authority during the Cripple Creek affair but now seemed to be working overtime to cover his mistakes.

Several wheelmen were present including the well-known Jack Davis. Davis was thoroughly disgusted with the way the Secretary had discharged his duty—and came out and said so directly to Thompson. The crowd grinned as the Secretary turned and walked over to the corral again. Finally, Charlie found a pail for the water, and bowing to the crowd in his most theatrical manner, made an effort to enter the corral gate. But Thompson was there, and endeavored to keep Charlie from going in. By this time Charlie was looking for gore. He brushed the official away and triumphantly made for the bull. His objective was to use a large, colored blanket which he held in his hand; shake it in the animal's face, to show the audience how dexterously he could avoid being caught by the bull's two-inch horns, while placing the water where he could get it.

Thompson was thoroughly riled at this juncture, and in spite of his warnings to desist from entering the corral—owing to the viciousness of the bull—Thompson made a line straight for ye plainsman, while Charlie stood pat alongside the animal. Thompson evidently miscalculated his distance from the corral gate. The bull did not. The bull raised his head—then lowered it, and with a low snort, made a move as if to approach Thompson, leaving Charlie for the last. This move took the Secretary quite by surprise and he regained the gate at a fast clip, while the crowd squealed with delight. This turn of events delighted ye cowboy Charlie, protected as he was by the vicious bull. Then

Thompson, now that he had gotten that far, was determined to go the entire distance in spite of the bull or anything else; he had an image to defend. By a little maneuvering, Charlie was almost in Thompson's grasp, and the Secretary made a grab for him. Thompson failed to get a good hold and Charlie dodged to the other side of the bull. Thompson followed closely but was totally unmindful of the powerful bull with his evil disposition.

The Secretary finally caught Charlie, but Charlie struggled hard while Thompson raised his trusty cane most threateningly. Ye plainsman was thoroughly riled, and with clenched fists made an effort to "thump the pudding" out of him and settle matters at once. But Thompson was ready for him—and Charlie's blow was not landed. Then the obnoxious little man signaled to two detectives, who marched Charlie out of the gate, but not before Charlie let fly with the pail in his grasp. The water landed fully in Thompson's face. Charlie figured further fighting was useless. A tremendous crowd followed him as Charlie was put in a car between two sleuths. Carlos Garcia occupied a rear car. They were followed by at least 100 men and boys who clung to the back and sides of the horse-drawn vehicles.

Those entertainers who were left at the park continued with the programme, but the evening's performance was canceled. On the way to the justice's office, Charlie informed the officers that he had been granted permission by Chief of Police Goulding to water the bull, and thought his actions were perfectly all right. He was taken before Justice Cater and was given bail in the sum of $300 for his appearance. Garcia was also admitted to bail. The charge in both cases was cruelty to animals. H. H. Blonger signed all three bonds. After signing his bond, Charlie requested permission to swear out a writ of habeas corpus against Agent Thompson for interfering with his show, but was told he would have to wait until the next morning. Several days later Judge Crowell dismissed all charges against Charlie in the Police Court. Ye cowboy had gotten off scot-free once again. By this time he had cooled his heels and apparently dropped the charges against Thompson.

During the time Charlie was around the Denver Wheel Club Park, he completely mastered the Winchester from a bicycle after one month's practice. Crack wheelmen had said they would "give him six months," then predicted he would "give it up as too big an undertaking." But the Arizona man thought differently; no one had ever been able to convince Charlie some things were impossible. When he was ready, he gave a private performance to Colonel Stockings and his friends which proved all of them wrong. While riding at a four-minute pace around the bicycle track, Charlie shot eggs and glass balls as fast as they were thrown into the air with a heavy Winchester, without once touching the handle bars, or, it was reported, "with as much ease as Buffalo Bill could from terra firma."

Before leaving Colorado Springs, Charlie produced without any interference one more Wild West exhibition. His show was "under a cloud because of the Gillett affair," said the press, but they were given a grand reception. The fact that he lived up to his reputation is verified by these kind words from the press:

"Arizona Charlie, the Winchester Wizard, was the feature of the day. His marksmanship appeared little short of marvelous. Mounted on a galloping pony, he followed his brother, Kid Meadows, circling about the field, and shot eggs offhand as tossed into the air. Small dirt balls, barely perceptible to the eye 50 yards away, were dissolved into clouds of dust as rapidly as they could be thrown. In this performance, Arizona Charlie used two rifles. Mr. Meadows is not the debonair, slender young scout of the novel. He is as tall as a two-story building with a basement, and his figure shows strength in every line. His hair is closely cropped, contrary to dime-novel tradition. In his corduroy suit and wide *sombrero,* seated astride a gaily comparison pony, he appears the lineal descendent of the centaurs. His riding is as perfect as his rifle shooting.

"Arizona Charlie, and his brother, Kid Meadows, ride like centaurs, shoot like centaurs, and like no others but the Meadows Brothers."

Charlie's hair was not really close-cropped; it was pinned up under his sombrero. The notoriety surrounding the affair at Gillett worked wonders with the popularity of ye plainsman. During the time he was in Colorado Springs, he won new laurels and the medal for the "all-round cowboy contest." Charlie's prestige was enormous.

Before the show left the Springs, J. J. Harris, a Denver man who was well known as a ball player with numerous friends and admirers, engaged Charlie and his show to perform with him at Rover Park in Pueblo, Colorado. Harris brought along his fine string of racing ponies, and also booked Professor Ivy Baldwin, as well as others for an exhibition.

The local law officers were warned ahead of time to "look out for an invasion of Gillett bullfighters into Pueblo County." So when Harris announced the exhibition, including glass-ball shooting by Arizona Charlie, there was considerable excitement in police and sheriff circles. Harris had a somewhat difficult time getting a license because of the Gillett affair, and was required to pay a $100 guarantee that there would be no cruelty. Also, Harris thought it about time for officials to "stop interfering with a legitimate enterprise." "More interference at this time," he said, "would be looked upon by the public as a political trick to catch votes."

Charlie and Kid were conspicuous on the streets—as they moved about taking care of the business connected with their show. They were constantly followed by a crowd absorbed in curiosity over their previous notoriety. One reporter inquired as to Charlie's height, to which Charlie replied: "I am two inches taller than Lincoln, who was accustomed to saying he was 'six-foot-four and never wore socks.'"

The following endorsement from the Lake County Branch of the Colorado Humane Society finally satisfied all criticism of Charlie's show, when they said:

"To all agents of the Colorado Humane Society, and to whom it may concern:

When Mr. Meadows, 'Arizona Charlie' arrived in Leadville announcing his intentions to soon give a Wild West exhibition in this city, a bad impression, to draw it mildly, had preceded him. On October 7, I sought to interview him, asking information of the character of the proposed entertainment. When same was outlined and discussed, I requested the act of roping, riding, and tying down of steers be omitted.

Being satisfied with a promise, the county commissioners were approached; the case stated that the obtained promise was to back me in every reasonable particular. The Sheriff of Lake County also agreed to have a posse on the ground to stop any act that I considered cruel.

I was present at the exhibitions on October 13 and 14, with a captious spirit and a desire or inclination to make trouble. Every act was closely watched, and the animals were closely inspected, but I am pleased to report no opportunity for interference presented itself. Mr. Meadows' promise regarding the steers was religiously kept.

I write this not to commit the Lake County Branch to any endorsement of the humanity of Wild West shows, or exhibitions of that character, in general, but that the facts regarding the Colorado Humane Society's part in Mr. Meadows' Leadville engagement may be easily accessible, and no misconception in regard to it obtained. I am bound to speak for the man as I found him.

Yours respectfully,

Jno. Whitton, Agent
Lake County Branch
Colorado Humane Society"

Following his Pueblo and Leadville appearances, Charlie took his show to Hot Springs, Arkansas, the land where his forefathers lived. A complete Wild West show was given, and he threw in a few chariot races with break-neck specialties—as an interlude. The audiences accepted his show in its entirety, welcoming Charlie so heartily as to approach an ovation. The audiences were astounded at his expertise with the Winchester, and he petrified them by shooting glass balls nestled in Mae Melbourne's hair with chilling accuracy. With a fleet wild horse, he surpassed the most preposterous exaggerations. But during one *William Tell Act*, Charlie failed to hold his head steady and came close to joining his ancestors—when a bullet meant for the apple atop his plumage, instead plowed a superficial furrow half across the cowpuncher's scalp. This was the only significant wound he was ever known to receive.

Arizona Charlie, Crackshot from a Bicycle, 1896

Denver Wheel Club Park

At home his family was experiencing difficult times. A severe Depression and the Panic of the 90's, still raging across the nation, had left great numbers of people destitute. Only the year before, the tariff had been removed from cattle, allowing Mexican cattle free entry into the United States; and, like many cowmen, Charlie's brother-in-law, Tom Beach, went broke. Tom herded his cattle to Holbrook, Arizona, then shipped them to Fort Morgan, Colorado by rail, and sold them for a few dollars. Always a Democrat before, Tom was heard to say, "Fried rats—and stewed cats—are good enough for Democrats."

After the murderous attack by the Apaches on his family, Charlie had made two promises—one to himself, and one to his mother—to avenge the deaths of his father and brother, Henry; and for his mother, to look out for the welfare of the other members of his family. Thirteen long years had passed and nothing had been accomplished regarding his Indian depredations claim. He wrote the following letter to Judge DeWitt from the Hotel Irma in Hot Springs, Arkansas:

Judge DeWitt
Washington, D.C.

Dear Sir:

I am the administrator of the J. M. Meadows estate, Tonto Basin, Arizona, which has a claim of $34,000 in depredations committed July 15, 1882. I was unable to meet you when you were in Phoenix last winter. I am very anxious to prove up this claim as the witnesses are passing away, and a number of heirs are sadly in need of their portion. The claim is a very good one, and since the father and oldest brother were killed at the time by the Indians, many of the heirs have been compelled to care for themselves. Please let me hear from you.

C. Meadows

nent was apparently unexpected by the
people who crowded into the grand-
ds, but the cowboy evidently antici-
d a row of some sort and made prep-

age look at the secretary, who ha
vated his cane in no compromising
ner and sneered. He allowed hims
be led to the grand stand, follow
a hundred of the crowd who had

SECRETARY THOMSON ARRESTING ARIZONA CHARLIE.

tions accordingly. Secretary Thomson
the Humane society acted as the stick
ich was thoroughly thrust into the hive
bees, and the consequences were some-
ng not on the programme. The secre-
y considered it his duty to be on the
unds during the thrilling cowboy show,

pell mell over the benches to see the
When near the outside gate Charlie si
fied his desire to tell the spectators
although he was temporarily out of
show, the performance would cont
right along, and for the people to
their seats. Suddenly the cowboy stop
"Let me go over to the office," said

Arizona Charlie, Article from a Newspaper

Arizona Charlie's Summer Attraction

Charlie Meadows, Hot Springs, Arkansas, 1896

CHAPTER 16

1896-1897
MORE INDIAN TROUBLES

Charlie returned to Arizona early in 1896 and again found the Tonto Basin torn with turmoil. The Cibicue and Canyon Creek Apaches were on the warpath. Many had joined Juan Dazin's band, subsisting mostly by depredating upon adjacent ranchers and "leveling tribute" against freighters crossing the reservation. All this trouble directly affected Charlie as he now had a large herd of stock, in partnership with fellow cowman, Bill Brodie.

Meanwhile, bands of Indians roamed the countryside making threats against the lives of ranchers. The condition became so desperate that the settlers considered banding together for protection or abandoning their ranches altogether. A call was made for all available men to join in apprehension of the rampaging renegades. Charlie, never missing a good fight, quickly joined the scouts and lawmen in their fight to preserve lives and property.

"Serious trouble developed when three deputies went to Chief Cooley's camp (brother of Nantangotayz) to arrest the offending Indians," reported the *Arizona Silver Belt* of February 8, 1896. Unsuccessful, the trio tried to leave peacefully to seek help from the military. The Indians, "bent on mischief," gathered closely around the officers, with Chief Nantangotayz attempting to grab the reins of Deputy Ketcherside's horse. Failing this, he grabbed Deputy Voris' bridle with one hand; his Winchester, which hung from the side of his saddle, with the other; and attempted to draw his gun from its holster. Deputy Voris grabbed the Indian's wrist but could not break his hold on the gun. About this time, other Indians standing on an adjacent hillside fired a shot. Realizing the situation was desperate, and knowing the Chief had the better of him, Deputy Voris, drew his six-shooter and fired. Nantangotayz threw his head back in time for the bullet to miss him, but Deputy Voris was quicker, and placing the gun against the Indian's breast, fired again. This ended the bloody career of the Indian who met his retribution in his attempt to murder the Gila County officers, "and his summary death was cause for rejoicing all over the territory," reported the press.

The Indians projected a very ugly disposition from that time on. Chief Cooley made the threat that—if the men who killed his brother "were not locked up"—he was going to be "a very bad Indian." During the cleanup of this serious situation, Charlie helped even the score with the Apache, being directly involved in the demise of Chief Juan Dazin. Although Charlie professed to be the "King of Scalpers," and left his heirs a buckskin poke full of Apache scalps, he was also a past master at leg-pulling. Also, it is likely a good part of them were purchased; it amused him to play on the tenderfoot's innocence.

This was also the year that daring Frank Prothero, famous tracker, apprehended the murderers of the Gribble party, who were carrying gold bullion from the famous Vulture Mine to Phoenix. From the beginning Frank out-trailed the Indian trackers, and never stopped, often going alone for days at a time without eating, until he ran the murderers down to earth; he killed their leader, Innocente Valenzuela, and recovered the $8,000 bar of gold bullion. Frank was never afraid of having a "few button holes worked into his carcass," it was said.

Scenes of rapine and slaughter by the hostile Indians, as well as the lawless white man's rule, prompted Charlie and Kid to consider looking for property in Arapahoe County, Colorado. Charlie concluded that judgment would be awarded soon—because Congress had appropriated all that money for Indian depredations. The Meadows Brothers still had stock, numbering 800 head on Sidella Creek, which Charlie and Kid intended to move to Colorado.

Welcome News at Last

On January 12, 1897, word finally came through from the Assistant Attorney General, Harry Peyton, that Charlie's long-standing claim amounting to $34,000 had been considered by the Department of Justice, and would be settled sometime in the latter part of February. Charlie heartily welcomed this news. But, as it turned out, it wasn't that easy; witnesses had to be examined on his behalf. Charlie submitted the following names to District Attorney Dewitt: Deputy Sheriff Frank Prothero; Chief of Scouts, Al Sieber; Fred Platten, soldier of "F" troop of the 6th Cavalry; John Hicks, William Houston, L.P. Nash, Robert Sigsby, Colonel Chaffee, Ed Tewksbury, J.W. Frakes (a noted bullwhacker of his day), and brother, Jake Meadows, lawman.

Ed Tewksbury had been released from jail after serving three years, having been tried three times for the murder of Tom Graham. John Rhodes was also a suspect. Tom Graham was the last member of the feuding Grahams, and Ed was now the lone survivor of the Tewksbury clan who were involved in the Pleasant Valley War.

The Court of Inquiry was scheduled for May. Charlie put on some Wild West exhibitions in Yuma during the interim. Kid was gored badly during one bull-teasing event, and Rosalie urged him to give up the perilous sport. Mae, warm and comfortable to be around, enjoyed life shared with the Meadows Family, as well as with her own family in Santa Cruz. Mae never pressured Charlie into getting married and played her hand carefully. Her skin was exquisite, she bathed it in whipping cream; her lips were red, like the sweet wine of life; and her voice was soft and caressing, like the south wind in the moonlight—but Charlie was not ready to take the big step.

Fiesta de Los Angeles

An urgent request came for Arizona Charlie's Wild West to join with the festivities at the Annual *Fiesta de Los Angeles*, with performances scheduled to begin April 20. This gave Charlie enough time to accept before depositions were to begin in May. He responded with enthusiasm.

Everyone had heard of Charlie's prowess as a bullfighter. He did not wish to disappoint them so he attempted to get Carlos Garcia, along with a carload of Mexican fighting bulls—but that part fell through for obvious reasons. Even though a genuine bullfight had been advertised, a record crowd came out to witness a lot of fun. Fun is what they got. The crowd, thirsty for gore, expected to see a real bullfight when they came, but no one objected to the hilarious show presented. Although they might not have gotten what they came for—they were satisfied. The old Hassayamper managed to put together a show in record time.

The crowd, in good humor, told the Arizona man to "let 'er go." Charlie nodded to the boys in the truck who had been waiting for his signal. Immediately, the big, four-horse truck moved through the entrance gate and bore down upon the exhibition pen which stood right in the middle of the main enclosure. On the bed of the conveyance lay a shackled member of the mean bovine tribe. By another nod from Charlie, the truckman backed the lumbering vehicle into the exhibition pen, then "cut the thongs that held him and permitted him to stand forth in all his bullish beauty," reported the *Los Angeles Times*.

The jovial audience gave him a good, generous round of applause, but it was as "pearls cast before swine." The bull did not like what he saw and wanted none of it. He had no appreciation for bull-fighting society. He pawed up a few clouds of dust, kicked at the clouds a time or two, and then relaxed into stubborn inactivity. Charlie spurned the suggestion the bull might be suffering from "ennui."

Pending the loosening-up period, ye "head of the Arizona delegation" gave an exhibition of fancy shooting. Then Charlie broke glass balls stuck out on the ends of wires from Mae Melbourne's hair. Some spectators thought the pretty lady should have known better. But Mae trusted Charlie's expertise and did not exhibit any qualms during the performance.

The bull still didn't show any belligerent signs, so cowboy Charlie put a boy who wanted to get into the act on the back of a bucking horse. The boy was quickly bucked off into the dust, which the kid thought hilarious. This seemed to please the other cowboys, but only whetted the appetite of the audience for some real "cowboy gore." Then the crowd let out a clamorous cry for bull and blood.

The Arizona man was ever-ready to meet the demands of the public. He gave the order and five "bullfighters," leaping to the fore, looked through the cracks of the fence at the aloof bull—who did not seem to care. Then, one of Charlie's cowboys had the nerve to climb over the fence and flaunt a red rag in the bull's insolent face. One by one, the whole troupe of cowboys dropped in on him, and he still appeared not to care. Suddenly, wild excitement and great activity prevailed, as the crowd laid their money on the spirited bull. The animal suddenly had found himself a likely subject and charged the "red flaunters" up and down the pen at an accelerated clip. This action drew wild cheers from the audience. The regulation safety barriers saved the cowboys. Of course, the bull had no chance; but it must be said that he finally showed a willingness to fight, which was "ridiculously absent" in the ranks of his tormentors. Charlie's remark was, "It was all in the act, don'cherknow, all in the act."

Then Charlie introduced a "fighter" stuffed with straw until he "bulged like an inflated circus tent." The clown stumbled into the ring and fell, purposely, in the center. The crowd roared with delight. The enraged beast was upon him in an instant, and the funny man's retreat was covered with a shower of bearded wheat and old clothes. By then the bull was worked up into a frenzy, but the "bullfighters" did not want to carry the thing too far. Kid had already had a bad experience in Yuma, but he did gallop up and down in front of the spectators bestride the pride of some dairy farm. The bull seemed to enjoy it, and so did the crowd.

Charlie always concluded his performances at their height, so the Arizona man salaamed very low—and told the audience the show was over.

Hard Words to Accept

Back in Arizona for the examinations, the first witnesses in the government inquiry were Charlie, his brother, lawman Jake Meadows, and deputy Frank Prothero. Their testimonies were given between May 3-5, in the offices of Charlie's attorney, Frank Cox, in the Thibedo Building in Phoenix. DeWitt blasted Charlie with 309 questions and 20 redirected questions; his testimony took a day and a half.

The remaining witnesses testified at a later date, with final testimony given on June 7. Some of the witnesses could not be reached: Sigsby was away in Canada; William Houston had returned to Visalia, California; Chaffee was at Fort Leavenworth, Kansas; and L. P. Nash was in the mountains. These men were vital witnesses; Charlie could have used their testimonies.

Following examination of the others, District Attorney DeWitt, the man Charlie had hoped would bring his claim to fruition, instead embarked on a dragnet investigation bent with intentions of shooting holes in ye Arizona Man's claim.

In that "sly coyote's" report to Acting Assistant General Charlie Russell, Washington, D. C., the following words were taken from its content:

> "The claim was assigned to me with instructions to afford the claimant an opportunity to examine witnesses at Phoenix, Arizona. At that place the administer or claimant appeared and submitted the testimony of himself and witnesses, all of whom were by me carefully cross-examined. The claimant and one witness, to wit, Frank Prothero, had evidently schooled themselves to a systematic drilling, and to my chagrin, I was unable to make any considerable impression upon them in my cross-examination. I felt keenly the discomfiture, and concluded to go to the bottom of the alleged loss, feeling confident that a fraud of considerable proportions somewhere lurked in the premises. My examination of the two witnesses above mentioned, fixed with certainty every foot of the trail over

> which the stock was alleged to have been taken, and every milestone of the way over which animals were slain, so that in light of the disclosures herewith transmitted, in the form of affidavits, no possible avenue of escape is left open to the witnesses, either in modification or explanation of their testimony.
>
> Immediately after the claimant closed his case, I began a systematic dragnet investigation, and while often times being misled, at the expense of a tiresome trip and money, quite generally at all points found some clues of importance. I investigated at Phoenix, Tucson, and at Mesa; also at Buckeye, some forty miles across the desert by carriage from Tucson and all along the Gila Valley. At all of the places, especially Mesa and Buckeye, some general knowledge was obtained, not such as was especially sought after. I was in quest of some one or more persons, other than the soldiery, who had passed over the trail of the Indians, cattle and horses between the home of Meadows and Chevelon fork, the place of the last stand of the redskins, and spot where the battle was fought. It was between these points on the trail and on the battlefield where Meadows and the creature, Prothero, made their stand and the stock was slain.
>
> I have deemed it proper that a reasonable accurate photograph of the things and surroundings should be spread upon the record; to the end that the assistant who follows me may be spared the task which befell to my lot, and go the final overthrow of this bad claim well equipped.
>
> W. S. DeWitt
> District Attorney
> U.S. Government"

While this letter was discouraging, it was not as hopeless as a previous one Charlie had received sometime earlier, which read:

> Now comes the Assistant Attorney General and, after leave of the court first had and obtained, for plea to declaration herein says that the claimant ought not to have and maintain his aforesaid action for the reason that at the date of the depredation alleged the defendant Indians were not in amity with the United States; and the court is therefore without jurisdiction to hear and determine this cause. And this the defendants are ready to verify.
>
> Assistant Attorney General
> John G. Thompson

At any rate, Charlie's ire was thoroughly aroused. If this claim did not qualify, whose did? Charlie found that growing hair on an apple seemed easier than collecting this judgment. He ordered his attorney to try again because he did not give up easily.

The Family in Yuma

Tom and Maggie homesteaded their ranch in the Yuma Valley after the government opened up the land to settlers in 1897. Brother Jake helped clear the brush while Tom punched down a well and bolted on a pump. Then, the two men started to make adobes.

They cleaned off the ground and put down a post in the center of a twenty-foot circle. To this they attached a pole, with a heavy loop of wire around the post in the center. Double trees were hooked to each other with a stick in between, and a longer stick went to the top of the post that was over a long nail. This allowed the stick to go around holding the horses the same distance from the center at all times.

Buckets of water were pumped, carried out, and poured into the space the horses walked. The horses took a dim view of all this at first, but finally settled into making mud. The men scattered straw all around where the horses walked in the circle. Tom's young sons, Tom Jr., and Jess, thought this was to keep the horses' feet clean. Then the men tested the mud: if it was too stiff, water was added; and if it was too sloppy, dirt was added. Boards were cut for molds, about 16 inches by 10 inches, by 6 inches thick. Tom wanted to make sure the walls were thick enough to cool them from the torrid summer heat—and strong enough not to fall down. Willow saplings were laid on top, then covered with bunches of arrow weed—an inviting haven for the likes of a tarantula, or possibly a scorpion or two. The floor was then wet and tamped down. Tom and Jess were not quite sure they would like living in the mud this way.

Mobley and Jake went to the Southern Pacific yards and got a long railroad tie; they hitched it to four horses and dragged it over the land to break up the sage brush and creosote weeds, which, called "greasewood," grew as high as eight feet. This was the rich bottom land of the Colorado River. The *mesquite* trees were as large as oaks, which Tom cut into three-foot lengths, hauled to the pumping plant, and exchanged for his irrigation water, or traded for groceries at Sanguinetti's Store.

Charlie hoped and prayed the depredations money would come through soon to relieve his family of these desperate times.

About this same time, that old Chaparral Fox, Frank Prothero, struck gold in a big way some six miles from Adono Pump. Twenty feet of shaft showed a well-defined ledge five feet wide, ranging in value from $25-$150 per ton of free milling ore. Frank immediately put on a force of Phoenix men and began developing the "Yellow Log," the name for his new strike. Everything Frank did, made front-page news; this find was as big as any known in Arizona at that time.

Arizona Charlie in the Yukon

CHAPTER 17

1897-1899
AN ADVENTURE THAT MOVED THE WORLD

While Frank Prothero was digging out his Mother Lode, banner headlines were announcing the news of "Gold! Gold in the Klondike, tons of it!" History was dawning abruptly and momentously in the Yukon wilderness, and a whole new frontier lay open. News spread across the universe like a prairie fire. There was an instant stampede that moved the world. No other word could stir the souls of men, nor cause them to abandon their homes, families, fields and jobs. It was certain that a great gold rush of such proportions would never be repeated in all its wild, uninhibited action and color.

Because the entire world was suffering severe economic shock, the continent went insane with excitement. Ye Arizona man's depredations claim was quickly forgotten. The word "gold" held a certain seductive charm, one that stirred an uncontrollable wanderlust. The very scent of gold, and the romance of such an odyssey, served as a spur that drove him on to the perilous journey. He chomped at the bit to get started.

The Klondike was the last frontier for the Americans; it did not take Charlie long to formulate his plans. Charlie had no trouble convincing eight of his cattlemen friends to accompany him on this great adventure. Frank Prothero was not one of them, because he had already discovered his *El Dorado*.

"My party consisted of A. E. Ruff, Del Bishop, Bill Hempstead, Al Ford, D. Fischer, B. Anson, H. Beaudry, and A. Alkeveitch, one of the best assayers and mining experts on the coast," Charlie reported. "All of these men were experienced in woodcraft and inured to the hardships of the wilds. We planned our expedition carefully, allowing a wide margin for error." The trip represented the very summit of Charlie's hopes and dreams.

Mae, herself the daughter of a "49er," felt her pulse quicken with an ever-growing desire to make her way to the land of great riches, as both her father and Charlie's father had done many years earlier. Mae was a woman of dauntless courage, so, despite remonstrances from her friends, she joined Charlie's party along with two other women. Newspapers of that time indicate Charlie and Mae married sometime prior to this trip, though records of their union have never been found. Charlie's first wife, Marion Mae, fell out of his mind like a stone into a well.

Charlie made a hurried trip to San Francisco to purchase his outfit and arrange passage for a party of twelve. Included were 200 *burros* which, with the help of a crew of Mexicans and Indians, were gathered up along the Gila River bottom. A grubstake for two years, roughly 1,200 pounds per person, and several tons of supplies and equipment also were obtained for their journey. Other provisions included the essential tools well suited to a sporting man's itinerant life and flamboyant style—a rifle and a fancy pistol, and a generous supply of whiskey, dice and playing cards.

With their "war bags" packed with hard tack, coffee, dried beef and beans, the Arizona company left San Francisco on the steamer, *Coos Bay*, August 15, 1897, for Juneau, Alaska. This was one month and one day after the stampede began, when the steamship, *Elcelsior*, docked in San Francisco, loaded with the first gold from the richest placers in history. Their ship was packed to the gunwales with humans, animals, and cargo of every description. There were dogs, goats, oxen, horses and mules, and any other animal with four legs that could stand up and pull freight. Also, there were men of prominence with compelling ambition: bank presidents, brigadier generals, doctors and lawyers. There were tin-horn gamblers, confidence men, thieves and cut-throats. There were shopkeepers, sod busters, whores, camp followers and Arizona cowboys, all lured by the lust for that golden dust. Excitement was fever pitched.

Crowded conditions on the boat were deplorable; men and a few women huddled in a tightly packed, human cargo. The putrid odor of booze and sweaty, unwashed men assaulted the senses, with drinking and gambling heavy. Round after round of bawdy stories were told, and these were all Charlie's favorite pastimes.

At Juneau, Charlie transferred his gear to the steamer, *Queen,* for the awe-inspiring trip up the Lynn Canal's inside passage. The scenery was spectacular, with snowcapped mountains, heavy pine forest, rare birds, and cascading waterfalls—which helped ease the discomforts for the Arizona Company. After one night in Skagway, Charlie's outfit was taken by scow for the final lap to his destination of Dyea.

"Our first altercation occurred at Dyea, when I observed cargo being dumped helter-skelter into the flats of the bay," Charlie wrote. The Captain had refused to pay the exorbitant fee for lighterage to move cargo to the beach. Tempers flared, and "this Arizona man was compelled—at the point of my gun—to persuade the captain to unload my supplies according to contract."

There were many routes to the Klondike. The Alaska Exploration Company had offered direct passage by way of St. Michael and the Yukon River, but Charlie and his companions were a trifle late for that route. Those leaving after the first of August by that route were in danger of getting caught in the ice pack, when the Yukon River crawled into its icy grave for the winter. Then there was the "back door" route, overland from Edmonton, Canada; the "all-Canadian" route, via Ashcroft; and numerous other trails through Alaska. But most routes were wildly impractical, and there was no way of knowing how many lives were lost in their frenzied attempt to reach the goldfields.

Charlie and his companions chose the Dyea Trail, a few miles from Skagway, which was seldom closed; and the Chilkoot Pass, because the White Pass Trail out of Skagway was a "dead frost." "I had the biggest outfit of any man on the boat—and on the trail," he wrote.

Almost at the same time, Charlie learned that none other than Joe Wolfe's Cripple Creek accomplice, and Charlie's recent unwanted associate, confidence man Jefferson Randolph "Soapy" Smith, often called the "Wizard of Deceit," had arrived in Skagway with his cronies in crime: "Reverend" Bowers, Red Gibbs, Syd Dixon, George Wilder, "Slim Jim" Foster, "Kid" Jimmie Fresh, Van B. "Old Man" Tripplett, and Bill Saportas, all of whom had begun to set up their business geared to fraud and villainy. His facade of well-mannered demeanor, gentlemanly behavior, and personal fastidiousness, created increasing respect for Soapy from the unsuspecting townsfolk. "We'll dig our gold the easy way, from the pokes of successful sourdoughs," Soapy was known to have told his henchmen. Their paths never crossed, but a greenhorn Charlie was not; Soapy's cunning wit was no match for Charlie's dead shot. Soapy was well aware of this.

Conditions at Skagway and Dyea were tumultuous. The beaches were piled high with outfits, spewed from hundreds of boats of every description that had docked at their shores, some of which held more water than cargo. Each wild-eyed human being, boiling over with excitement and in a frenzied rush to get started, had the same purpose in mind—to tame the fierce wasteland and take the gold. The Arizona Company suffered a long delay because of a scene of *chaos*.

Dawson, Yukon Territory

Dyea Trail, Alaska

Soapy Smith at His Bar, "Jeff's Place," Skagway, Alaska

The Soapy Smith Gang

While on the trail writing his letter home, Charlie said: "Before we left Arizona, I learned that *burros* were selling as high as $1,000. I had good intentions of being a rich man before reaching the goldfields. If the jacks sold well, my plan was to return to Arizona and get more, and run a little 'gold mine' of my own right there on the trail. Some I sold for $600, but then the packing business also paid well—good packers getting from $40 to $70 a day. If that proved practical, we planned to establish a shuttle service with a regular route from Dyea to Lake Lindeman." At this point everything looked relatively simple to Charlie.

They packed 200 pounds to the horse; the first fourteen miles were easy going through wooded, floral terrain. The trail crossed the gravely Taiya River bed in several places, then past Indian cabins visible through the dense foliage along an old logging road. Approximately 600 miles lay between them, Dawson City and the gold fields.

Glaciers were hanging precariously between the rocky crags and crevices of the breastwork of the mountains, only a few miles on this idyllic trail. The trail grew worse, the packs heavier, and the stream beds colder, deeper, swifter, and harder to cross over. "I ran a miner's supply store, including a restaurant and liquor dispensary in my big tent all along the trail," Charlie wrote. "I made a good deal of money on the trail, as much, I would imagine, as any poor shivering Klondike miner, and that covers a multitude of mishaps." His carefully swaddled liquor, in canvas-covered cases, "went for six bits a drink," and "meals at $2.00 each, horseshoe nails as high as $1.00, hard tack at 50 cents a cake, coffee from 75 cents to $1.00 a cup, were about the ruling prices. One of my men gave $7.50 for a cup of coffee on one special occasion, and we camped one night above timberline where stove wood cost $1.00 a stick." It rained constantly and a cold wind blew, but "several times I was compelled to refuse men room in my tent at $5.00 each for a night's lodging." They slept cold on the ground with only a little lumber and spruce boughs between them and the mud.

There were diversions to combat the germs of worry. A card sharp and a dead shot, Charlie, like the notorious John Wesley Hardin, entertained by "signing" playing cards with bullets, as odors of bacon, muddy coffee—and dung floated through the chilled air.

In their rush many of these indiscriminate-looking, frontier inefficients misjudged the enormity of the task; they came ill-prepared to withstand the hardships of the trail, and most were compelled to turn back. Minds were stretched and intellects challenged. It was survival of the fittest; there was no place for greenhorns.

"Our first and most terrifying experience occurred just below Sheep Camp, a very tough hole, the last major stop before ascending the treacherous and icy summit of the Chilkoot Pass—the last four miles rising 3,200 feet alone. Owing to an unfortunate conflict with a glacier, in which our outfit came out second best, it cost me a dollar a pound to bring my stuff over the pass by Indian packers," Charlie wrote.

For more than fifty years this glacier had been watched by early travelers as it hung precariously between jagged peaks, but it had to wait for the old Hassayamper to come along before it loosened its hold. It all came about when earlier, warm summer winds melted the middle of the glacier, forming a lake in its center, causing it to crack. Then, at 6:30 one morning, the heavy winter winds sheared off a section; with a deafening roar, a raging torrent of water, uprooted trees, and boulders were sent down the canyon with the speed of an express train, flooding out their sleeping camp. Paralyzed with bowel-loosening fear, Charlie, Mae, and the others barely escaped with their lives. Charlie lost much of his magnificent outfit, including his prized liquor supply and some of his pack animals, in the resulting flood. Three others, one a "cousin" named Choynski, were not so fortunate and paid with their lives, leaving the caskets of their souls to moulder in the quagmire. It was the worst fright of Charlie's life; neither wild bulls nor fierce Indians were a match for it. Some gave up the struggle here. Charlie, too, was weak in the knees. To go on required a considerable amount of endurance and determination, but nothing seemed to dampen his enthusiasm for this adventure. It was his driving will, and his feverish refusal to be denied, that made him so unique. He seemed to thrive on the romance that danger would bring.

Charlie bemoaned the fact that he lost his prized collection of hats and his valuable pistol. Most of their clothes were lost in the sea of mud, and their blankets were soggy with muck. "I was able to put together another outfit by buying out disheartened tenderfeet who turned back," he wrote. The tenderfoot had no chance without fool luck. "Undaunted, courageous Mae purchased an entire outfit for herself and that of two other men in our party. These men entered into a grubstake agreement with her by which they were to give her half of everything they made." With their resurrected spirits, they struggled on in a slow-moving chain—crammed between narrow passes, groaning under the weight of their packs, as they sloshed their way through sleet, slush and snow. Here stampeders began to drop weighty pieces, heavy skillets, kettles and the like, and it was here that many tired and work-worn horses perished for lack of food. Restless men began to grumble, as they plodded their way over a trail that could break a strong man's heart.

At the foot of the Scales, at the boulder-strewn base of the summit, their last camp was made before climbing the 30-degree, glaciated, forbidding crest of the Chilkoot Pass. Most of their gear went over the pass by Indian packers—up the 1,200 "golden stairs" hacked into the steep ice. If a man was too poor to hire a packer, he climbed the pass forty times before he got his outfit to the summit. It was marked here, then the weary soul slid down the icy slope for another load. By the time he returned, his gear was usually covered with deep snow.

It was actually easier to reach the summit in the winter, for the steep pass was a mass of jagged boulders that lay beneath the snow. Sliding down the opposite side was said to be the easiest part of the whole trip. Mae learned to pack a horse, and throw a hitch as well as any man. With the two other ladies and a few of the men with the horses, she went around the pass on horseback through hock-high snow, the longer Peterson route. "With our five tons of supplies composed principally of a trading outfit, with which I intended to do business with the Indians at Tagish Lake, we moved just 34 miles in three weeks; the relaying of our gear, with each man carrying a 70-pound pack, swelled our hike to 200 miles, and it took eight men and seven horses to do it at that," Charlie said.

Beyond this treacherous pass, in a meadow-like valley, began a chain of glistening lakes and rivers. Borne of the snow melt from the glaciated peaks they had crossed, provided them with a waterway to navigate. The water then grew into the roaring Yukon River. "There at a body of water called Long Lake, a most unfortunate experience developed when my horses all died in one night from the poisonous grass," Charlie wrote. On the snow-covered shores of Lake Bennett and Lindemann, the greatest tent cities in the world sprang up. Here the second stage of their trek began.

Chilkoot Pass

Chilkoot Pass

At these lakes, the two connected by a short, violent stream called "One Mile River," men labored frantically building sawmills. "The greatest obstacle for us here," Charlie said, "was work, of which we had a long siege." His company worked at the height of their endurance—and in a frenzy of haste, building boats, fashioning oars, and hoisting sails to move their outfits through the series of lakes. Nails, pitch and oakum and other essentials for boat building were part of every standard pack.

The Arizona Company felled their own trees, split their own lumber, and built a fleet of three boats to float them north toward fortune and prosperity. "They were the greatest on the Yukon," Charlie wrote, as "no one had their equal, and no one left the lakes with as many as three boats. The first two freighters capable of carrying 5,000 pounds were the *Arizona* , the *Santa Cruz*, (Mae's home town), and the passenger ship the *Melbourne*.

"An evidence of prosperity presented itself at Lake Bennett when I refused an offer to throw hitch on thirty-one horses. At these lakes everyone had gone into winter quarters, and it was thought next to suicide to try to reach Dawson before breakup in the spring. But the Arizona Company, with the strength of desperation in a mad race with the ice, ran day and night to get there." From Lake Bennett in British Columbia, to Dawson and the goldfields, was still another 400 miles to the North. On leaving these lakes, this bizarre fleet bucked the great rivers—their fiercely swift currents, some even the treacherous Whitehorse Rapids and, ultimately, the 35-mile-long Lake LaBerge plus the Five-Finger Rapids of the Yukon River—before freeze-up.

"Back in the states, I was told later by the family, news reports told of mob law, starvation, mounted police turning people back, and so forth. These reports, as far as I was aware, were fakes—pure and simple. I neither saw nor heard of any of it, other than the strong, underworld tendencies Soapy Smith and his breed were exhibiting in Skagway," Charlie wrote.

On the American side, Soapy's men did not work the trail until after Charlie's party had gone through, fleecing stampeders in a variety of ways. On the Yukon side they felt safe, as those uniformed. "Champions of Justice," the Northwest Mounted Police, had stations every fifty miles. They stood ready for Soapy with Maxim guns had he dared cross into Yukon Territory.

Gale followed gale. Outside Tagish Lake, on a much-dreaded stretch of water called "Windy Arm," they suffered a devastating shipwreck and lost a valuable portion of their outfits. Disheartened, they were shivering and trembling—but never discouraged. "We faced our hardships and dangers without flinching, and laughed at misfortune and fate," Charlie said, and to quote Jack London, "the romance of the land and quest entered into their blood, and the spell gripped a hold on them and would not let go." With valorous determination, they pushed on up the Yukon River faster than salmon in spawning season, hoping to steal a march on the main horde of stampeders.

At Tagish Post they met a Canadian authority for the first time. Here the customs officer, supported by an attachment of Northwest Mountain Police, stopped all boats converging from the different trails to collect a customs tax.

The walls of Miles Canyon are of perpendicular basalt, standing almost a mile in height. In this narrow gorge of churning waters, which widens in the center into a huge basin, raged a violent whirlpool among jagged rocks and eddies. From there the canyon narrows to about thirty feet. People who chanced the canyon were thrown into the gushing Squaw and Whitehorse Rapids. Smaller boats often capsized, and many lost their lives during the first hectic months of the stampede.

Charlie, a man of wisdom and caution, chose not to subject his boats to the fierce currents, and the possible rupturing of their bottoms on the jagged rocks; instead, he portaged his little fleet on a tramway past the dangerous part. It took a special kind of man to "mush on."

In a single turn of the screw of fate, the stampeders were faced with a new and deadly threat—scurvy, which puffed at their flesh and ate at their bones. Many suffered the tortures of snow-blindness, others died of pneumonia, and as the chill penetrated more deeply, some died in the howling grips of blizzards and a few by their own hand. But the

Arizona Company—with its ability to grapple with the unexpected—came through intact, and pressed on relentlessly.

Navigating the 35-mile-long Lake LaBerge took a week. Where it was oft' times placid, Lake LaBerge surprisingly enough turned out to be one of their most difficult hurdles. The bitter cold—along with a portentous driving wind, which played havoc with their sails and rendered their oars useless—proved to be more of a problem than riding out the Whitehorse Rapids.

Drunken with weariness and straining at the oars, they plowed through ice-choked waters with sleet beating sharply at their flesh. Their lungs seared from the bitter cold and their knee joints stiffened like rusty pump handles, in a strange land and on an unknown river, until they reached Stewart River, 80 miles from Dawson. The mountain streams turned to mere trickles and ceased to feed the mother river. As the white fog of winter settled over the North, and a spectacular display of northern lights danced across the skies, the unfriendly river froze around them. They could go no farther. Under adverse conditions, Charlie's unfaltering courage and resourcefulness were a few of his many attributes, as he led his party. They unloaded their boats slowly and cautiously; the river ice could not be trusted. Whole sections sometimes gave way; humans, dogs, and outfits perished.

Even though they'd left a world of comforts and conveniences to come to an inhospitable land of ice and snow, to face impossible odds—and freeze to the very marrow of their bones—Charlie's words, "*fail we never knew, and quit we never did*!" had challenged them on. Others suffered the same misfortunes and all collapsed into insensibility, becoming prisoners on "Split-Up Island on ice-bound Stewart River.

The slightest grievance often could ignite into a quarrel. At this point, half-crazed partners, insane from fright and suffering, fought over nothing—sometimes splitting their battered and patched outfits in two, literally sawing their boats in half and going their own way; hence, the name, "Split-up Island." Splitting up usually proved to be a dreadful mistake.

Here, the Arizona Company along with others found plentiful fuel, and empty cabins—believed left by Harper and Ladue of the Alaska Commercial Company—which brightened the picture a bit. Yielding to fatigue, the camp bedded down and slept like corpses of drowned men, their shelters reeking with odors of drying long-johns, woolen shirts and sox, whiskey and chewing tobacco, sweat, and the curling smoke from wood burning in the cast-iron stoves.

In this motley group of "Cheechakos," at this temporary "tent" city, was a bright young man of twenty-one, who seemed much older than his years. He had a winning smile, a splendid personality, and a boundless imagination with keen insight into mankind's passion for adventure. Later, he became a famous novelist—his name was Jack London, the "Kipling of the Klondike." A great admirer of Kipling, Jack listened intently to Charlie's stories of his association with Kipling in another part of the world. During that first bitter winter on Stewart River, even though their politics were as far apart as the two poles, Jack's cabin was a gathering place for weary sourdoughs. Storytelling was the favorite pastime, and an inexhaustible collection of rare experiences, a dearth of fanciful, blood-curdling and easily disproved tales were spun.

"We were frozen in at the right time and place to get two claims and four half-interests on Henderson Creek," Charlie wrote. "While some of us built sleds to pull our goods the rest of the way, others prospected the Hootilinqua River." Rumor had it that there was gold in the sands, but it did not prove rich enough to make a strenuous effort pay off.

Eventually, camp was broken at Stewart, 80 miles from Dawson. Out of the thousands who left Skagway, "The Gateway to the Promised Land," the same time Charlie did, only a few haggard and hardy souls made it to Dawson that winter. The Arizona Company arrived the latter part of December utterly spent in mind and body. These were the brave men and women, the stalwart and strong, who had conquered the treacherous mountain passes, shared the risks of the trail and the unknown violent rivers, braved the bitter elements, and underscored every negative imaginable in the pursuit of life and treasure. Through heart-wrenching agony, each had learned lessons of a lifetime from his or her ordeal. Certainly, Charlie learned his, an experience he would never forget.

Many suffered from scurvy, and Jack London was one of the unfortunate. He was so crippled his gums commenced to separate from his teeth, and his body bent almost double. He was also one of the lucky ones, however, for his illness was treated in Dawson and he survived. His stay was a short one, but the trip was enough to give him inspiration for one of his many famous works, *The Call of the Wild.* Eventually, he built a crude boat, and with a partner sailed it the full length of the Yukon River to St. Michael and Norton Sound—some 1,700 miles, to catch a ship for San Francisco. Charlie's partner, Del Bishop, enjoyed a close friendship with Jack, and Del appears under his own name throughout London's book, *Daughter of the Snows.* Jack also sketched Charlie in several of his papers—*Jack London and the Klondike.*

At Dawson they found an enemy dreaded even more than the hostile wilderness; the meager monster called "famine." Neither gold nor money could buy food because there was none. All boats headed in that direction with food and supplies were stranded, some crushed and splintered in the frozen river. Most of the incoming Cheechakos had enough to get by until the spring thaw, but earlier inhabitants were already suffering from the ravages of scurvy, believed caused by the lack of vegetables in their diet. Some suggested the over-consumption of black coffee caused the disease, while others blamed irregular bathing habits. The only known means of treatment was to drink spruce tea and lime juice; or pluck the tender leaves of sour-dock or pepper, weeds that peeked through the rocky crags and crevices of the snow as the only visible vegetation, which was boiled and made into tea. Even though Dawson was on the ragged edge of famine, no one actually starved that winter, but only because they were warned and many fled during the fall.

In his letter home, Charlie wrote, "I scattered my men all around the unprospected parts. I bought, sold and located, claiming #50 above Bonanza Creek, #18 on Bear Creek, which was one of the richest in the gold belt, and two claims on 'Little Skookum'." A new law allowed a free miner a hill claim as well as a creek claim in every mining division, which increased the rights of those in the district to eight instead of four claims. Charlie was well established before the influx of new Cheechakos that spring, and he had several miners in his employ. Most people who waited out the winter at Lake Bennett and Lindemann, reaching the goldfields in 1898, found nothing left to stake.

When spring rolled around the willows and aspen burst into bud, big noisy mosquitoes, "with snouts as long as darning needles," attacked in great swarms. The river came alive with 7,124 boats, lined six deep along the water front; loaded with 30,000,000 pounds of food, liquor, and thousands of new gold-hungry miners bringing news from the "Outside." Dawson was an adult *metropolis*, its streets crowded not only with strangers, but with strange types of people. Of the 100,000 persons that actually started out, approximately 30,000 made it to the gold belt.

The city erupted with thousands of tents, and hastily built cabins that sprouted everywhere like daisies, crammed on a flat with scarcely enough room to accommodate a boom; they stretched along the slopes of Moosehide Mountain, overlooking Dawson, to the banks of the Yukon and Klondike Rivers. What the average sourdough called the *Klondike* was actually the *Thronduick*, which in the native Indian language meant "salmon." Once the ice had broken, the spawning season began; and a salmon belly made a good square meal for the hungry miner. By the summer of '98, 2,000 head of beef cattle successfully hoofed it into Dawson.

A human maelstrom of miners clogged the trails to the gold creeks, hoping to wrest their fortunes from the bosom of the earth. Sawmills hummed all day and all night at full capacity, erecting fast-rising buildings of all descriptions. Charlie said, "Life soon became all bustle, excitement and stampede. On the American side I bought one-sixth interest in the Alaska Placer and Coal Company, a very wealthy syndicate, from Messrs. Lyman Burrell, Andrew Nelson, Richard Aggasiz, Marcus Hamilton, and H. N. Brown. We owned 14 miles of rich placer diggings, an 80-acre island, 360 acres of rich coal land, and a big quartz ledge. My first four months in Dawson I had some $40,000 in paper, and 30 pounds of gold nuggets, some of which weighed over a pound each." The largest nugget discovered at that time weighed 35 ounces, found on *el Dorado* by W. Knuston.

Scores of dance halls, saloons, and gambling establishments sprang up. The establishments in Dawson were the mecca for the high-roller, with their glittery and riotous atmospheres: foggy with tobacco smoke, strongly impregnated with booze, and vibrating with throngs of sweaty stampeders. Men from all over the world, who were willing to "spit at the mark" for their whole pile, or cut cards for an *el Dorado* claim, were there in great numbers. Seated around the same gaming table were men from every class, well-dressed and new-made millionaires, and alongside of them, rough miners fresh from the diggings. During the night hours many a poke of gold nuggets or gold dust rapidly changed hands at games of faro, the favorite; black-jack, craps, and roulette. Few kept their wealth, laying their glittering heaps on the tables and spending lavishly as if Mother Nature would forever replenish the source.

With the stampede came the first ragtime music—with a piano or two packed over the trail in pieces, on the backs of weary stampeders. Looking on from the sidelines were always the dance hall girls, who earned their gold dancing with women-hungry miners, and who would sashay the men to the bar for drinks from which they derived a handsome percentage. It was said a man had to be pretty lonely to give most of them a second look. The saloons and dance halls, the center of social life, ran twenty-four hours a day but *never* on Sundays.

Front Street—Dawson, Yukon Territory

Front Street—Dawson, Yukon Territory

Front Street—Dawson, Yukon Territory

In these establishments, "Millionaire Klondike Kings" rubbed elbows with both rich and poor, and dozens of famous and colorful characters came alive. Many noted trekkers came from Arizona as Charlie had. Besides this famous cowboy, among them was Nellie Cashman—one of the most famous Western women of that period, and the only female mining expert in the United States at that time. Nellie was petite, with delicate features; with large, lustrous eyes; and hardly the type for such a rugged existence. She had prospected all over the coast and had just returned to Arizona from Alaska, when word came of the stampede. Known as the "Champion Woman Musher of the North," Nellie was asked by a reporter from an Arizona paper if she was going back to the Klondike. She said, "Indeed I am. I was in Alaska two years ago and would have stayed, but our provisions ran out and we were in a portion of the country where it was impossible to procure them in less than three months. Winter was coming on and I had to get out, leaving good paying gravel at that place."

Nellie's career stretched all the way from Virginia City, Nevada, where she ran a short-order restaurant at a rough-and-ready mining camp. From there she went to Tombstone, Arizona, when she operated the famed Russ House Hotel on "Tough Nut" Street during the silver strike. She made a fortune mining and prospecting in British Columbia, Mexico's Baja Peninsula, and Alaska, before joining the Klondike Stampede. Known for her kindness and generosity, Nellie grub-staked down-and-out prospectors and nursed many a miner of the scurvy. Her merciful compassion earned her the names, "Frontier Angel," "Miner's Angel," and "Saint of Sourdoughs." The miners held her in such high regard that "her entrance into a public place was a signal for every gentleman to rise and stand in respect."

Charlie's old friend and Indian scout, Captain Jack Crawford, "The Poet Scout," was there. Jack was noted for being able to write a poem on the spot. He had done his share for the Territory; his last active duty was as Chief of Scouts in Colonel Buell's 1880 expedition into Mexico against the Apache Chief Victorio. In Dawson, he was the proprietor of his own business, the "Wigwam," and sold everything from ice cream to hay.

Now, for a change of pace in personalities, the notorious "Buckskin Frank" Leslie made the trek as well. He was a famous, fast-draw gunslinger from Tombstone, and was responsible for a number of killings. A "lifer," he had just been released from the Yuma Territorial Prison, "a place that could really try a man's soul." His troubles stemmed from his fondness for good whiskey and fast women. But criminals did not last long in Dawson and he soon faded into obscurity. No one is sure what happened to him, but rumor had it that he committed suicide in San Francisco a few years later.

Other soon-to-be-famous personages included showmen, Sid Grauman, best known later for his famous "Grauman's Chinese Theatre" in Hollywood, where movie greats press their feet into wet cement; and Alexander Pantages, who later became the head of a chain of theatres, most notably the "Hollywood Pantages Theatre." Several future novelists later gained great recognition were there: Rex Beach, James Oliver Curwood, and Charlie's new friend, Jack London.

Tex Rickard was another classic example of the "rough and ready" Westerner who was a successful fortune hunter, life-long gambler and fight promoter in Madison Square Garden. Then, there were the Mizners: Addison, Edgar, William, and Wilson. Wilson, a piano player in Dawson, became a successful restaurateur and owner of the Hollywood and Los Angeles "Brown Derby" restaurants. Edgar was known as "the meanest and most arrogant man in Dawson."

During the first bitter winter of Charlie's arrival, he devised a scheme of producing a souvenir newspaper or illustrated journal, the *Klondike News*, designed expressly to glorify the Klondike Kings who made the first, large or significant finds. The paper brought the latest goldfield news, maps and locations, and other related subjects. Charlie was a resourceful man and wrote the prototype on brown wrapping paper. Of course, vainglorious Charlie had a good-sized article in his own paper about himself. Pictured in buckskins and *sombrero*, with a rifle thrust across his shoulders, it read in part, "The luckiest of all the 1897 pilgrims to the Klondike, is the King of Cowboys, Arizona Charlie, rancher, miner, Wild West showman and all-round frontiersman, so famous in the Southwest as an Indian fighter, and known the world over as the 'greatest horseman on earth'. The history of Arizona Charlie is familiar to all the English-speaking world. His youth was passed amid all the excitement and turmoil incidental to strife and discord in an unsettled community, where the embers of Indian contention 'smoldered until it burst into warfare.' A child of the plains raised on horseback, by birth and early association insensibly inured to hardship and danger, he was without knowing or intending it, making himself nationally famous.

"During the last six years he has been twice around the world, and has been entertained by almost every crowned head under the Sun. He is a shrewd businessman, modest and unassuming and free from the common faults of the typical frontiersman."

Each article or biographical sketch was accompanied by a picture of the subject in the review. Ye Arizona man was the manager with a 75% interest; Virgil Moore, an attorney whom everyone called "Judge," acted as editor; and Warren C. Wilkens, a short, stocky gentleman was his artist and photographer. Each individual portrayed paid handsomely for this exposure; with our "persistent rainbow chaser," Arizona Charlie, deriving some $50,000 for his first-time publishing venture, said to be "a record in journalism." Only one issue was printed, but it proved to the old cowpuncher that all that glittered was not always found on the creeks.

Mae was Charlie's wife, and everyone knew that, but any woman in Dawson could have her choice of at least fifty men. There was a long line of females—but a shortage of good women, and only about fifty altogether. Many a miner found Mae beautiful, intelligent, and exceedingly charming. Among these men was Charlie's old Arizona friend, Curly Monroe, who, like Charlie, roamed the same territory as a cowboy, and who the sourdoughs called the "Chief of Stampeders."

Curly got an early start in the Klondike and had accumulated great wealth. "His cozy cabin had all the comforts a mortal heart could wish for," and in the evenings Mae and Charlie found his warm hearth a gathering place for friends. Curly was a famous cook, and outright handsome—if one could imagine him without all those whiskers. He was a good catch. A picture in Charlie's famous scrapbook shows three men looking over Charlie and Mae's shoulders at several giant nuggets, as they sat around Curly Monroe's cabin table.

Almost immediately after the *News* was written, Charlie and three friends left Mae in Dawson while they proceeded by dog team for the "Outside" and San Francisco with his precious cargo sealed in a can, to have the journal printed and to purchase equipment. Charlie wrote: "I was publicity man and outside manager for the Alaska Placer and Coal Company, of which I was a partner, and my mission held a three-way purpose. I was to purchase the necessary equipment for my new partnership, a well-borer and tackling machinery to develop and work the new properties, and a small steamer to run between the Seventy Mile and Mission Creek districts. Then, too, I was to seek a large syndicate that might possibly take hold of the properties and provide working capital necessary for speedy workings of the properties by improved methods. I was convinced that, within two years, developments there would astound the world."

Virgil Moore and a man named Carlisle, accompanied Charlie to the "Outside." They spent just 23 days going out over the ice by dog team this time, which was quite a difference, when not pulling freight. For Charlie, driving a set of malamutes was much like driving a team of horses. The dogs were trained to respond to "Gee" and "Haw" in the same way. By sheer fate they were just three days behind another dreadful avalanche; a second far crueler tragedy, again at Sheep Camp, April 3, 1898, that claimed another 64 stampeders. Charlie seemed to lead a charmed life.

At Skagway, described by many as "the worst hell-hole on earth," Charlie and his partners found "Soapy" Smith in brazen and lawless control as "dictator" of his well-built empire of crime, and operating from his notorious saloon, "Jeff's Place," headquarters for his countless illegal operations and misdeeds. One of his most common practices was to invite unsuspecting miners, returning from the goldfields, out back to view an eagle he had chained to a perch in the courtyard. Since the area also served as a urinal, this led those going out back to say "they were going to see the eagle." In time, "seeing the eagle" meant getting slugged, rolled, and relieved of their buckskin poke of gold dust. The unsuspecting miner found himself in the alley, without redress in lawless Skagway.

Upon Charlie's arrival in the States, news came of Congress declaring war on Spain, and the organizing of Teddy Roosevelt's Rough Riders. Teddy, at that time was the irrepressible Assistant Secretary of the Navy, as well as Lieutenant Colonel of the regiment. Many of Charlie's old cowboy pards—who had ridden and dared and fought together, were signing up with the Rough Riders for the Cuban campaign. The Middleton boys, Prescott's boy sheriff and politician, "Bucky" O'Neill, and Charlie's old roping rival, Tom Horn, were among them. Bucky was the first to sign up and was commissioned as Captain of Troop "A." A "foolhardy cuss," the darkly handsome Irishman was the "personification of the *beau ideal* Rough Rider." Bucky did not make that dramatic charge up San Juan Hill. He refused to take cover while reassuring his men, and was killed by sniper fire on July 1, 1898, bringing his colorful career to an abrupt end. Only 38, Bucky was a national hero, and "his relentless pursuit and capture of the Canyon Diablo train robbers, already assured Bucky his place in the Arizona Valhalla of heroes," said one account. Bucky's statue on a spirited horse stands as a memorial to him and other heroes of yesteryear in the courthouse plaza in Prescott, Arizona.

Tom Horn was in charge of a pack train, as he and Charlie had been during the Apache trouble in 1882. Charlie's friend, and one-time backer of the bullfight at Cripple Creek, Brigadier General Sherman M. Bell, who at the time of the bullfight was a constable at Cripple Creek, led the advance up San Juan (Kettle) Hill. Sherman Bell was one of Colorado's most colorful military figures and a national hero. Colonel Theodore Roosevelt once said if he could have only one soldier in his regiment, he would pick Sherman Bell. "On the whole," Roosevelt said, "I think trooper Sherman M. Bell was the gamiest man in a regiment of game men. He showed himself in every emergency absolutely fearless, trustworthy and with singularly good and cool judgment. I cannot speak too highly of him."

Of course, Charlie was all "fired up" to join; he was always ready for a good fight. But the timing was bad. He had made a commitment to Mae as well as to his partners waiting in Dawson, and he also had the business of getting the *News* published and distributed.

With his mission accomplished and a long visit with Mae's family in Santa Cruz, Charlie returned to the land of the *aurora borealis* in time to celebrate the demise of the "scourge of Skagway," Soapy Smith, victim of his own knavery—done in by gunfire exchange with Frank Reid, vigilante member of the committee of 101 formed to throw the corrupt gang out. Soapy's men were rounded up, and stability replaced disorder in the famous Alaskan coastal town. The old West's lawless element had enjoyed its final fling.

Soon after his return, a "Statement of Claim" was served to the Arizona gentleman by the Supreme Court of the Northwest Territories, Provisional District of the Yukon, brought about by Benjamin Seitz. "On or about the 7th day of January, 1898," the document read, "the plaintiff and defendant, Charles Meadows and C. Wilkens, entered into an agreement to become partners together for the purpose of preparing and publishing an illustrated paper portraying and describing the places of interest, prominent men and resources of the Klondike region."

In his statement to the court, Charlie said, "No agreement of the sort was made with Mr. Seitz as alleged in the statement of claim. But I did offer him 10% of the net profits upon all work he might do being in character described in his statement of claim, but the plaintiff did not perform the work, nor did he solicit advertisements or anything else to entitle him to get the 10% profit." It is not the only time Charlie was summoned to court over the *News*. Others were anxious to cash in on a good thing.

A writ of summons was issued on November 7, 1898, by the Territorial Court, between John B. Wickery and defendants Charles Meadows, Virgil Moore and W. C. Wilkens. On, or about the 10th day of August, 1897, Mr. Wickery stated that Mr. Wilkens entered into a written partnership with him on the trail to the Klondike, for the purpose of becoming partners in *all* business transactions and adventures which either of them might enter into in the Yukon Territory. Mr. Wilkens was to receive 20% of the profits of the *Klondike News* partnership, and Mr. Wickery sought to collect 10% of Mr. Wilken's share. The plaintiff stated that "huge amounts of money had been collected for publication of the paper, and there remained according to the list given him by Mr. Wilkens, promissory notes for advertisements in the sum of $21,310." But they neglected to give him any part of the monies received, and he was seeking his share of those monies. The outcome of these two cases is unknown.

Charlie, like all the others, then turned his attention to a desperate search for the Mother Lode.

On January 10, 1898, Dawson was the scene of much excitement; on the quiet side, rumors were astir that a typical gold stampede was in progress. It was bitter cold and men could be seen grouped in saloons, gambling establishments, and on street corners discussing something highly secretive. If word got out, there would not have been enough claims to go around. Every dog team was pressed into service, packed and ready to go at a moment's notice. Klondikers, "Nigger Jim" Daugherty and his friends, Sam Stanley, Billy Chappell, and a dozen of their cronies, had their eye on what they were positive was the Mother Lode.

Charlie got wind of their scheme. He thought he had what was the Mother Lode, and his plan was to head them off. By 2 a.m. in the morning the temperature was 60 below, but the stampede began in earnest. At least fifty sleds moved quickly down the frozen river ice, in the ghostly peace of the frigid night, in pursuit of the lead team. Others had the same idea—but all available dog teams had been taken before Charlie made his decision to go. Being a wise and resourceful man, he secured an ox which was known for speed and endurance on the trail, loaded him up, and bundled up in his parka with fur muffled up to the eyeballs; he then downed a chill-chaser. Thus equipped, he dashed post- haste up the frozen Yukon River into the tranquil silence of the immense, snow-covered wilderness—a good 12 miles before he was convinced they were not going his way. He stopped at a convenient place, and after waiting a considerable time, he returned to town when his cigarette supply became exhausted. A good ribbing was his only reward.

Charlie later learned the group reached a place called the "18-mile roadhouse," bought the whole place, including the edibles, and remained out of the cold until the others gave up their chase. Then horror struck. Even though they had staked their claims, the price they paid was enormous. The 60-below temperature caused one man to lose both feet, and left several others severely maimed. Few, if any, returned to the tundra they had staked at such a high cost.

Property values sky-rocketed in Dawson, with building lots which sold for $100 the summer before now going from $20,000 to $40,000. Speculation ran high and money was plentiful, bringing from 10-15% per month with gilt-edged security. Charlie, with a shrewd eye for good opportunity, moved to capitalize on the city's boom early by purchasing a sizable lot on Third Street, later renamed King Street, right across from the new post office. He reasoned, "What a marvelous place for a profitable enterprise."

"Mae invested her money wisely in real estate too," Charlie said. "Her grubstakes yielded her rich returns, with interests located on Hunker, Bear and Dominion Creeks, and Skookum Gulch. Her city properties were accounted very valuable with the rapid growth of Dawson, and with her claims she was soon worth $100,000." Mae was said to be one of the best-dressed and fashionable young women in town.

The folks of the Klondike were practically shut-ins eight months out of the year, and remote from the advantages enjoyed on the "Outside." They needed recreation and amusements during the harsh winter months. It was readily seen by the Arizona man that most of the gold ended up in the saloons and gambling establishments, where lonesome sourdoughs spent their wealth on Yukon "hooch," women, and high living. One by one, saloons, dance halls, and theatres multiplied as the entertainment business flourished and became a gold mine in itself. The Opera House was Dawson's first theatre. It was quite small, but elaborate. Then the Pavilion opened its doors in June of 1898, the Tivoli in August, and the luxury resort, the Monte Carlo, in October.

During the never-to-be-forgotten winter of '98-'99, Dawson was almost completely consumed by fire, when dancehall girl, Belle Mitchell, (it was said), left a candle burning in a block of wood. Flames leaped up fiercely and half of Front Street went up in the blaze. The Green Tree and Worden Hotels burned to the ground. The Pioneer, Northern, *Bodega*, and Dominion saloons were reduced to ashes. The Monte Carlo was badly damaged, and the Opera House, Tivoli and Aurora Theatres were completely destroyed. The fire did not stop until it had burned most of Paradise Alley. Shooting, fighting, and rowdyism were not tolerated by the Northwest Mounted Police, but the governing powers closed their eyes to the scarlet face of vice.

Front Page of Charlie's "Klondike News"

W. C. Wilkens and Arizona Charlie

Charlie, Pre-Opening Night at Charlie's Grand Opera House

Dinner for 40 Friends at the Grand Opera House

Almost immediately, the town began rebuilding—and burgeoning with new arrivals and old smelly sorts, who tramped the crowded streets with an agglomeration of horses, mules, *burros* and dogs floundering through the ooze and slime of a putrid mixture of mud and fresh, steaming horse dung. "The summers were very sickly," Charlie wrote. Dawson, a city of haphazard sanitation, seemed not to have time to come up with a good plan for coping with the sewage.

Charlie was a picturesque figure on the streets of Dawson, his long auburn hair and buckskins made him stand out among the motley horde of sourdoughs, and it was hard to find a man in all of Dawson who had not run into the Arizona man in some other part of the world. Charlie was an enterprising man, and visions of easy money danced in his head. The stage was in his blood and he dreamed once more of its glamour. Soon he was planning the most elaborate theatre and opera house in all the Northwest. He envisioned it to rival those on the "Outside," and wanted it to be the grandest, most elegant establishment of its kind.

The gold belt was 60 miles wide and 70 miles long. The whole territory, although not so rich, was even more extensive for it was believed 10 years' work would not make a mark upon the ground. So he wanted his theatre to be strong enough to withstand the brutal blasts of the elements. Not yet 40, he firmly believed that this was where he would be for a long time—his pot at the end of the rainbow. He was an entrepreneur who passionately believed in his product, who wanted to bring the best theatrical companies available from San Francisco to present first-class entertainment. This is the way he did things.

He contracted Mr. C. H. Albertson, a well-known architect from Portland, Oregon, who came over the trail along with him, to design and build the structure. The "Grand Opera House" went up in six months when lumber was at a premium. Lumber was used to shore up the mines, as well as for housing, and as fuel for the steamboats. Charlie obtained two, old, wrecked steamboats from the Alaska Commercial Company and used them for the front and facing of his building. The architecture was a combination of the traditional, European-style opera house and the less elaborate frontier theatre. The second and third floors contained horseshoe balconies, which used a system of 7/8" diameter steel rods whereby the two horseshoe balconies were suspended from the roof structure, and "attested to a very resourceful mind of the architect," said the *Klondike Nugget*. These balconies had small boxes, hung with lace tie-back curtains. Then, there was the fancy dress circle for the "Klondike Kings." The "Royal Box," constructed for "King" Charles and his friends, was across the back on the third level. To the front of the building—on the second level were two suites, one for the host or hostess and the other for the visiting star of the show. Pictures sent home revealed Charlie and Mae enjoying very commodious quarters.

The star's room was wallpapered in a dazzling combination of red and gold, the plush carpeting with a design of large red roses, and the furniture was golden oak. There were lace Nottingham curtains at the windows, and the room was complete with a flowered rose—bowl, pitcher, and chamber pot.

The upper floor contained a large room for the different fraternal orders, and was used sometimes for hotel space. Some are quick to suggest that these rooms and others were set aside for amorous interludes with women of easy virtue; but the real truth is that hotel space in Dawson was almost non-existent, and Charlie had to provide living space for the theatrical companies that came from San Francisco. Although there were prostitutes in Dawson, the dancehall girl was not exactly one of their number. She was paid to dance with the miner, make him happy, and shill drinks for the house. Although she flirted outrageously, and some of the miners kept them as mistresses, few were daring of dress and flexible of morals. Paradise Alley and Louse Town provided enough girls for the woman-hungry miner in Dawson.

Behind Charlie's handsome and highly polished "Rochester Bar," was a fine mural of the Miles Canyon Rapids; and Yukon scenes painted by artist Art Buell surrounded the outside railing of the first balcony. A crimson red curtain draped the stage, and rich brocade-designed wallpaper graced the walls with a European air of elegance. The theatre was heated by wood-burning stoves, with heat from the flues warming the upper stories. A wood-burning stove was also placed under the stage. Behind the stage were several dressing rooms for the actors and chorus. Chairs were a problem. Charlie had to make-do with 500 straight-backed kitchen chairs—with satin headrests and cushions. The building held many more, but with standing room only. It was the largest and most glamorous theatre in all the Northwest.

These were the halcyon days of the "Gay Nineties," and Dawson became known as the "Paris of the North." The finest cigars, gowns, and perfumes from Paris, imported wine and exotic foods made their way there. Charlie wanted his theatre to reflect this opulence, and when finished, it was magnificent by Dawson's standards—the biggest and best theatrical establishment of its kind north of San Francisco and west of Winnipeg. This was the supreme emblem of his achievement.

In San Francisco, Charlie's old manager, Charles Gore, took care of arranging stock companies and supplied him with some of the finest theatrical artists on the coast. The theatre was not quite ready for a Grand Opening, but he had a deadline for a celebration on the Fourth of July, that grand American holiday—Independence Day. The city was wild with excitement. Captain Jack Crawford, along with Charlie, gave an entertainment for the throngs who crowded the streets during the day. That evening he celebrated the occasion by giving a lavish preview banquet at the theatre for forty of his closest friends, and placed a complimentary ticket for the grand opening, plus a crisp Canadian $100 Banknote at each plate. He always believed in sharing his success with others, and this is the way he did it—his flamboyant way.

Two weeks later, his "Grand Opening" advertisement welcomed everyone to:

THE BIG STAMPEDE
TO THE GRAND...
TUESDAY, JULY 18, 1899

"To The Amusement Seeking Public—Arizona Charlie
Sends You Greetings. He Will Open the Grand On The
Above Date With The Grand Spectacular Production,
"*LA SEIGE INFERNO*"

40—Shapely Ladies—40

You are especially invited to join the Masque Ball and drink all the hooch and wine you can pay for. No limit to this game. Come early and get in the bald-headed row. See the best vaudeville house West of Chicago. '*LA SEIGE INFERNO*.' Replete with new scenery, dazzling wardrobe, and mechanical effects." C. Meadows, Proprietor and Manager

Opening night was mildly *chaotic*. The town turned out *en masse* to honor the occasion in a blaze of glory and calcium lights. Representatives of the "nobility" were there, along with many of Dawson's "Four Hundred," and a goodly portion of the common sourdough. A couple of stray malamutes livened up the entertainment, which was said to be a "howling" success in more ways than one. The audience had different ways of expressing their appreciation, and howling was simply one way they displayed their good feeling. Among the famous characters who passed through its doors that evening were Sid Grauman, Wilson Mizner, and the Dawson waiter, Alexander Pantages.

It was a grand occasion, and the tall, long-legged Arizona man was simply in his element. Dressed in a tuxedo with rich furs and his finest Stetson, sparkling cuff links and the gorgeous diamond ring he had won for roping in Arizona, his photograph projected the part of the successful *entrepreneur.* Mae never looked so exquisite. Her voluptuous hour-glass figure was gowned in flesh-colored *Parisienne* lace, and a garland of nuggets, a gift from Charlie, adorned her lovely neck. Even his bartenders wore immaculate white aprons and shirts, hard-starched collars and bow ties, diamond cuff links and stick pins—all of which were in keeping with the grandeur, along with their hair carefully oiled, and parted with pomade, waxed and curled mustaches.

On the first level, Champagne brought $5 a bottle, but the price went up with the price of the seat. The champagne in the dress circle commanded $50. The music was under the direction of "Professor" Adolph P. Friemuth and his eleven-piece orchestra. The crowd, hungry for entertainment, was in a most enthusiastic mood and "applauded to the echo" any effort made by the performers that appealed to their fancy. They paid little attention to the scenery, which was still a trifle damp. They knew of Charlie's prowess as an Indian fighter and were more interested in seeing just how he could handle a bevy of chorus girls.

"The ballet, which was the crowning glory of the whole show, consisted of a variety of shapeliness and loveliness to satisfy any and all tastes. It was especially enjoyed by the wide-eyed, woman-hungry occupants in the bald-headed row, with several of these gentlemen appearing to be troubled with the chronic ailment known as 'elongation of the neck,'" reported the *Klondike Nugget*..

Some slight difficulties were experienced at times with the stage settings, but these trivial matters and annoyances seemed to heighten the delight of the merry-making crowd. George Hillyer and Frank Simons came to Dawson in the summer of 1899 expressly for the purpose of painting scenery for Charlie, and both were prominent in theatrical circles as actors of some note.

The cast and programme consisted of the following mortals and immortals: Alchemist, a Wizard in league with Satan; King of Inferno, played by Walter Voorhees Demonface Spitfire, in the employ of both Tittania and Zamiel, played by W. C. Campbell Golden Rule, a fairy, played by Mae Lewis and Tittania, Queen of the Water, done by Evaline. There were a number of fairies, *et cetera.* The play consisted of three acts.

"The second act, where Queen Tittania, drawn in a luxurious barge by a pair of swans, comes on the scene, somewhat worked against the grain of a few in the audience," reported the *Nugget.* "The beauteous Queen alighted gracefully and with great dignity of Royalty, then advanced to the front of the stage, while her humble subjects, drawn up on either side, did homage to their sovereign as she passed. But then, instead of addressing her subjects upon the grave and lofty matters of State, she in all regality belted out the masterpiece of harmony entitled, *'All Coons Look Alike to Me.'"*

Will Howard showed off his Zouave baton drill and juggling. Voorhees and Davis presented a refined musical act, and W. C. Campbell delighted the audience with his trick bicycle riding. The beautiful serpentine dancer, Pauline Claire, also entertained with a Dutch song and dance, Mae Lewis gave a banjo and dance act, and Earl Rogers was excellent on the flying trapeze. The evening was packed with excitement and well received by the merry-making crowd.

It was reported that Big Alex McDonald, who had just bought more than a mile of claims on *El Dorado* and Bonanza Creeks, and "Swiftwater" Bill, who bought a cargo of eggs to prevent his sweetheart, "a comely strumpet" named Gussie Lamore who had jilted him, from having a ham and egg breakfast, were shoved out of the spotlight by this theatrically handsome Arizona man. The Grand Opera House was on everyone's lips and the center of Goldtown's festivities. Charlie took in $12,000 opening night alone, and was admired for his *entrepreneurial* zeal. He had reached his professional maturity—and basked in the glory of his success.

After the initial opening, a variety of entertainments were offered in the following months, including tear-jerking melodramas, vaudeville-type performances, concerts, and sporting events. Chorus line and specialty acts were always available and ever popular.

One of the most appealing production attempts, although there was some miscasting, was the dramatic vehicle *Camille*.

Charlie's trademark was his familiar buckskins and *sombrero*. Before each performance he would mount the stage, and in his most elegant manner, *sombrero* in hand, make a grand sweeping bow before the curtain; and in a voice grand with as much gravity as he could muster, announced the evening's attractions. Those were the glorious days that remained so vivid in his memories.

Plays of the frontier and pioneer days were also popular favorites. Charlie staged the play, *The Arizona Scout,* designing it after the play, *The Scout,* originated by his Wild West showman friend, "Doc" Carver. Doc was often called the "Evil Spirit of the Plains," because of his part in this famous role. Charlie's version was an ambitious attempt, and everything advertised was faithfully presented. The theatre was packed from cellar to garret on the opening night of *The Arizona Scout.* Everyone came to see Charlie's expert marksmanship and the horse that dropped into the tank of water, and they were not disappointed. In fact, they got more thrills than the management intended to offer. Charlie took a dunking that was not on the program and narrowly escaped injury because someone pulled the rope too soon. Instead of having the curtain go down while he hung precariously in the air by the railings, he fell with his horse a distance of 14 feet into an eight-foot tank of water, to the infinite delight of all those present.

Charlie was the "Evil Spirit of the Plains." He was to "kill off" a band of Indians in order to rescue the Lily of the West, or words to that effect. She was bound to stakes at the side of the stage near the footlights. The stage had been "filled with the smell of gun powder, and piled high with dead Indians." They had affected the release of the maiden, then the "long-haired gentleman from Arizona" directed the girl to mount his horse and ride to safety while he captured a pony belonging to the Indians, and as she rode away he was to follow, disappearing up a run under the flies.

The setting was a road that wound around a mountain and further back and higher up, made very effective and realistic by the expertise of the stage carpenter. It crossed a deep chasm spanned by a rustic bridge, underneath which roared—according to the play, a raging mountain torrent. The tank, placed below the bridge, lent realism, and was just long enough to admit the pony that dropped into it. The bridge was swung by hinges and parted in the center in order for the horse to drop through into the turbulent waters below, where he swam nightly with a very realistic effort, the scout was to catch the railing which does not fall, then swing to the opposite bank with the aid of a rope, while the curtain went down.

That particular night he rescued the maiden, rode triumphantly up the hill toward the bridge—where the Indians could be seen hacking the bridge away so vigorously with their tomahawks. When the Evil Spirit crossed it, the bridge would fall. Charlie came firing as he rode, and as he went up the bridge he attempted to put his revolver into its holster with one hand, while he reached for the rail with the other. He grabbed for the rail—but missed it, and along with his horse plunged down into the tank to the great delight of the audience. Charlie didn't think it so hilarious. He fell somewhat to the left of the horse and slipped down underneath him. The tank had a false bottom, which, when the curtain was down, was raised by pulleys until the horse could get a foothold, and then lifted up to the level of the stage. The panic-stricken stage hands pulled them out, but not until Charlie had suffered several painful injuries. Dripping, and with *sombrero* in hand, the flamboyant showman took his bows, then got into dry clothes and stayed with the play until the curtain went down. Friends and practical jokers, Curly Monroe and Waterfront Brown, were suspected of cutting the rope almost in two.

The whole evening had a jinx on it. The shooting act in which Charlie shot glass balls from betwixt Mae's fingers and from her hair—didn't work out too well. Everyone gasped, for they remembered the fate of Frank Fayne's wife and trembled for Mae's safety. During this act, Mae was seen shaking her hand after a shot. A divided bullet was found to have caused an injury to the tip of her thumb. The following night Charlie found himself missing time and again in unusual fashion as he shot glass bottles from a shelf. An examination revealed the fact that the first bullet had stuck in the muzzle, and each succeeding shot just jammed the barrel more solid with lead. Mae lost interest in the shooting acts after that, and never participated in them again.

Fire, the very nemesis of every mining camp, swept Dawson two more times, but each time the Grand was spared. Many traveling players appeared there, and *Old Homestead* and *Pygmalion* were two very ambitious renditions. When outside shows were not available, "ye erstwhile purveyor of vaudeville theatricals" would mount the stage in his familiar buckskins and *sombrero*, and dazzle the audience with a lively display of lassoing and sharp-shooting, and kick up his heels in a dance routine as the "Arizona Kicker," to the infinite amusement of those present. He was the star attraction and he loved every minute of it.

Mae was always by Charlie's side, gowned in one of her beautiful costumes—and sang and danced to the enjoyment of the crowd. As the evening's performances drew to a close, usually about midnight, the chairs and benches were pushed back; the orchestra would render the grand old songs in ragtime, and Mae and Charlie would lead the crowd in waltzes, polkas, square dances and one-steps, to the popular sounds of "There'll Be a Hot Time in the Old Town Tonight," "Put Your Arms Around Me Honey," and all the familiar tunes of the day. The miners paid a dollar for the privilege of dancing with the girls of the stage, who rushed them to the bar at every interval. Most of these girls were involved in tempestuous love affairs with saloon keepers, dance hall proprietors, and wealthy gamblers, but when it came to tall and handsome Charlie, Mae let it be known he was taken. Lively faro games—Charlie's favorite, played for high stakes, and went on continuously in the saloon. The gaiety went on until almost dawn.

The ordinary sourdough was an avid sports fan, and prize fighting was the most patronized indoor sport among the miners. Boxing contests sometimes took place right after the evening's performances and caused no little furor amongst the ladies of position in the town; they believed it was a "sin" not only because it was a profane sport, but because it brought about heavy betting. The better fights brought $25 a ticket, but big money was always made from betting and bar sales.

Charlie had billed a prize fight one evening and sold every inch of space that could hold a chair or a pair of broganned feet. The box office held a fortune in gold dust and coin. Then horrifying news reached his ears that one of the fighters had turned "yellow" and wouldn't show up. Charlie was in a fit of despair. He was going to have to return all that gold dust and coin, and that he was not prepared to do. He had a young man working as a swamper in his saloon by the name of Alexander Pantages, and Pan learned of his boss' desperate plight. Pan, rather short and stocky, fought as a welterweight in San Francisco. "I'll save the pot for you, Charlie. I'll fight that guy myself." Then Charlie asked him, "What do you know about fighting, Pan?" Pan said "Not a thing—except for a few, rough tumbles I've taken, but you've been a good boss, Charlie, and I'll take a licking for you right now."

Pan made true his promise. He hopped into the ring with the other fighter and kayoed him in just a few minutes. Charlie was so grateful that he gave Pan a ten-percent interest in his theatre.

At the same time coal from Charlie's company, the Alaska Placer and Coal Company, was a godsend to the thousands of boats that plied the Yukon River, that were experiencing difficulty in obtaining enough wood for fuel. At $50 a cord, Dawson businesses and homes were also glad his company could assure them fuel. Their coal, somewhat brittle, had a brilliant luster and contained some pyrite and amber. It was all lignitic, but it was thought it would not bear transportation to any great distance, without turning to dust. In addition to the boats, thousands of cabins and businesses to heat, the outlook for Charlie's company was excellent.

Palace Grand, 1899

CHAPTER 18

1899-1902
MASS EXODUS

Dawson City was still prospering as a boomtown when the shocking word came that an exciting gold rush was on in Nome, Alaska. "Gold," they said, "can be found right in the sand on the beach and scooped up in buckets." Disillusioned Klondikers, who had not found riches in Dawson, and were working for wages, saw this as their chance to make their fortunes. Then, too, Canadian duty was being collected by the Northwest Mounted Police on all ore excavated, and soon rich claims were the only ones worth the trouble. Only six months after the Grand was built, Charlie watched in disbelief as 8,000 miners left Dawson in droves to coax the yellow ore from the bowels of the earth at Nome. Even "Judge" Virgil Moore, Charlie's partner in the News, left with his family for Nome, on the *John Cudahy*, to open law offices there.

Running a theatre was not a shoestring business venture. In addition to the large investment in his building, furnishings and liquor stock, there were salaries for the bartenders, theatre staff, and gaming-room attendants. Performers averaged $150 a week, and musicians $20 a day. The better-known actors and actresses commanded a much higher scale. With the departure of thousands, a puritanical spirit of reform and cultural improvement gathered strength, with a half dozen women—whose position and reputation were unassailable, expressing their proper indignation in the serving of liquor inside theatres. Without liquor sales and the drop in attendance, it was extremely doubtful that Charlie could operate his theatre on a profitable basis. Dawson playhouses, from all appearances, appeared doomed.

Charlie, however, had not been idle. He could not believe he was out of business and refused to be licked. He took advantage of the quiet times and made structural changes in his theatre—mainly separating the Rochester Bar entirely from the main part of the theatre. Then he changed its name from the Grand Opera House to the "Palace Grand Theatre," and announced everything would be run "first class." Dawson was a society city, so he hosted benefits and socials—such as the St. Mary's Hospital Fair, the St. Andrew's Ball, and the Benefit for the Widows and Orphans of the Transvaal. The *nouveau riche*—and anyone at all who cared to go or could gather the proper habiliment, attended the St. Andrew's Ball. It was a magnificent evening—with an impressive display of fancy evening gowns and swallow-tail coats.

Then, for a short run, Charlie leased the theatre out to "Nigger Jim" Daugherty and Murray Eads for the six-day foot races. In October he leased the theatre for a month to his stage manager, George Hillyer. Hillyer produced several classical plays such as Goethe's drama, *Faust, My Partner*, a play of frontier days, and *Two Orphans*, which was one of the finest productions ever attempted in Dawson. Chair seats were usually $.50 and box seats, $1. But it never was quite the same again. The "whoop-em-up" days appeared to be gone.

Nome was short on playhouses. A gigantic scheme entered the *entrepreneurial* mind of the Arizona cowboy. If the people couldn't come to the playhouse, why not take the playhouse to the people? Charlie approached Mr. Albertson, the builder, with the idea of moving the structure down the Yukon River—over 1,700 miles to the beach at Nome.

Mr. Albertson, who for several previous months had been erecting Government buildings in Dawson, was excited about the undertaking. He had moved houses before—but never on water. Nevertheless, he assured Charlie of the feasibility of the plan and clearly demonstrated it to him. So a deal was consummated between the two men for the most "gigantic undertaking in land, lumber, and marine" history. Charlie's plan was to move the Palace Grand on the opening of the river that next summer—as soon as navigation was fairly able to get through. "My plan is to take a good dramatic company—comprising the best talent that can be had in Dawson, with entertainments aboard given at various mining towns down the river," Charlie said to a *Nugget* reporter. "I also plan for a large number of passengers and their outfits. As Nome is short on playhouses, I am well satisfied my venture will prove to be a profitable one from a financial point of view," he affirmed. This proposal caused no small stir in Dawson theatrical circles.

In speaking to the same *Nugget* reporter, Mr. Albertson explained that "a great many people think it is a foolhardy proposition, but let me tell you, I know what I am contracting to do. I planned and built the Palace Grand and know just how substantially it is put together, and I know it will stand the trip and never start a nail."

The Palace Grand was 40 feet wide and 100 feet long; and 34 feet from sills to comb; three full stories; and its weight, without furniture and fixtures, was very close to 52 tons.

"My plan for floating the building," Mr. Albertson continued, "is to construct four scows, each 20x40 feet. The scows will be shaped with round bottoms something after the pattern of a Whitehall boat. They will have bulwarks, keelheads, and keelstones, and will be very strong and perfectly water tight." The building was to be solidly attached to the scows, but would rest on a large bolster which was to be attached pivot fashion to the scows, without in any way disturbing the equilibrium of the building. "The motive power will be a steam tug which will be in front, while 14 men with large sweeps will 'steady on the stern,' the sweeps doing service as a rudder for the big craft," Mr. Albertson said. The whole shebang sounded like something out of *Ripley's Believe It or Not.* He finished his interview by saying, "It will be necessary to put from 12 to 20 tons of ballast on the first floor to hold her steady, but there may be sufficient passengers and freight to serve as ballast."

The Klondike Nugget's comment on this giant undertaking was, "In the meantime movements will be watched in the big project with no small degree of interest. The removal of the Palace Grand from Dawson will deprive the city of its finest theatrical building. But the owner is confident of the successful issue of the undertaking, and it is most earnestly hoped by his friends that he is not reckoning without his host. Arizona Charlie is a plunger, and his theory of 'nothing ventured, nothing achieved' will either make or break him this time. 'Tis hoped it will be the former.'" Charlie was impatient to get started.

Julius Ullman, a fairly well-known painter in Dawson, was drawn to the Klondike not only by the lure of gold, but for adventure, excitement—and interesting subjects to paint. Charlie commissioned Ullman to paint Mae in the flesh-colored *Parisienne* gown he adored seeing her wear. He promised to pay Ullman $1,500 for his work. The painting turned out beautifully and did justice to Mae's voluptuous charms and feminine pulchritude—Charlie was extremely pleased with the result after a month's sittings. Charlie felt it was worth every penny—but being a little "short of cash" at that particular moment, he asked Ullman to please wait for his money.

Palace Grand, February 5, 1900

Saint Andrew's Ball

Kathleen Rockwell, "Klondike Kate"

Captain Jack Crawford, the Poet Scout, 1898

It was Christmas of 1899, and the elaborately framed work was hung for all to see on a prominent wall inside the Palace Grand. Friends dropped in to view the "masterpiece," which was toasted with good cheer. One day Ullman walked into the theatre while Charlie and Mae were exhibiting the work to some admiring visitors. Ullman somewhat "flushed" with liquor to muster up his courage, awkwardly cleared his throat and demanded his money. It was somewhat embarrassing for Charlie, but he offered Ullman $500 on account. Ullman was not pleased with that sum and demanded the whole amount—immediately! The Arizona man's attention was momentarily drawn in another direction, but Ullman thought Charlie was purposely ignoring him. He came forward—drew out his pocket knife and proceeded to slash the painting to shreds. Charlie was dumbfounded and speechless. Mae fainted. Ullman turned and stalked out; his sense of moral rectitude finally satisfied.

Charlie had the reputation of being a very shrewd businessman, always holding on to his money as long as he could—unless it was to throw away as he pleased to make an impression, or to have a good time with his friends—yet he had many of those frivolous moments.

As the long winter wore on, disturbing reports from Nome filtered in. As usual, with all gold rushes, it occurred too late for the influx of new miners who came when the best ground had already been staked by the early comers. By the summer of 1899, $3,000,000 had already been removed from the beaches and creeks. Charlie began to have grave doubts. Practically no law existed in Nome, he was to learn. Claim jumping and theft were rampant. Mob law ruled. Then too, Nome was continually exposed to the wrath of the Bering Sea; and to storms which bore down from the South with wild fury, driving huge waves on shore, gobbling up buildings, machinery and supplies in the raging surf. Many lives were lost—and the main street of town was wiped clean and swept away.

Charlie deliberated on the situation as it stood. Mob law could be dealt with—but he had concern about the Sea. He wondered what would happen once the scows entered the angry Bering Sea between the mouth of the Yukon River and the sands at Nome. He was afraid the fourteen men and the "sweeps" in that position would be entirely worthless, and the Palace Grand could very well be swept clear to Siberia. An adventurer he was; a greenhorn he was not; and he was not about to make his first tactical blunder. By all appearances, Nome's day in gold rush history was limited just like all other stampedes. He concluded that one way to avoid trouble was not to be there when it happened. And, as it happened, his assessment of the situation was accurate. In two short years Nome's beaches had been picked clean; 20,000 miners pulled out for other gold fields, and a big percentage went home. Only 5,000 miners remained to work the tundra.

The Darling of Dawson

The Arizona man's energies as a showman continued, and he strove to bring top-of-the-line, first-class entertainments to the Palace Grand. That spring a very young actress named Kitty Rockwell worked her way to the northwest where she joined the Savoy Theatrical Company. She danced and sang with a French flair, and Charlie immediately booked her for the Palace Grand. Kitty was given the Star's plush suite and it was in this theatre that she reached the peak of her career, becoming famous as *Klondike Kate*.

Kitty had flame-colored tresses, blue eyes with a complexion of peaches and cream. Her costumes were from Paris, her lingerie was French and handmade. Her dresses and pink tights were covered with rhinestones and pearls, spangles and sequins. She sang old ballads and songs the sourdoughs loved to hear. A skit well received meant pouches of gold dust—the floral tribute of the Yukon, thrown at her feet. Two of her hit numbers were *She's More to be Pitied Than Censured*, and *A Man Was the Cause of It All*. Business prospered, the rafters rang once more with the Arizona man's eloquence, and the Palace Grand once again became the center of Goldtown's festivities.

Kate's grandest production was the *Cake Walk*. She wore a beautiful crown of lighted candles upon her flame-colored tresses, as she performed a breathtaking flame act, with swirling yards and yards of billowing fabric around her as she danced her whirlwind number. Flame-colored spotlights of coal oil carbon illuminated the subject. Kate made $200 a week for her performances and often cleared another $500 for champagne sales. She became a big hit with the sourdoughs and everyone loved her. She was the highest paid singer in the Klondike; the "bright star" of the Palace Grand footlights. She was the Queen of the North, the Darling of Dawson and the Flower of the North, but to most people she was known as Klondike Kate.

On the nights Kate did not perform, two other bright stars of the Palace Grand firmament, Cad Wilson, a popular songbird, and Diamond Tooth Gertie, entertained with humorous songs, as they rustled their flounces and furbelows in high-stepping dances. As they swirled about the stage, Gertie flashed a diamond filling in her front tooth, and wore an interesting snake bracelet that wound around her arm from shoulder to wrist. As the two made their graceful exit from the stage, some shapely leg was shown—and off went their garters, which were then tossed into the miners sitting in the "bald-headed row," in a teasing sort of way.

When Kate first arrived in Dawson, she wore an engagement ring and expected her *fiance* to follow. But he got as far as Seattle and died of a cerebral hemorrhage. But Kate was a girl who could have any man in town she wanted. Like all the local men, Alex Pantages was enamored with her—and in time she fell in love with the Little Greek. As Kate became wealthier, she helped Pan open his own Orpheum Theatre, and Charlie lost his hard-working saloon partner, welterweight champ, and the finest actress in all the Northwest.

The flamboyant *entrepreneur* suddenly found himself without a show manager. George Hillyer was an inmate of the Territorial Barracks because Mae had pressed charges against him for theft when he was found leaving their rooms in the Palace Grand with her expensive gold coin bracelet in his hands. It was hard for Charlie to believe that Hillyer, whom he had brought to Dawson with Frank Simons expressly for the purpose of working solely for him as a scenery painter and stage manager, would be accused of a crime in the very building Hillyer made his prominence.

Ye Arizona man took over the theatre once more, and with Frank Simons and Ed Holden, past owner of the Monte Carlo, they were the sole proprietors of the "All-Star Sapho Company." Together they staged the outstanding production, *Just Behind the Scenes*, with a brilliant cast of players. Performing were the six incomparable Peri Sisters, Julia, Amy, Ida, Lillian, Margie and Mamie; and the famous O'Briens, Eddie and Ana; and Miss Alice Jennings. Accompanying them was a marvelous acrobat, Seymour; Miss Marion Tracy, a monologist; Minona, Jacqueline, and Ida Rossiter, Queen of Song. Mabel Pearl, and John Cassidy rounded out a very delightful production.

During the summer of 1900, the Palace Grand was a scene of a grand masquerade ball—a riot of fun. That same month some beefy masculinity engaged in a wrestling match, and soon afterward a heavyweight boxing exhibition was staged between Frank P. Slavin, "The Sydney Slasher," from Australia, and a man named Perkins. Slavin was remembered as the only heavyweight fighter the great John L. Sullivan refused to meet! Following the summer sporting events, Charlie produced "The Crown of Success"—the play, *The Lily of Kilarney*—which filled the playhouse to capacity. Then, a satire based on the amorous exploits of Klondike millionaire, Swiftwater Bill Gates, entitled, *Stillwater Willie's Wedding Night,* delighted a very noisy crowd.

Afternoon animatoscope moving pictures—the rage at that time—were shown and consisted mostly of the latest world championship prize fights and other sporting events, as well as world news. A mixture of kerosene and oil was used to run the projector. Unable to get this fluid, Charlie resorted to gasoline of low volume, but it exploded, burned the projector and badly burned the arms of the projectionist. He had to close his matinee and return all the gold dust and coin.

W. R. Jackson of Whitehorse, leased the theatre from Charlie for a long run and changed its name temporarily to the *Savoy* . Then ye Arizona cowpuncher, said to be the "tallest man in town," was elected "crown flue inspector," at an annual salary of $20,000.

Along with the honor came the title, "Royal Shoe Black." Then Charlie toyed with the idea of arranging a Klondike exhibit at the Paris Exposition in 1900; one of the features to be $1,000,000 in gold dust taken from the *New El Dorado*. He even had agents in Paris working on the preliminaries. But as each day passed and each month progressed, less and less gold was found and more and more stampeders left town for new gold *digs*. Little by little, life seemed to seep out of Dawson—and the Palace Grand, and with it died one of the most flamboyant periods in American history.

A Fresh Scent, A New Adventure

It was 1901, and now the Palace Grand was a noose around Charlie's neck. Being a man with a vivid imagination, broad vision and a restless spirit, once again the call of the wild beckoned. There seemed to be no limits to his adventurous pursuits. A grandiose scheme agitated his fertile brain; a bold and quixotic scheme that had intrigued him since it first reached his ears in 1893. He was excited as a bloodhound after a fresh scent.

Three miles from the western coast of Mexico, less than a day's journey from the boundary of California, in the gulf, is the "cannibal" island of *Tiburon*, or Shark Island, of which, at that time, was less known than any other spot on the face of the earth so close to civilization.

In speaking to a reporter from the *Seattle Post Intelligencer*, Charlie said, "R. E. L. Robinson, a historian and writer of some note—who had on several occasions interviewed me for his paper, the *San Francisco Examiner*, told me in 1893 that he had heard the story of the probability of Cortez' cache of Montezuma's treasure being buried on the Island." This treasure was supposed to have consisted of 19,000,000 gold *pesos* valued at $12 each of our money, which was taken from Mexico when Cortez was driven from the land, and not a dollar of which was recovered when he returned from Vera Cruz with reinforcements and stormed to recapture the city.

"Robinson claimed to have traced the treasure to the west coast of Mexico. He believed it disappeared at the same time as the schooner, *El Platto,* which he was convinced was taken to *Angel de la Guardia* ("Guardian Angel"), a small island near Tiburon, and from there being pressed by the enemy, or fearful of discovery, it was taken to Tiburon," said Charlie. "It was another idea that the vessel might have been foundered and the money lost in the Straits of *El Infernillo* ("Channel of Little Hell"). Robinson believed that the stranded vessel discovered by Padre Salvatierro in 1709 at the north end of Tiburon and then looted and torn up by savages, was none other than the treasure ship.

"The island is approximately 35 miles in length, and from 8 to 20 miles in width. The natives are known as Kunkaak, and are called *Seri* by the Mexicans. There are many stories of their origin. Some claim they are descendants of the Welsh, others that they are Patagonians. It has been claimed they are Asiatics, and still others say they are descendents of the Moors—but whatever they are—they are savage cannibals," Charlie said. "Ever since the 16th century no force of Mexican government has been able to subdue the fierce tribe which peoples it. They know of no law—and have no ruler other than that of their own choosing."

In his interview with the reporter from the *Seattle Post Intelligencer*, Charlie went on to say, "The Robinson party of four left Yuma back in May of 1894 in a small sailing craft, the *Examiner,* down the Colorado River to visit the island of Tiburon in interest of their paper." Charlie was invited to accompany them that year. The expedition was an exciting one for Charlie, but the timing was bad. "Arizona Charlie's Historical Wild West" had just been organized, and Charlie was ready to leave Phoenix on his first tour.

"They went from the mouth of the river to the Island of Angel de la Guardia," he continued, "where they found roads well macadamized and the ruins of fine structures. They proceeded across the bay to Tiburon and made a landing at Fresh Water Bay, camping where Ugarte had 165 years before. The party found a village inhabited by Indians that were friendly. One of the party, a man named Clark, remained with the Indians alone on shore that night. Robinson and Logan, the following morning, went hunting with a party of four Islanders who allowed them to carry their guns. When about a quarter of a mile from camp, Clark, who was at camp, heard a shot and recognized Logan's voice calling for help.

"About that time Clark and his companion, O'Brien, noticed four Seri rowing in a skiff toward the Robinson party's launch as fast as they could. O'Brien did not wait to ascertain their mission, but pointed a shotgun at the Indians, which frightened them and they took flight. Clark and O'Brien got their launch under way as soon as possible and made for Guaymas, where they reported the matter to Mexican authorities. Some of them returned with the men to the scene, but would not set foot on the island. It was generally believed my friends, Robinson and Logan, were roasted and eaten by the Seri." That was one time Charlie was in the right place at the right time, and another reason he seemed to bear a charmed life. The newspaper, *El Eco Fronterizo*, published in Nogales, Mexico, gave an account of the murders, saying, "The Seri Indians who inhabit Tiburon are extremely savage and barbarous. We recommend their extermination by the Mexican Government."

"Shortly after that episode," Charlie went on, "a sailor from the *Junk World* in San Diego by the name of John Johnson, and Captain Porter with the schooner, *World*, while hunting for prized King Egret feathers and pearls, were camped on the east side of the island. They were surprised by a large party of Seri. After a desperate fight in which Porter killed seven Indians and after he was mortally wounded, he and his companion were overpowered. Their bodies were never found, but the story of their death was told in Mexico by a friendly Indian guide, who told of how his employers were massacred by the Seri; he believed the body of Porter was devoured by the savages.

"Then a man by the name of James McCuen, a cattleman from Hermosillo, spoke of a Seri woman who was drunk—that told him of seven white men that were being held captives on Tiburon, and this gave rise that among them might be Lieutenant Robinson and Mr. Logan. I did not think this, as the Seri are without sentiment of any kind; therefore it is reasonable to presume that any white man captured would be put to death and eaten," reasoned Charlie.

There had been other men who landed on the inhospitable shore of Tiburon who were never heard from nor seen again. Some had reached the island after shipwreck, while others had gone in quest of treasure or minerals. "But I am a man who is not afraid of the devil with his horns sharpened," Charlie said. Of Charlie's courage, there could be no question; it had been put to the test on too many occasions to admit doubt. The prospect of such an odyssey was enough to stir the blood of the reporter from the *Intelligencer*.

"My plan is to gather a force of cowboys and give the natives battle with modern rifles, the fire of which no savage would withstand. I can find any number of men who would go along with me just for the deviltry of it—men who are trained to use firearms and who are not afraid of anything on earth. I intend to get a grant from the Mexican Government on condition that I capture it from the natives and pay for it at a reasonable price. Then I intend to colonize it. I have no doubt whatever that both placer and quartz mines will be found there." And surely Charlie didn't forget about Cortez' cache of Montezuma's treasure he thought might be buried there.

"Dr. Lyon, a friend of mine from Los Angeles, who was a member of Professor McGee's geodic expedition, and the only one known to have gotten away from the island alive, said some of the black sand assayed out at $1,800 per ton, and there were placers of which could not be determined under the circumstances. I have plans of putting a line of steamers on the Colorado River connecting with the Southern Pacific Railway in Yuma, Arizona, and making regular trips to the island—a distance of but 125 miles from the city. The place would be a mecca for sportsmen and globetrotters, as it abounds in game, and along the shores the best sports fishing in the world is obtainable. My idea also includes a possible 'Monte Carlo' on the island. There is no reason why the island cannot support such a place as is on the island of Montevideo in the Mediterranean. And besides all these favorable prospects—it would be a great stock-raising country. I am dead serious in the matter, and have spent hours mapping out my scheme and planning my expedition. I have sent representatives to Mexico and have their reports in my hands."

For a man of courage and imagination it offered a field of boundless opportunities, and for Charlie, the prospect smacked of intrigue. It was at this time he put his "Theatre on the Frontier," the Palace Grand, up for sale. Once he had made up his mind to leave Dawson, he could hardly wait to get moving on this new adventure. When his business was completed there—he planned to leave for Mexico to lay his plans before General Torres, and Governor Ysbell of Sonora.

The Klondike Nugget got wind of his scheme. He understood the value of advertising as a proper method of working up a scheme, and welcomed their story. The front page of the October 17, 1901, issue ran a story and a large caricature of Charlie, by artist Art Buell. It showed Charlie sitting on a barrel—his throne—clad only in a towel gathered round him, side-gun holsters, and a large Mexican *sombrero* on his head—with a crown perched on top. He held a banner on a staff in his left hand with wording: "Long May Arizona Reign." Beneath the caricature it read: "High on a Throne of Royal State, Which Far Outshone the Wealth of Ormas or of Ind, Arizona Exalted Sat." The article read:

"Arizona Charlie is about to start on an adventure which will make the world ring with his name if he accomplishes the enterprise upon which he is bent. He proposes to do no less than capture from a savage tribe the island of Tiburon in the Gulf of California. Should he accomplish his task, he will occupy an envious position for he will be a potentate of no small magnitude over a territory larger than any of the kingdoms of the Old World, and his fame will live when the name of many a king has been erased from the memory of man or records of history. Mr. Meadows' plan is to gather a force of cowboys and give the natives battle with modern rifles, the fire of which he says no savage can withstand. Whether Mr. Meadows will accomplish the task of subduing the natives remains to be seen, but that he has dreamed and dreamed for years of possibilities of conquest, and that he means the attempt—there is no question of doubt."

Others said his flamboyant scheme was "wild," "crazy," and "impossible." But Charlie was nevertheless besieged with applicants and "could have filled a steamboat," he said. But he was determined to take just 40 men with 40 shares, and they had to be the real thing. Alex Pantages was interested in the trip from a showman's perspective.

While he stayed on in Dawson to sell his theatre, the *greatest pride of his life*, and wind up his business affairs, Mae preceded him to the "Outside," for an indefinite stay with her family in Santa Cruz, California. She left on the steamer, *Canadian,* with actors Eddie and Ana O'Brien and their family. Charlie was to meet her there later.

A quick sale of the theatre was negotiated with James Hall. There were several James Halls, but this was the one from #17 *El Dorado*, a realtor and the former owner of the Green Tree Hotel. Hall had no plans to run the theatre; he leased it to a man by the name of Murray Eads, who promptly changed its name again to the "Auditorium." Three five-point games of 7-Up were played to determine the method of payment—gold or *cheechako*. Currency of the realm won—the sale price being $17,000. A few years later, on his way out of the North, Murray Eads drowned when his ship, believed to be the *Princess Sophia,* sank.

Charlie enjoyed several rounds of pleasure and good-bye parties with his friends, who toast after toast, drank to the success of his new venture. His farewell send-off on October 21, 1901, on the small primitive steamer, *Nora*, her last voyage out before freeze-up, was long remembered. Those good-byes rang in his ears for the rest of his life. Pantages was there, and Charlie gave him his word he would keep him informed of events as they transpired. Most expressed envy he was leaving, and many sent out messages to those waiting at home.

By then the sun had departed for its winter hibernation, and Arctic darkness settled over the city. But once you've felt the *lure and the spell* of the Yukon, your feelings are always to return someday. Charlie never got around to returning, but it was the ultimate adventure of his life.

At Whitehorse he connected with the new White Pass and Yukon Railroad, and left for Skagway, Alaska. Although there had been several critical periods in his rags-to-riches life, Dawson was one of his most profitable ventures. He left the Yukon wilderness with a bundle of cash and two bulging sacks of gold.

Charlie was on a winning streak, and before leaving Mae in Santa Cruz once more, he dallied with the "little God" Faro, and when the old traveler cashed in his chips, he had won $12,000 to the good. He felt he had just dealt himself a royal flush in the game of life, and the whole world was a jackpot.

Arizona Charlie, San Francisco, 1898

CHAPTER 19

1902
KING OF TIBURON

While Mae stayed on in Santa Cruz, Charlie proceeded with his plans and arrangements for the expedition. Money was burning a hole in his pockets, so he bought two city blocks in Yuma—where he and Mae intended to put down their roots—and a good quartz mine in Mazatlan. Steers were selling in Mazatlan for $1.59 a head; how could anyone go wrong? Mazatlan, he heard, was also short on playhouses. There were so many good opportunities there that he decided to make a trip to check them out. He took the Duke Sisters and a comedian by the name of Mullaly with him. The Duke Sisters were remembered by Dawsonites for their outstanding engagement at the Standard Theatre. They left on the steamer *Santiago* for Sinaloa, Mexico, on January 11, 1902. On the way he sent his first correspondence to Pantages, informing him of his plans—and his big win at faro.

Meantime, news came informing Charlie that the U.S. Government had been trying without success to locate him since 1899. In his excitement he had neglected to inform his attorney, Silas Hare, of his forwarding address. It looked like his associate, Frank Cox, had gone to bat for him and a settlement would be awarded soon in his depredations case. Everything seemed to be going in the right direction for Charlie.

Show business in Mazatlan did not prove to be a good idea, but he bought all the cattle in the country. Then the big problem of getting them to market confronted him. For more than twenty years cattlemen had been attempting to move cattle from this section of Mexico, but at $1.59 a head, this Arizona cowpuncher was determined to find a way. This was the problem that brought him back to Los Angeles. Dressed in Wild West garb, he hired a cab, and his first characteristic gesture was to throw coins to the crowd who followed. It was his way of telling everyone Arizona Charlie was in town. After all, he was a celebrity, and a hero had to maintain his aura, don't you know.

A steamship company, whose vessels plied the Gulf of Mexico, contracted to ship the cattle from Mazatlan, but it was found the boats could not make the landing because of high surf, nor was there any point within reach at which shipments could be made. While he pondered his dilemma at the Nadeau Hotel in Los Angeles, a brilliant scheme or two entered his calculating brain. He could drive the cattle north to Sonora, and ship by rail from there. But that would have necessitated crossing the Yaqui River, through hostile Yaqui Indian country, with the certainty of attack by the fierce tribe, and loss of cattle—if nothing worse. Then, he hit on the idea of shipping the cattle on large lighters through the length of the Gulf of California, up the Colorado River to Yuma. From Yuma they would be shipped by rail to Los Angeles and San Francisco. It is not known how Charlie solved this problem. It surely was a unique case; Charlie never gave up on his ambitions. His thoughts then turned back to his expedition, and he was soon enmeshed in his ornate scheme.

His first order of the day was to meet with the Mexican Consul, General Guillermo Andrade, of Los Angeles. In 1888, when the Generals of the Mexican Army were carving Mexico up and dividing it among themselves and their relatives, President don Jose de la Cruz Profirio Diaz contracted to give General Andrade about 2,000,000 acres of Colorado River bottom land in Sonora, and the islands of Tiburon and Angel de la Guardia for services rendered. At the age of 75, Andrade decided to pass the settlement and exploration of Tiburon over to younger individuals.

"With the General," Charlie said, "I made a contract to purchase two-thirds of the island for $50,000, due in ten yearly payments, and a refusal of a lease for the other one third for ten years with the Mexican Government. I am to give 15% of the mining interests to the Governor of Sonora and General Andrade, and two Mexican bankers from Nogales. This is for the first expedition only. Thereafter, the mining interests are to be held by the forty shareholders. In addition to the purchase price, I am to establish ten families on the island and colonize it after gaining possession by subduing the natives. This seems the easiest part of the whole scheme. I don't expect to do much fighting. One look at the arsenal we intend to take—will, I feel, send them flying.

"I have started construction of a small battleship to carry my little party of invaders down the Colorado River and out to the Gulf of California to the islands. Two rapid-fire Maxim guns are to be mounted on the deck, and in the armory will be Mauser rifles. Mauser rapid-fire pistols and shotguns are for hunting small game or for fighting at close range if necessary. Each man will have his own rifle as well, and brace of revolvers and hunting knife; ornaments that for long habit have been indispensable—even when on a peace mission. Stores and provisions are planned to last several months.

"For all the war-like preparations, I am still confident my large force will overwhelm the Indians and they will be glad to make peace. If I thought there would be great danger, I would abandon the trip. There was a time when all I asked was there be a bit of the element of danger. But I am well enough fixed now that I do not need to take any such chances."

He was busier than a one-armed cowboy saddling a green bronc. If things came to a showdown, and he couldn't civilize the whole tribe, he planned on returning with their warm, bloody scalps dangling at his belt. He seemed to actually relish the danger. He was hoping to conquer so he could fulfill his option to buy the land, find the treasure, and become as rich as an Oriental potentate.

Charlie's scheme drew great publicity. He was obsessed with the dream of creating his own "empire," and referred to Tiburon as "my island," and his friends jocularly called him "King of Tiburon." A standard letter was sent out to several of his friends still in Dawson, offering glowing inducements to join his expedition.

"I knew them to be 'rugged' individuals," he said. "I laid it all on the line—the dangers and the rewards." It was explained to all that the Indians were a "bad lot"—that they used both poisoned arrows and spears. It was reported that a rattlesnake was allowed to strike a deer's liver and the arrows were then dipped into it. "There are 15 to 18 hardy men already recruited that are willing to take responsibility for the Indians, so that any member who doesn't want to be a target for one of those poison arrows can stay out of harm's way. I intend to build a rock fort on the north end of the island and delegate night watches," he told them. "I promise to pay the entire expense from starting point—San Pedro, California, or Yuma, to the island and return.

"Two conspicuous members of my company are Del Lewis, Sheriff of Cochise County, Arizona, and J. H. Thompson, Sheriff of Gila County, Arizona. Nothing more is needed in proof of courage of these two men than the statement that they both lived to serve out their terms of office. In fact, Thompson was the first man who ever lived to serve the term of Sheriff of Gila County. His predecessors all 'died in discharge of their duties' when attempting to make the arrest of some outlaws that formerly had things their way in both Cochise and Gila Counties." Lewis and Thompson, like Charlie, were crack shots—and involved in the wars with the Apaches. Thompson rid his county of bad men, while Lewis ran the outlaws out of his county and lived so peaceably he feared he might become lazy.

Then there was Charlie Cowles, who gained frontier fame as a member of the Earp gang. Dr. W. H. Lyon, of Professor McGee's expedition, was a prominent shareholder. Charlie had several later partnerships with him. His old manager, Charles Gore of San Francisco; Dawsonites, Frank Slaven (the Sydney Slasher), former champion James Russell, Tom Rockwell, Captain Norris and Frank Berry, were shareholders. The group also included his nephew, John Arnold, of Randsburg, California, and Phoenix personalities, Tom Sparks, Huse Ward, and Major McClintock. Many others from Los Angeles and San Francisco bought shares in the company.

Then to add a favorable note to the whole expedition, the Mexican Government of Sonora, under Governor Ysbell, volunteered to have Commander Emilio Kosterlitsky, a famous Russian Pole—and righthand man of President Porfirio Diaz—and as many of his *Rurales* and scouts as thought necessary to assist Charlie's expedition and to remove the danger of international complications which might arise if an armed party other than the Mexican soldiers were to land on the inhospitable shore.

Men who were survivors of the California Gulf islands, and who had the opportunity to observe the natives of Tiburon disagreed with Charlie's views on the ease with which the island could be taken. One of these was Captain Lew Harris who with the schooner, *Emma and Louise*, navigated the Gulf in the guano trade among the islands. These are the words of caution he gave to Charlie, as reported in the *Los Angeles Sunday Herald* of August 31, 1902:

"We had intended to go ashore at Tiburon and prospect for gold, but for a variety of reasons we changed our minds. For one thing, I never lost any wild-eyed cannibals with painted bellies, and I don't care to find any. I learned while in the southern country that Lieutenant R. E. L. Robinson and his partner, Logan, were surely killed and probably eaten by the Seris on Tiburon. I talked with a survivor of the party, a Mexican, who gave me details of the case. I went to Tiburon, anchored off shore and saw the Indians, and believed their story. Such ferocious, repulsive and dirty people that I have ever seen. After a few days at Pelican Island, near Tiburon, we learned enough about the natives to satisfy us that we were right in giving them the cold shoulder, and went north."

Charlie was a man who was quite familiar with the history of that party. Robinson had been the reporter that gave out the story about Charlie's "fight" with Geronimo. Charlie had gone through varied rough times and experiences without a scratch, and Harris' tale did not lessen his plans one whit. Charlie had such a large and certain opinion of his own place in the cosmos, few seemed capable of denying him the position of authority into which he insinuated himself. "If Robinson and Logan are alive and held captive in the fastness of Tiburon," Charlie told a reporter, "then this Arizona man plans to release them and return them to civilization. It is my intention to go into the interior and explore every part of the island, cannibals or no cannibals! They are a giant race it is true, but they are not brave men I am told, and this bunch of Arizona cowpunchers are going to be able to handle them and bring back scientific proofs of wealth." By this time Charlie was besieged with applicants to join his expedition. But he screened out each and every one of them by their hardihood and to his qualifications. It was no place for a greenhorn, but for men whose natures craved the wildest freedom.

Charlie spent considerable time in San Francisco, gathering stores, signing up shareholders and meeting with the press. *The San Francisco Examiner Magazine* section of August 17, 1902, presented a long column about the colorful Arizona man. A few excerpts from their article follows:

"Arizona Charlie, most picturesque and daring frontiersman in all the West, has entered upon a new role in his very adventuresome, interesting and creditable career. As admiral of a miniature home-made battleship, manned by nineteen souls only a degree less dauntless than himself, he proposes to do that which no man has ever succeeded in doing. He has set forth upon a perilous and self-imposed mission, in attempting to perform where he, with his companions may be eaten by cannibals. For Arizona Charlie, in his queer little battleship, means to conquer the ferocious Seri Indians of Tiburon Island.

"Will the handful become mouthfuls? Will he lead his expedition to victory across the *Angustura del Infierno* ("Hell's Narrow Path"), that narrow stretch of water that boils like a tea kettle when the tide is in—and glides gulfward like a snake when the tide is out? Or will he make for himself a chapter unique in the world's history as a man who subdued the Seri savages, who for centuries have terrorized all comers?

"That a man should come forward with a cool proposition to buy this island after risking his life to blaze the way to possession of it, is one of the marvels that Mexico cannot understand but is quite willing to accept.

"Arizona Charlie is a cowboy of the best type, a gentleman as cultured as he is brave and handsome. He is a splendid specimen of physical development, six-foot-six in his stocking feet, and there is nothing in his modest demeanor to indicate the record he has made on the range."

President Theodore Roosevelt was the only rancher-cowboy to ever make it to the White House. In Arizona, after his organization of the Rough Riders, he had the reputation of being an *fervent jingo*, with an insatiable lust for life. Charlie was convinced he should send Roosevelt an invitation to accompany him on his expedition and lead the advance of Isla Tiburon. Roosevelt's presence, he figured, would give him all the publicity he would ever need, and Charlie never stood in the way of a good story. The following invitation was sent:

> "To Theodore Roosevelt, President of the United States. Arizona Charlie invites you to accompany him on an expedition to Tiburon Island, Mexico, October 1, 1902."

These words were engraved on a small silver shield, or plate, to which Charlie attached an Apache scalp. Charlie had very little difficulty suborning the press. "You should have seen the face on the bug-eyed reporter from the *Los Angeles Times* when I told him I had personally lifted the 'receipt for a good Apache' in Pleasant Valley in 1884," Charlie said.

The invitation caused no small sensation at the White House. Roosevelt could not go, and he suggested Charlie might be in violation of neutrality laws, and that there could be serious international complications. However, Presidential indifference did not discourage Charlie's ambitions. He had a zest for risky enterprise.

Charles Meadows, Yuma, Arizona

The Elia, Charles Meadows' Boat

The red tape with the Mexican officials took longer than Charlie expected, and his starting date had to be moved. Meantime he bought an elegant yacht, the *Elia*, in San Francisco, a sloop of 11 tons, and had it beautifully outfitted. Some of his friends were anxious to help him try it. He shipped the yacht to the gulf, and full of fire and enthusiasm, organized a scouting party and decided to go to Tiburon, sail around the island and investigate possible watering places or other problems they might incur on the larger expedition.

They all met at Hermosillo, and then proceeded to Guaymas on the western coast of Mexico. The water in the gentle bay has the hue, iridescence, and sparkle of gems; it is a paradise for fishermen. The serious work of the trip commenced. His party of seven included his brother, Jake Meadows, Marshal of Yuma; his nephew, John Arnold, of Randsburg; Ed DeHaven of San Diego; Warner Weakley, Frank Wells, George Fugard, and the "King of Tiburon," Charlie. Ed DeHaven, wealthy Alaska miner, described the trip in detail to a reporter from the *Seattle Post Intelligencer* saying:

"Whenever the word 'Tiburon' was mentioned, no one would go with us or sell us an outfit. A Yaqui Indian was hired, but he backed out when he learned our destination, saying, 'I would not go for a million dollars.' For years the Papagos, the Indian tribe living nearby, and the Seris had been fighting each other; and the Seris always triumphed. Several times the Mexicans had attempted to make a landing on the island, but were so badly beaten they gave up all ideas of ever making the attempt again. Consequently, all the inhabitants in the country were completely cowed."

In reciting his experiences to the reporter, Charlie recounted that "we first touched the island of Tassie, in Bahia Kino Bay, and from there we shot straight for Tiburon. We traveled along the shore quite a distance, trying to see some signs of life. We circumnavigated the island for 13 days before we saw a small column of smoke and struck straight for it. These were some of the coast tribe who allowed their women to visit Hermosillo where they traded gold nuggets for provisions. They were friendly, but at first suspicious. We took out a bottle of wine, offered one Indian a drink, but he would not imbibe until he saw the members of our party drink, then he could not get enough. When we inquired about the interior, they appeared anxious to have us go with them to see for ourselves. After a consultation we decided to go—made fast everything in the launch—and started. The Seri supposed we were going without firearms, and we let them think so. We traveled with them eight miles and they appeared very glad to conduct us. All of a sudden out of a clump of bushes came another party of Seri. This ferocious-looking group were armed with bows and arrows and looked like fighting bucks. They spoke to the party with us, and at a command from me, our party drew out guns from our shirt fronts and presented a front to the savages. That was all they wanted. They seemed to fly before us, and it was not necessary to fire a shot. Just what their intentions were—we never knew. They did not stop to explain.

"They were the only ones of the 51 Seri we encouraged who gave us any idea they were hostile, but had we gone in the interior, our fate would probably have been that of those who had gone before us. The hostile Seri with murderous instinct we intend to tame or exterminate on our next expedition."

Before weighing anchor at Guaymas, Charlie wrote friends in Los Angeles and San Francisco, informing them that he intended only to sail about the island, and then make haste up the Colorado River, where he would be expected in about fifteen days. He wrote, "If the party is not heard from in fifteen days from date of sail, you may conclude that we have failed and have been eaten by the Seris!"

Once there, they were not content in looking on from the boat; and the fifteen days passed quickly with not a word heard of their little expedition. Charlie's friends were about to organize their own expedition to the Gulf of California in search of the missing explorers. After all those weeks had passed with no news of her husband, Mae gave Charlie up for dead. Then Charlie got a telegram through that eased her anxiety:

Cape Lobos, via Heroica Caborca, Mexico, October 12.

"All well. Will be home in ten days." C. Meadows.

"We did a little trading with the friendlier Indians and obtained a number of their poisonous arrows and a peculiar bamboo boat, all of which we put on exhibit in Los Angeles. The island was covered with the usual desert vegetation and fine grass which ye cowpuncher thought would make excellent grazing ground. The Seri subsisted totally on raw food, and all their game was run down by foot. Their feet are as swift as a dog's. The island is full of deer. One day we shot one and tossing the Indians a hind quarter, they proceeded to devour it raw. They seemed to live mostly on fish and turtles. When they catch any game they wish to eat, they simply tear it apart and eat it while the warm blood is still dripping from it. In the waters of the straits there are pearls of great value. The seas are rich with an abundance of fish, including yellowtail, *bonita*, skipjack, and the larger sea life—porpoise, bottleneck dolphin, huge sharks, manta rays, gigantic Jewfish, and black sea bass with mouths large enough to 'swallow a beer keg.' And, the island was alive with four kinds of rattlesnakes.

"The climate was excellent, never reaching over 100 degrees, and never falling below 50 degrees. At the south end of the island there is a stream called *Arroyo Carrizal,* in which the water undoubtedly sinks into the sand during the greater part of the year. What looked like permanent water to us was found on the east side of the island, and the latter I should imagine aggregated at least two-thirds of the area.

"We did not examine the pearls in the possession of the Indians, but saw many. They know of their intrinsic worth, and the same is the case with gold. They know it is good to buy food, and that was all. They grow no grain, and seemed to know nothing about agriculture.

"Their homes were little more than a place in the sand where they slept and ate—just rude, flimsy hovels of *mesquite* and *tules*, or *Palo Verde* brush piled up in circles about the holes dug in the sand. Here and there they decorated the brush with a few large turtle shells laid on top. They had no huts or teepees, in fact their shelter was no better than what pigs live in in Arizona. They were a sad-looking bunch of ragamuffins, unspeakably filthy; their faces and lips hideously tattooed with blue coloring matter, and their foreheads were daubed with white bird guano."

The scenery on Charlie's voyage home by way of the Colorado River delta was a riot of wildlife. Besides birds of over 160 species, including osprey, perigrin falcon, black brant, gilded flicker, ladder-backed woodpecker, and the white-winged dove, there were mountain sheep, beaver, two species of wild pig, lynx, wild cat, coyote and jaguar.

There were fish that "leaped like tuna," turtles of immense dimensions, clams "big enough to hold a man's foot in their jaws," great oyster beds, deer as big as cattle with "horns as wide as *mesquite,*" lions of immense size, and wild boar that could "lay open a horse's belly with one single upthrust of his snout." There were flocks of geese, ducks, and wild chickens that fairly blackened the skies when in flight. Charlie portrayed "a sportsman's paradise never before seen by this cowboy in all my worldly travels."

Charlie busily spent the next few weeks between Yuma, the Lick House in San Francisco, and Los Angeles, gathering stores and organizing his major expedition, then on to Seattle to sign up the last of the forty shareholders. There were numerous callers in his rooms at the Northern Hotel in Seattle. "Meadows is a character within himself," said the *Intelligencer,* and "he delighted all in a recital of his experiences since he had left Seattle in August to visit the man-eaters of the Gulf of California." "Then the viper stung!" Charlie loudly exclaimed.

He was met in San Francisco by General Torres, who informed him that strong-man President Diaz had issued a warning: General Andrade was not to sell any part of Tiburon under their agreement—and if a scientific expedition proceeded, it would be with side arms only. Such restrictions rendered Charlie's plans unattainable—and the whole expedition had to be scrapped. Charlie could not believe his efforts had been for naught. The bitter disappointment was enough to twirl ye cowboy's rowels, and blast his horse right out from under him. But Charlie swallowed his *chagrin*, for nothing could discourage his ambitions nor dampen his enthusiasm for adventure.

Charlie with Yellow Boy, Yuma, Arizona

CHAPTER 20

1902-1906
KING OF HOG ISLAND

"No one has ever given a satisfactory explanation of why they want to come back to the hot, mosquito-bitten misery of Yuma," Charlie once remarked. "You cannot imagine the vast clouds of mosquitos we had to contend with that arrived promptly after the spring floods."

Then the venomous *Genus Crotalus* (rattlesnake) and the *Dipsossaurus Dorsalis* (Desert Iguana) held steadfast their right to live there. Few Indians liked the locale well enough to make it their all-year home. Kit Carson pronounced the general area "so desolate and God-forsaken, that a wolf could not even make a living on it." An Eastern newspaper, in describing Yuma, said, "The city is built of mud, and inhabited by Mexicans, naked Indians, and Americans. [Aren't the Indians the "real" Americans?] This is the hottest place in the world; so hot in the summertime that wings melt off mosquitoes, and flies die from the excessive heat of the scorching sun. The Indians cover themselves with mud, the Mexicans crawl into their huts while the Americans stand in the Colorado River and keep drunk the rest of the time to avoid death by melting." It was even said by some 'that the horned toads carried canteens.'

"The glorious sunshine and purity of air is believed by many to be the solution, while others claim the profound stillness or the very bigness of the desert around them caused the longing to return," Charlie said. But Yuma at first blush seemed something a little less than heaven on earth, and hardly the popular desert oasis it is today.

There are several reasons why Charlie came back to Yuma. Yuma lay like a crusted sore on the banks of the Colorado River. The river springs from the confluence of two major headwaters: one, the Green River in Wyoming; and the other, the Grand, born of the snow melt in the Colorado Rockies. It winds its majestic way through the Grand Canyon for hundreds of miles before reaching Yuma, where it joins the Gila River. Then it flows another twenty miles to Sonora, Mexico, and from there spills into the Gulf of California.

But it wasn't the water that brought Charlie back. The Colorado River was of reddish color, and carried with it immense quantities of sand and mud. It was "too thick to drink and too thin to plow." The Yumans drew a pail of it each evening, and by morning—after the mud had settled—they were able to dip from the top for cooking and drinking.

Charlie had no intentions of drying up on the desert. He was a gambler. His scheme was the gulf; the clear and sparkling waters of the Colorado River Delta; and the waters around the islands of Tiburon and Angel de la Guardia where the "greatest hunting and fishing in the world was obtainable." Then, too, Arizona was known for having the greatest natural resources, and rich gold mining was one of Yuma's main activities. The fact that Arizona won all the best mineral awards at the World's Columbian Exposition was all the inspiration Charlie needed. He was always searching for the lucky break of locating some fabulous *cache* of riches. Then, of course, Yuma was where some of his family were living.

Yuma was a wide open, "hell-bent for leather" western town. The main street of any community is usually the hub of activity, and the main street in Yuma was no exception. It was extremely wide to accommodate the turning around of large freight wagons, and there, at every third door that made up the one-and-a-half blocks of Main Street, stood a saloon—seventeen in all. According to a remark made by Charlie's old friend, Police Chief Henry Levy, "Charlie enjoyed riding his horse in and out the swinging doors of Pat Sullivan's, the Ruby Saloon, and all the rest," seeking company of old friends full of amiability and good talk. Then next door to the Huling's Sunshine "tonsorial parlour," in the rear, was the dandiest little card room this side of Dawson City.

By this time the family's fortune had greatly improved and Charlie seemed more relaxed. The City Marshal, Jake, gave a fine stag dinner at his residence in Charlie's honor. The long table was beautifully decorated and loaded with baked beefsheads, tongues, and good red beans—with plenty of sauces and a fancy array of side dishes. The cakes were choice, with decoration of artistic form—and served with blushing lemonade. There was a keg of good red wine that everyone sampled. Even though it was a stag party, the ladies were remembered with generous slices of cake. The main topic of conversation dealt with the *bolas*, kris, and stag horns gathered on Charlie's world tour and on display.

In the fall of 1900, while Charlie was still in Dawson, brother James homesteaded a 160-acre ranch in the Yuma Valley, and took a bride, Miss Gertrude Haraszthy, granddaughter of politically self-exiled Hungarian Count Agoston Haraszthy, father of modern California viniculture. Their romance took place on the famous old paddlewheeler that served Yuma for transporting supplies across the Colorado River during the week, and as a pleasure boat on Sundays. James a born farmer, raised mostly alfalfa, with an area devoted to fresh vegetables and a small orchard; he always had a few beehives to provide honey. On the side, James raised ostriches which was one of the major industries during the early years. James spent hours patiently preparing their feathers for market, popular at the time for making milady's hats and dresses.

James and Gertrude's first home was a tent structure of canvas and screen with a wooden floor. Baths were taken in large galvanized tubs and heated on a wood-burning stove. All their milk and eggs were provided by their own cows and chickens; pigs and cows were raised and slaughtered for meat. However, like all the Meadows family, dry red beans cooked with bacon back was their main diet. Perishable food was kept in coolers, fashioned from burlap sacks wrapped around wooden frames and hung from shade trees, with an *olla* above filled with water to drip slowly down the sides, to keep food cool as it evaporated.

That same year the Mobley Meadows and Tom Beach families, along with the Gillett and Van Horn families, pioneered the Imperial Valley in California—the dry desert land no man coveted. The Van Horn and Gillett families had come from the Salt River Valley, all having heard of the development to start on the Colorado River desert in the Imperial Valley. The three families met on the muddy bank of the Colorado River in Yuma, and wondered how in the world they were going to get across the swollen water. The five men decided to build a crude raft, and within a week they managed to fashion one large and sturdy enough to carry a small load that could be poled across the swift current. It took more than a week of laborious trips—with the help of some experienced Yuma Indians—to carry the families with a total of 17 children, teams and wagons, several crates of chickens and what implements they could carry, which included two Fresno scrapers, five cows and one bull. Fearing the children—all under the age of 10 years—would fall through the cracks in the raft, a rowboat was borrowed to take them across in shifts.

Jake Meadows

Jake, Charlie, and James Meadows

The Tom and Maggie Beach Family

Rosalie, Carlos, and Mobley "Kid" Meadows

Safely across the river, the three venturesome families found themselves on Mexican territory, facing three terribly important-looking officials. Lists and manifests carefully in order (the *rurales* checked out every line) everything appeared alright—but wait! "Where are the chickens?" asked the officers. Of all things, the chickens were not listed. The men were compelled to send the chickens all the way back to Yuma; then ship them to Flowing Wells. One of the men had to make the long trip back with a team to pick up the chickens and return to camp. After that, they kept the chickens north of the line.

The three families were the first immigrants to cross. All went to work immediately for the California Development Company, which was the first construction work done on the main canal system that soon brought water to the fertile Imperial Valley from the Colorado River. With a plow Mr. Gillett broke the first furrow of the canal, and the Van Horns, Mobley Meadows, Thomas Beach and Dennis Dean handled the scrapers. The Van Horn scrapers were the first of thousands that eventually were turning dirt. Tom was superintendent of construction at an unheard of salary of $300 per month. Tom and a man named C. N. Perry succeeded in throwing the first barrier across the rampaging Colorado River during flood stage; this was deemed a "most remarkable achievement," even though it held for only a short time. "They came close in an effort in which experts still marvel," said Otis B. Tout in his book, *The First Thirty Years in Imperial Valley*.

Mobley and Tom planted the first crops of sorghum, barley and milo *maize*, and sold the first load of feed marketed in the valley. Maggie gave birth to the first white girl born in The Valley, at the construction camp on the *mesquite*-banked Cameron Lake, naming the child Cameron after the lake. Since the new construction, Cameron Lake no longer exists as it was the result of the flooding from the Colorado River. Maggie and the other women, set up a rolling commissary and followed the crew for a year, feeding 32 men and managing 17 children at the same time. Three boys and two girls now made up the Tom Beach family. Tom eventually had his own farm and built the first frame home in the Valley. He was later a valley real estate broker and was instrumental in establishing the towns of Niland and Calipatria.

This valley settled by those hard-working pioneers is now the land God remembered, with his "great munificence in richness of soil and lavishness of water"—and has proved to be one of the most productive farming areas in the world, the "agricultural marvel of the age."

Comfortably rich, Charlie and Mae built their frame home in Yuma on First Street; modest by today's standards, but much more prestigious than the usual canvas and screen home—or the original mud and thatched Indian hut that made up the town. To ward off the rays of the blazing sun, they covered their acreage with cottonwood trees and referred to their place as "Headquarters." Throughout the years, Headquarters became the center of considerable activity. Down the main canal, Charlie had another ranch, part of which composed "Meadows Park," where his baseball-on-horseback team was headquartered. "Punk" a nondescript white dog with black blotches was his loving mascot. Punk and Charlie were inseparable.

Mae enjoyed loving her brood of kittens, and her position as a leading member of Yuma's polite society. Dressed in her elegant Dawson wardrobe, she was the envy of the female gender. Charlie was active as a Yuma "booster," striving to create a better image for their town. As "Mr. Yuma," as some called him, he said: "I subdivided West Yuma; laid out the boulevard system, and converted this rattlesnake den and jack-rabbit pasture into a land of shade and flowers, where now nestles herein more than 200 homes."

From the Tonto Basin Charlie gathered 100 head of cattle and 15 head of horses from his herd in partnership with fellow cowman, Bill Brodie, and rode herd to his ranch in Yuma. Mae wouldn't have pigs around, but Charlie appreciated a good hunk of bacon in his beans, or a chop of some kind occasionally, so he settled a group of those "that wallow in the mud" on an islet in the Colorado River, close to his ranch, and became, as he called himself, "King of Hog Island."

When Charlie first came back to Yuma, perhaps the most famous gold mine here was the "King of Arizona," established in 1899. Some of its ore assayed out as high as $3,000 a ton, and was one of the richest ever discovered in Arizona. Felix Mayhew was a miner and ran a saloon on the side. Everyone in town knew Felix; make no mistake about it, Mayhew was one really salty *hombre*. Charlie, in his haunts, made Felix's acquaintance and they hit it off well together. With the help of a Mexican sweetheart, Felix and another fellow named Nick Larsen, along with "Brass Band" Bill Smith and the DeCorse boys, discovered their own rich claim, the "North Star." Whether Charlie had a stake in this mine has not been proven.

"Felix" said Charlie, "was one big, handsome *hombre*, with bushy head, glinty eyes, and a red twisted smile—who wasn't afraid of an acre of evils." At one time Felix had been a running mate with Burt Alvord and Billy Stiles, famous Arizona outlaws, but that was long before Charlie knew him.

Charlie Buys His First Iron Monster

There were only wagon roads leading out of Yuma. Before the advent of the automobile, travel to remote communities was both difficult and arduous. If one couldn't reach a destination by horse and wagon, one had to get there by boat or rail. Charlie and Mae frequently vacationed in Los Angeles, especially during the hot summers, and enjoyed vaudeville performances as the guests of Alexander Pantages at his Hollywood theatre.

One day a man by the name of Seth Hartley of nearby Somerton chugged into Yuma from California in the first gas buggy ever seen in Yuma. The funny looking contraption, which was a Reo, caused considerable laughter up and down Main Street. Some people even went so far as to predict that the auto would never take the place of the horse. But Charlie was one man who was greatly impressed. He had to own one, no matter what the price. Over a little liquid persuasion in a local saloon, Charlie managed to wheedle Hartley into parting with his pride and joy for $1,500.

Following a few quick instructions for its operation, Charlie hopped into the iron monster with mining crony Nick Larsen as passenger and took off. Recalling the event, Charlie remarked to a woman reporter from the *Morning Sun*: "We set out down Main Street, and I never before realized that so much traffic traversed that Appian Way of Yuma. That was before the street was paved—bumps-nothing-but-bumps, foot-loose *burros*, *burros* with Indians astride them, wagons and more wagons."

After touring the whole of Yuma showing off his new toy, Charlie discovered he hadn't learned how to stop the danged thing. So the two men ran the flivver around the block a few times—then out to the mesa, where Charlie thought he could bring it to a stop against a sand dune. But the contraption finally belched and stalled on its own, then ran out of gas. The two friends had to walk back to town, where they took a good ribbing. The noisy thing was prone to breakdowns, and as Charlie was a genuine lover of the equine clan, it hardly took the place of his horse, so he was rarely seen about town in it. Eventually, he sold the troublesome thing.

Later, the old plank road came into being across the vast sand dunes that separated Yuma from the Imperial Valley. It consisted of 2 x 12 planks held together by metal bands placed side by side, forming a 14-inch ribbon of wood for each side of wheels, with a stretch in between of 2-3 feet. Ever so often a set of side tracks were placed for passing. Keeping the car on the tracks proved to be a constant test of nerves and skill, with autos often bogging down in the sand.

Mae was twelve years younger than Charlie and in the prime of womanhood, but they were never blessed with children. Charlie realized just how much this meant to her, when one day, while glancing through his famous scrapbook, he discovered someone had taken a razor blade and carved Marion Mae's face from a group photo of Harmston's Company in Australia. It was Marion Mae who had his child—wherever she was, and that Mae could never forget. With each sunrise Mae piled it on, and her once wasp waist and voluptuous curves disappeared into a straight over-stout form, which didn't help her self image much either.

A Railroad Departure

It was well into November of 1903, when Charlie learned his old arch-rival, Tom Horn, had met his rendezvous with destiny in far off Wyoming. One of the finest ropers in Arizona, Tom was hung by the neck until his body was dead—and his soul swung into eternity for a crime he did not commit. The odds were that Tom would be found innocent of the death of a young boy who died at the hands of an unknown assailant. Both honorable and brave, Tom played an important part in Arizona's history: first, as a packer along with Charlie; then as a government scout; interpreter; and Chief of Scouts under both Generals Crook and Miles. He also played a prominent part in bringing Geronimo's band to the famous conference with General Crook at *Cañon de los Embudos* ("tunnel canyon").

Tom went to Cuba with Roosevelt's Rough Riders, and when he returned, he found employment in Wyoming with the big cattle interests as a range detective aimed at wiping out cattle thievery. But Tom was not bereft of influential friends. Al Sieber said, "A more faithful and honorable man I have never met in my life." Considerable money was given in his defense, but the deck was stacked against him by his enemies, cattlemen from whose ranges he recovered stolen stock. All gave damaging testimony; he was swiftly framed. Several members of the jury had reason to despise him; the whole case was quickly railroaded through and Tom became a tragic victim of circumstance.

Charlie Whips the Bush

The lure for the riot of wild life on the Colorado River delta sports paradise constantly beckoned, and with his sloop, *Elia*, Charlie made numerous excursions with friends to the gulf island to hunt and fish. On one ten-day trip to San Felipe, 40 miles below Montague Island, with Charles Cowles and Gus Olinger, a great and experienced seaman who had at one time piloted his boat as far as Alaska, they caught spawning sea bass weighing 70-90 pounds that could be had for the taking, and seven immense sea turtles. On that trip they were able to recover part of the goods stolen from them on a previous trip. At that time a Yaqui Indian who Charlie had left to guard the boat, swam ashore when four escaped convicts from the Yuma jail made their way down river, boarded Charlie's boat, and attempted to sail away. The Indian ran a considerable distance to give Charlie the warning. Charlie organized a party of Cocopah Indians at once, and with their assistance "whipped the bush" about the mouth of the Colorado River on both sides of the International Line.

The tide was too low and the convicts could not get the boat over the bar. So they contented themselves by carrying off everything they could take with them, including blankets, utensils, clothing, guns, revolvers, and ammunition—"well capable of meeting up with a brigade of Mexican Army," reported the morning press.

Charlie learned that the thieves were escapees from the Yuma Territorial Prison, and only three could be accounted for. The three had endeavored to cross the California desert to Calexico, but in doing so, one of them, a fellow with a wooden leg, was abandoned. He had stripped off every tattered thread of his clothing and had apparently laid down to die. Later, he was found by a man passing with a team.

From San Felipe, Charlie's mining interest took them to an onyx quarry where they obtained some fine specimens; one, weighing about 900 pounds, was shipped by way of Calexico and put on display at the Gandolpho Hotel in Yuma.

Fate's Cruel Blow

Charlie was unable to go to the Gulf Islands on Gus Olinger's next excursion. Once again, he escaped fate's cruel blow. Gus and his boat, along with Henry Miller, former Principal of Yuma High School, mysteriously disappeared. Gus was from Los Angeles, and like Charlie, kept his boat stored at Montague Island at the mouth of the Colorado where it empties into the gulf. Olinger, impressed with Charlie's tales of great oyster beds in the waters surrounding Tiburon, and vast growths of sponges around the Isla del Angel de la Guardia, relayed his knowledge to a Los Angeles syndicate who hired him and their representative, Miller, to investigate. Miller was also to seek a mountain believed to contain radium that Charlie believed to be there, and prospect for gold and silver deposits. They intended to harvest enough sponges to pay for the trip and open up a new line of commercial enterprises.

Because Olinger was a qualified seaman and had made a trip or two with Charlie into these waters, many of his friends feared he had been caught in a storm that swept the gulf at that time and would head for the island. After a few weeks an appeal was made to the Mexican Consul in Los Angeles, doughty General Guillermo Andrade, by the syndicate. Governor Ysbell of Sonora dispatched a relief party to the area in search of the two men. They found nothing.

Charlie, along with others who had studied the incidents, held to the theory that the two men made a landing on Tiburon and were decoyed away from their guns by the wily savages and then slain—and possibly eaten by those cannibals, the Seris. General Andrade held the same opinion.

Charlie with Will Rogers, *Circa* 1905

Charlie with His Niece, Florence, at Hog Island

In the Interim

Finally, after 14 years of passing through the United States Supreme Court system, the minions of the law were sadly disappointed when Charlie's attorney informed him that the moment he had long been waiting for had arrived, and a check of $68,000 for Indian depredations would be soon on the way. The amount covered 14 years of interest and attorney's fees. Although it had been needed more in earlier years, Charlie was the happiest cowboy under desert skies the day he was able to split the windfall with his heirs.

Charlie again dabbled in show business. In 1905, he traveled for two weeks displaying an early movie machine called the "Magic Lantern," showing the Jeffreys-Corbett fight. Stella, his niece, went along and performed with a magician. She was tied in a mail bag, and when the rope that was tied to her feet was loosened, she came up singing, "Goodnight My Starlight."

During that same year, Rosalie became seriously ill. Jake took a lawman's job in the Imperial Valley and moved his family there so his wife, Martha, could help Rosalie with the children. At this time Charlie's energies were spent on mineral and mining schemes and big game hunting. Except for a few pets and buggy horses, Charlie moved his remaining animals to the Imperial Valley along with Jake's.

The following years were filled with heartache. Even though Charlie was not one to dwell on the reality of death, a mysterious stroke of God's will that seemed unjustifiable, took the beautiful Rosalie—only 30, a lady champion *equestrienne* who rode her steed over life's greatest hurdle. As if that was not enough sorrow, Maggie's little girl, Cameron, died from diphtheria. No matter how they all tried to reason with this double tragedy, Charlie and Mae grieved right along with the Mobley Meadows and Tom Beach families.

About the same time, Charlie learned that his old pard, Texas Jack, Jr., still a young man in his forties, was struck down by death in South Africa. Charlie and Jack were unable to keep their pact for a reunion. Charlie regretted this. But it can be assumed that Charlie thought "perhaps someday—when I'm booted and spurred and ready to ride out, we'll be reunited again." Then on April 13, 1906, San Francisco suffered a devastating earthquake, and the family all trembled for sister, Mary Arnold, until word was received of her safety.

CHAPTER 21

1906
THE VALLEY HORNET

The Arizona gentleman became active in civic and governmental affairs, problems and improvements concerning his town, and the reclamation of Yuma's bottom lands and their proposed irrigation system—by the planned Laguna Dam Project and its canal system. He also was the creator of a boulevard system for Yuma, forever leaving his footprints in the stream of Yuma history.

Now Charlie was as "modest as a hazed freshman," and as "polished as a Fifth Avenue Swell," and his conversation was that of a cultured traveler. He had always been a man for men to follow—and he was therefore shattered by real and fanciful "slights."

There were a few "hungry lawyers," as he called them, and politicians who objected to a newcomer taking a leading voice as strong as his, when before they had the privilege of running little old Yuma their way—right or wrong.

In 1906, these "Apostles of the Bar," and hard-lined individuals of the town attempted to slow the Arizona man down by having him dragged into court for personal property violation, to wit—the crime of "perjury." The whole blamed matter concerned the number of cattle and horses in his pasture the preceding year. "All" had been moved to Imperial Valley along with Jake's cattle, except for his pets and buggy horses.

Simultaneously, Mae and her sister, Emma, who jointly owned some ranch lands together, had a property dispute. One of the above-mentioned attorneys was W. F. Timmons, Emma's lawyer. A heavy-set man addicted to the hard use of alcohol, he also took a great interest in politics; and his "accomplice," pawn broker Eddie Frankel, was Emma's new love interest. This same attorney proceeded to make a Federal case out of a minor squabble.

The tax evasion case against Charlie was finally dismissed on a technicality, but Mae's property dispute led to an altercation that made front-page news in the Yuma papers for some time, dragging Charlie's name and that of his wife, down in the mud.

Charlie, in describing the trouble, said: "Yours truly was accused of pointing a gun at the inebriated lawyer's face, and Mae was accused of beating him with a "buggy whip." I was not allowed to present my side of the fracas in court, and figured I got less than a fair shake, don'cherknow."

Smarting at the accusation—and in order to clear their good names in a case brought against them for assault and battery, garrulous Charlie put out the first edition of his extremely controversial newspaper, the *Valley Hornet*. It was in the way of a newsletter to the public, and was published on November 3, 1906, part of which follows:

"Some two months ago the people of Yuma were startled by the sensational report that a prominent and peaceable citizen had been attacked in the suburbs by a drunken ruffian and an infuriated woman, and while the former held the victim at the point of a gun, the latter introduced a 'horse-whip.'

"Now, the undersigned happened to be that 'drunken ruffian,' and as I have been arrested four times for that and other charges arising out of it, and as promptly released on each occasion without an opportunity of making a statement in court, which, in my discretion I withheld for such an opportunity, I now feel that in justice to my family, and for the edification and enlightenment of the Independent Order of the Good Templars, I owe an explanation.

"In making this statement I shall not ask you to take my word for all or any part of it, but will cite to you the proofs in each instance; and if I fail in any instance, I bind myself by these presents, and over my signature, to deed to the town of Yuma, Block 56 of said town (valued at $3,000, and for which negotiations are now on for sale to the town council). If you are skeptical, come to me for proofs.

"To begin with, I have been unjustly censured by some good people who have heard only one side of the case; and have been both persecuted and prosecuted by a few policy-playing time-servers who seek to cover the faults of a raving and drunken maniac by blasting the reputation of a lawful, and, I believe, an honorable citizen of Arizona, and no stranger to its citizens and the public; and I ask in justice to take my record from the time I made for the borders of civilization 29 years ago before there were roads or trails on the outskirts of the Apache reservation. There I settled with my parents until the smoldering embers of contention between the Indians and settlers burst into warfare. It was the first time in my life I ever raised a hand or voice against a human being when I fought beside my father and brothers, and saw my relatives fall around me fairly riddled into sausage meat before my eyes in fierce and deadly conflict. And when I saw my loving mother die of a broken heart from this terrible tragedy, it seemed as if the last ray of sunshine had gone out of my life forever; and I became a wanderer on the face of the earth. In strange lands and under foreign flags, without recommendation or introduction, belonging to no order of organization, never raising a distress sign or seeking a favor, or asking a dollar from a fellowman, but going independently on my own merits and resources, I carried the name of *Arizona* all over four continents, and brought it home untarnished.

"Follow me from the South Sea Islands and to the Antipodes, through Java, farther to India, Sumatra and Burma. Through the Philippines, China and Japan, across Canada and Europe, and from the Arctic Ocean to Panama, and if you find one blot against the name of *Charles Meadows*, bring your deed and I'll sign.

"Tired at last of wandering, I selected from the broad expanse of this globe a home in the little law-abiding town of Yuma. For four years I have lived among you and have harmed no man intentionally. Here's the trouble: I committed the unpardonable crime of refusing point blank to be robbed of $500 in broad daylight in the streets of Yuma. A hungry lawyer and the proprietor of an unlicensed pawn shop coveted the prize. They exhausted every trick in the trade, and finally hid their heads beneath the petticoats of a good, but feeble-minded woman, and already had her in the shadow of the penitentiary when the unwritten law stepped in."

The *Valley Hornet* is quoted at length here to give the reader an idea of Charlie's extremely extraverted and loquacious nature. Charlie goes on to say, "In the office of that law firm sat the King of Hypocrites, shielded by a Masonic emblem; parading the white badge of temperance, he reclined on a soda fountain with a bottle of bourbon in his back pocket and a roll of grafted bills in front of him—quite an easy position I assure you—very different from that of the little woman whose whole sole object in life has been to attend to her own affairs, and who spent a long and sleepless night coming from San Francisco on an urgent telegram to find this imminent lawyer and prominent citizen sitting by an electric fan with her obstinate husband's $500 in one hand and leading her ill-advised sister to the penitentiary with the other, all for a $500 fee. Do you wonder that in his drunken delirium his conscience told him that he had been to the whipping post? But our brother never drinks—it was the other 'fellow' that was drunk.

"Kind reader, here is where you win a city block. I have never posed as a society model or a saint, and I have probably contributed more to the saloon licenses of Arizona than any man in it. I have drunk wine with the nobility of the Old World, and *mescal* with the Peons of Mexico. I have bought and paid for enough drinks to float the new California Development's dredge—but I have never carried a bottle of whiskey in my pocket and a white ribbon in my buttonhole, and if you can furnish me proof that I was ever under the influence of liquor, I'll sign. Prove that I have ever had an altercation with, or raised a hand against a white man, and Block 56 is yours.

"Now let me tell you exactly what happened on the Mesa Road that night. I met lawyer W. F. Timmons, on the Blue Rock Road, and while I shook an angry finger (not a pistol) in his face and told him emphatically, and I meant what I said, that unless he returned that money to me before court opened the following morning, neither he nor his pawn shop accomplice would live to get inside the courtroom. If Timmons was struck over the face, it was with a lady's umbrella, and not a horsewhip, which was no part of my fight. I picked up from the mesa wreck a broken buggy and a shattered parasol, and what

Timmons got was the fear of God Almighty put in his heart. If he was not already drunk, why was he returning to town at that hour after going home?

"At the appointed time of the trial the following morning, not a soul darkened the doors of the Justice Court. When Timmons failed to show up, his client, brother Eddie (Little Ickey) Frankel (Emma's friend), called in a reputable attorney, who told him unless he had some claim on that money to return it at once to the owner—and get a receipt.

"This closed the first chapter in the celebrated case which occupied three places on the Justice Court docket, and two in the District Court. It also took up about half the time of the last grand jury.

"Timmons was certainly 'going some' that night, or I lose a city block. He barricaded himself in his office with a shotgun and a revolver. He told his friends how he had watched me come from the mesa and hide in a woodpile across the street. Nor would he be pacified until a committee went to the spot designated and pulled a drunken Mexican from a barrel. At last my 'brother' Henry Wupperman, an attorney, came to the rescue. He went to the Meadows *hacienda* and found Charlie asleep in his bed.

"Sullivan took me to Timmon's office that afternoon. Timmons said his clients had quit, his associates had thrown him down, and his heart was about to quit beating. When he offered his outstretched hand what could an honorable man do in front of a prostrate foe but shake it. He saw me to the train, and begged my pardon and my wife's forgiveness for the misstatements he had made in the papers. I went on my vacation thinking all was well, but 'methinks' while my back was turned the viper stung! On my return the grand jury handed me two small packages, and I believe they were perfectly justified in their minds from the evidence, such as it was, and they had no particular reason to doubt it.

"As to Ransom D. Breedlove, let me say right here that I have known him for a long time as an honest and upright man and a good neighbor. He was entitled to stay with Bill Timmons, and if he had at any turn of the road I should have lost the high esteem I have held for him and his family. And if brother Bill Timmons does see things a little crooked when he is in his cups, I'll take his bare word when he is sober rather than that of a majority of the last grand jury, and so will you Mr. Voter, after you have heard me.

"Those grand jurors, when they convened, must have taken an obligation to faithfully look into the criminal affairs of the county. They were cited to a case on the county records that has been examined by a number of experts, several lawyers, and some twenty citizens, and they all agree that it presents a clear *prima facie* case of felony against W. F. Timmons. If, when that was presented to the grand jury, one good old brother made a speech and a motion to ignore it without an investigation, and another seconded it, and eight others voted, 'Aye,' what do you think of their solemn obligations?

"The man who made the motion said it would look like blackmail, and was afraid of criticism. Great guns! Gentlemen, can these charges be true or are they political fodder? It has been printed now several days and no one has denied it. If true, the names of those 10 men should be printed and posted on the very page of the county record that carried the $250 discrepancy, and go down in history as the 'men who were afraid.'

"As to the four pious old spavins who got up and swore that they were unbiased and unprejudiced in my case—you have my sympathy, old boys. You swore long and strong, but with the little judge there was nothing doing. There was a barrier of honor in front of him that could not get over with 'high signs.' You were separated from your bankroll, as it were. You winced like whining puppies under the piercing glance of that magnetic little judge. He knows a lobster when he sees one—that is everyday business with him. He had you located before you uttered the second sentence, and I never talk about anyone either, but from the decision he gave, I suspect he thought you were swearing through your bonnets. Why, you old suckers, if you were biased why didn't you say so? Everybody in the courtroom but myself wanted you to. I pulled attorney Tom Malloy's coattail off trying to prevent him from rounding you up. Little Jimmie stood Tom Malloy's cross fire like a major, and swore until he was blacker in the face than Timmon's record. When he left the stand he felt bigger than Jon Shanssey, in fact so big that he had to go plumb outside to change his mind. Then Brown thought Jimmie was too good a friend of mine, and he recalled him. Jimmie went this time with a gallop. He said he never liked me much anyhow, and that he was 'prejudiced' just like all other good people like himself! Everything was quiet for a minute, then Judge Campbell laughed—Brown turned red, Tom Malloy reached for his tee, and I burst a collar button gritting my teeth. Timmons drew a free breath, and on the square, Little Jimmie didn't look six inches high this time when he waddled off the stand, and he felt lighter than the Ainsworth vote when it is counted.

"This man Timmons had me arrested because he got drunk—and I didn't get a look in, or a drink, or a smell. He got all the booze and had a rip-roaring good time, and I couldn't get a grand juror to look in his direction. Now, if I am arrested four times for shaking my finger in Timmons face for $500, what would happen to me if I had gone as strong as Dunc DeVane did when he stuck a rusty pistol under Brother Patterson's nose and brought him in in a dog trot with $3,000? Just shift the cut on me and find the ratio. Answer: Counting finger and pistol equal, six indictments please. And let me say right here that had Dunc DeVane been on the last grand jury, and had been cited to a $250 steal charged to Brother Bill Timmons, or any other Brother, I will stake 'four' city blocks they would have thought there was a hornet's nest knocked down in their midst before they would have adjourned without an investigation.

"But, say there, Charlie, how about that little tax affair? You know Tom Malloy knocked that out on a technicality. The taxpayers are not very pleased about that, and it is not too late for the supervisors and the stock inspector to work you over again. You may be King of Hog Island, and have some stock on neutral ground, but how about that 85 head in the pasture on May 1, 1905?

"Four horses, two cows, Meadows; one filly, Hickey; one stray bull, three horses, McClelland, all taxes paid; one buggy horse, Eddie Frankel, taxes "not" paid. What! Did Brother Eddie Frankel take the oath and forget to pay on his horse and buggy? (Do you want the proofs?) But who hollered 'wolf.'

"Ah, Mr. Grand Juror, did you not hear the busy little footsteps of little Eddie Fagin on the outside when he led that little orphan girl, who is without a protector on earth, to the doors of the grand jury room, and coached her into making a willful statement that 70 head of stock were on that place. You don't need the proofs. No child has the interest of the county enough at heart to make a statement without undue persuasion. She was not mistaken. She cared for and named every animal on that place. Of the horses there were Dick, Norton, Chappo, Princess, and Nancy Hanks. Of the cattle, there was Diller and Grandma. Who found the other sixty-two? Show me another one, and I will pack my blanket and get out of town tonight. Jim Graham swore he'd never heard of this case until it came up in the grand jury room that day. He didn't know that the little school girl was kept out of school that day at the sacrifice of her veracity. He did not send for her.

"Brother Patterson did this county out of about $60,000 and caused the untimely death of some old people. That might have been bad management and no fault of his. But can you imagine a degenerate descendent of Abraham and Montezuma outside the walls of the penitentiary, and sitting beside you in a lodge from who has carried faganism to the home of orphans, and willfully or deliberately polluted the innocent, unprotected school child? This little Brother Ickey has Brother Bill skinned the full length of the boulevard. He got me indicted because I paid my taxes and he didn't pay his. And he made a child I raised, fed and clothed for 10 years prove to the grand jury that I was a felon. He doesn't have to pay his taxes and hock-shop license, that fellow. And there is still that $250 discrepancy on the county records, and several other small precincts that would never have come in if it had not been for him.

"He has enough work already in sight for a special grand jury. There are a lot of people in this valley from Missouri, and those 10 grand jurors have got to show them. You wouldn't hand Charlie anything that you wouldn't hand Brother Eddie—would you, with all conditions equal and Eddie carrying weight (a horse and buggy)?

"I have made some sarcastic remarks in this statement about the Masonic lodge, for which I ask forgiveness. I have always regarded it as the grandest secret organization on earth, and I happen to know—with very few exceptions, that its members are sober, honest, God-fearing men; but gentlemen, there are beneath your banner some who are using your cloak to cover their tracks of sin and lawlessness; unless you cleanse your ranks you will bring down on your order the wrath of your best members, and all the law-abiding citizens of this community. If you will take the Pattersons, the Timmons, Frankels and some others, please take me.

"I will go at the lightning Express like a bull at a red flag. Then if I stand before you with tears rolling down my cheeks, and tell you I am a train robber and I need money, and that the old dirty expressman lambasted me over the head with an umbrella and shook his fist in my face and made me give up the money; then if you exonerate me, and prosecute that express company, I will agree to turn over the transcontinental lines to Bryan before the next presidential election.

"Some two months ago I was making daily visits to Joe Redondo's office answering charges and giving bonds, etc. I chanced to see a case where Bill Timmons was working the order over time.

"There was a civil suit going on and Bill was making a masterly plea for his client. He was addressing his entire argument to an old decrepit man who sat in the corner with a Masonic button on. When the jury took a ballot, 11 men voted for the verdict. The man with the button 'stood pat,' and kept standing pat until everyone got hungry, then the verdict came.

"Mexican stand-off, the horny hand of toil whom I had seen swallowing dust, as he followed a scraper for two weeks leveling a man's yard, walked home. He paid half the cost, lost all his money—but saved his life. Then the next night I saw Brother Bill Timmons and the man with the button and the man who had the yard leveled, and another good Brother (the man who shot Mrs. Dunn's old pet buggy horse because he liked hay) all going up to the Good Templar's Lodge. They were carrying ice-cream freezers and going up to take charge of their classes to teach the little children to be good and honest and true and sober. It may be all right for you mothers, but I felt the effect of one of your pupils on the grand jury. Me for anti-Roosevelt as long as you keep that class of teachers.

"Mothers, do you think for one moment that those brazen old hypocritic scoundrels are patting your little children on the head and feeding them candy and ice cream because they are interested in their welfare? Not for a moment. They want your cloak of protection and your husband's vote.

"Purify your ranks and set an example for other orders, oust those hypocritic scoundrels and show that you are not afraid as the grand jury was.

"Before the ink is dry on these pages you will hear a wail go up. Watch where the shoe pinches, and see who is denouncing the author and why. Because he did not rob the county of $250, shoot a defenseless horse, hang a grand jury and beat a laborer out of his earnings, or rob an orphan school girl of her veracity?

"This Arizona man is not afraid of criticism or to fulfill his sworn duty, and furthermore, he is not afraid of God, man, or the Devil, so long as he knows he is in the right. And if the time ever comes that he will have to play the policy game or practice hypocrisy and rob and steal and hide beneath the spotless banner of fraternalism, then Charlie will pack his traps and 'hike' to the sinks of the Colorado and rear his family on roots and grass nuts. But Charlie, you sling a "nasty" quill. Watch me, this is only the first edition. I am on the trail of the imposter. And if my pen were the candle of Satan dipped in an oiling, seething vat of prussic acid and vitrol, and had I the talent of Braun and the immaculate gall of Bill Timmons, I could not do justice to the subject."

Yours fraternally,
C. Meadows.

WANTED—25 ARMED MEN AT ONCE FOR BODYGUARDS. APPLY TO HIS ROYAL HIGHNESS, KING CHARLES I, OF HOG ISLAND.

Charlie's *Valley Hornet* made quite a sensational entrance into the journalism field—and stung like hornets do, causing no small stir in the little old town of Yuma.

Mobley with Deputies and Dog, "Punk"

CHAPTER 22

1907
THE HOT AIR NAVIGATION COMPANY

There was no place on the face of the earth that had such a variety and quantity of big game as the great valley of the Colorado River and the Gulf of California, and the Arizona gentleman's interest in this sportsman's paradise never waned. In 1907, the "Hot Air Navigation Company" was formed with friends, Felix Mayhew and Bill Buck. They provided easy and speedy transportation for sports and pleasure parties down the Nile of America, to America's greatest hunting and fishing grounds, on the steamer, the *Felix Mayhew*, the two naphtha launches, the *Gee Whiz*, and *Cracker-Jack*, and the two luxury yachts, the *Elia*, and the *Two Republics*. Comfortable house boats were constructed for eating and sleeping quarters, and a commodious club house provided.

Ten-day excursions were also made to the Gulf Islands, and sight-seeing tours of the sulphur mines, the Aztec ruins, Cocopah Indian villages, and into the spawning waters of the famous tuna, tarpon, papagallo, and a dozen other varieties of game fishing sporting in the shallows of the gulf. They also furnished Indian guides and trained horses for pig-sticking. Special attention and reduced rates were given for large parties.

The remoteness of this region, and the difficulty of penetrating it for any distance made it one of the most remarkable game refuges known in America at that time. Small game was not much of a problem, but the horned and hairy heads, the main fruits of their hunting, were difficult to bring out of the remote recesses, back channels, and mud-land archipelagos that made travel next to impossible. Mules seemed the answer, but they proved unmudworthy, so few of the larger trophies were ever retrieved, and that proved to be the only weak link of the whole undertaking.

The Hot Air Navigation Company hosted parties for many distinguished notables from all over the world on excursions down the "American Nile." Charlie's reputation as a host was unrivaled, and one card in his possession reads:

> "The Countess of Meherenc of St. Pierre
> St. Brienc, France.
>
> Thanks to Mr. and Mrs. Charles Meadows for their nice reception, she sends them the photos of the trip down the Colorado.
>
> With best wishes. . . ."

Over the years Charlie and Mae entertained many old friends from the Klondike days, and others from all over the world, at Headquarters, including renowned American personalities, Buffalo Bill, Zane Grey, and Will Rogers.

First Sheriff Mobley Meadows

During the floods of 1904-1905, Mobley became a hero. The capricious Colorado River, without which the Imperial Valley could not have been built, became a raging cataract and went on a rampage that threatened the destruction of the whole canal project. Flood waters eroded the banks and spilled over into the farmlands around the towns of Calexico and Mexicali.

An obstruction of solid rock diverted the flow down the main street of the town of Calexico, threatening its destruction. A substantial reward was offered to anyone who would blast out the obstruction, but there was no rush of volunteers. Then, Mobley stepped forward and volunteered for the ticklish job. No one knew how he intended to do it. A boat could not ford that current. To the amazement of all, Mobley walked calmly up the river bank for some distance and dived into the water with a charge of blasting powder on his back. The strong current forced him downstream as everyone panicked, but he was a powerful swimmer and made headway fast across. Wild shouts went up, "he's made it." Mobley planted the charge and drifted downstream beyond the force of the following blast which cleared the obstruction and saved the town. He was an instant hero. A few chests swelled in Charlie's lordly *hacienda* that night.

Mobley's winning ways and marvelous exploits gained him wide popularity. On August 6, 1907, Imperial Valley was chartered following its divorce from San Diego County. The brave, work-toughened pioneers were still conquering the harshest of all American frontiers of heat, sand, and desolation, when they chose Mobley Meadows as their "first sheriff," and his whole bi-partisan ticket carried except for the assessor. Old Charlie fairly "burst" his suspenders.

At first the sheriff's office was in a brick restaurant building. A county jail with four cells for prisoners and quarters for the sheriff was ordered built by the supervisors and put on Mobley's property. A sign read: "County Jail—Keep out." This was notice for loafers and not meant for the prisoners. But then a continual disturbance by drunken inmates prompted Mobley to drag the jail out of earshot so he could relax in peace. It has been said that when the brothers dropped in, they all sat around and picked flies off the ceiling with their guns. Mobley made Charlie's old friend and partner, Bill Buck, his chief deputy.

Mobley was said to be a typical sheriff—all bone and muscle. He was quick on the draw, yet kind in his dealings with law violators, often tracking murderers over the desert, sand dunes, and across miles of mountains for long days. He also saved the lives of numerous prospectors because of his uncanny knowledge of the arid expanses.

Jake was town marshal, but when Mobley was elected sheriff, he swore Jake in as a deputy. But all was not tranquil in 1907. After a short illness, death claimed Jake's wife, Martha, still a young woman in her thirties. Like his brother, Mobley, Jake was left with three small children to rear. He never seemed to recover from his loss. The following year grief was renewed with the passing of their sister, Rhoda Kansas. Death, Charlie knew, was part of life, but why was it coming so early and so often for the women in the family? For Charlie, each day Mae lived was a blessed day of grace.

Charles Meadows, Colorado River Fishing Excursion

Photo #79
Chief of the Tiburones with Arizona Charlie

Charlie Standing Near the Chief of the Tiburones

Arizona Charlie on His Horse with Dog, "Punk"

CHAPTER 23

1908-1910
THE GREATEST *VAQUERO*

In the Spring of 1908, when a seven-day visit by Theodore Roosevelt's Great Atlantic White Fleet was expected to arrive in Los Angeles after their world cruise, people thrilled with patriotism, and began dusting off the Stars and Stripes in preparation for a gigantic welcoming. Two local promoters, Los Angeles boxing instructor, Van Court, and the General Manager of the far-famed Vaquero Club, Jack Hendrickson, and his committee, took into consideration the sailors' love of sports and combined their efforts. They envisioned a wild west entertainment to accompany the sports activities.

Arizona Charlie was Mr. Hendrickson's idea of the "greatest *vaquero* of all time," and he requested his talents. Charlie was indeed flattered that he was still considered in the arena of all-time greats. It had been a long time, but he felt he still retained his old-time agility, and this opportunity pleased the long-shanked cowboy. He accepted willingly.

Charlie's job was to round up other western men with known skill and a band of fierce-looking Pima and Cocopah Indians. His brother, Sheriff Mobley Meadows, of Imperial County, California, and known trick-rider of the west, was his first choice. Then Captain Rynning, former Rough Rider, and the Captain of the Arizona Rangers, who at the time was the tough warden of the Yuma Territorial Prison, was next on his list. Miss Mollie Nesbitt, the beauteous "Desert Queen," and Charlie's very rich mining crony, Felix Mayhew, were willing additions. Felix had recently sold his North Star mine; lit his cigars with $20 bills; took a bride, Mrs. Carmelita Romero, a widow, and was then occupying an upholstered chair on Easy Street watching the common herd go by. It was "clover" for Felix; nothing was too good for him. He rented his own plush Pullman car equipped with all the necessary creature comforts, and transported all of them, including Felix's partner, Nick Larsen, to Los Angeles, where he ensconced them in the impressively elegant Hollenbeck Hotel. This magnificent hotel "had it all" when it came to the red-carpet treatment.

Nick Larsen, also a big winner in the North Star, said, "These box canyons sure do limit your lookout a whole lot. I just can't get use to being hemmed in like this." Nick, of course, meant the "skyscrapers" that broke the view along Main Street.

"That's corral dust, Nick," was Charlie's reply, "You'll get in all kinds of habits like removing your boots and *sombrero* before going to bed. You'll get the habit until you can't sleep good in your hunting shirt and chaps." Nick sported a sparkler on his lapel that could put your eye out.

Charlie was mobbed by reporters from the local dailies; one commented, "Charlie is so horsey he singles, fox-trots, or canters, but he 'never' walks."

Los Angeles was the most beautiful town around and its citizens had gone all out to make it the most attractive spectacle that eyes could behold, in their welcome to the men of the "red, white and blue."

"Fling out your banners—high and wide, seaward and skyward, let them float," was the word given by the *Los Angeles Times*. And they were flung—from spire to steeple, and from turret to battlement; their colors shining in masses at every vantage point Los Angeles afforded. "There was more patriotism to the cubic foot than air, and it glowed as warmly as the rays of sun in springtime. Mother Nature went out of her way to make the occasion one to be remembered for pleasantness; the daytimes brilliant, and the evenings lighted by a full moon. The enthusiasm of that moment was caught like an epidemic and sparked like a prairie fire, until the whole city was enveloped in a mass of color," said the *Times*.

Lawns were stuck with flags; flags floated from every tall and every small building, dingy factory and residences from cottage to mansion. It was red, white and blue everywhere, and banners fluttered in the breeze "in wild, bewildering profusion."

"Real men of the west, several of whom have had a hand in the making of frontier history will take part," said the *Los Angeles Times* of April 18, 1908. "Captain Rynning, former Rough Rider, and Captain of the Arizona Rangers, will take part as a rider and marksman. 'Arizona Charlie' Meadows, whose name is known throughout the southwest, and whose gun carries several notches, and his brother, Sheriff Mobley Meadows of Imperial County will participate."

Hordes of people were transported to the seashore each day to witness the arrival of the fleet and to visit the ships on board. Steam and electric lines carried 75,000 people alone. Hundreds of others arrived at the seashore by automobile, carriage, rig, and tally-ho. Spectators packed the bluffs overlooking the sea, and beach, waiting excitingly for the arrival of the fleet. At seven o'clock in the evening, searchlights alerted the vast throng of the 16 arriving battleships which still lay offshore in broadside semi-obscurity. At 8 p.m., the battleship *Connecticut* led with the first show of lights, with the others following; each vessel dressed in glory from stem to stern with brilliance reaching in an arc from Long Beach to San Pedro. "It was hilarious to see the blessed women then begin to straighten their hats, pull down their belts, and haul taut their rigging in a panic to perfect their toilet before the arrival on shore of the Admiral," commented the *Los Angeles Examiner*.

Each day 3,500 blue-jackets were allowed on shore at one time, all overwhelmed at the elaborate welcome in their honor. By order of the Admiral, commanding concerts were given four mornings of the festivities by the combined bands of each squadron. Amateur boxing tournaments for the championship of Southern California, were given each morning, with the honorable James J. Jeffries—at the time a temporarily undefeated heavyweight champion retired—chosen unanimously as referee. Fence, foils, sabers, and broadsword exhibitions were put on by the sailors with a purse given, and a loving cup presented to the battleship on which they served.

The morning program also included a balloon ascension and a parachute jump by Monsieur Leroyzex, introducing the big red, white and blue parachute, "America"; a slide for life, hanging on by his teeth, by Senor Pepe; a high-dive by famous flying diver, "Kid" Lewis; a bicycle high wire across Chutes Lake by Professor Williams; and the hazardous revolving ladder act by the Aldo Brothers.

At noon each day, a Spanish barbecue—which was a gastronomical success, served 3,500 men all at one time and was thoroughly enjoyed by the Jack tars; 5,000 pounds of Spanish beans, 3,500 rolls, 300 pounds of butter, 500 gallons of coffee, and 100 boxes of oranges were served. The band blared and 450 ladies sang the "Star Spangled Banner" the strains of which were almost completely drowned out by the soul-stirring cheers of the intensely jubilant blue-jackets; every hat doffed as the magnificent American flag was unfurled. Then led by three bands, Arizona Charlie and 150 participants of the Wild West Show acted as honorary escort to Agricultural Park, and put on a show that was welcomed so heartily as to approach an ovation—putting Buffalo Bill's show in the "skate class," the *Times* reported.

At Agricultural Park, a typical western town, "The Gulch," was built. It included a noisy blacksmith shop, complete with anvil and hammer; Peat's Saloon and Dance Hall, complete with gambling and alive with the drone of the roulette wheel and the clinking of bottles. There was a combination general store and undertaking parlour with all the "fixin's," Pike County jail with its bad men, and Sing Lee's Laundry, that helped fill the town. They had a judge, a sheriff played by the noted actor, Lewis Stone, and his deputies; several loafers, gamblers, miners, bartenders, and a "pianer" artist who played ragtime in the saloon. In another part of the grounds, there was a band that played music for dancing.

As a start to the program, while everything was apparently peaceful in the little camp, six cowboys, led by Arizona Charlie in lavish accoutrement, came dashing in on horseback with their six-shooters popping. Wild yips from the cowpunchers, while shrill responses came from the vivacious cowgirls, accompanied the mad race of excitement and daring, which stirred the blood of the yelling mob of blue-jackets. Then the entire company, along with the *Vaquero* Club, hurtled down the track on the wings of the wind. The great grandstand was banked solid with uniforms of blue, and the lower enclosure near the fence was crowded with thousands of civilians who wanted to see the fun along with the sailors. When Frank Wright broke out the flag in front of the bandstand, all the boys in blue sprang to their feet, off went their caps again, and out came a prolonged cheer that fairly made the broncos dance. One burly blue-jacket sprang to his feet, after the crowd had settled down for the fun, and yelled out, "Maties, three cheers for the Vaquero Club and the Wild Westers," reported the *Los Angeles Examiner.* It was the grandest patriotic and inspirational display of enthusiasm in all of Charlie's experiences.

Then, the crowd settled back to witness the deeds and daring patterned after those who made the west famous, and every face wore a broad grin of anticipation. The shooting up of the little frontier town was the curtain raiser, and it certainly aroused the blue-jackets to a height of enthusiasm from which they did not descend for the remainder of the afternoon. Each day there was bronco busting, mounted tug-of-war contests, fancy and trick riding, Indian dancing, a realistic hold-up, and some exciting steer roping and riding.

The sailors "had their all." The first appearance of Arizona's howling, shooting, galloping bunch of cowpunchers set every man in blue on the edge of his seat, and the responding roar that went up testified that a "touch of wild frontier" was just what the sailors from the roaring main wanted. Every "puncher" did his best to escape breaking his neck, but only by a hairbreadth, and the spirited ponies lent every possible effort to bring about actual results. At each narrow escape, the Jack-tars groaned in disappointment and cheered for the cowboys to do it some more. Charlie was in his element.

The broncos bucked until they were sore, the wild bulls were extremely wild, the stage coach was held up each day, the highwaymen were shot, roped, and unmercifully tortured, and ye crack shots, the "best rifle and revolver shots in the west," A. C. Freeman, William Norman, and Arizona Charlie, pulverized glass balls, and "all went along merrily in bad man's land," reported the press.

"Wild Horse" Hill rode a wild steer that he afterwards claimed someone had fed red pepper. At "first heave" both the steer and Wild Horse went into the air. The steer came down and galloped off—but Hill was still up there—"all sprawled out." He hit the ground so hard "he fairly echoed." But a real cowboy isn't scared off that easily. He caught the steer again and rode him until he "fairly heaved."

Of course, when the stage coach was held up each day the driver was carrying a million dollars in bullion and a stage full of tenderfeet, which only asked for trouble, and, of course, they generally got it. The plot revolved around young men and women gathering each day at the Gulch for a jolly good time; strolling in and out of the various stores in the little frontier town. The stage arrives, bringing in a "blawsted, bloomin' Hinglishman" in his usual tweeds and argyles. The wild and woolly westerners see him and pepper his heels until he finally retreats into the Gulch Hotel. The mail was thrown off, the passengers unloaded, a few new ones put aboard, and—with a "swinging whoop," a sharp crack of the lash, and popping of pistols—the journey was on again.

All went well for a time, then came the "bold, bad, masked highwaymen." They stopped the coach, rifled it of the express box, took other valuables, and fled with their loot. Miss Theresa Talamantes, a dark-eyed, olive-skinned *senorita*, and champion woman rider of Southern California, happened to be aboard the stage on her way to an exclusive boarding school. And, of course, she just happened to have her saddle horse along. The robbers had gone but a short distance, when Miss Talamantes took off for the saloon in town and aroused the cowboys who were soon in pursuit of the bandits.

Naturally, in a short time they were captured and placed in Pike County Jail. Their leader managed to escape, but while opening the box containing the treasure, he was surprised and killed in a revolver duel. The robbers were identified and sentenced to hang. Meanwhile, several Indians that were strolling about, arrived, and while amusing the cowpunchers with their dances, the prisoners escaped from jail. One of them, with the assistance of a "*vaquero* sweetheart," succeeded in evading the bullets of the posse, while the other was shot to death. The exciting drama ended with a roar of approval from the sailors. "Diamond Dick never wrote anything as thrilling as their show," reported the *Los Angeles Times*.

The Belasco Theatre group scored heavily in the stage robbery; one actor having the honor of being a much-shot robber, while another played the part of a "perturbed tweedy Englishman" inside the coach. His name was Harry Earle. Then actor Charlie Ruggles, who, on the Belasco stage played both "good," and "bad" guy parts, dashed in on his horse and grabbed off the "greased goose."

Pulling on the goose was not as easy as it looked. The feathered foul was hung on a wire across a track by the feet, and a bunch of reckless cowboys whooped up and down grabbing at the dead bird. This particular day the best of the cowboys went after the goose. One got the neck, the next got a little more of the same thing. Then a half dozen drew feathers, after which a more lucky cowboy took away a wing. Then Charlie Ruggles came along in a pretty pink shirt—with a natty brown silk handkerchief flopping out of the pocket. Ruggles was on a "quick little nag" that split the atmosphere. On his second try the matinee idol reached up and carried away what was left of the goose amid whoops from the boys in the fleet.

During one performance, Archie Freeman, from the Belasco Theatre group, took the honors in the ring-tilting contest, and the following day Arizona Charlie and Wild Horse Hill played the torynado game as easily as if it were "kiss in the ring," said the *Times*, and took the honors, positively astonishing the boys from the roaring main.

Miss Nesbitt, the "Desert Queen" charming in her costume, appeared on a white horse, and as she sped along, she threw glass balls as Arizona Charlie came on a fleet horse behind her and shot them all in rapid succession. Then she went on a quarter-mile run with the cowboys all pursuing her. The lucky man who overtook her was awarded the prize of a kiss. The sailors in the stands all responded with "Yum, Yum, Yum," but Miss Nesbitt rode away and arrived at the station in the Gulch all alone. It took several bottles of "hooch" to calm down the disappointed horde of pursuers when they finally stampeded the Gulch.

Mobley Meadows presented some extra fancy horsemanship, when he put his mount through many extraordinary stunts that drew swells of applause. Then friend, Felix Mayhew, donned a sailor's uniform and rode a steer with "horns wide enough to span the Los Angeles River in flood stage, all decked out to resemble 'Little Billy the Goat,'" said the *Times*. This was otherwise known as the mascot for the ship, *Louisiana*, and Felix got round after round of applause for his pluck and comedy antics. The boys in blue seemed fully aware of the joke, but—to their supreme delight—the provost guard did not tumble to the fact that Felix was only a "prairie schooner" sailor. Two of the Naval Shore Patrol Police went to the barrier determined to arrest the sailor for creating a disturbance. A Los Angeles policeman finally put them wise. The two took the joke in good stead, but one remarked that if Felix had been a real sailor he would have lost four-months' pay for breaking into the show. Felix was absolutely fearless; and his comedy acts fairly brought down the house.

There were several hairbreadth escapes. Miss Nesbitt, who had taken such a prominent part in the program during the week, augmented the program later by riding a wild steer. The animal bucked and bolted in a vain endeavor to shake off its fair rider, but his efforts were futile, and in a frenzy, arose and fell backward. The Vaquero Club members as well as the cowboys were petrified for a moment, and a cry of alarm arose from the thousands of spectators who witnessed her performance. But Miss Nesbitt quickly leaped aside and was unharmed. Cool and undisturbed, she bowed and smiled, and waved to the audience amid a thunderous applause.

At the opening of one afternoon performance, Captain Jack Hendrickson of the *Vaquero* Club met with a horrifying accident. As he hurtled down the track, his horse plunged—alarmed by the volley of rifle shots from the cowboy's guns and the shrill screams of the cowgirls—swerved slightly, and then dashed underneath a scaffold. A cross beam caught Hendrickson square across the chest and threw him from his saddle. The force of the impact was so great that the main beam was snapped clean through its center. There was a groan of sympathy from the assembled crowd when the prostrate Hendrickson was picked up and carried into the general store of the miniature town. In a few minutes, a little unsteady and pale, he reappeared unassisted and was greeted with wild cheers. He made a few announcements of succeeding events, but twice during the afternoon he fainted.

There were boys from every vessel in the four harbors. The boys from the *Main*, the *Alabama*, the *Missouri*, and the *Kentucky* mingled with the boys from the *Vermont*, the *Connecticut*, and other ships. But their eyes and their interests were concentrated on the thrilling show that was taking place.

"It was all so realistic to the blue jackets," said the *Los Angeles Times*, "when the long-legged, picturesquely-attired man from Arizona gave his remarkable exhibition of crack rifle shooting; breaking nearly every glass ball thrown into the air, the sailors applauded uproariously. Little they thought or cared of the trick behind the game."

The program was varied each day, and on the whole was "most excellent," as the papers told it; the Vaquero Club had done itself proud in arranging such a mammoth production, and, it was said over and over, that the Arizona delegation's part "was exceptionally well done."

Buffalo Bill Shows in Yuma

That fall Charlie returned to Los Angeles to meet with his old compatriot, Buffalo Bill. They had a good visit, a few snorts of "tanglefoot," and dinner. Charlie's purpose was to prevail upon Buffalo Bill to stop in at Yuma for a day and give the Yumans a show. Buffalo Bill promised to work on it. In a few days he was able to change his schedule and sent Charlie the following telegram—which is self-explanatory:

> Charles Meadows, Yuma, Arizona.
>
> Referring to our conversation about giving a show in your city. If the Mayor and citizens desire it, will give them a Wild West Show Sunday. See manager Ernest Cook on arrival of my first train Sunday.
>
> Best wishes, W. F. Cody.

Charlie immediately got busy and had the valley thoroughly billed the following morning. The performance was given at Charlie's "Meadows Ball Park Grounds," Sunday afternoon, October 19, 1908. It was seldom Yuma got any of the big shows, and the people there were extremely grateful to Charlie for the solicitation of his old-time friend.

Buffalo Bill's Wild West was the excitement of the hour. His special train arrived at ten o'clock that morning, and a large crowd lined the tracks from the depot to the freight yard to watch the unloading of his interesting paraphernalia. All the old settlers—Indians and Mexicans—turned out to watch the picture of the "good old days" as portrayed by the Wild West Show. The Indians were no less eager and enthusiastic than the others. Buffalo Bill invited all the children from the Indian School to be his guests at the afternoon's performance, and they watched with animation and glee written all over their little faces. The older Indians crowded the benches beside the children and showed the keenest enjoyment in the Indian scenes, ambuscades and dances.

At least 1,000 people came out to view Buffalo Bill's Wild West Show, even though the morning paper and the billing Charlie had done were the only media of advertising.

Ye cowpuncher, along with his friend, Felix Mayhew, rode in the exciting cowboy scenes to the delight of the Yuma citizens. They rode like the champions they were, and there was nothing prettier on the field than their horses. Felix was mounted on a splendid black sorrel, a gift from partner, Nick Larsen, and Charlie was on a beautiful white mount. The "notorious" Pearl Hart, a hard wretch, and past inmate of the Yuma Territorial Prison, "whose code of morals was the honor of thieves, and of decency she knew not of which," rode as a female rough rider.

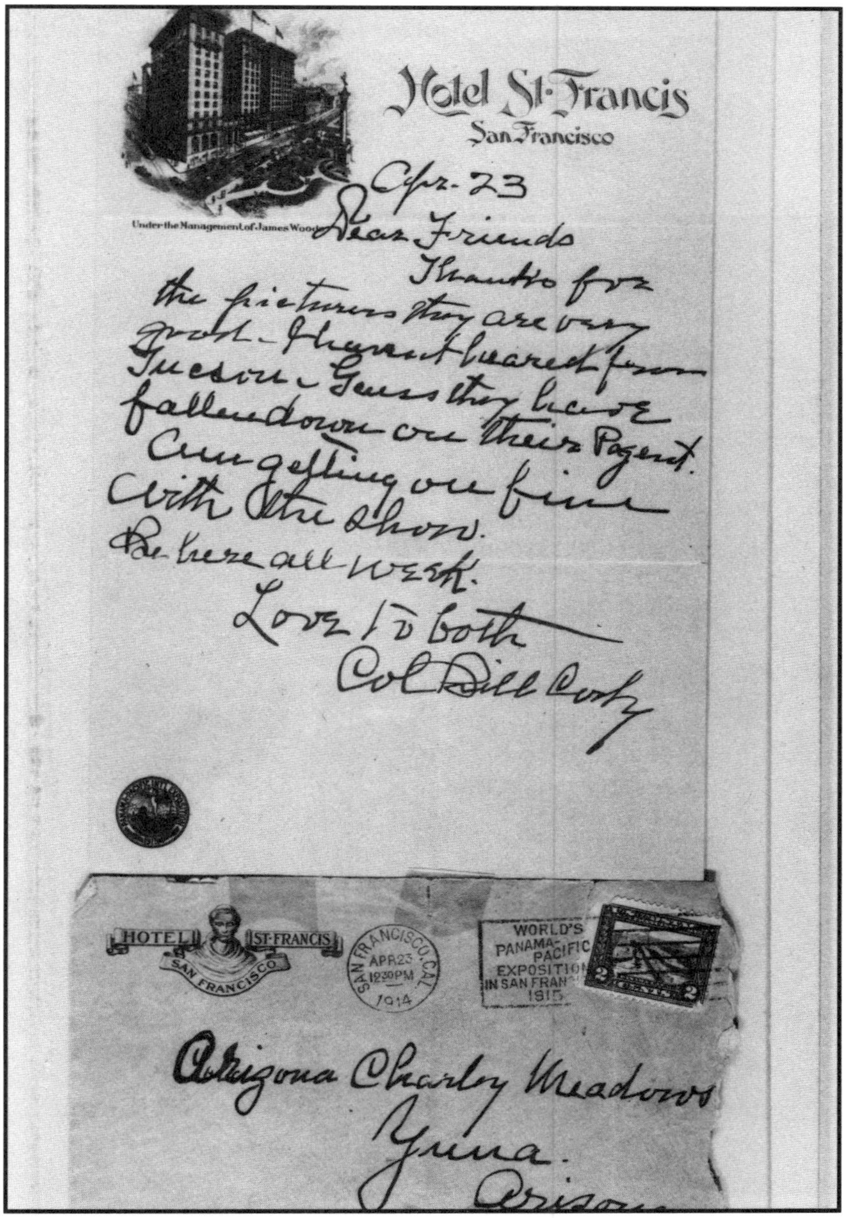

Hotel St. Francis
San Francisco
Under the Management of James Woods

Apr. 23
Dear Friends
Thanks for the pictures they are very good – I havent heard from Tucson – Guess they have fallen down on their Pageant.
Am getting on fine with the show.
Be here all week.
Love to both
Col Bill Cody

HOTEL ST. FRANCIS
SAN FRANCISCO
SAN FRANCISCO, CAL. APR 23 12:30 PM 1914
WORLD'S PANAMA-PACIFIC EXPOSITION IN SAN FRAN 1915

Arizona Charley Meadows
Yuma.
Arizon

A Letter from Buffalo Bill

Barbecue for Buffalo Bill

Charlie with Buffalo Bill, *Circa* 1910

Ida Mae McKamish Meadows, "Mae Melbourne"
(Charlie's Second Wife)

After the show, Charlie gave a great bull's head barbecue "for the Colonel, a few star performers, and some of his friends," at Headquarters. And as usual, Charlie's hospitality, with Mae's help, was a huge success.

Soon afterward, Felix's beautiful black sorrel met with a tragic accident. Grazing in an adjoining lot—separated only by a picket fence which he attempted to scale—the horse landed with his flank on the sharp pickets. He was so badly injured that Felix had to shoot him.

Other than a few short tours with a kaleidoscope of entertainers, including a magician—and a "magic lantern," from which Charlie presented minute-long vignettes—the old cowboy had reached the finale of his career. At age fifty, Charlie certainly would not have been the young romantic lead who would keep customers flocking to the movie houses to see the western films then aborning. It was at this time that Charlie bobbed his long hair, when it started to turn grey.

A Difficult Period

The cloak of death still hung low over the Meadows family, with 1910 marked by more sadness. That year Jake died tragically from gunshot wounds inflicted under mysterious circumstances in the jail area of the El Centro Court House. Before expiring, his last words to his son were, "A woman shot me, remember son, your father never killed a man." Jake's three children were left orphans. The shock knocked Charlie's world to its foundations. He was still gripped in a fog of unreason when a message came informing him that sister, Rose, had passed away in San Francisco of blood poisoning. The loss of so many loved ones suddenly brought him face to face with life, and he passed through the turning wheel of time in a kind of narcosis. Of the twelve siblings, now there were only seven left.

During the difficult period that followed, Charlie received the following letter from his old friend, Bill Cody, written from Watsonville, California, on October 4, 1910:

Dear Charlie and Mrs. Meadows,

Am coming, head me off at Yuma. You bet I'll be glad to see you and the ranch.

Your friend,
W. F. Cody

Buffalo Bill announced "I am coming" before arriving for all his scheduled appearances, and when he arrived he always announced, "I am here."

Buffalo Bill had what he thought were valuable mining interests at Campo Bonito, at Oracle, just outside Tucson. He spent most of 1910 at his Oracle mine, so he visited Charlie at his Yuma Headquarters frequently that year. His profits from a partnership and successful tour at Madison Square Garden amounted to $40,000, and he sunk most of this money into his mine. By 1911, his mine was producing tungsten, but the following years production costs proved too large for a profitable venture, and Charlie saw less of him after that. Friends like Buffalo Bill helped Charlie recover his old-time spirit.

The flames of ambition that had sent Charlie on his incredible journeys were now burning lower at the age of 50.

Mae Meadows with Buffalo Bill, *Circa* 1910

CHAPTER 24

1911-1915
GATEWAY TO THE GREAT SOUTHWEST

Yuma Valley was extremely fertile as the result of years of silt deposited by the overflowing of the Colorado River, but irrigation was inadequate and development slow.

The prospect of an opening of these lands by the government as well as others affected by the laws providing for the expenditure of about $25,000,000 in irrigation projects, moved intended settlers by the hundreds to besiege the local land office in Los Angeles, and the Interior Department in Washington, for information. Ye Yuma man was one of these people.

Water was to be diverted from the Colorado River by the proposed Laguna Dam Project and its sluiceways about ten miles northeast of Yuma, into two canals: one on each side of the river. The canal on the Arizona side would have an initial capacity of 1,600 second feet, and the one on the California side, 200 second feet. These canals were to irrigate all the bottom lands of the Colorado and Gila Rivers between Laguna Dam and the Mexican boundary in Arizona, an area of 84,000 acres, and the bottom lands of the Yuma Indian Reservation in California, an area of 17,000 acres.

Under the provisions act, the land was allotted to only actual settlers, to no one of which more than 160 acres was to be sold. The cost of irrigation works were to be assessed upon the lands and paid for in ten equal installments, the first being due when water was ready for delivery. The distribution of water, collection of annual payments, and maintenance charges was to be through the Yuma County Water Users Association, an organization formed by the land users of the district. The plan called for the construction of levees to protect—and a drainage system to remove surplus water from low-lying areas.

Because settlers were to be given ten years to complete their payments, it was expected that they would be able from the start to make their payments with returns from the soil. The project had been expected to be completed by 1911, but there was considerable foot dragging. At the time, Charlie was involved in several mineral and mining schemes as well—with Geologist H. W. Lyon. The following letter from Dr. Lyon confirming their business dealings was sent April 14, 1911, from Washington, D. C.:

> Dear Mr. Meadows,
>
> Your letter received. I called on Dr. Gomez, but could get very little out of him. He speaks very little English, but has some attorneys here, one of them speaks Spanish and interprets for him. They are afraid to say much. Gomez has been in jail here, and his attorneys are wrote [*sic*] up in the papers occasionally. The attorney's address is Hopkins and Hopkins, Hibbs Building, 723 15th, N. W. They said he was not in a position to take up such a proposition as that was not his end of the work, but for you to see Gustav Maders, 437 Main Street, San Antonio, Texas, and that he was in a position to handle it. I gave them your address and they wrote Maders about you.
>
> Have not received the samples of phosphate of lime and gypsum, yet am looking for them every day.
>
> I have looked into the reclamation proposition quite thoroughly and find we have got a systematic skinning clear case of a school boy doing a man-sized job. Things are moving slowly, but I believe we will get something done. The U.S. Reclamation Service is misrepresenting things here—and there also. Cameron is helping all he can and stands well with the departments. He was appointed on four committees; that is more than any other member of Congress got.

Hope you are doing well. Your old friend, Cody, shows here next Monday and Tuesday. Advertised positively his last appearance in the saddle. Don't know when I'll get away from here,

Yours truly,

H. W. Lyon

Buffalo Bill had announced his retirement many times before, so it can be presumed that Charlie "was inclined to hoot" at that part of Dr. Lyon's letter.

When the water was finally turned on, there was no lack of applicants, and Charlie was one of the first in line. Yuma celebrated. People lined dusty Main Street in their Sunday best for a big parade. In their pride, Yumans cut and hauled palm fronds and decorated the streets with potted trees and flags to commemorate the Colorado River, the "greatest irrigation power river in America." Yuma proclaimed itself to be the "Gateway to the Great Southwest."

With the opening of the new canal system, Yuma was no longer a major seaport and the old Colorado River boat fleet settled into a watery graveyard at Port Yzbell—in Mexico. Charlie made fewer hunting trips into the lower mud lands.

On January 23, 1911, a revolution broke out in Mexico, and President Diaz's government was overthrown. A band of "fervid" insurgents—which included several radical American citizens, and a group of so-called revolutionists from Mexico under the leadership of William Stanley—took possession of Mexicali and set up their own government. Governor Vega of Lower California sent a force of Federal troops to oust the intruders who had built themselves trenches along New River chasm. The United States Government also sent a troop of cavalry from San Diego to protect the border. The revolutionists left to re-assess their position. They returned again on January 29, took possession of the town and killed the jailer who refused to turn over the keys. Mobley swore in fifty deputies, all experienced cowboys and horsemen. Charlie, of course, was not to be left behind—and joined the party, all leaving immediately for the border.

The original insurgents were then joined by some 200 recruits, thirty of whom were Americans. The Federal troops finally arrived and were quickly repulsed by the entrenched insurgents, who fired across the New River chasm at the approaching column of troops under the command of Colonel Vega. The revolutionists' loss was five killed and three wounded in the fight that followed. The Federals' loss was three killed and seventeen wounded. Charlie and Mobley, along with a few of the other recruits, visited the battlefield area under the Red Cross flag and searched for the wounded, discovering one Federal who was left behind.

Two months later, on April 8, 1912, the Federals returned 400 strong under Colonel Mayol. The insurrecto band under William Stanley had dwindled to seventy. With "dare-devil audacity," Stanley made a bold attack with what few men he had left and threw such a fright into the Federal troops that they pulled out. But Stanley himself was killed during the battle by a bullet to the head, and eleven of his men were either killed or wounded. Several detachments of United States Government troops and thousands of curious citizens from around the Imperial Valley watched the conflict with Charlie and Mobley, which took place within a mile of the boundary. Stanley's dream of a Socialist domain with himself as governor failed; and Mobley returned home with his men.

Arizona Celebrates With a Bang!

On Valentine's Day, February 14, 1912, after a long bitter struggle, President Taft signed the proclamation admitting Arizona to the Union as the 48th state. The President's official message began by announcing, "I have this morning signed the proclamation declaring Arizona a state. . . ." Forty-eight sticks of dynamite were discharged in Bisbee, Arizona; in Globe a cannon boomed forty-eight times; and in Prescott toasts and pistol shots echoed their full approval on Whiskey Row. In Phoenix cannons boomed, bells tolled and sirens wailed, as an impressive band led a long motorcade that escorted Governor-elect George W. P. Hunt to the State Capitol for his inaugural address. All Arizona celebrated.

Also, 1912 was a very good year for Charlie. It was about this time his beloved "Yellow Boy," a beautiful palomino horse, entered his life. Charlie, Punk, and Yellow Boy were inseparable.

Return of a Brother

As summer was fading into fall the following year, the citizens of Seattle, San Francisco, and other coastal communities opened their morning newspapers to read about a man with a decided limp, caught as a stowaway on a recent ship. The man was to be sent back to Australia if he couldn't come up with the needed fare. Then Mobley received a wire which read along these lines:

Dear brother,

Please send me some money fast, or I'll be sent back to Australia.

Your brother,

John.

After an absence of twenty-three years, John had come home at last, entering the country illegally—and the whole state of California seemed to know about it. The Indian episode in Phoenix had long been forgotten, but now John was suffering from old Indian wounds as a result of the Diamond Valley attack of 1882. First—fragments of the clay pipe he had in his breast pocket, which diverted the bullet—were dug out of his back in Australia. Now, a bullet fragment lay festering away close to a bone in his leg. Unable to work for some time, an Australian doctor had recommended amputation. If such drastic action had to be taken, John preferred having it done at home where he could be near his family for support.

In Seattle, intense interest in the story was shown by a reader when the article disclosed that John's brothers were the noted Sheriff of Imperial County, California, and another the famous "Arizona Charlie" Meadows, Wild West Showman. From this reader came a letter to Mobley which read something like this:

Dear Sheriff Meadows,

I have reason to believe I am the child of your brother, Arizona Charlie Meadows. I was told by my mother at a young age that my father was dead. If this is not the case, please kindly put me in touch with him.

Sincerely,

M. Meadows.

Mobley rushed to Seattle to bail John out, and when he returned he found the letter waiting. But Mobley was busy with "sheriffing," and couldn't get around to answering it immediately—or get over to Yuma to give Charlie the "bolt out of the blue" news. He was busy apprehending criminals. It was an important case, and the following "dime novel episode" which he enacted in real life, took place in the wildest part of Riverside County, with Mobley the "hero of the hour."

Sheriff Meadows and three other men surrounded a gang of horse thieves, when Mobley discovered that one of the gang had a 30-30 rifle drawn on him; but taking all chances going, he suddenly threw up his own 44, the two shooting simultaneously. Mobley escaped injury, while the bullet from his own gun tore away the thumb of the horse thief, and then passed through the side of his neck. It took a fraction of a second, but it was a decisive battle. The other two horse thieves threw up their hands and surrendered when Mobley commanded them to do so.

In the overflow lands, north of the line of Imperial Valley, the party struck the trail of the thieves. Leading westward to the river and through a thicket of arrow weed, it became impossible to see for any distance. Following the trail with difficulty, the lawmen came to a deep slough; on the opposite side of the murky water, they could see the horse thieves. Light of heel, Mobley moved quietly toward the gang and found the men on horseback; they apparently had been frightened by the slight rustle that he made. As Mobley looked up, he saw the man who had the bead on him, Monroe, and that is when he fired.

From the time the posse left Imperial Valley that Sunday morning until their return, Sheriff Meadows and his men had been without sleep for three days. For that time, they had traveled 309 miles by automobile, and 20 miles on foot through dense underbrush. A fifth man remained at large for some time before being apprehended.

Several weeks later Mobley got over to Yuma and informed Charlie that he had a twenty-one year-old son who wanted to contact him. After Charlie recovered from the initial shock, he contemplated his next move. He wasn't quite sure after all those years how this bit of news was going to fit into his life. He knew the child would be a boy, and, of course, he had to let Mae in on the news. She had to know, but that revelation drew a silent heat wave that pretty near melted the waxed smile from the Old Hassayamper's handle-bar moustache.

Then Mobley received a follow-up letter from the Kid that put an entirely new light on the subject. Mobley answered the letter with the following reply:

Office of the Sheriff
Imperial County, California
El Centro, Ca.
Dec. 23, 1913

Miss Marion Mae Meadows, Seattle, Wash.

Dear niece, I received your first letter some time in October, and was waiting until I saw my brother, Charlie, who lives in Yuma, Arizona, before answering it, and had almost forgotten about it until a few days ago when I was over to Yuma and was talking to him. I gave him the wrong information. I thought you were a "boy."

I am writing Charlie Meadows tonight, also sending him your letters and you will likely hear from him soon. Wishing you a Merry Christmas and a Happy New Year.

Yours truly,

Mobley Meadows.

It appears that Charlie stalled somewhat here before meeting his long-lost daughter. Mae, no doubt, put out her "horns" when it came to inviting Marion to Headquarters. Charlie and Marion did some corresponding, but to keep peace with Mae it was some time before the two met. But when Charlie did set eyes on her for the first time—there was no doubt in his mind that she was his own—she resembled him in so many characteristics, from the cowlick on the top of her head to the tips of her long Meadows' toes.

That coming April, Charlie received another letter from his good friend, Buffalo Bill, written from his suite in the Hotel St. Francis, San Francisco:

April 23, 1914

Dear friends,

Thanks for the pictures, they are very good. I haven't heard from Tucson, guess they have fallen down on their pageant. Am getting along fine with the show. Be here all week.

Colonel Bill Cody.

Colonel Cody was never one to write a very "newsy" letter. From San Francisco, Buffalo Bill's tour route took him to Seattle. Cody had learned from Charlie that his long-lost daughter, Marion, was living there. Buffalo Bill sent Marion the following letter:

May 24, 1914

Dear Miss Meadows,

Received your card, also letter from my old friend, your father. I want to see you. He gave me a different address than you. Let me know if you get this. Come see me—or call me tomorrow, Saturday, at this hotel.

Yours,

W. F. Cody.

In his letter to Marion, Buffalo Bill enclosed a complimentary box seat ticket to his show; this was about Colonel Cody's last performance. To satisfy his creditors, property was disposed of at public auction in Denver, Colorado, by order of the United States District Court. Just how much of his millions he had left was uncertain; his profits at the last had dwindled, and he had made several very bad investments. However, he held on to his mine at Oracle, and still had other valuable properties.

Doheny Comes to John's Rescue

Following the amputation of his leg, John Valentine looked up his old Arizona mining partner, Edward Doheny. Doheny at this time was fabulously wealthy and wanted to help John get back into "life" in the United States. So "Good Samaritan" Doheny, bought John a big chicken ranch in Arcadia, California, and gave him a handsome monthly allowance. "What are old friends for, anyhow," was Edward Doheny's feeling. But John, like all the Meadows Brothers, loved to gamble, and had a fondness for potent liquid fortification. The two didn't mix well, and this time liquor proved to be his eventual undoing for he lost the chicken ranch to gambling debts. Doheny had no intention of making the same mistake twice, and thereafter gave John only a monthly allowance. Tom and Maggie took him into their Los Angeles home for a time, and when he was able, John took a room in a Los Angeles hotel.

Charlie and Mobley Show Their Nerve

In 1914, President Woodrow Wilson gave orders to Huerta of Mexico to salute the American flag, and later ordered Vera Cruz taken by the Untied States Marines. The Imperial Valley became alarmed because just across the border there were 600 Federal Troops with machine guns. Mobley swore in fifty deputies to guard the borders of the Imperial Valley. In case of hostilities between the two countries, the canal system below the line would be in the hands of the enemy. Steps were taken to save the valley by declaring north and south of the line neutral territory. Had hostilities broken out, Americans would have invaded Mexico to protect our water supply. Mediation finally quelled the war scare, and after a brief stay, Mobley and his deputies, and a regiment of one hundred other citizens organized for the emergency, were sent home.

Sometime during this emergency, Mobley called on Charlie. "Load your arsenal and come help me rescue the Little brothers." The Littles had a spread on the border, and the Mexicans were holding them captive. When it came to a fight, Charlie always possessed more than the average vigor and spirit. So the two brothers drove down to Mexico—all bluster and bluff—in Charlie's cut down flivver, through thorny tangles of *mesquite*, arrow weed and *ocotillo*. If the two brothers had not shown nerves of steel, they would have been overpowered. The bluff paid off and the men were able to bring out the Little brothers.

Charles and Mobley Meadows

Charles Meadows, Age 71

Mobley Meadows

A Heavy Load to Carry

The year 1915 was studded with floods, earthquakes, and personal tragedy for Charlie. In February, Yuma suffered its worst flood in history. Gophers inundated the levees, and due to these pesky critters, the town literally floated in the Colorado River waters.

One event that year was favorable. Mobley had been re-elected sheriff. Novelist Harold Bell Wright had come to the valley some years before to write and to raise thoroughbred horses. Tom Beach managed all of Mr. Wright's properties. Mr. Wright perhaps gave the desert its widest publicity when he wrote the book, *The Winning of Barbara Worth*, a novel which depicts the beginning of the Imperial Valley, published in 1911. The characters for his novel were taken from real-life pioneers who posed for a series of mural paintings depicting the characters that tell the story of Barbara Worth. These were hung along the walls of the new Barbara Worth Hotel lobby. One of the characters was done in sculpture form, and for this striking statue, pioneer Mobley Meadows was chosen to pose. The figure is shown kneeling at the brim of a dry water hole, holding an empty canteen and apparently asking the question, "What shall I do now?" The sculpture was started in March of 1915, right after the big floods, and done by Miss Ella Buchanan sister of the mural artist.

Mr. Wright, in giving credit to the early Imperial Valley pioneers, said: "Some day, perhaps when the world is much older and very much wiser, civilization will erect a proper monument to the memory of such men as these. But just now civilization is too greedily quarreling over its newly acquired wealth to acknowledge its debt of honor to those who made this wealth possible."

For the sculpture, first a plastina sketch was made, then the large figure was modeled in clay and cast in plaster; the final cast being in concrete. The statue was placed on the mezzanine floor of the Barbara Worth Hotel, a gift to the valley by Mr. Harold Bell Wright. Two months later, a strong earthquake rocked the desert floor and the statue fell through the skylight to the lobby below, damaging the nose. It was later moved to the sheriff's office in El Centro, where for years it was admired by those who loved and respected their sheriff.

Then—the following month—on the evening of July 13, 1915, Charlie received the unsettling message that Mobley lay gravely ill in the St. Thomas Hospital in Imperial Valley. This was cause for "great" pain. Charlie sweated bullets; the anguish he felt could not be measured. With a heavy heart, he and James drove the 60 miles to the valley in grim silence, nervously groping their way in the darkness over the vast sand dunes on the old plank road.

Mobley had suffered a similar attack once before, but this time depths of pain shuddered through his giant body. Before the brothers reached the hospital, Mobley had passed away. Charlie's world "crumbled." Crazed with grief he wept until no more tears could come; his throat twisted into a knot that fairly strangled him, and his heart was broken in pieces too small to mend. He was his brother, yet like a son, and his death Charlie could not accept. Like Charlie, Mobley too had braved the perils of life and emerged unscathed. "Why did this have to happen to him," Charlie must have asked over and over. Mobley was only thirty-nine and in the prime of his life. Charlie was not alone in his grief; the announcement of his death threw Yuma and the whole Imperial Valley into grievous shock.

The sun beat down unmercifully on July 15, 1915, as business houses closed and a thousand mourning friends and relatives of the departed sheriff gathered in an open-air chapel to pay their final honors. Mobley's body had laid in state during the morning hours, attended by the El Centro Fire Department and a dozen white-gloved Masons the crepe badge of mourning was upon the sleeve of each. An organ was installed under a permanent roof, a wealth of flowers were banked, and a pulpit and chairs were reserved for the mourning family and brother Masons of the deceased. Canvass was stretched over some pepper trees, but only afforded shade for a few.

After the casket was set in place, soft sobs could be heard as the immediate family and other close relatives took their places. On a rude table close by sat the men the sheriff had selected as his deputies, and drawn to them by the common loss of a brother officer, were policemen from every town in the valley. "Their Captain had gone, and they felt," said the *Daily El Centro Progress.*

Judge Franklin Cole, a close, long-time friend of the sheriff, gave the eulogy. "He was deeply affected as he related the attachment of himself and others to the sheriff, and he portrayed the admirable personal qualities of his friend," the *Progress* reported.

The "beautiful and reverent" exercises of the Masonic Lodge followed, with Paul D. Swing, Worshipful Master of the El Centro Lodge presiding. "His affection for the late sheriff several times made it necessary for him to pause—that control of his voice might be recovered," said the press.

At a few minutes after three o'clock, fire bells tolled. Six men carried the flower-crested casket between a line of aproned Masons and placed it on a bier. Then a cavalcade of sixty automobiles, led by the hearse, "swept out into the open country, and what had been mortal of Mobley Meadows, was consigned to its earthly resting place in Evergreen Cemetery." It was "the greatest procession ever seen in the county," said the *Progress.*

The following words were taken out of context from the *Imperial Valley Press*, which devoted several columns to the memory of Sheriff Mobley Meadows:

"The sudden passing of Sheriff Mobley Meadows has come with a shock to the whole county. He was still a young man, but in his life in California and Arizona, there had been crowded a strenuous frontier experience that had developed the peculiar gifts that made him the ideal man for the position he held. Kindly, modest in his instincts; quick, quiet, and unafraid of facing bad men, he was a terror to evil-doers and at the same time endeared himself to others as few men do."

Known as "Honest Mobley," the *New York Times* pronounced Mobley Meadows to be the "last of the fabulous old-time frontier sheriffs."

Mobley was in his office preparing civil papers when his first pains came. He loved the outdoors; he had always been an outdoorsman. His plan was to drive to his ranch that evening, and gather supplies in preparation for a camping and hunting trip with Lieutenant Governor Eishelman, and W. O. Hamilton. Awaiting his dinner in the jail, he was seized so suddenly with excruciating pain his body fairly doubled up. Almost beside himself in agony—and with a loud gasp he mumbled through tight lips, "Oh God, "kill me! kill me!"

Mobley was rushed to the hospital and the doctor was called—and his pain was momentarily alleviated. His only words were, "Prop me up." But his condition grew alarmingly grave and he lapsed into unconsciousness. At 10:20 that night, with one last convulsive gasp, Mobley expired.

At the coroner's inquest, and after a postmortem examination, his death was attributed to peritonitis brought on by ulcers. That was the general belief, until a few months later, during a trial against Richard Ford and Herman Suhr, the leaders of the I. W. W. (Independent Workers of the World), for murder and sabotage of California crops in order to gain freedom of two jailed members—an admission was voluntarily made by one member that the credit for Mobley's demise by "poison" should go to them. An unidentified newspaper reported:

"They finally got our old friend of Imperial Valley. This rat had dodged everything for the last five years, from poison to bullets, but he finally fell and died after four hours of terrible agony from poison of some kind," bragged a member of the Union. "This skunk who used to sell rebels, men and women, to the Mexican Government and take them over the line and shoot them. He lived five years too long, but we finally got him."

Of course, those charges against the sheriff were not true. His fearlessness and keen marksmanship were credited by the citizens of Imperial Valley in keeping peace with the Union known as the "Wobblies," who tried to stir up trouble in the early 1900's. Mobley once shot it out with one I. W. W. member entrenched in the remote desert area, and took the man into custody after wounding him in the leg.

The Wobblies put out stickers bearing inscriptions: "As long as Ford and Suhr are in jail, beware of California fruit." Their campaign of sabotage in California resulted in the destruction of $10,000,000 worth of crops annually for several years.

All the things that Mobley loved tore at Charlie's heart because he was no longer there to enjoy them. Along the way, Charlie's friend and side-kick, Felix Mayhew, met misfortune when he was killed in an auto accident with Yuma druggist, Homer J. Smith. Charlie was convinced the danged "iron monsters" could never take the place of the horse—and he knew it could have very well been him in that car with Felix that day. Again, Charlie was in the right place at the right time. Punk was the next to go, and with a broken heart Charlie laid him to rest under a giant cottonwood tree. It seemed to him that those he loved—could not live.

CHAPTER 25

1916
CHARLIE BARBS THE DART

Agonizing over Mobley's death seemed to change Charlie. Consumed with the stress of his emotions, he was unable to abide by criticism. Whenever things didn't go right for him—he would rant, rave and wheedle until he got his way.

President Woodrow Wilson's war preparedness policies, the exploits of Pancho Villa, and the Mexican border incidents were of passing interest only to the readers of the *Morning Sun* in the summer of 1916. No doubt the citizens of Yuma about this time were a little crazy with the heat, for the merciless sun glared like a shield of red-hot brass. The big news was the assault case Charlie was involved in with a neighbor, an Englishman by the name of Willoughby Woodiwiss.

"My worst fault, I'll admit," Charlie said, "was an attack of chronic vibration of the jawbone." Well—at least Charlie was the first to admit his own faults. This fact resulted in a whole peck of trouble for Charlie, and led to the publication of the Arizona man's second issue of the *Valley Hornet*. Sensational political history preceded its publication, which was printed on September 11, 1916, two days before the primary elections, and amounting to, at least in one instance the changing of public sentiment. But Charlie always said, "When I believe I am in the right, I am not afraid of God, man, or the devil with his horns sharpened."

Charlie's own unvarnished account of the trouble that ensued is directly quoted from his *Valley Hornet*:

"Now old man Spade," [he called himself that—and you will soon learn why] "he is of Scotch-Irish and German extraction, and in the face of war conditions, the name of Meadows became the subject of inquiry from the John Coyotte neighbor." Americans at that time were finding it difficult to be neutral in fact, as well as in name. "When the news reached Yuma that Captain Keonig's periscope had shown up in Chesapeake Bay, this old man Spade's tongue got into high speed, and his jaw brake slipped and refused to hold. I was skidding down Main Street with my front exhaust wide open when it exploded in front of John Coyote's 'soaps suds' joint with the startling information that I was a descendant of Kaiser William and a first cousin of Captain Koenig.

"All this and more, too, John Coyote heard. Peeved to perfection he went forthwith and tanked up on forty-rod aquifortes; went home, got his axe and cut down old Spade's fence and liberated his cattle in the streets to roam *ad-lib*; finally laying down in front of the home of John Coyote, where Spade and his hired man had just spent two days building a yard fence—free gratis.

"I thought nothing of my cattle being out. They never stayed inside a fence unless it was in some other man's field. But when the zanjero called Mr. Spade up to meet him at the flume to get his regular Wednesday morning apportionment of the 'God-given, silt-laden silvery,' Spade discovered his fence had been whittled down. When he inquired of J. Coyote as to who the whittler was, about all I heard were things we would not like to put in a society journal such as this. There was much talk about a 'yellow-bellied Yankee,' London prize fight rules, and 'foit like a mon.' The whitefeather recruit spat into his hands, shook his fist, pawed at the earth and roared like a two-year-old bull.

"It didn't look good to this old man on a yellow horse with a shovel on his shoulder. He had seen a humped back with a pegged head like that once before that could whip his weight in wild cats. So I let my tongue run free and suggested pitting an Indian against the brave Britain. To this suggestion John Greyback went all a-tremble, straining his fetters with suppressed rage.

"When conscription began, John Coyote's hair stood on end, his heart leaped up into his throat, and his face took on a delicate hue of lemon peel. He took the next boat out of Britain. It seems a fellow never gets rid of a thing like that.

"The old man on a yellow horse hung his shovel on his shoulder and rode away, singing sweetly, 'Your mother never raised her boy to be a soldier,' and brought up that old 'whitefeather' business.

"Anyhow, the brave trench-ducker fanned down Colorado Street, and in about fifty yards overtook Mr. Spade and was dragging him from his horse when just then something happened. I think you can guess the result. The shovel fell off old Spade's shoulder, hit John Skunk Coyote on the head—cutting a small swath near his right ear. Mrs. J. Coyote ran out of the house with a revolver with all intent of 'winging me if I would fight,' as she put it to the court, while all the while J. Skunk Whitefeather loosed the strings of profanity and fairly outdid himself calling me all the names in the dictionary and a few others.

"Now Mr. and Mrs. John Skunk Whitefeather Coyote," Charlie continued, "were extremely English, don'cherknow, and their dialogue in court came over quite hilariously. J. Coyote's 'little' wife was sixteen stones six; 224 pounds American measure; her horizontal had outgrown her perpendicular; in other words she had "out latt-a-too-ted her longitude" and in the heavy sand stone like a duck.

"This new American recruit tried to raise a disturbance with every man of German name that he could make the acquaintance of. He condemned this country by sections and said President Wilson was as yellow, don'cherknow, as a blawsted canary just because he wouldn't say 'sickum Kaiser' with a few hundred thousand young Americans for cannon fodder at Verdun.

"Whitefeather and his 'roarin', rootin', tootin', shootin' filly from West Yuma appeared in Judge Jones' court, accompanied by his counsel, 'Sis' Lindeman, the preacher-lawyer-boy-wonder. Sis was all English, too, don'cherknow, and had his hand-me-down pants rolled half-way up to his knees. In aping the English, he represented something like a cross between a straddle bug and a tired man going for his pay check.

"He had seen Pete Robertson and Judge Baker chew tobacco in court, and to show that he was there with the legal stuff, he poked a quid in his right jaw as big as a dwarf apple. One side looked like the jaw of a well-fed gopher, while the other resembled Ike Turner's belly after the forty-second day of fasting.

"He had given a constable a well-prepared list for jurors and they were all in. It looked like a reunion of the best old plugs on carts in the good old farm days when booze was king. There were down-and-out saloon men of the big-bellied, bald-headed, soiled vest and red tie variety; down and out politicians, blind pig operators and their patrons. And then there were three good, big, nice athletic-looking gentlemen."

Now, all this and more too came out in this issue of Charlie's *Valley Hornet*, and he mentioned that "if any juror took offense to the above, he was one of the last named."

Charlie wrote several paragraphs demeaning the British. He, no doubt, knew little of his ancestors before his great grandparents, or he would have known that the Meadows name originated in England, and his forefathers came from there also.

Charlie continued his *Hornet* by saying, "The defendants were primed with about four fingers of chemical busthead, and three grains of Doc Knotts' snow tablets. What the defendants said no one seemed to understand, except that she was the 'Original Kalamity Kate,' and full of shoat. She was excused early, retired and took her seat, took another Doc Knotts' snow tablet and continued to give evidence all through the trial, *ad lib.*

"The British lion then took the stand. When he reached that part of the evidence where he demanded of old Spade to get down and 'foit like a mon,' the jury set up a titter, and from that time on John Whitefeather was all hero. He had called the old man with the shovel everything there was in the dictionary, chased him all over Hell's Half-acre (more tee hee from the jury) and was finally pulling him off his horse and taking the shovel away, when the horse's haunches, don'cherknow, knocked him down.

"The Tee-Hee brothers got into a regular ha! ha! by that time, and when the lion was reminded that the day before he had sworn that the farmer had 'come an overhand lick' down on his bean and knocked him down, he still hung to the horse's haunches and thought he might have gotten a bit of a scratch when he pulled the shovel away from the enemy. He crummed his head all over both sides and on top for a full minute, and finally located what he said was a bit of a scratch above the right ear, for which the poor old farmer was to cough up $5,000.

"The big display of legal talent showed in the preacher-lawyer when ye accused was put on the stand. After it was ascertained that ye witness was a resident of Yuma, State of Arizona, and that his true name was Charles Meadows, the boy wonder shifted his quid to the other side of his face, carefully straightened up his stack of law books and volplaned one at a cuspidor at about a six-foot range. He shot a little scattering, but he made a fairly good hit, and looked well satisfied, as much to say, "That's got Senator Ives beat."

"The jury looked on admiringly, first at the cuspidor and then along the space to the chair and into the boy wonder's open continence.

"First question: "What kind of stock business are you in, and if so, how many cattle stock did you have in said pasture on said day in said town county of Yuma, State of Arizona?"

"My answer: "Are you defending an Englishman or prosecuting a bunch of cattle? If the latter, I motion that you issue a bench warrant for the bell cow and bring her to court."

"At this the audience set up a roar of laughter. The judge pounded on the table, and the Tee-Hee brothers in the jury box could see nothing funny; the teacher-lawyer turned purple, swallowed half his cud, sowed up over the cuspidor like a razor-backed sow in a hail storm, and coughed up the remaining brain tablet. Then he submitted his case. The jury filed out shortly with the verdict of "not guilty." Aside from that—and like the little boy who slept too soundly, they had nothing to say.

"Each had a peculiar sheep-killing look, that indicated that about a half roll of toilet paper and a wet towel would fill their immediate need. Except for the three perfect gentlemen referred to, and honestly, they walked as though they had been galded."

Of course, Charlie pressed charges against "J. Coyote" for disturbing the peace, reducing his fence to splinters, and letting his cattle roam free, which started the scrap in the first place. But because Charlie went to the Woodiwiss place voluntarily, this seemed to eliminate the element of disturbance in the minds of the jury, who were somewhat prejudiced—the way Charlie saw it. The defendant "swore on a stack of Bibles as high as dung piles on Main Street," and Charlie lost his case.

Well, he felt unduly chastised, don't you know. One day he stopped in at the quarry where his old friend, George Edwards, was living. The Mexicans had pushed Charlie's cattle up the river, and he was moving them back down. Edwards was cooking a large caldron of rabbits and quail, and asked Charlie to stay for supper. They got to talking politics—with Charlie still fuming over earlier events. The whole town was "full of lousy, drunken, cowardly, black-stub, pipe-sucking degenerates," he said, that were running for public office with the primary elections only days away. Three of these men were involved in the two lawsuits: C.A. Lindeman, attorney for the defense; Judge Jonathon C. Jones was the Democratic candidate for Justice of the Peace of the first precinct of Yuma; and Clement H. Coleman, the Republican candidate for County Attorney.

"This was enough to make this old cowpuncher eat his lariat and spurs, and swallow his cinch rings whole, then strike for a job of herding sheep or editing another newspaper. If you think old Charlie could forget all this, it would have been when his pencil hand was amputated, his tongue extricated, and his mouth sewed up with cat-gut," he said.

It was doubtful that Charlie entertained any serious political aspirations, but he always liked to dally in journalism, so a newspaper it was. His mental processes became activated, and these three men, Woodiwiss and the others, became targets for Charlie's vitrolic pen—with the second known issue of the *Valley Hornet.* The *Hornet* was so in demand, it sold for as much as $5 as far away as San Diego.

W. H. Shorey and B. F. Fly publishers of the *Yuma Daily Examiner*, printed the *Hornet* for Charlie. The two had themselves only a scant few months earlier, been arraigned on criminal charges brought on by William Webb, publisher of the *Gadsden Clarion*, for their vituperative commentary, and were out on bond. Mr. Webb was referred to in the *Examiner* as a "white-slaver, possessed of a diseased brain, an idiot, an ass, disreputable liar, ungrateful cur, living in open adultery with a woman in 1915." These derogatory statements were not only published in one paper, but repeated in the leading daily. Well, as you can see, this type of commentary set the journalistic tone for that period. But not in many years had anything caused so great a sensation as Charlie's second issue of the *Hornet*—which was known for its "deadly sting." The *Hornet* this time was published under a fictitious name. His opening editorial for the September 11, 1916, issue of the paper follows:

Salutory

"With this issue of the *Valley Hornet*, Charles Meadows, former editor and owner steps out, and I Sting, present editor and proprietor steps in.

The *Valley Hornet* will occupy a unique place in the journalistic field. It is the only journal in the whole wide world that does not depend on advertising, subscriptions or contributions for its existence, and is written for the sole amusement of the author, who has no fads or pet schemes for reforming the universe, and no public axe to grind. The author has no sectarian ties, no political hobby, belongs to no fraternal organization, and has no wares to market. The distant hum of the office bee has ever been heard in the crown of his bonnet, and he has decided not to stand a stallion or open a blind pig.

In view of these facts, kind reader, you may expect a fair field and no favorites.

It is not the policy of this paper to dig into the closets of its neighbors and drag out the family skeleton, or take the name of an honest man in vain. Not one line of racy or social scandal or neighborhood gossip will receive space in this paper.

The public servant who abuses his trust, the boodler and grafter, the hypocrite, the imposter, the county treasury looters, the bull-duster and the four-flusher, will feel the stinger of the *Hornet,* and will be held up to the public in their true light, and handled with an ungloved hand.

The phrases, 'It has been said,' 'We are informed,' 'The report is current,' 'There are rumors to the effect,' will not be employed in this publication.

It must be known fact, and there is no interest on earth that can be advanced in these columns through fraud or lie. No city, county, or government printing, no mercantile or whisky trust advertisers, or political putty-head subscribers are depended upon for our coffee and doughnuts.

If it is your opinion, the editor of such a journal is entitled to live outside of our Governor Hunt's road camps, give us your friendly support; just stand by and keep the dogs off and let us see a moving picture of the man or set of men who will undertake to denounce or suppress this publication.

It may be that the truth will press down hard on the corns of your pet candidate; in that event, just forget it, for he will forget you when the election is over. Moreover, it will be the truth and should be told, and if you are half-way honest, you will not advocate the cause of the evil-doer.

The *Valley Hornet* will be printed from time to time during the campaign, and on later dates when conditions demand it."

I. Sting

"I made it plain that you would have to be a square shooter if you vote or play politics in Yuma County from that time on, and that old stuff wouldn't work any more," Charlie said in the *Hornet*. He continued by saying:

"The first illegal voter, and every other one would be promptly arrested and taken before a justice that would give him or her what is due them, and the registration officer that did the illegal registering should be pinched on each count and properly punished, if it cost the county $10,000. Clean politics and square shooting from that time on. And if anyone ran on illegal votes, he was a crook and had no right to public office.

"Now the *Royal Arch* was a 'highfalutin,' high-sounding name and might have been construed as a fraternal organization of European featherhead or Oriental potentates. When simmered down to a cold, hard-boiled fact, it meant only a union of tall liquor dealers, bartenders, and saloon porters. They were not banded together as a trust to charge exorbitant prices or otherwise mistreat anyone, but for their own protection, mostly to prevent prohibition fanatics from passing laws that would compel the retailers to open and close three times a week, and remain closed over part of Saturday and Sunday. The head of the *Royal Arch* was some prominent distiller of the past, who, in national politics, dictated to the smaller fries who and what candidate they should vote for.

"In local politics, the grand ruler passed out the word as to who was safe. When it comes to voting, this order voted to a man, regardless of politics, as one. When politics were evenly balanced, they easily turned the elections to suit their own desires. In this way they then had control of local officers and courts, until the people, disgusted with the procedure, voted them out of business. And thereby brings a tale! Two years earlier, C. H. Coleman, attorney for the *Royal Arch* circle, was nominated by the Republican party for County Attorney, and Judge J. H. Westover was nominated for the same office by the Democrats. While Colonel Westover was making a clean ticket and seldom mentioning his own cause, exponents of the *Royal Arch* were circulating the report among prohibition people that the Democratic candidate was canvassing the county in a portable saloon!

"When election day came, presidents of banks, ministers, principals and teachers in the schools, and leading taxpayers, saw in the voting booths their votes killed by saloon porters, drunken bartenders, whores and mashers.

"When the vote was counted, it was found that the state was dry, and on the first day of January, Yuma County was found to have $87,000 worth of *Royal Arch* booze, and a *Royal Arch* county attorney.

"After that day, three full-fledged saloons opened on Main Street under the eyes of the county attorney. Booze worth $87,000 was sold at the exorbitant price of two dollars a pint. A colored boot-black, Mexican peon, or stable boy that interfered or cut into the trade as a competitor, was promptly prosecuted and floated out of town.

"Thanks go to the able assistant, who had the interest of the county at heart, and whose guiding hand protected the taxpayers and the county affairs in general. There is no doubt but what if he had been given the whip hand at the beginning, this form of lawlessness would have been brought up with a nautical jerk the first month of service.

"With Coleman it was just a *Royal Arch* tail wagging a political dog, and he was just about the frailest sister that ever graced a county attorney's office. His knowledge was limited to crossing and double crossing, and it was doubtful if he could distinguish between a subpoena and a search warrant, or the Constitution of the United States and a receipted wash bill.

"It was a certainty that the voters would at the coming election put a screw and cotter pin cinch on his political career. Nothing was more certain than that the Republican party had some good material and good deserving candidates who would lose a hundred votes by associating their good names with this moral degenerate and mental misfit on the ticket."

So Charlie, with a penchant for the verbal low-blow, addressed a whole column to Clement Coleman:

"Mr. Coleman: You entered your official career a top-notcher on the Republican ticket. You will go out at the next general election a tail-ender, receiving the least number of votes of any candidate of the Republican ticket. Several hundred of your constituents have migrated mostly to Mexicali and Tijuana, where they will vote for Pancho Villa in the next Mexican Presidential election. You have not the chance of a no-legged man in a marathon race or a cut dog at a fighting carnival."

Not satisfied with that, Charlie barbed the dart further by saying:

"Your weight, and you are a featherweight at that, is breaking the backs of several good, honest, efficient, worthy candidates on your ticket. Several of these candidates could get in by the skin of their teeth, if they can run without carrying weight. The *Hornet* man controls more votes than any man in Yuma county, and would like to cast his support to several Republican candidates, but, under the present conditions cannot honestly do it. It is just a case of old dog Tray."

Now when it came to that "Old Skunkmonger," Jonathon P. Jones, Charlie pleaded with every mother to read the following article:

"Two years ago, 1914, a mother burro with a ten-day-old baby found her way into Judge Jones' front yard. The mother was engaged in the pastime of licking the label off one of the many tin cans that adorned the filthy premises. Jones appeared on the scene with a heavy four-pronged pitchfork. The agile mother made her escape at the gate; the little one following in the distance. When it reached the corner, this old yellow-hearted villain thrust the fork with all his force into the little animal's neck. Benumbed with pain, it drug the fork in a circle until the old skunk-monger extracted it. This little animal was not much bigger than a full-grown jack-rabbit and had been presented to a little orphan girl who prized it dearly. It never lived to reach its home, three blocks away."

Now, tender-hearted Charlie was a lover of the equine clan, and this act just about did it for him. He proceeded to assail Judge Jones with withering denunciation as follows:

"I brand any man that will deliberately commit such an offense as that of a cold-blooded murderer at heart! Only the law and society will prevent him from murdering a child. So I ask every true Democrat and every candidate, and every friend of a candidate to knife the old hypocrite at the primaries, and that every candidate that is known to favor him be harpooned! Any party that would place a murderous, old treasury-looting skunkmonger on its ticket is entitled to go down in ignominious defeat!

"Eight years ago, Jonathon P. Jones was racing a fat bacon rind up and down a buck saw, fiddling on a *mesquite* stick one day and hauling his merchandise to town the next, at two bucks a load. He was the leading light in the Socialist party and a fairly good citizen. When he renounced his faith and politics for official position and filthy lucre, he proved himself to be the old snake in the grass that he really is."

That didn't seem to be quite harsh enough, so Charlie dragged in Jones' family and friends:

"A hundred and fifty dollars per month and the trimmings was fine doings for the wood merchant. If he had been contented with that, but he had hardly gotten the county udder between his teeth and in the mouth of his family until he fell victim to that terrible contagion, 'Get rich quick.' He played hot and fast until he soon found himself so balled up, until every pee-wee politician and shoestring shyster in town held a club over his head. With Jones as Justice, his son as poundmaster, one daughter as interpreter, and another as Clerk, Old Yuma, or Jonesville, is doing quite well, thank you.

"So I pleaded with the voters. Can you afford to vote for this man, caught red-handed stealing the county funds, and whose moral and social conduct has made him the most loathsome and degraded white man in Yuma County?"

Then the opposition's attorney, C. A. Lindeman, didn't miss the brunt of Charlie's indignation—receiving the following blistering rhetoric:

"Some years ago when the Reverend Lindy Lindeman, dressed in a long-tailed coat and wearing a white tie, lit on the sandy banks of the silvery Colorado with a Bible under his arm, he was the most sanctimonious sonofaseacock that ever coaxed a nickle of candy from the chubby hand of an infant, or maced a yellow-legged chicken from the table of a poor widow. He was the prohibitionist prohibitioner that ever preached in a pulpit or hid a gallon of busthead under a haystack. And dry! If dry was a toy boat, this Reverend Lindy would have been the English Navy before the Kaiser's hell-divers got to it. He was superlatively dry when he got into the Reclamation Service; so much so that a man, who was known to ever drink a glass of beer or hoist a highball, couldn't ever buy water for irrigating purposes, if his reverendship could prevent it.

"The Reverend Lindy was not so much to look at in those days. He had the 'pink pills for pale people' complexion, and the restless, watery eye, and nervous disposition so characteristic of young men who were left alone too much when they were first verging manhood. His appearance was that of a young man that should have had some worldly advice from a father and the attention of a physician. All in all, he somewhat resembled a cross between Judge Jones with his spinach trimmed, and a six-month's false conception.

"He made his debut at one of the local churches on his first Sunday evening in Yuma. Like a lame parrot making a sneak on a rotten peanut, he shambled up into the Amen corner, where he sat with eyes bulged out like a young heifer delivering her first calf."

There seemed no end to Charlie's grievances, and Lindeman got more than his share as Charlie continued to smite him in the following way:

"There he sat and groaned like a government mule in the last stages of colic. When collections were called for, and the nickles, dimes and quarters began to hit the plate, it sure looked good to 'Willie.' If these old-time mossback preachers could gather in the lucre in such bunches, what he could do with his up-to-date Eastern ideas of drawing the mazula from the pockets of the Arizona heathen?

"At the close of the services it was announced that the boy preacher would occupy the pulpit the following Sunday morning. When Old Sol shone in all his glorious splendor on the seventh day, the Reverend Father Lindeman was there, spic and span, with a pint of busthead in his left pocket for bracer, and an extra high, crowned hat with which to gather in the contributions. The text was, 'Wine is a Mocker, and Strong Drink is Raging, so, touch not; taste not; handle not.'

"At the conclusion, the Reverend Father woke up to what was left of his audience and announced that the following Sunday evening the text would be, 'When Moses Lifted Up the Serpent in the Wilderness.' That his first sermon would be devoted to Christ, but that the following Sunday everyone would be expected to decorate the *sombrero*, *'pagele jente,'* or words to that effect.

"When the next Sunday rolled around, Father Lindeman wrapped a shot sack—that would hold about $200 in silver—around his bracer flask, and got his hide over to the House of God. Just a minute late, in order to keep the congregation waiting and at attention, when he entered the church.

"When he entered—he found the church overflowing with empty seats—and aside from that, there was nobody home but the janitor who explained, after an hour's wait, that there probably was some misunderstanding amongst the churchgoers.

"Law business looked like the best legal way to steal a living, so this moral vacuum and hark from the tomb lallypalooser and mental miscarriage, broke into the game with the zeal that registered 200 in the shade.

"Lil' Lindy developed symptoms of office-heading hysteria. Indeed, it is said that some of his associates were playing peeping Tom on the boy wonder one evening and found him in front of a six-foot mirror with three hats on the dresser. He was changing hats with both hands, bowing and addressing himself first as County Attorney, then as Superior Judge Lindeman, and last as Governor!"

Well, there was much more. In fact, some twenty columns altogether of vindictiveness, but that was the heaviest onslaught of offensive rhetoric in the whole content. You can imagine how this charged up the Yuma atmosphere on the eye of the elections.

"Of course, they got a little naggy and sassy about it," Charlie admitted. That Sunday evening about 8:30, after the *Hornet* hit the streets, Alfred Jones, son of that old "skunkmonger," attacked the old cowboy in front of the Arizona Hotel. Jones knocked Charlie down and administered such a severe beating, he was barely able to get home. Charlie was much bigger, indeed, but showed no willingness to fight. It was hardly a fair match; Alfred Jones was a young fellow, and Charlie was fifty-six old.

Chief of Police, Henry Levy, arrested Jones and fined him ten dollars for the offense, the money being paid by a check from C. A. Lindeman. Charlie thought that a little odd—John "Whitefeather" wanted $5,000 from the "poor old farmer" for a lesser injury.

Following the beating—late that day, a warrant was sworn out by C. A. Lindeman, charging Charlie with criminal libel. Charlie was in default of $1,200 bonds, which he was unable to post until the next day. This fact naturally led to the subsequent commitment of ye citizen to the city *juzgado* for a night, by Constable Purtell and Chief of Police Levy. There came three cases of libel altogether, and it seemed to Charlie that there was a pattern each time of serving warrants at the end of the day; which kept him in jail overnight until friends could post bail the next day.

A complaint of criminal libel was also issued against W. H. Shorey, publisher of the *Yuma Examiner,* by C. A. Lindeman, who charged Shorey of being in "collusion" with Charlie, and "willfully and maliciously" printing the *Hornet* for him. Even the arrest of the newsstand proprietor who handled the *Hornet* was contemplated.

Well, the opposition retained all the lawyers in the town of Yuma, and it seemed unlikely Charlie could find one to defend him. Partners in the same law firms did not want to step on any toes. So, Charlie filed for a continuance until after the coming elections.

On January 22 and April 7, the cases came to trial. When the jury returned in less than ten minutes in each instance, with a verdict of *not guilty*, spectators burst into applause. Once again, Charlie had charmed himself out of another mess.

Had Charlie not been born a cowboy-showman he may have followed the journalism field. But now he had grown weary of perpetual recrimination and laid down his prolific pen. The *Hornet's* venom had subsided, and no trace of later issues have been found.

Charlie's scurrilous publication became well known, and was of general interest and discussion for months. It surprised his friends, of which he had many, created a political upheaval, and embarrassed Mae, who, as the respectable wife of one of Yuma's richest men, was a prominent hostess in its social circle. It was some time before brother James got around to speaking to Charlie again. Others either loved him or hated him. But newspaper items of that day report that Yuma was not the peaceable, quiet town it is today.

CHAPTER 26

1916-1923
A RETURN TO NORMALCY

Charlie threw himself back into reclamation work. The following letter from brother-in-law, Tom Beach, written from his Los Angeles Lands Office, with Imperial Valley properties his specialty, and his lingo—"I talk dirt—and I sell dirt"—suggests Charlie had another scheme up his sleeve that would keep him in the public eye.

October 19, 1916

Mr. Charles Meadows,
Yuma, Arizona

Dear Charles,

The *Times* man has just left my office. He is very much interested and says this will make a cracking big story, but he objects to going into it without more data, for the same reason that Mr. Lawson objects to having his name used; that is on account criticism that would naturally come about if the story was not backed up with the proper data. Now he is not an engineer, but he knows what he wants; at least, he thinks I do. He says that he would like to have a sketch to put in his story, or the data sufficient to make one from. He should have a profile from mesa to mesa, showing the elevation of the mesas, as well as the elevation of the hills at the river. I don't mean that it would be necessary for an engineer to make a cross section. I am sure the Reclamation Service has all the data necessary, including elevations, distances, etc. Mr. Lawson could have some of his boys draft a rough sketch showing the area covered by the reservoir, the depth of the water, etc. This, of course, could be estimated approximately. I realize that it would be impossible to get all the data absolutely correct, but Mr. Hayden appreciates the importance of this story and refuses to write up a big story on guess work. I have gotten him so deeply interested that he wants to write a story that the jack-leg engineers, that Mr. Lawson refers to, cannot criticize and tear it to pieces. He doesn't want to put the proposition before the people, and especially through the *Los Angeles Times*, that can be criticized by anyone, so he must have the data.

Mr. Lawson will know just what is necessary. Mr. Hayden is very busy at present. I suggest we go over Sunday, but he says he hasn't had a Sunday off for nine weeks; and he doesn't think it will be possible for him to come to Yuma, but if you can get Mr. Lawson to prepare the data, wire me; and I will see Mr. Chandler and have him send him (Mr. Hayden) over there. You can tell Mr. Lawson he need not hesitate to talk to Mr. Hayden, as he will not be quoted anywhere in the newspapers, even as giving us this data, if he objects.

I am sure Mr. Hayden can get the data he wants, he will get up the best story on water conservation that ever was written in Southern California. I will have to admit that the further I go into it, the more interested I am getting myself.

Yours truly,

Tom

It is not known how this story turned out, but it proves that little grass grew under Charlie's feet while he waited for his libel cases to be tried.

The Noblest Spartan

Tired of fighting the natives, the old Hassayamper sold some of his town property next to Headquarters; and lit into the jungle of giant arrow weed and *mesquite* on his ranch in the rich bottom lands at the confluence of the Gila and Colorado Rivers; and became a hard-working "son of the soil," settling down in a nitch where a man's private affairs weren't every pesky critter's business. "I burned my way into this hermetic habitat," Charlie said, which he shared with a covey of quail. "I cleared a small piece of my 160-acre parcel, the soil so rich you could put ten-penny nails in the ground and reap a crop of bolts, and on this land I placed a small bunch of those that cheweth the cud, and with my saddle horses hitched to a plow and scraper, meandered a small stream from the chocolate-colored, silt-laden water from the North Laguna Project."

Charlie's skin turned darker than a mule's wet hide, and quickly took on the look of a dried onion. He loved every creature that bathed under the blazing sun, and fed every bony, decrepit horse that wandered the burning sands. The local newspaper referred to him as possibly the "the noblest Spartan of them all," because he fed a whole bag of apples to a starving horse on the desert.

His herd multiplied, and "I bought up and improved adjacent land, and now I am the holder of the largest single body of land in the county," Charlie said.

On some of this choice land—which the soil was simply marvelous in its productiveness, he put in an experimental crop of cotton, and set aside one acre devoted to a trial crop of sweet potatoes; the resulting crop nigh incredible! When those monstrous roots were harvested, some weighed as much as six to seven pounds each! Some called him the "versatile genius of First Street." Those words were more flattering than the names he had been called only a few months previous. When he harvested some 2,000 pounds of this crop from one acre, he set aside the seed from which he grew twenty acres of this fine crop the following year, and the "finest ever seen in Yuma."

Between chores, Charlie made time for his friends, one crusty old miner crony by the name of "Frenchy" La Rue. Because of some trouble with a claim jumper, Frenchy couldn't leave his digs unattended. So, Charlie made numerous trips into the Kofa Mountains with bags of grub for his friend. Charlie assured Frenchy that if the pesky "rascal" ever showed his face in Yuma, he'd have to reckon with old Charlie first.

On February 10, 1917, at the age of seventy-two, and after long ill health attributed to uremic poisoning, Buffalo Bill passed on to join his many friends who had gathered long since in the unknown arena of another life. A high-minded gentleman, and a valued friend, Buffalo Bill's visits were sadly missed at Charlie's Yuma Headquarters.

Then—in 1918—when all seemed tranquil, death again intervened. A wire from Maggie in Los Angeles notified Charlie of John Valentine's untimely and tragic death from gunshot wounds delivered by an unknown assassin. His hotel room, found in considerable disarray, indicated that robbery was apparently the motive. John and Charlie had been through so much—yet had been apart so many years, and Charlie was sorry for that. He knew we all must go the way of the flesh, but this was another tragedy Charlie found difficult to understand or accept. James was then the only brother he had left. The following year Mobley's son, Carlos, Charlie's namesake, a young man of only twenty-one, passed on, a victim of tuberculosis, leaving his young wife, Mary, a widow, with their young son.

Zane Grey Visits Headquarters

Zane Grey, the famous western fiction writer came to Yuma purposely to interview Charlie and others concerning the facts relating to the Pleasant Valley War, for his book, *To The Last Man*. There was still much secrecy concerning the facts of the feud because of the bitter hatred that still existed amongst the descendants of those killed, who were still living in Pleasant Valley and adjacent Arizona localities. Grey found Charlie's lips sealed. While Grey was in Yuma, he got an inspiration for another book, *Stairs of Sand*, published in 1928, and in that book he characterizes the old onion-skinned sidewinder like this:

"Arizona Charlie, a local character, whom Merryvale knew by sight, appeared with a group of friends, all bent on conviviality. He stood head and shoulders above the crowd, a picturesque frontiersman in cowboy regalia, red of face, blinking of eye, with a mouth that was a thin hard line except for when he smiled."

Grey was an avid trophy hunter, and shared the same passion for adventure that Charlie did. His interest in Charlie's tales of Tiburon, and the fabulous hunting and fishing excursions Charlie had made there—never ceased to intrigue him. However, Grey was not too eager to accompany Charlie on a planned trip to Tiburon. The following letter from his home in Atladena, California, suggests he and Charlie shared a friendship, both having lived in Tonto Basin at different times:

February 25, 1921

Dear Mr. Meadows,

I am sending you by parcel post three of my books. Hope you like them. When I get around to it I will read all the clippings, etc., you lent me, to learn all I can about Tiburon Island.

I have found since I have been here that Salisbury has a ranch at Guaymas, and has been to Tiburon several times. I greatly fear that conditions have changed there since you visited it. As soon as I can interview someone who has been there recently, I will let you know. As a matter of fact, however, Lower California and the Gulf Islands interest me much more than this island.

With best regards and hoping to hear from you about your proposed trip.

Yours sincerely,

Zane Grey

Grey appeared to be a little frightened of the "man-eaters" on Tiburon, and there is no indication that Charlie ever returned there himself. Perhaps he was only going if Grey accompanied him.

A Visit Back to Wonderland

George Edwards, a long-time friend of Charlie's, said Charlie was never seen in a car—he was always around town riding his horse. By this time the old pioneer accepted the automobile as a necessity, and in 1923, bought a new one. He and Mae made a trip "back to my old stomping grounds," he said in an interview with a reporter from the *Yuma Morning Sun* —"a trip to wonderland, where we visited spots brim full of memories of exciting times in the early history of Arizona."

It is the same old story: "Distance lends enchantment. I do not regret travelling over one hundred thousand miles and spending several times that many dollars (that's the best "windy" Charlie has told yet) sightseeing in foreign lands and distant climates, looking over nature's wonders and man's architectural achievements. "But," Charlie marvelled, "to return and find at my very door, a splendid boulevard to the Grand Canyon, a wonderland that surpasses all the beauty, splendour and grandeur that I have seen before, indicates that the joke is on me.

"Leaving Yuma, the Gateway City, one rides for a few miles through orange and date orchards, that soon fade from view as we find ourselves speeding over the Painted Desert," he described. "I would say to the tourist, delay not, unless you are prepared to come again and stay. Writers describe the mirage, the turquoise sky, the copper, purple and heliotrope colorings, but no one has given a satisfactory explanation of why they want to come back and stay.

"I have seen the barren desert regions of Australia and Africa, and the Great Plains of Russia, and was never inoculated by the desert bug until I reached Southwestern Arizona," said Charlie. There is no indication whatsoever that Charlie saw either Africa or Russia. Again romance entered his story, but typical of the old cowboy's tendency to exaggerate. Yet, he captured Arizona's enchantment:

"It seems not so long ago that I remember Phoenix as a small Mexican village, built of adobe shacks. It is now a city with all the metropolitan airs. The United States Reclamation Service's construction of the Roosevelt Dam, the largest irrigation project in the world, has brought under a high state of cultivation 300,000 acres of rich land. A thousand miles of main canals serve 6,000 farms that support a population of 100,000.

"The roads through the Salt River Valley are now paved. An hour's ride through Tempe and Mesa, and we are again on the Painted Desert travelling over the old Apache Trail, the oldest highway in America. The scenery along this route is superb!

"I have seen the handiwork of man in the Temple of Jacka on the Island of Java, the Rangoon Pagoda in Father India, the pyramids of Egypt, the Eiffel Tower, the Great Wall, the Statue of Liberty, and the Brooklyn Bridge, but in point of interest and benefit of mankind with me, the Roosevelt Dam is ace. Fifteen miles above the dam on Tonto Creek, the desert fades and a luxuriant growth of green waving grass and beautiful flowers marks the contrast. Box elder, juniper, and live oak were the timber growth. In one hour we were in Payson, amongst the pines and cedars.

"Payson is a summer resort with several hundred permanent residents who are devoted mostly to mining and grazing. The women have that wonderful peach-glow complexion and step like they are on springs. Men are the "He" type; big, brave and good, but who wouldn't be in such a climate and such surroundings and scenes.

"Frontier days brought out men who owned their own herds and vied in friendly contest for supremacy in cowboy exercises of skill and daring. They were real men, mounted on trained horses, handling sure-enough denizens of the range.

"Tonto Basin is a beautiful park. To the north it breaks off in the Black Mesa, or Mogollon Mountains, in a half-moon circle something like a thousand feet perpendicular, the top of which the Salt River and the Little Colorado meet."

From Payson Charlie sped up Strawberry Hill to the rim of the Mogollon mesa, making the trip in an hour. In the old days the trip took many hours, while "playful Indians amused themselves taking pot-shots at the travelers."

"There were many side issues to this route, near and very attractive. Fossel Creek, that furnishes Prescott with light and power, bursts in one body from a huge limestone cliff and is probably the largest spring in existence. The petrified forests and cliff dwellings are only a few hours' drive from the main boulevard. One hour's drive brought us to the summit of the reserve, to the edge of Coconino Forest by Mormon Lake and Flagstaff. The whole country at this time was a waving field of luxurious grass and wild flowers. The forest seemed grand and unlimited in every direction. Hundreds of droves of wild turkey, many hundred deer, and several thousand antelope have disappeared since I lived there. No estimate could be placed on the value of these beautiful, harmless, mild-eyed creatures, if they could have been allowed to remain.

"As long as man makes the laws—and arms and ammunition, there will be open season for their extermination. There was some consolation in seeing in their place thousands of well-bred, white-faced cattle fairly rolling in tallow.

"On the brink of the Grand Canyon, the 'Garden of the Gods,' was now a modern hotel and and a road of some twenty miles long skirted the rim of the gorge; the cliffs which in the sunlight glow with ruddy fire. In natural scenery I have seen the Alps, the mountains and forests of New Zealand, Niagara Falls, Yellowstone Park, Sequoia and Yosemite Parks. I have seen the inland sea of Alaska, its great glaciers, lofty peaks and mighty rivers; there is a way of describing them all, but words to give an accurate description of this Great King of Gorges—is not in the English vocabulary."

CHAPTER 27

1926-1932
HERMIT OF THE PAINTED DESERT

For Charlie, 1926 was another year of grief. Bitter news came informing him that sister, Sarah, had died tragically in a violent automobile explosion in a Calexico service station. Seated in the back seat of the car with her baby grandson in her arms, the two were consumed in the blazing inferno. Charlie was clutched in a fit of despair. Tragedy had struck so many of his loved ones in such horrifyingly unnatural ways, yet he had risked his life 101 different times, and always came through unscathed. Why were the innocent always the victims? Only four of the twelve siblings were left.

Charlie was almost impossible to get along with after this dreadful tragedy. He had a streak of cussedness a mile and forty inches long. He and Mae were always out of sorts with one another, and she didn't see things as Charlie did anymore. Whenever Charlie mentioned his daughter, Marion, Mae arched like a wild cat about to pounce on a lizard. She loved the seashore, so whenever it got too hot in Yuma—either with Charlie or the weather, she would go on an extended vacation to Santa Monica, California, and stay by the beach for the duration. One time Mae did not come back. Eventually, they made a settlement and separated for good.

During the lonesome months that followed, Charlie was like a tumbleweed—drifting before the wind; a hermit of the painted desert. Each day about noon, Charlie rode to town to pick up his mail; an imposing figure on his palomino horse, Yellow Boy; dressed in western finery, with large *sombrero*, and a sequined ribband on his tunic with the name "Charlie" emblazoned on it.

Then Marion, who dared not come around before, made several visits to Headquarters. Charlie took his daughter on several Gulf Island excursions and they grew to know each other better. He was an amazing man, and Marion resented her mother for keeping her father from her for so many years. She spent hours listening to her father relive his grandiose adventures, and feasted on every page of his famous scrapbook. Marion noticed her mother's picture had been carved out of a young group photo taken of Harmston's Company in Australia. Charlie tried to explain Mae's jealousy. Sometime later he found Mae's head had been severed from her body in a photo taken in Monroe's cabin in Dawson.

Even though Marion had never forgiven her mother for telling her Charlie was dead, she arranged a reunion between her parents. It had been thirty-four years, and the very thought made Charlie panicky. Finally, he consented.

Both Charlie and Marion Mae were somewhat uneasily speechless that day in Yuma, their mouths considerably agape. He could scarcely contain himself at the sight of dismay on her face. She, no doubt, was startled to see such a gray, gaunt, sun-parched and long shanked old desert rat, when she possibly expected to see the same tall, handsome and stalwart *vaquero* of many years ago. All the while she was taking him in, he muttered a few guttural symbols and found himself surveying her now overly-stout matronly figure with a calculating eye, wondering whatever attracted them to each other. But after a loosening up period, a sentimental spark between the two ignited, as they re-lived the romance and thrilling adventures they shared over three decades earlier. The two kept up a line of communication from then on. Possibly Marion Mae did believe he died when the newspapers reported him missing on Tiburon in 1902. She married twice again, and had two more children, but now, she too was alone. They seemed to have so much in common.

A Sorrowful Time

Charlie was never a man known to cry, especially in the presence of others. He had his raw-hide toughness, but he was tender-hearted and sentimental, and there were a few times in his colorful life that were exceptions.

Yellow Boy was Charlie's whole life—now that he was alone—and his favorite equine friend. They had been together a long time, and to Charlie he was the closest to his heart. Everyone commented on how beautiful Yellow Boy was, and how regal Charlie looked in his saddle. If Charlie wasn't on Yellow Boy's back, Yellow Boy was following Charlie around the ranch like a devoted child.

Charlie made daily trips to Hog Island to care for his pigs, donning mud boots, and crossing the shallow waters that divided the tiny islet from his property. The islet was just big enough for Charlie and the pigs, not roomy enough for a horse—so Yellow Boy was never allowed there.

One day Yellow Boy started to follow Charlie through the water—and Charlie ordered him to go back, but he kept coming. Somewhat annoyed that he disobeyed him this time, Charlie shot—what he believed to be well over the horse's head—to frighten him so he would go back. But, dear Lord, he missed, and he hit Yellow Boy square in the head! Stunned—with the blood fairly draining from his body and a dreadful sinking feeling in his heart—Charlie reeled in disbelief. Casting his eyes heavenward, he prayed it was all a dream. He frantically begged Yellow Boy to get up, but he just lay there quivering and senseless. In his delirium Charlie knew his only recourse was to put his beloved friend out of his agony, so with great pain he delivered him his quietus with a final shot. In an instant there was a single convulsion, and the horse was dead. Engulfed with grief, and half out of his mind, Charlie stumbled home and into the arms of his niece, Florence, and wept until he was exhausted. Something vital had been taken out of him; the guilt was more than he could bear—and life was not worth living for a long while. He could, for the rest of his life, only speak of Yellow Boy with a choking utterance.

Charlie had always been a crack-shot, and never before had an accident of this kind happened. But his eyes were failing—according to friend, George Edwards; he was no longer the King of the Cowboys—or the Winchester Wizard, he was only King of Hog Island.

A Pioneer Gets Ruffled

On April 14, 1927, Charlie joined the Arizona Pioneer's Association. The basis for his qualification was his residence in Arizona for thirty-five years or longer. Except for time out here and there for his many adventures, Charlie had been a resident of Arizona for over fifty years. In October of 1927, Charlie learned of a proposed plan to erect a statue in Skeleton Canyon, in the Old Chiefton Geronimo's memory, by the Hollywood Motion Picture Industry.

Now this revelation ruffled every tuft of Charlie's fevered brow, and sent the short hairs a-prickle on the back of his neck.

A formal protest was written by ye Arizona pioneer to Mr. Charles Clark, President of the Arizona Pioneer's Association, as follows:

Dear Mr. Clark,

According to a dispatch from Los Angeles, September 20, "Geronimo, defender of the soil," is to have a monument erected in Skeleton Canyon, Arizona. It will depict Geronimo in characteristic pose mounted on a bronco.

The necessary funds are to be raised wholly within the motion picture industry, and the project is to be sponsored by the American Ethnographic Society, of which G. C. Turner is president.

Just why Hollywood should sidestep their own Badge Bandit, and Hammer Queen and cross the burning sands of desert to present us a delayed tribute in the shape of a monument to our murderous old Geronimo can be attributed only to a horse sense of the historical Thompson colt variety.

Following the monument there will, of course, be a motion picture, something of the vanishing American complex. This will be extremely educational to the coming generations in showing the harshness of their forefathers in driving old Geronimo from the soil.

A mental test of those answering the call in the World War brought out the fact that 52,000 men of draft age had only the mentality of six-year-old children. Even if the promoters, contributors, and sponsors of this monumental enormity were among this mentally deficient number, for immaculate gall, intestinal stamina and unadulterated disregard for other people's feelings—we are compelled to give them one hundred percent.

Geronimo left a string of white widows and orphans that are still living in the neighborhood of Skeleton Canyon; pioneers who, in days gone by, returned to their firesides only to find their wives and children killed and mutilated by the murderous old Geronimo and his cut-throat followers; the climate in Skeleton Canyon will no doubt prove quite rigorous for a Geronimo statue.

Since the soil defender will feel we should not butt in and take it away from them, and that it would be the right thing to let the contributors retain it and set it up in their own home town. It would be a crime to mention in the same breath the names of such Knights and defenders of the road as Joaquin Murietta and Vasquez, with that of old Geronimo, but, a group showing the Hammer Queen, posed over her prostrate victim with uplifted hammer; the Badge Bandit, with his victim lashed to a telephone pole; and old Geronimo in characteristic pose, holding an infant at arm's length in one hand and a bloody scalping knife in the other, with its mother bleeding and dying at its feet, should satisfy the statuesque cravings of the monumental maniacs!

Charles Meadows

A Lonesome Cowboy

In the year of 1931, James suffered a fatal stroke. The two brothers, Charlie and James, had not always seen eye to eye; Charlie admitted that. Sometimes Charlie's public disputes were humiliating to James, and he was sorry for this. But the most vivid memories of his life were those adventurous times spent in the early days when he and his brothers were all together, roaming the mountains and deserts of Arizona. They were a close family, but now his brothers were all gone—and he missed them so very much.

Like all the Meadows Brothers, when he was younger, James thought he could lick anyone he chose to fight. In earlier Yuma years, James had a running feud with the local blacksmith, S. F. Moore. He lost to Moore several times. Moore would hunt him down, and, when he found him—give him a sound beating. The last time Moore attacked James was in front of Harry Marshall's Barber Shop. After the beating, James had Moore put under a $3,500 peace bond.

Now, there were only three of the twelve siblings left; Charlie and two sisters, Maggie and Mary. In the twilight of his life, Charlie had a few complaints, but nothing that appeared serious. His varicose veins were bothersome, but who ever heard of anyone dying of that. A nagging hernia and a clumsy truss were aggravating, his eyesight was not too keen, and the doctor said he had a minor heart problem. Charlie had seen much life and had done a great deal of real living, but his life was "charmed," and he was convinced he was too ornery to die.

Alone with his thoughts, he heard less and less from old friends who shared in the days of hazard and hardship, and the glorious and exciting times still vivid in the old cowpuncher's memories. Raking over the embers of long-dead years, Charlie's thoughts turned to the frenzied epic of the Klondike gold rush; dreams as clear as real life. So he wrote to the *Dawson News*, inquiring of his old friend, Jack McQuesten, a most prominent figure in early Yukon history, and no man more beloved in all the north, only to learn Jack had passed to the great beyond more than twenty-two years before in California.

It seemed to Charlie that everyone was gone. Without Yellow Boy he was lonely. Other than a few nieces and nephews, he had no family in Yuma. Charlie looked forward to letters from Marion Mae; and from time to time their daughter, Marion, came to stay for a time with him. He missed a woman around the house; he did not want to grow old all alone.

Eighty acres of his land was leased for a crop of *maize*. In a letter to Marion Mae he said, "and I am not to be burdened with any labor or expense—and I get one-third of the bin." The rest of his acreage was in sweet potatoes and Bermuda grass. Charlie devoted more and more time to his small garden at Headquarters, and during his leisure hours he lounged in Oriental garb—old dress he brought from Southeast Asia many years before. His mode of dress often disturbed the neighbor woman who lived across the way. She never liked him much after his horses breached the fence and ate the tops off her garden. Charlie always had a good answer for her complaints. He told her the garden would only come back better than ever.

One of her most urgent complaints was that Charlie worked in his garden on hot days in nothing but a towel gathered around him—held together by a large safety pin. From long habit he always kept his rifle by his side, and a large *sombrero* on his head. She got rather panicky that he might lose the scanty outfit. So she got on the wire to her landlord, Ray Lewis, who said her gasp could be heard clear over to Mose Hibbard's snake farm. Ray informed her, if she would back away from her window—she needn't have to worry.

A Splendid Invitation

In June 1931, Charlie was bombarded with mountains of mail—and messages over the wire, by relatives, classmates, the Chamber of Commerce, the rodeo committee, Native Daughters of the Golden West, and the Bull Moose, requesting his presence at the biggest round-up and rodeo ever attempted in his little old home town of Visalia, or anywhere else in California. It was the third annual Visalia Moose Lodge Rodeo and Fiesta, and about the biggest celebration that ever happened there.

A change of scenery, Charlie thought, was just what the doctor ordered, and he would not have missed this event if he had to go by muleback.

Charlie had a fairly decent Model T Ford, called "Lizzie," and he chomped at the bit to get started back to the place he first saw the light of day some seventy-one years before. The trip, however, was against the dissuasive appeals of sister, Maggie, and friends, who kept warning the old pioneer, "You've got to take better care of yourself, Charlie, or you're not going to be around long, remember your heart." Others brought up his failing eyesight, and another his sore legs, just more signs of age taking its place. The old Hassayamper, though grizzled, still stood tall, straight as an arrow, and his long fingers—large at the knuckles, showed strength as the result of years of roping. He was far from entering the big corral in the sky, and always came back with the retort, "It'll be a snowy day in Yuma, Arizona, the day I die."

Charlie's bags were quickly packed with his most colorful beaded and braided vestments of the *vaquero*. He put a little spit and polish on his boots; grabbed the big hat Buffalo Bill had given him years before, and headed out for Visalia. He was all alone in Lizzie. He was happier than an old hound dog who had just made his first retreat from the fiery darts of a porcupine. He made one short stop in the San Fernando Valley—near Los Angeles, to say hello to Maggie.

Charlie Steals the Glory

What a time Charlie had in Visalia! He had the honor of being asked to ride in the parade as Grand Marshal, but he preferred to watch this time; he'd always led the parades and never got to see one. But with a little persuasion, he consented to ride part way—as far as the Lincoln Oval, with his Honor, Mayor Rufus J. Bagby; Walter Hunsaker, Chairman of the Governor's Reception Committee Gene Goodfriend, the General Chairman; and George Tschumy, Chairman of the Reception Committee; Charlie got off and viewed the rest of the parade and rodeo with his niece, Sadie, (daughter of Rhoda and Abe McGinnis) and her husband, Rufus, and their daughter, Thelma.

Now this old rope wrangler stole plenty of glory from the rodeo performers—Governor Rolph of California; Governor "Alfalfa" Bill Murray of Oklahoma; and Governor Fred Balzer of Nevada—when he was introduced to the crowd. The thrill for the Arizona gentleman was magnificent; he loved being Arizona Charlie, and soaked up the swell of applause. Clay Carr—another hometown boy, who was the 1930 World's Champion, who thrilled the gallery of spectators with his daring bronc riding and bulldogging—received a hearty ovation to equal that for Charlie.

While the oily broncs were tossing the cowhands around, to the amazement of the crowd, an exciting surprise unfolded overhead. Amelia Earhart, the famous American aviatrix, was circling the sky over the arena, waving salutations to the throng below from her queer-looking autogyro as she dipped over the park. The daring pilot was flying from Oakland to Los Angeles, testing the practicality of the flying windmill as transportation.

A maelstrom of murky clouds swirling overhead made the day ideal for the rodeo. Abe Lefton, a talented and witty announcer, kept the audience in a perfect uproar, and western music was furnished by the Arizona Wranglers and the Ranch Hour Boys of Hollywood.

The Arizona cowpuncher got plenty of enjoyment out of meeting old-time friends and Visalia relatives. A little fun was poked by the Arizona man at old John Bennett and his Missus, who along with Charlie and a few others held reserved seats right alongside Governor Rolph of California in the grandstand. Now John was an "old-time cousin" who hadn't recognized the weaseled and lined old gent. He and his Missus were just a "trifle excited," and all keyed up, honored guests, and seated amongst other honored guests right in the middle of things; Arizona Wranglers "Slicker," "Nubbins," and "Irontail," right in front of them, and Mayor Bagby and Governor Jimmie to the side.

"Let me see your Annie Oakely's," were Charlie's words—according to the *Visalia Daily Delta*. He said them sort of belligerently, as he leaned his big arm hard on old John's shoulder. Old John had his tickets still in his hands, so excited he hadn't thought about putting them in his pockets.

"These stubs don't call for those seats," was Charlie's next line. "You can't sit here."

Old John was flustered at first, but backed up by his Missus, had to be shown. The Arizona Wranglers had nothing on the wrangle that ensued. Charlie got a little bit personal and insisted Old John "get out" and take his wife with him. Spectators in the rapidly filling grandstand were intently watching the row, and police were seen elbowing their way toward the commotion. A showman right to the end, Charlie especially enjoyed the audience he was attracting.

Old John was now trembling with suppressed anger, and wanted to know "Who in the Sam Hill are you, you big slab-sided horned toad?" Charlie came back with a crack about "certain folk who couldn't ride Rebel John with a double cinch," passing themselves off as pioneers. (Rebel John was a famous race horse of the Visalia country over fifty years before. Cinches are belly bands, or girths that go under the horse.) It was the reference to the cinch that got Old John a-going.

Old John "squared off" and was starting a "roundhouse swing" at Charlie's mid-section, but the old cowboy held him just out of range.

"You know what we do with fellows like you down in my country? Why we hog-tie you and feed you to the coyotes," Charlie proclaimed, all this within earshot of the reporter from the *Visalia Times Delta*.

"Where do you come from—and who in the heck are you?"

"I'm Arizona Charlie Meadows, from Yuma, Arizona, how are you 'cousin' John?" John was so excited to see the old cowboy he could hardly keep his eyes on the show. The old publicity-loving showman had not lost his knack for baiting the press.

Charlie was the house guest of his niece, Sadie Connelly, and her husband, Rufus. The old desert coyote didn't want to be a bother too long, so after a few days visiting with friends and relatives, Charlie headed back home to Yuma, where his sweet potato crop waited to be harvested, and his big acreage of Bermuda grass was due to be threshed. But first he detoured past the old family homestead, the place of his birth. The old adobe house (an historical landmark) that his father had built of hand-made bricks, had been torn down recently, which was sad for him, but the giant valley oak he was born under more than seventy-years before—was still standing. As he whipped down the interstate he marvelled at the distant jagged peaks where he prospected as a boy, and a maze of touching memory visions preyed at his heart as his mind searched the scenes of his glorious youth.

Moving rapidly down the highway, his thoughts turned to Marion Mae. He was lonely once again. He and Marion Mae had talked of a "last stand" in their many letters, and the prospect of their reunion now cluttered his mind. Marion, of course, would not be happy, he thought. She might "boom" their plans. She wouldn't like her mother "stepping in" and taking her father away from her again. Marion Mae had told him they would have to "be careful." He thought of the "Morgan Place" that was up for sale. But it was the Great Depression Years, and Morgan wanted more than Charlie could afford. When he got home he'd try to make a trade with Morgan; Marion Mae would like it there, he thought. But if she came she would bring along her other daughter and her family . . . it would be a wonderful place to bring up her grandchildren. He would buy the older girl her own saddle . . . a beautiful one he already had his eye on, and groom her to be an "Arizona Princess." He could hardly wait to get home and "work" on Morgan. He would have that ranch, "trade or no trade." Besides, a geologist had told him that "oil on that very place showed better than any place in Arizona." He'd "bend all efforts to get some sheep," he thought . . . he had all the grass needed to feed them. He could hardly wait to get back home and write to Marion Mae and tell her about his marvelous trip, and his plans for their future life together. There was only one small detail clouding the way. Mae had never bothered to get a divorce. But he'd get Marion Mae's garden started anyway . . . they'd work it out some way.

Overcast skies that had threatened for several days—followed him out of town—then turned into black clouds that hung like a blanket of lead on the horizon. A terrible summer storm was brewing—a thing hitherto unknown in that region in the month of June. Then a heavy thunder clap bore down upon him; the heavens opened up and he suddenly found himself driving in a drenching rain with visibility practically nil. Old Lizzie skidded a mile and forty inches and buckled up like an accordion in the roadside ditch. Now Charlie figured none of this would have happened had he been on his horse, but as usual it was not his time, and he struggled free of the shambles—a little scratched and shook up, but all in one piece.

Back in Yuma after a week, Charlie had plenty of flap from his old friends, who had that "I told you so" attitude. Old timer, George Edwards, scolded by saying, "Charlie, you idiot, you won't be around long if you go on many trips like that one." Charlie came back with the usual, "I've been kicking along better than ever, my good friend. It'll be a snowy day in Yuma, Arizona that day they plant this old Hassayamper!"

New Headstone Contributed by Dawson City, and the Klondike and Yukon Visitor's Association

EPILOGUE

On December 9, 1932, at the age of 72, and with all the history of his life written into the lines of his face, Arizona Charlie, the "World's Most Persistent Rainbow Chaser" reached the end of his earthly trail, departing on his last great adventure, a romantic echo of the glorious past. The night of the day he was buried, *snow fell on Yuma*. It was the *first snow* recorded in the eighty-year history of the United States Weather Bureau there.

Arizona Charlie was the tragic victim of his own error in judgment. Refusing to see a doctor for relief, he opened his troublesome varicose veins with a pocket knife. After losing considerable blood he was unable to keep up the heart action; an ignoble way to die for such an astonishing man. Three of the six pallbearers included, Doc Knotts, Archie Griffen, and Joe Balch.

Charlie died intestate. His daughter, Marion, with him in his final days, was awarded his vast ranch lands. In 1944, she died of cancer. His nephew, Johnny, in charge of her estate, had Charlie's remains removed from the Old Desert Cemetery and placed next to Marion's plot in the new Desert Lawn Cemetery nearby—at her request. For fifty-four years a weathered granite marker plate rested at the head of his silent grave, pitted by the swirling sands of time that had all but obliterated his familiar name. The man on horseback still rides tall in the saddle.

Dawson City, suspended in time, recalls the spirit of some 100,000 men and women who challenged the odds; all expecting to strike it rich in the hectic days of the Klondike Stampede. In 1951, Walter Dinsdale, Canadian Minister of Northern Affairs, presented a bill in the House of Commons for the restoration of Charlie's Palace Grand Theatre, once the pride of Dawson City. During the spirited debate, outraged liberals with an eye on votes in the coming election, complained to Parliament that Dawson needed a hospital more than a monument to a gaudy past.

But, undeterred, the conservative majority "whooped" through an appropriation bill, "and a fine thing too," editorialized Toronto's *Globe and Mail*. "May Arizona Charlie's be rebuilt to its former splendour; let ragtime music tinkle again in the Red Feather Saloon . . . Let the Bonanza Belle again paddle her way up the Yukon River, and by all means, bring back the girls . . ."

And the spirit of Arizona Charlie came back into the spotlight of history. The Department of Northern Affairs and National Resources considered Charlie's place part of its new "Northern Vision" policy; grubstaked the town for $385,000, and made the Palace Grand a National Historic Site of Canada. The restoration of its original splendour was completed in time for the Gold Rush Festival of 1962, commemorating a segment of Canada's history in which thousands of Americans shared. Close to $750,000 was invested in preparation for the festival, and 2,500 travel agencies across America and Canada booked tours.

Visitors were put up in two beached sternwheelers, where ragtime Bob Starch and his honky-tonk piano entertained, and in a tent city set up on the edge of town much like the miners of '98. (But with the comforts of flooring and beds.)

The Honorable Walter Dinsdale, and stage star, Beatrice Lillie, officially opened the Gold Rush Festival prior to the main attraction at the Palace Grand. They "whooped" it up at Charlie's place opening night. After a toast to Arizona Charlie, veteran stage master, Bert Lahr, guided a complete Broadway cast in the premiere performance of *Foxy*, to a thunderous standing ovation, and it might have been gold rush 1897 all over again. Co-starring with Bert Lahr was Larry Blyden.

The musical comedy was written especially for the occasion by Ring Lardner and Ian McClellen Hunter, and Johnnie Mercer provided the exquisite lyrics of wit and spice. The program was based on a lot of gold-rush nonsense, rolled in with a little slapstick and romance. Comedian Bert Lahr in the title role came off with some fancy soft shoe shuffling, mugged and sang his heart out, and clowned around in a polka dot nightgown. He switched his act from gold prospector to English Squire, and from villian to lover for a delightful and amusing three hours.

It was quite a night for the 700 Dawson residents and crowds of out-of-town visitors. There was a mixture of black tie and evening dress, combined with old prospectors sporting long beards and plaid shirts. Among them, seated in the "Royal Box" near the stage, was Black Mike Winage, 92, a grizzled and bearded leftover from the trail of '98.

Today in the land where strong men still lust for that golden dust, there is life in the old place yet. Charlie's Palace Grand Theatre presents the *Gaslight Follies*, which is the main attraction of Dawson City, attracting some forty to sixty thousand visitors from all over the world each year during summer season. What a thrill it was for me to give the toast to Charlie from its stage in 1980, on the eighty-first birthday of the theatre! There—along with Klondike Kate, who made her fame upon his stage; George Carmack, who discovered the gold; "Soapy" Smith, who fleeced it; Robert Service who wrote the verse; and Jack London, who told the story—Charlie's name is legend. In Whitehorse, the Capitol of the Yukon, and in British Columbia, a chain of first-class restaurants bears his name.

Sometime in 1933, an unidentified Los Angeles newspaper reported that Cecil B. DeMille, Hollywood Motion Picture Director, loaded his big yacht with machine guns and rifles, and headed for Tiburon Island in the Gulf of California, to discover again the cannibals said to be there by Arizona Charlie some thirty years before. The result of the trip is not known, other than the fact the party returned safely. At that time it was reported that some believed the Seri Indians to be a "harmless lot," easily bribed with a generous supply of tequila, unless "scared blacker than they are by pith-helmeted explorers desiring to pot a few cannibals for publicity."

The report said: "Newspaper files of about thirty years ago contain the record of Charles Meadows, the Buffalo Bill then of Yuma, and tell of his expedition to Tiburon. Meadows was a wild-west showman, a real cowboy, six-gun expert, who could do more roping in a minute than Will Rogers could talk in an hour."

That same year, Don Alberto Maas went across the length of Tiburon, took photographs of the natives (as Charlie had also done); and with a little supply of tequila was heartily greeted; and probably could have elected himself King, and stayed and founded a dynasty. And he came back without being served as "steaks or chops" and published his findings.

Until 1956, the Mexican Government allowed the Seris to remain on Tiburon, with the strict condition that they give up cannibalism. Then a couple of Mexican fisherman disappeared, and the Mexican Army moved in and re-located the whole Seri tribe, then numbering 220, to the mainland of Sonora. Today a few live on a beach near Kino, and a few at Desomboque, near Punta Sargents. The girls and unattached women still paint their cheeks with bright stripes.

In 1978, Tiburon was set aside by the Mexican Government as a wildlife sanctuary. The Mexican and United States Governments agreed to work together to study and manage wildlife they share.

In 1947, Mr. Anthony Gibbon, District Editor of the *Oil Weekly*, published by the Gulf Publishing Company, Tulsa, Oklahoma, wrote to Charlie's nephew, Johnnie, requesting the following information:

Dear Mr. Meadows:

> Mr. George B. Gross, Business Manager of the *Yuma Daily Sun*, advised me that you had in your possession a scrap book kept by your Uncle, Mr. Arizona Charlie Meadows. I am trying to obtain some information about his trip to the Island of Tiburon, and would appreciate it if you will lend me the scrap book. Needless to say, I will take good care of same, and will return it to you after I have scanned it. My interest in Tiburon stems from a report which I received many years ago that your uncle had discovered some pitchblende which is an important source of uranium. I am gathering all information possible so as to pass it along to

our government. As you know, all uranium ores have been nationalized both by the United States and Mexican Governments, and therefore this is not a question of profit but purely a patriotic gesture in which I trust you will share. I am sure that you are as anxious as I am that the United States be informed of any sources of uranium and that we do whatever we can to keep such sources or information from unfriendly governments.

Trusting that you will cooperate by loaning the scrapbook if you have it, or advising me where I can obtain it, if you haven't got it, I beg to remain,

Sincerely yours,

Anthony Gibbon
District Editor
The Oil Weekly

There was no such information in Charlie's scrapbook, and it is doubtful the treasured and fragile family heirloom would have been loaned.

The World's Oldest Continuous Rodeo celebrated its 100th year in 1984 at Payson, Arizona. This Rodeo draws contestants and visitors each year from all over the world. Honorable recognition was given Arizona Charlie Meadows, originator of the *first* Payson rodeo in 1884.

Near Payson, at a place called "Whispering Pines," the oldest apple and pear trees in Arizona still stand and bear fruit, planted there in the early 1880's by John Moberly Meadows. Below these trees, a spring banked in water cress still bursts forth and flows into the East Verde River, part of the old Diamond Valley Ranch.

In Yuma, Arizona, a friend of Charlie's by the name of Harry Knight told reporter Tate Cooper, in 1972, "Charlie was an individualist who always did pretty much as he pleased. He was a big talker, had many friends and many enemies. Charlie just wasn't an ordinary man."

A personal telephone interview with Charlie's old neighbor, Ruby Adair, 88 years old at the time in 1982, said, "Charlie had a great sense of humor. I was very fond of him and still remember how attractive he was when he rode. He sat so erect and looked like royalty."

During a visit with Charlie's niece, Florence Pennington, in her nineties in 1982, she said, "Charlie was an exotic man."

Percy L. Bonabrake, remembering Charlie, wrote in the September, 1956, issue of the *Los Angeles Corral*: "Charlie was a pleasant sort of fellow to meet; one of those fellows you like at once; always chasing rainbows; considerable of a daredevil; and liked to have fun. He was said to have been the best roper in Arizona, and even at this date when old timers meet and the subject of roping comes up, Arizona Charlie and his feats with a rope will be sure to be mentioned."

In a letter to this writer in 1982, Mr. Leo K. Murphy of Yuma said that, after Charlie died, a man named George Kilroy took him out to Charlie's First Street home where his daughter Marion lived and showed him a room full of memorabilia. Amongst the collection were four saddle medals with the inscriptions, "Charlie Meadows, World's Champion Cowboy."

Mr. Kilroy, who had spent twenty years as a newspaper reporter, mostly in the Klondike region, and worked in Yuma as a reporter between the years of 1920-25, wrote many stories about Charlie. When Kilroy returned to Yuma in 1936 to check with the weather bureau about Charlie and the snow story, Mr. Murphy became acquainted with him.

Mr. Murphy said to me in his letter, "When George Kilroy passed away, I made a trip to Montana to ask Kilroy's daughter to sell the story of Charlie to me. 'My dad died a drunk,' Kilroy's daughter said. 'I threw out reams and reams of junk written about a Charlie.' When I told her she had destroyed a *fortune*, she laughed and said, 'So what?'"

Early in 1985, Conrad Boyce, actor, for six years had been portraying the Wild West showman in shows sponsored by the Yukon Visitor's Association, both on stage at Charlie's Palace Grand, as well as the *Arizona Charlie, Follow Your Dream* Show at recreational vehicle parks throughout Arizona, and at Palm Springs, California in the interest of tourism, visited Yuma's Desert Lawn Cemetery to look up the old pioneer's grave. He was astounded that the wording on Charlie's granite headstone could not be read. Also he was disappointed that the people of Yuma were not more aware of Arizona Charlie. Upon the suggestion of his wife, Bonny, he decided to raise money to replace the deteriorated headstone with a new bronze one to indicate the role Charlie played in history.

In August, 1985, R. Barry Redfern, Executive Director of the Yukon Visitor's Association, announced to the writer that funding had been allocated for the memorial through the efforts of Mayor Peter Jenkins, and the citizens of Dawson City; the Yukon Visitor's Association; the Klondike Visitor's Association, Mr. Conrad Boyce, and others.

Conrad Boyce and the *Arizona Charlie, Follow Your Dream Show* finished their tour of Yuma on the fifteenth of February, 1986, and the dedication of the memorial plaque was made at 2 p.m. that afternoon at the Desert Lawn Cemetery. Services were performed by the Reverend William D. Watkins of the Sierra Vista Presbyterian Church. Speakers included Senator Jones Osborn of Arizona, Mayor Peter Jenkins of Dawson City, Conrad Boyce and Jean Beach King, who also unveiled the plaque.

It didn't quite snow, but the heavens were listening. As the ceremony began, the blue skies disappeared and tiny droplets fell, requiring the acquisition of a canopy. The droplets grew steadily into a heavy downpour, the first rain to fall in a week. It was quite a thrill, considering Yuma receives only three inches of rain each season, and never two Saturdays in a row. When the ceremony was finished, the rain turned off like a spigot; the sun came out and the skies turned blue again. Always larger than life, this was Charlie's grandest performance. The old headstone was taken back to Dawson City to find its final resting place.

John Moorish, an old time Yuman, and an interested spectator at the event, remembered Charlie quite well. "I ran into him when I was farming in the Gila Valley. Charlie was running some cattle and they got into my alfalfa, so I put them into my cattle pen. Charlie pointed out that it was open range, and if I didn't want them in my field I could very well put up a fence." I asked Mr. Moorish what he did about that, and he replied, "I put up a fence; he was wearing a six-shooter when he told me that." But I guess they became friends. Mr. Moorish went on to say, "Bill Westerbeek and I used to make a little wine in the 1920's-30's and Charlie used to help us drink it."

Down an almost extinct and rutty dirt road, situated in a remote desert corner of Arizona, not far from Yuma—and very close to the borders of Mexico and California, a place called "Arizona Charlie's Floral Gardens" can be found. Ruins of some ten to fifteen miniature monuments, each surrounded by a low rubble of rock; and two large thrones crafted of cement, glass and stone—defaced by vandals and the elements over the years—rise ghost-like amidst sage brush, mesquite and boulders, against a barren and rocky mountainside. Seated on one throne is a headless figure of a man with long legs and broken arms. At the head of the other throne is a flat stone shaped and painted with a hog's head, an eternal reminder that once a "King" left his footprints here.

In the Yuma Territorial Museum, a beaded gauntlet, cuff and pocket from one of Charlie's show costumes, and an over-sized pistol belonging to him may be found in the vaults.

Marion Mae Murray Meadows Lesh, Charlie's first wife of a few months, was readying to leave her nursing home business behind and rejoin Charlie in Yuma when she learned of his death. She passed away on October 11, 1939, at seventy years of age, and is buried in Bend, Oregon.

Ida Mae McKamish (Melbourne) Meadows, Charlie's second wife of twenty-eight years, passed away in Los Angeles December 21, 1960, at age eighty-eight, and is buried in Santa Monica, California.

My grandmother, Maggie Meadows Beach, who fought off Indians at the age of thirteen, "could have been a heroine of any one of Zane Grey's novels with a Tonto Basin local," said writer-historian, and seventh sheriff of Imperial Valley, Herbert Hughes, in one of his books. She died in Los Angeles, California in 1934, at age sixty-five. Her ashes were spread in the Mogollon Mountains near the East Verde River, Arizona, close to the old family homestead.

Mary Angelina Meadows Arnold Bostick, the first born and the last to die of the twelve children of John M. and Margaret Meadows, died a natural death of old age in San Francisco in 1939, at the age of ninety.

The life-sized statue of Sheriff Mobley Meadows, Imperial Valley's first sheriff, now takes the spotlight among the many attractions at the California Midwinter Fairgrounds in Imperial. Mounted on a concrete pedestal, the statue now guards the entrance to the colorful museum of the Imperial Valley Pioneer Society, which draws thousands of visitors, students and historians yearly.

Currently, in Skagway, Alaska, Mr. Dennis Corrington, of Corrington's Alaskan Ivory, has had a scrimshaw history of Arizona Charlie carved on an Ivory tusk. Thirty others, out of a projected forty-nine, each representing a separate chapter in Alaska history, have been completed and will soon be displayed in Mr. Corrington's own private Skagway museum.

On April 22, 1988, in Las Vegas, Nevada, an "Arizona Charlie's" Hotel and Casino owned and operated by Ernest Becker Enterprises opened its doors, complete with a replica of the facade of Charlie's Palace Grand Theatre in Dawson City, Yukon.

Jean Beach King

Palace Grand before Restoration

BIBLIOGRAPHY

The Bibliography includes research and documents that spand a period prior to 1860 through 1988. Frequently, sources and dates were not possible for the author to obtain. There has been an attempt to clarify these references and identify those dates and sources that were unknown. However, some information was included that the author believed would be of value to the reader that was not completely referenced.

NOTES
SOME OF THE FOLLOWING MATERIALS ARE PROPERTY OF THE AUTHOR

Chapter 1.

1. The U.S. Civil War, which raged throughout the Northern and Southern States that lay predominantly east of the Mississippi, was as heartfelt, though not nearly as bloody in the Western States. Histories and historical viewpoints give little or no mention of the West's involvement in the heated conflict.
2. According to Annie Mitchell, Tulare County Historian and resident of Visalia, in her book, "*King of Tulares*," in one day five hundred mustangs were corralled on the San Joaquin near Fresno. The June 19, 1862 edition of the *Visalia Daily Delta*, corroborates this by stating: "Wild mustangs seem to be plentiful in our vicinity." It is very likely that Charlie became as proficient with the horse and lasso as he did, learning through first-hand experiences with the abundance of wild horses on the Tulare Plains.
3. A terrible rainstorm that year flooded the Meadows' adobe home with water. Mobley was being born, so John Meadows raised the bed off the floor by ropes attached to the rafters.
4. According to a report presented at the Tonto Grazing Conference in 1926, John Valentine was the first man to bring cattle into Tonto Basin at Tonto Creek.

Chapter 2.

1. Strawberry Hill is located at the present site of Strawberry, a small mountain hamlet north of Payson. This is the site of the oldest standing schoolhouse in Arizona, the Strawberry School, which opened its doors in early 1886.
2. Victorio had urged peace until the Army moved his people from a reservation on their original homeland in New Mexico to San Carlos in 1877. Turning renegade, he led 250 warriors in a bloody rampage that left 400 whites dead before he was killed in 1880.
3. Old records indicate Frank Prothero came from the family of Virgil Prothero. One Prothero family member is mentioned to be married to a Meadows woman. This would indicate, though not conclusively, that Charlie may have been related to Frank through marriage.

Chapter 3.

1. According to Dan L. Thrapp, in his article, "War on Cibicue", (*True West Magazine,* 1964) the name of this Indian is not known precisely, "most old records state it as Noch-ay-del-klinne, but they contain enough variations to account for his soldier-given nickname of "Bobby-do-klinney." Bobby was a somewhat effeminate, pale skinned White Mountain Apache who enlisted with General Crook's first group of Apache scouts, but was later discharged, disappearing into obscurity. A number of years later he emerged into prominence among his people, travelling to Washington, D.C., where he received the Congressional Medal of Honor. Soon after, he went to Santa Fe and, already having gained the reputation of a mystic and dreamer, became impressed with

the teachings of missionaries there, particularly the "periodic withdrawals of Christ for meditation and the story of the resurrection." When he returned to the White Mountains, two chiefs within the tribe had simultaneously killed each other, as Bobby had foretold, and thus, the pale mystic was hailed by his fellow tribe members as a divine prophet.

2. This is a decidedly different story than the one reported by a Mrs. Richeson to the *Arizona Republican* of April 13, 1921. Mrs. Richeson said that she "recalled the tragedy well," and went on to state that the Meadows father, two daughters, and two sons were "murdered in cold blood" and from evidence, "they had all been cruelly tortured before being put to death."
3. Sidella is located 1 1/2 miles up the East Verde River from the Payson-Pine bridge and was named after Henry Siddle, who was the first settler on this land. In early 1880, Mr. Siddle sat on a hill and watched the Apaches burn down his house.

Chapter 4.

1. Prescott may contest this revelation, recently disputed by Fay Ward, an old-time cowboy and rodeo buff, who couldn't find mention of the contest in the old Prescott newspapers. But the family has in their possession a saddle medal as proof. Some suggest Charlie had the date changed on the medal as a joke on posterity. And there are some who refer to the medal as a belt buckle. But those in the know will tell you it is designed to fit on the four corners of the saddle. This is only one of several in Charlie's collection.
   Even though Charlie was accused of telling "half truths" and "windies," and drinking the Hassaymampa almost dry, the "sin" of the cowboys in those days, (with those boys it was difficult to get into a serious conversation that didn't end up as a contest for the position of the "world's champion bullshitter,") I cannot believe Charlie had any reason to fake the medal. His contemporaries were the only ones he wished to impress, but they would have known and he would have been ballyhooed out of the territory.

Chapter 5.

1. This story was almost believable, but later, after extensive research, I learned Geronimo was never captured, he surrendered, and it wasn't in Eastern Arizona, it was in Skeleton Canyon, in the southern part, where on that exact date Geronimo was talking with General Miles concerning his surrender.
   Mr. Dan Thrapp, author-historian, disputes this story in his book, "*Al Sieber, Chief of Scouts*." Mr. Thrapp also stated in a letter to me, "Geronimo was never captured, never stood trial for anything, and never had a fight with cowboys in Battle Creek Canyon or anywhere else. This is just one of the yarns spread for the benefit of the tenderfoot."

Chapter 6.

1. According to Will C. Barnes, in his manuscript, "The Pleasant Valley War of 1887,"—"What little written history there is on the subject (the Tewksbury-Graham Feud) is mostly a mass of conjecture. . .little. . .will stand close investigation." Therefore, no attempt will be made here to offer a definitive version of the feud, but rather, to offer incidences of same in the lives of Charlie and his brother, John V. Meadows.

Chapter 7.

1. To avenge the death of a kinsman was for long more than a right, it was a religious duty. William A. Robeson, *Civilization and the Growth of Law*.
2. Old timer, Louie Pyle, told the story in 1968 of Zach Booth, and one of the younger Meadows boys, believed to be Jake. Louie thought the boys might have been drunk. Zach carried somewhat of a wild reputation and was a "hard man when crossed." He held an old dog between his legs and ordered Jake to shoot the dog. Jake shot the dog alright, the bullet first going through Zach's hand. Louie, after all those years, still remembered seeing a big rock on the west side of the Verde near Sidella, with the name "Meadows" carved into it.
3. There is a similarity between this contest and a previous one between Charlie and Tom Horn. I have found that old newspapers often garbled their reportage, and it makes one wonder. However, the times taken were similar, but the former contest made no mention of lady riders, horse racing, etc., and one event took place in Phoenix, while the other was held in Payson—several months apart.

Chapter 9.

1. The Apache Kid remained at large until May of 1895, and his reign of terror ended after a cowboy's Winchester found its mark. But that was after the Kid had killed Buck Taylor, a top hand of that period, who had been a member of another posse.
2. A series of misfortunes gave Cripple Creek its name. A valued calf belonging to the original settler by the name of Levi Welty, stepped into a prairie dog hole and broke its leg. Then Levi Welty, while chopping wood, cut his foot so badly he was laid up for months. His son, George, was fixing the ruined roof when he fell and injured his back. Then a horse reared and fell on a hired hand. Then, Levi Welty while dismounting his horse, accidentally discharged his revolver which permanently paralyzed the second finger of his hand.
   Two big fires in less than a week in April of 1896, burned most of Cripple Creek's business district and left 5,000 people homeless.

Chapter 14.

1. Arnica, an herb from Aster family used as an anti-irritant and tincture, similar in use and, most importantly, color to that of iodine.
2. This was the height of the bicycle craze. Although the development of the bicycle—of many odd sorts—began in 1816, the first rideable bicycle was not invented until 1842. With the coming of the automobile around 1895, cycling as a utility began to die out, only to continue as a popular sport. The cycle industry boomed; cycle clubs flourished, with bicycles equipped with roller drive and pneumatic wheels.

Chapter 17.

1. The artist's caption reads, "Ormas," however the correct spelling is "Or'mazd," "Or'muzd," or "Auramazda" who is the principal God of the Persion religion Zoarastrianism. The religion teaches that Or'mazd, principle of good, lord of light and goodness, the supreme deity, creator of the world, and guardian of mankind, was ceaselessly against Ahriman who represented evil, darkness and savagery.
   "Ind" is used here as a poetical term meaning Charlie outshone all the wealth of "India," or the "Indies."
2. There are no records available indicating when Yuma became a village, but in 1849 the U.S. Government established on Indian Hill a military post known as Fort Yuma. By 1875, Arizona was a rough territory and the Territorial Legislature voted $25,000 to build a territorial prison in Yuma. First the town was called Colorado City, then became Arizona City, and finally Yuma.

The following places were helpful in locating material and information:

Alaska:

Alaska State Library, Juneau; and the University of Alaska, Fairbanks.

Arizona:

Yuma City-County Library; Arizona State Historical Society; Yuma County Historical Society; Yuma Territorial Prison Museum; State ofArizona Department of Library, Archives and Public Records; Sharlot Hall Museum, Prescott; The Recorder of Yavapai County, Prescott; Century House Museum, Yuma; Northern Arizona University, Flagstaff; Pima Regional Library Service; Arizona State University, Tempe; University of Arizona, Tucson; City of Phoenix Parks, Recreation and Library Department-Public Library; Clerk of Superior Court, Yuma; and the Museum of Northern Arizona.

Australia-New Zealand:

Victoria College, Burwood Campus, Victoria, Australia; University of Sydney Library; Riverina College of Advanced Education, Wagga Wagga, New South Wales, Australia; The Alexander Turnbull Library, Wellington, New Zealand; Department of Local Government, State Library Division, Adelaide, Australia; John Oxley Library, Brisbane, Queensland; Victorian Arts Center Trust, Melbourne, Australia; Canterbury Public Library, Christchurch, New Zealand; State Library of New South Wales, Mitchell Library, Sydney, Australia; Sydney Opera House Trust; National Library of Australia, Canberra; State Library of Victoria, Melbourne, Australia; The National Library of New Zealand; Auckland Public Library, New Zealand; The National Trust of Australia, New South Wales; Mitchell Library, Sydney; State Library Division, University of Queensland; Royal Australian Historical Society; General Assembly Library, Wellington, New Zealand.

California:

University of California, Berkeley; University of California, Irvine; Tulare Public Library; Tulare County Historical Society; Tulare County Free Library System; California Historical Society, San Francisco; Los Angeles Public Library; Southern California Answering Service, Los Angeles; Metropolitan Cooperative Library System, Pasadena; Granada Hills Library; California State Library, Sacramento; El Centro Public Library; San Francisco Public Library; The Fresno Bee, Fresno; and the Huntington Library, San Marino.

Canada and The Yukon:

Public Archives of Canada, Ottawa; Metropolitan Toronto Library Board, Toronto; Parks Canada; Dawson City Museum, Yukon; Government of Yukon, Whitehorse; Yukon Visitor's Association; Yukon Archives, Whitehorse; Klondike Visitor's Association.

Colorado:

Colorado Historical Society, Denver; University of Colorado, Boulder; Denver Public Library; State of Colorado Division of Archives and Public Records.

Court Records:

County Clerk, Santa Cruz, California; Administration Office of the Courts, San Francisco; Clerk of the District Court, Colorado Springs, Colorado, Yuma District Court, and the Supreme Court of the Northwest Territories.

England:

Richmond College, Surrey, England; American International College of London, Surrey, England.

Texas:

Texas State Library, Austin; Amon Carter Museum, Fort Worth.

Washington:

University of Washington, Northwest Collections, Suzallo Library; Shorey Book Store, Seattle; Seattle Public Library.

Miscellaneous:

The Free Library of Philadelphia; Newberry Library, Chicago; Buffalo Bill Museum, Cody, Wyoming; Circus World Museum, Baraboo, Wisconsin; Will Rogers Memorial, Claremore, Oklahoma; The New York Public Library; Chicago Public Library; Illinois State Library, Special Collections; Memphis State University Library, Memphis, Tennessee; U.S.Postal Service, Bend, Oregon; Office of the Local Civil Registrar, Bulacan, Philippines; Ringling Museum of the Circus, Sarasota, Florida; Harvard Theatre Collection, Memphis State University; Flint Public Library, Michigan.

NEWSPAPER SOURCES

ALASKA WEEKLY	July 24, 1931; May 15, 1931; February 5, 1932; December 16, 1932
APACHE REVIEW	August 30, 1884; December 12, 1888; April 24, 1889
ARIZONA CHAMPION	August 30, 1884, September 13, 1884; October 27, December 1, 1888; April 27, 1889
ARIZONA DAILY GAZETTE	December 23, 1892; January 1, 13, 1893; February 14, 18, 1893; March 14, 24, 26, December 14, December 28, 1893; October 20, 27, 1894; January 5, 6, 17, 1895; September 5, 1923; July 3, 1962
ARIZONA ENTERPRISE	April 4, 1891; December 9, 1892
ARIZONA REPUBLIC	January 5-17, May 24, August 12, October 30, November 9, December 16, 19, 1890; January 9, April 8, 1891; July 19, August 3, September 2, 9, October 28, 1892; March 26, 29, September 12, 1893; April 15, May 4-5, September 9, October 27, 1893; June 6, July 24, August 1517, October 2, 13, 24, 26, 27, November 13, 1894; January 5-6, 1895; April 13, 1921; April 13, October 11, 1927; July 3, 1962; May 4, 19, 20, 1964;
ARIZONA SENTINEL	September 11, 1902; March, 1903; October, 1907; March, 1912; August, 1913; July, 1915; January, 1931
ARIZONA SILVER BELT	March 19, October 15, 1887; July 4, August 14, 25, 1888; March 30, 1889; November 8, 14, 15, 1890; June 18, April 9, August 6, 13, 20, September 10, October 8, 1892; January 7, April 1, December 27, 1893; October 27, 1894; January 6, 1895; January 11, February 8, May 7, 21, September 24, 1896; September 27, 1897; January 30, September, 1902; March, 1903; March, 1912; January, 1931, July 8, 15, 22, 1982
AUCKLAND NEWS, N.Z.	October 1, 25, 1890
BRISBANE COURIER, Aust.	February 13, 16, 19, 1891
CALIFORNIAN	June 10, 1893; October 19, 1894
CHARTERS TOWERS TIMES,Aust.	April 16, 17, 1891
CHRISTCHURCH PRESS, N.Z.	October 14, 21-22, 1890
CRIPPLE CREEK TIMES	August 24, 1895
COCONINO WEEKLY SUN	December 15, 1892
COLORADO SPRINGS GAZETTE	August 6, 18, 23-29, September 4, 1895
COOKTOWN INDEPENDENT, Aust.	May 13, 1891
COURIER	May 15, 1964
DAILY NEWS	August 25, 1895, July 28, 1929, November 18, 1933; May 11, 1936; January 10, 1942;
DAILY STAR	August 1, 1882, November 25, 1888, May 26, 1894, June 22, November 27, 1894
DAWSON NEWS	September 23, 26, October 13, 18, November, 7, 14, 28, 29, 30, December 4, 1899; August, 15, 1931

EL CENTRO PROGRESS	July 14, 16, 18, 1915
EPITAPH	August 27, 1887
EVENING POST, Aust.	October 8-20, 1890
GRAHAM COUNTY BULLETIN	October 19, 1894
GRAPHIC	April 11, 1908
HOOFS AND HORNS	April, 1888
IMPERIAL VALLEY PRESS	July 15, 1915
KLONDIKE NEWS	April, 1898
KLONDIKE NUGGET	September 3, 1898; January 4, 14, June 21, 28, July 22, August 30, September 23, 27, December 9, December 30, 1899; January 17, 21, February 4, March 8, 1900; August 17, September 27, October 16, 17, 19, 1901; February 13, August 29, December 11, 1902
LOS ANGELES EXAMINER	April 1897; April 18-24, 1908, February 18, 1936; July 24, 1962
LOS ANGELES HERALD	May, 1893; August 31, 1902; July, 1962; July 24, 1964
LOS ANGELES TIMES	September 10, 1892; May 24, 28, 1893; April 12, May 24, 1894; April 18, 19, 24, 1897; July 23, August 31, 1902; April 9, 1905; April 18-24, 1908; May 16, 1915
MAITLAND MERCURY, Aust.	January 22, 1891
MANAWATU HERALD, Aust.	September 15, 23, 29, October 9, 10, 11, 14, 1890
MARYBOROUGH CHRONICLE, Aust.	March 21, 1891
MOGOLLON ADVISER,	August 15, 1984
NATIONAL POLICE GAZETTE, NY	October 20, 1888; August 30, 1890; December 10, 1892
NEWSCASTLE CHRONICLE, Aust.	January 7, 11, 12, 14, 16, 19, 22, 1891
NEW YORK TIMES	September 3, 1966
OAKLAND TRIBUNE	September 7, 1930
OLYMPIAN	April, 1894
PHOENIX GAZETTE	July 18, 1882; July 2, October 1, February 6, 1884; August 21, 1890; January 1, March 14, 1893; January, July, 1894; August, 1896; January, 1897, September 5, 1923; July 3, March 29, 1962
PHOENIX HERALD	July 10-17, 19, 1882; December 10, 15, 1887; July, 1897; April, 1888
PRESCOTT JOURNAL MINER	December 12, 1888; July, 1897
PRESCOTT MORNING COURIER	August 5, 1882; July 31, 1890
POST PRESS	December 11, 1902
PUEBLO PRESS	October 24, 1895
QUEENSLAND TELEGRAPH, Aust.	March-April, 1891
ROCKY MOUNTAIN NEWS	August 17, 24, 25, 26, September 30, 1895; July 19, 1896; October 3, 1901
ROCKHAMPTON NEWS, Aust.	April, 1891
ST. JOHN'S HERALD	January 10, October 31, 1889
SALT LAKE CITY TRIBUNE	July 5, 1896
SAN DIEGO UNION	September 26, 1954, June 12, 1957
SAN FRANCISCO BULLETIN	November 25, 1902
SAN FRANCISCO CHRONICLE	February 6, March 14, 1893; May 20, 24, 28, June 18, 24, 26, 27, 1894; October, 17, 20, 1902; October,

	1905; April, 1908
SAN FRANCISCO EXAMINER	January, May, June, 1893; May 27, 29, 30, June 15, 1894; May 11, 1898, August 17, 1902; April, 1908
SAN JOSE DAILY MERCURY	April 30, May 20, 24, 25, 26, 1894
SANTA CRUZ SENTINEL	June 15, July 11, 19, 20, 26, 29, 31, 1894; December 3, 1897; April 19, 24, May 11, 1898
SATURDAY REVIEW	October, 1894
SEATTLE POST INTELLIGENCER	December 7, 1902
SOUTHLAND TIMES, Aust.	December 6, 1890
SPOKESMAN REVIEW	January 13, 1897
STRAITS INDEPENDANT AND PENANG CHRONICLE	September, 1891
SUN	January 27, 1966
TELEGRAM	July 3, 1962
TRAVEL NEWS	April 1962; May 1962; June 27, 1962
TUCSON DAILY STAR	July 20, August 1, 1882; April 25, October 27, November 25, December, 1888; April 25, 1893; May 26, June 22, November 27, 1894;
TULARE COUNTY TIMES	July 28, 1882; March 26, 1891
VALLEY HORNET	November 3, 1906; September 11, 1916
VISALIA DAILY DELTA	June 10, 11, 12, 1893; January 13, 1961
VISALIA TIMES DELTA	April 25, 1874; August 16, 1912; August 19, 1930; June 1931; January 13, May 31, 1951; October 31, 1952, June 25, 1959
VISALIAN	April, 1891
WAR CRY	September 22, 1894
YUKON STAR	July 18, 1980
YUMA ARIZONA SENTINEL	September 17, 1902; March 25, 1903; February 20, April 17, June 12, June 19, August 14, 1907; April 22, August 5, October 10, 1908; August 5, 1909; June 30, October 13, 1910; July 21, 1911; March 14, 1912; August 14, 1913; July 15, August 12, October 7, 1915; September 12, 1916; January 13, June 22, December 13-14, 1931
YUMA DAILY SUN	July 5, 14, 1916; March 29, 1944; January 27, October 27, 1966
YUMA MORNING SUN	August 9, 1896; April 21, 1898; October 10, 1908; March 14, 1911; January 22, July 1, 5, 6, 14, 22, September 4, 12, 13, 14, 15, 16, 20, October, 1916; April 20, 1917; November 26, 1919; September 4, 1923; October 9, 1927; September 14, 1928; June 18, 1931; October 27, 1954; December 11, 13, 1932; October 27, 1954; January 27, 1966

PUBLISHED SOURCES

ALASKA LIFE — *Little Known Facts About the Life and Death of Skagway's Soapy Smith.* April, 1942
Facts and Fiction in Alaska History. April, 1942

ALASKA SPORTSMAN — *From Ketchikan to Barrow.* July, 1961
The Real Soapy Smith, November ,1947

ADAMS, RAMON F. — *Western Words.* (Dictionary) University of Oklahoma, Press, Norman, 1968

ADNEY, EDWIN TAPPAN — *The Klondike Stampede of 1897-1898* . New York, New York, 1900

ALDERSON, NOVA. — *Frontier Literature: A Fast Draw on Navajo Nick, and Tombstone Tom, and Arizona Charlie.* Arizoniana, Summer, 1961

ARIZONA BRAND BOOK — 1898, 1916, 1920

ARIZONA HISTORICAL REVIEW — *Tom Horn, Chief of Scouts.* January, 1931
The Apache's Last Stand. April, 1929

ARIZONIANA — Summer, 1961

ARMSTRONG Major Newel, A.D. — *Yukon Yesterdays.* John Long Ltd., London, 1936

ATWOOD, FRED N. — *Dawson Night Life Wasn't So Tough.* Alaska Life, December, 1941

BARNES, WILL C. — *The Pleasant Valley War of 1887,* Arizona Historical Society Review, October 1931, January 1932

BEACH, REX — *Personal Exposures.* Harper, 1940

BEER, THOMAS — *The Mauve Decade.* Knopf, 1926

BERG, HELEN — *The Doll of Dawson.* Alaska Sportsman, February 1944

BERTON, PIERRE — *Stampede For Gold,* N. D.
Klondike. (Revised) McClelland and Stewart, Canada, 1978

BLAISDELL, LOWELL L. — *The Desert Revolution, Baja, California, 1911.* University of Wisconsin Press, 1962

BONABRAKE, PERCY — *Arizona Charlie (Charles Meadows).* Los Angeles Corral, September, 1956

BOOTH, MICHAEL R. — *Gold Rush Theatres in the Klondike.* The Beaver, Spring, 1962

BOSTOCK, E. H. — *Menageries, Circuses and Theatres.* Arno, 1927

BOURKE, JOHN — *On the Border With Crook.* Rio Grande Press, 1962

BRANDA, ELDON STEPHEN — *Handbook of Texas.* VII, Texas State Historical Society, Austin, Texas, 1976

BRANDA, WM. and MILLARDE — *The Hell Hole: Arizona Territorial Prison, 1875-1909*

BROWNE, J. ROSS — *Adventures in the Apache Country.* University of Arizona Press, Tucson, Arizona, 1974

BURKE, JOHN — *Buffalo Bill -The Noblest Whiteskin.* G. P. Putnam Sons, New York, N. D.

BURNS, WALTER NOBLE — *Tombstone,* Doubleday, Garden City, New York, 1927

BUSH, SAM STONE — *The Rush To The Klondike Goldfields,* Review of Reviews. August 1897, March, 1898

CHINDALL, GEORGE L. — *History of the Circus.* Caxton Printers Ltd., Caldwell, Idaho, 1959

COLLEY, CHARLES C. — *Documents of Southwestern History.* Arizona Historical Society, N. D.

COLLIER, SANDRA — *The Palace Grand.* Alaska Magazine, March, 1978

COLORADO MAGAZINE — *Nate Salsbury and the Wild West Show.* July, 1955
Wild West at Windsor, July, 1955
Colorado Festivals, July, 1953

CORY, HARRY THOMAS — *Imperial Valley and the Salton Sink.* S. F. Newbegin, 1915

CRAMPTON, C. GREGORY — *Land of Living Rock.* Alfred A. Knopf, New York, 1922

CROFT-COOK, RUPERT — *Circus - A World History.* McMillan, 1913

CROWE, ROSALIE and BRICKERHOFF, SIDNEY — *Early Yuma.* Northland Press, Flagstaff,Arizona Yuma Historical Society, 1976

DAVIS, MARY LEE — *Sourdough Gold: The Log of a Yukon Adventure.* W.A. Wilde Co., Boston, 1949

DAY, DONALD — *The Autobiography of Will Rogers.* Selected and Edited by Donald Day. Houghten Mifflin Co., 1949

DeGARZA, TED and SMITH, WM. NEIL — *The Seri Indians, A Primitive People of Tiburon Island In The Gulf of California.* Northland Press, Flagstaff, AZ, 1970

DESERT MAGAZINE — *The Seris.* August, 1981

DOBYNS, HENRY F. — *Apache People,* 1971

DUNN, J. P. — *Massacres of the Mountains.* New York, 1886

EARP, JOSEPHINE — *I Married Wyatt Earp.* University of Arizona Press, Tucson, AZ 1976

EWING — *Six Faces Of Mexico.* University Of Arizona Press, Tucson, Arizona, N. D.

FARNSWORTH, HARRIET — *Remnants of the Old West.* Naylor Co., 1965
Cowboys of Old Yavapai. Frontier Times, July, 1967

FISHER, JONATHON — *A Desert Casts Its Spell.* International Wildlife, December, 1980

FORBES, B. C. — *Men Who Are Making The West,* N. D.

FORREST, EARLE — *Arizona's Dark and Bloody Ground. Caxton Printers, Idaho, 1936*

FOSTER, HARRIS — *The Look of the Old West.* Viking Press, 1955

FREEMAN, LEWIS R. — *Down the Grand Canyon by Mule Team and Scow.* William Heineman Ltd., London, 1924

FRONTIER TIMES — *Swift Justice On Chilkoot Pass.* July 1967

FULLER, O.T. — *Bright Lights Under Midnight Dome . Dawson City, July 1, 1899*

GARD, WAYNE — *Frontier Justice,* N..D.

GARLAND, HAMLIN — *Trail of the Gold Seekers.* MacMillan, New York, 1899.

GARRETT, R. M. and ROGATNICK, R. M. — *The Palace Grand.* Parks Canada Research Division, April 11, 1962

GIBBS, RAFE — *Bullfight U.S.A.* Esquire Magazine, 1947.

GREAVES, GEOFF — *The Circus Comes to Town. Nostalgia of Australian Big Tops.* A. H. and A. W. Reed

Pty. Ltd., Sydney, Australia, N. D.

GREENLEAF, J. CAMERON — *Captain Jack Crawford, The Poet Scout.* Arizoniana, Summer 1961

GRIFFEN, CHARLES ELDRIGE — *Four Years in Europe with Buffalo Bill.* 1908

HALLIGAN'S ILLUSTRATED WORLD'S FAIR — *Buffalo Bill's Wild West at the Columbian Exposition*, 1893

HAMILTON, WALTER R. — *The Yukon Story.* Vancouver, 1964

HAMLIN, C. W. — *Old Times in the Yukon.* Wetzel, 1928

HAYES, JESS — *Boots and Bullets.* University of Arizona Press. Tucson, AZ 1970

Sheriff Thompson's Day. 1968

HAYNE and TAYLOR — *The Pioneers of the Klondike.* S. Low Marston, 1897.

HEMINGWAY, BILL — *Soapy Smith, King of the Con Men.* Empire Magazine, July 2, 1970

HERBERT, J. — *The Palace Grand Theatre.* National Historic Sites Division, Canada, N. D.

HERNER, CHARLES — *Arizona Roughriders.* University of Arizona Press, Arizona Board of Regents, Tucson, 1970

HINTON AND GODSELL — *The Yukon,* N. D.

HITCHCOCK, MARY E. — *Two Women in the Klondike.* C.P. Putnam and Sons. New York, 1899

HOFFMAN, EDNA EVANS — *Written With Fire.* Holt, Rhinehart and Winston, 1962

HOPGOOD, CEDRIC — *Circus at Worlds End.* Angus and Robertson, Sydney, Australia 1947

HORN, TOM — *The Life of Tom Horn, A Vindication* (Reprint.) Crown Publishers, New York, 1977

HUGHES, HERBERT — *Picacho, Placers & Pistols.* Southwest Printers, 1973

HUNT, FRASER — *Cap Mossman, Last of the Great Cowmen.* Hastings, New York, 1951

INTERNATIONAL WILDLIFE — *A Desert Casts Its Spell.* November-December, 1980

JARVIS, W. H. P. — *The Great Goldrush - A Tale of the Klondike.* MacMillan, 1913

JENNINGS, WALTER WILSON — *A Dozen Captains of Industry.* Vantage Press, New York, N. D.

JOHNSTON, PHILIP — Dismal Days in Pleasant Valley. West Ways, August, 1953

KELLOGG, VIRGIL R. — *Matadors Walked The Streets Of Gillett.* Frontier Times, April-May, 1972

KIBBEY, LEO P. — *California, the Civil War and the Indian Problem.* Journal of the West, 1981

KING, FRANK M. — *Wrangling the Past.* Trails End Publishing, Pasadena, California, 1946

Pioneer Western Empire Builders. Trails End Publishers, 1946

KNEASS, AMELIA — *The Flogging at Sheep Camp.* Alaskan Sportsman, October, 1946

KNOX, BOB and WILMA — *Follow the Klondike Gold Trail.* Better Camping. March, 1966

KOREBER, A. L. — *Seri.* Published by Southwest Museum, 1931

LAMAR, HOWARD R. — *The Reader's Encyclopedia of the American West.* Thomas Crowell Co., New York., 1934

LEADERBRAND, ROSS — *Where They Took Their Pleasure*. Westways, June 1965

LEONARD, ELIZABETH JANE and CODY, JULIA — *Buffalo Bill - King of the Old West*. New York

LEWIS, OSCAR — *War In The West. 1861-1865. Chapter 6, Press & Pulpit*. Doubleday & Co., New York, 1961

LOCKWOOD, FRANCIS CUMMINS — *Pioneer Days in Arizona*. McMillan Co.,New York, 1932
Arizona Characters. Los Angeles, 1928

LOGAN, HERSCHEL C. — *Buckskin and Satin*. The Stackpole Co., Harrisburg, Pennsylvania, 1954

LONDON, JACK — *Tales of Adventure*. Edited by Irving Shephard. Doubleday & Company., Inc. Garden City, New York, 1956
The Unabridged Jack London. Running Press, Philadelphia, Pennsylvania, 1981
Burning Daylight. MacMillan & Company, New York, 1945
Daughter of the Snows. Archer House, Inc., New York, Edited by J.O. Evans, 1963
The God of His Fathers. Arno, 1901

LOVE, FRANK — *From Brothel to Boomtown - Yuma's Naughty Past*. Little London Press. Colorado Springs, Colorado, 1981

LUNG, EDWARD — *Glittering Fortunes and Empty Pokes*. Alaska Sportsman, February 1952

LYNCH, JEREMIAH — *Three Years in the Klondike*. Edward Arnold. London, 1904

McCALLUM, PAT — *Klondike Outpost*.. Westways Magazine, April, 1977

McLAUGHLIN, DENIS — *Wild and Wooly*. An Encyclopedia of the Old West, Doubleday & Co., Garden City, New York, 1975

MARTINSON, ELLA LUNG — *Trail to Northstar Gold*. Binfords and Mort. Portland, Oregon, 1969
Black Sand and Gold. Binfords and Mort., Portland, Oregon, 1978

MASON, JOHN — *Bullfight at Gillett*. Real West Magazine. January, 1961

MAZULLA, FRED M. and JO — *The First 100 Years Cripple Creek & Pike's Peak_Region*. A.B. Hirschfield Press, Denver, Colorado, 1956

MEADOR, VICTOR P. and BERNAL M. — *Our Meador Families in Colonial America*. Kansas City, Missouri, July 1983

MEADOWS, DON — *The Genesis of Arizona Charlie*. Westerner's Brand Book, Los Angeles Corral, Book 7, N. D.

MEDILL, ROBERT B. — *Klondike Diary*. Beattle Company, 1949

MENFREE, EUGENE, and DODGE, FRED A. — *History of Tulare & Kings Counties, California*. Historic Record. Los Angeles, 1913

METTLER, J. P. — *The Last Renegade*. Tonto Trails Magazine. Winter, 1971

MILES, GENERAL NELSON. A. — *Personal Recollections and Observations*. The Werner Co., New York, 1897.

	Serving the Republic. Harper and Brothers, New York, 1911.
MITCHELL, ANNIE	*King of the Tulares*. Visalia, California, 1941
	Visalia, Her First Fifty Years. Visalia, California
MUNN, HENRY T.	*Prairie Trails and Arctic Byways*. Hurst & Blackett Ltd., London, 1932
MURDOCH, JOHN R.	*Arizona Characters in Silhouette*. Tempe, Arizona, 1939
MURPHY, IRA	*A Brief History of Payson*. Payson, Arizona, 1983
NATIONAL GEOGRAPHIC	*Seri*. October 1919, November 1922
NEWSWEEK	*The Americas*. April 16, 1932
NOBLE, MARGUERITE	*Filaree*. Random House, New York, 1979
NORTH, DICK	*Swift Justice on Chilkoot Pass*.. Frontier Times, June-July, 1967
NORTH MAGAZINE	Special Klondike Issue. May-June, 1962
O'CONNER, RICHARD	*High Jinks On The Klondike*. New York, 1954
	Wild Bill Hickok. Doubleday & Co., Garden City, New York, N. D.
OGILVIE, WILLIAM	*Early Days On The Yukon*.. John Layne Co. Ottawa, Canada, 1913.
PHILLIPS, R. A. J.	*The Klondike Legend*. Canadian Geographical Journal, March, 1962
PORTER, SAMUEL THOMAS	*Silver Rush at Mineral King, CA. 1873-1882*. (2nd edition)
RAND & MCNALLEY & CO.'S	*A Week At The Fair*., World Columbian-Exposition Chicago, 1893
RETALLACK, ATHOL	*Paris of the North*. Unknown Source, N. D.
RIM COUNTRY HISTORY	Northern Gila County Historical Society, Payson, Arizona, N. D.
RITCHIE, WARD	*The Dohenys of Los Angeles*. 1974
ROBERTSON, WM. MORRIS	*Yukon Memories*. Toronto, 1930
ROBINSON, GIL	*Old Wagon Show Days*. Brockwell, Cincinnati. 1925
ROCKWELL, KATE	*I Was Queen of the Klondike*. Alaska Sportsman, August, 1944
ROGERS, WILL	*The Autobiography of Will Rogers*. Selected and Edited by Donald Day, Houghton Mifflin Co., Boston, 1949
RUSSELL, BANKSON	*The Klondike Nugget*. Caxton Ltd., 1935
RUSSELL, DON	*Lives and Legends of Buffalo Bill*. University of Oklahoma Press, 1960
	The Wild West, a History of the Wild West Shows. Ammon Carter Museum of Western Art, Fort Worth, Texas, 1970
RYAN, GERALD	*Little Known Facts About the Life and Death of Soapy Smith*. Alaska Life, April, 1942
ST. LEON, MARK	(extract from) *The Circus in Australia*.. 1841-Mahroonga, Aust., 1981
SANDOVAL, ROBERT	*"Once There was a Bullfight"*. Empire Magazine. Aug. 18, 1974
SELL, HB and WEYBRIGHT, V.	*Buffalo Bill and the Wild West*
SIMPICH, FREDERICK	*"A Mexican Land of Canaan."* National Geographic, October, 1919

SPRAGUE, MARSHAL — *Money Mountain, Chapter - A Lot of Bull.* Little Brown & Co., Boston, 1953

SUNSET TRAVEL GUIDE — *Kino Bay, Land of the Seri Indians.* Lane Publishers, Menlo Park, California, N. D.

TEBBEL, JOHN and JAMISON, KEITH — *The American Indian Wars.* Harper Bros., New York, 1960

THRAPP, DAN L. — *"War on Cibicue."* True West Magazine. April, 1964

Al Seiber, Chief of Scouts. University of Oklahoma Press, 1964

The Conquest of Apacheria. University of Oklahoma Press, 1967

TIME LIFE BOOKS — *The Old West.* N. D.

Alaska. Alexandria, Virginia, N. D.

TOLLEMACHE, STRATFORD — *Reminiscences of the Yukon.* E. Arnold, 1912

TOUT, OTIS B. — *The First Thirty Years in Imperial Valley. 1901-1931*

TRAVEL NEWS — *Canadian Government Travel Bureau*, Ottowa, April, 1962

TRIMBLE, MARSHALL — *Arizona Adventure.* Golden West Publishers. Phoenix, Arizona, 1982

TYHERLEIGH, MIKE — *Foxey Casts Sails for Dawson.* Canadian Travel News, Ottawa, 1962.

UNRUH, JOHN D. J. — *The Plains Across.* University of Illinois Press, 1979

WALSH, RICHARD J. and SALISBURY, MILTON — *The Making of Buffalo Bill.* A. L. Burt Co., New York, N. D.

WAGNER, JAY C. — *Arizona Territory, 1863-1912.* University of Arizona Press, Tucson, 1970

WALKER, FRANKLIN — *Jack London in the Klondike.* The Bodely Head Ltd. Toronto, 1966

WALTERS — *Tombstone Yesterday,* N. D.

WELLMAN, PAUL I. — *Indian Wars of the West,* N. D.

WESTERMEIER, CLIFFORD P. — *Trailing the Cowboy.* Caxton Printers. Caldwell, Idaho, 1955

"Cowboy Sports and the Humane Society." *Colorado Magazine.* Denver, Colorado, October, 1949

WETMORE, HELEN CODY — *Buffalo Bill, Last of the Great Scouts.* University of Nebraska Press, April, 1965

WESTOVER, WILLIAM — *Yuma Footprints.* Arizona Pioneer's Historical Society, Tucson, 1966

WICKERSHAM, JAMES — *Old Yukon Tales, Trails, and Trials.* Washington Law Book Company, Washington, 1938

WILLSON, ROSCOE G. — "As a Robber the King was a Dud." *Arizona Days and Ways*, April 7, 1963

WINN, BESS — "Alaska's First Lady of the Stage." *Alaska Life,* Oct, 1942

WINSLOW, KATHRYN — *Big Pan Out.* New York, 1951

WIRTH, GEORGE — *Round the World with a Circus.* Melbourne, Australia, N. D.

WIRTH, PHILIP — *The Life of Philip Wirth.* Troedel and Cooper,

Melbourne, Aust., 1934

WOODBURY, DAVID O. — *The Colorado Conquest,* N. D.

WOODY, CLARA T. and MILTON SCHWARTZ — *Globe, Arizona..* Tucson, Arizona Historical Society, 1977

WYLEY, RUFUS K. — *Arizona, The History of a Frontier State.* Hobson and Herr, Phoenix, Arizona, 1950

YOST, NELLIE SNYDER — *Buffalo Bill, His Family, Friends, Fame, Failures, and Fortunes.* Swallow Press, Chicago, N. D.

YOUNG, SAMUEL HALL — *Klondike Clan.* Fleming H. Revel Co., New York, 1916

CORRESPONDENCE

Beach, Margaret Meadows	Letter to her brother, Charles Meadows, regarding Indian attack of 1882. Century House Museum, Yuma, Arizona, January 23, 1932
	Letter to her niece, Sadie Connelly, regarding Charlie's death. December 18,1932. Ron Loving Collection (original)
Beach, Thomas Sr.	Letter to Charles Meadows, regarding water project. October 19, 1916 (original)
Butler, Frank	Husband of Annie Oakley, and member of Buffalo Bill's Company. Letter to Charles Meadows, regarding the show. April, 1893
Cody, Col. Wm. F.	Letter to Charles Meadows, October 10, 1910, from Watsonville, California.
	Letter to Charles Meadows from San Francisco, April 23, 1914
	Letter to Charlie's Daughter, Marion Meadows, from Seattle, Washington, May 24, 1914
Dewitt, S. W.	U. S. Government Attorney. Letter to Honorable Charles W. Russell, regarding Indian Depredations Claim. June 10, 1897
Forrest, Earle	Author of "Arizona's Dark and Bloody Ground." Letter to Johnny Meadows, regarding papers belonging to John V. Meadows, Coronor and Justice of the Peace during the Pleasant Valley War, February 28, 1935
	Letters to Ida Meadows Gregory, regarding her uncle, Charles Meadows. September 28, October 28, 1965
Gregory, Ida Meadows	Letters between her and the Arizona Historical Society, throughout 1965
	Letters to Earle Forest, October 24, September 20, 1965
Grey, Zane	Western fiction writer. Letter to Charles Meadows from Altadena, California about Tiburon and Gulf of California. February 25, 1921. Milam Collection
Gulf Publishing Company	(The Oil News). Letter to Charles Meadows' nephew, Johnnie Meadows. About possible information in Charlie's scrapbook referring to uranium ores on Tiburon. March 25, 1947

Herbert, J. D.	Chief, Department of Northern Affairs and National Resources. Ottowa, Canada. Letters to Don Meadows regarding restoration of the Palace Grand Theatre, N. D.
Kellner, E. F., Jr.	Letter to Marion Meadows about friendship of his father and Charlie Meadows, July 6, 1942
Lyon, W. H.	Letter to Charles Meadows from Washington, D.C. about the Reclamation Act and mineral partnerships. April 14, 1911
Meadows, Charles	Letter to sister, Rhoda, July 17, 1882, about attack on the Meadows homestead by Apaches, and death of their father
	Letter to the Arizona State Historian, Effie Keen, *Circa* 1931
	Letter to Judge DeWitt regarding Indian Depredations Claim. March 16, 1895. Written from Mexico City
	Letter to Judge DeWitt, regarding Indian Depredations Claim. Written from Hot Springs, Arkansas, November 30, 1895
	Letter to Arizona Pioneer's Association, regarding Geronimo statue. Yuma Morning Sun, October 9, 1927
	Letter to his first wife, Marion Mae, July 21, 1932
Meadows, Marion	Letter to her half-sister, Alice Weeks, October 3, 1939
Meadows, Mobley	Letter to Marion Meadows. December 23, 1913
Murphy, Leo K.	Letter about George Kilroy story, Yuma Historical Society, December 8, 1964
Ryan, Pat M. Jr.	Associate Professor of Drama, History and Criticism, University of Arizona, Tucson. Letter to Mr. J. D. Herbert, Department of Northern Affairs and National Resources, Ottowa, Canada, April, 1961
U. S. Department of Justice	Inter-department correspondence in search of Charlie. February 12, 1900. Depredations Claim, #9147

Vyskel, Luvena Buchanan — Letter to Mr. Edwin P. Fitzhugh, regarding construction of the Mobley Meadows statue, November 4, 1949

Wentworth, Judge John W. — Letter to Charles Meadows and Frank Prothero, August 3, 1887

Wright, Harold Bell — Letter to Tom Beach, August 20, 1919

GOVERNMENT PAPERS

General Services Administration, Washington, D.C. Indian Depredations claim #9147. Petition December 1892

Canadian House of Commons, Department of Northern Affairs and National Resources. March 22, 1962. Parks Canada Research Division. Debate concerning restoration of the Palace Grand Theatre.

COURT CASES

SUPREME COURT OF THE NORTHWEST TERRITORIES. Statement of Claim between Benjamin A. Seitz, Plaintiff, and Charles Meadows, and C. Wilkens, Defendants.1898

SUPREME COURT OF THE NORTHWEST TERRITORIES. Writ of Summons. John B. Wickery, Plaintiff, vs Charles Meadows, Virgil Moore, and W. C. Wilkens, Defendants. August 10, 1898

DISTRICT COURT OF THE STATE OF COLORADO. Complaint. J. H. Wolfe, Plaintiff, and C. D. Smith Drug Company of St. Joseph, Missouri and M. F. Bowers, Sheriff of El Paso County, Defendants. March 2, 1896

EL PASO COUNTY JUSTICE COURT. F. M. Jeffry, Plaintiff, vs. Charles Kinney, J. H. Wolfe and C. M. Cranston, Defendants. February, 1896

TERRITORY OF ARIZONA, COUNTY OF YUMA, vs. Charles Meadows. Affidavit May 1, 1905. Charge of Perjury in connection with personal property. District Court Case #163. Not Guilty, October 15, 1906

THE SUPERIOR COURT OF YUMA COUNTY, STATE OF ARIZONA vs. Charles Meadows. Felony - Libel. # 664. October 11, 1916

SANTA CRUZ TOWNSHIP. Santa Cruz County, State of California. Warrant #2316. The People of the State of California vs. Charles Meadows. Charge - Felonious Embezzlement - brought by Frank and Mamie Gebhardt and S. Shaki. August 2, 1894

INTERVIEWS

Beach, Ross	Grand Nephew of Charles Meadows. Laguna Nigel, California, 1981-1986
Coffeen, Lavena	Her Memories of Charles Meadows. Yuma, Arizona, 1982
Hazelton, Drusilla	Member of Early Arizona Pioneer Family. Tonapah, Arizona, 1984
Huling, Cecil	Sunshine Barber Shop. Yuma, Arizona, 1982
Johannson, Ernie	Early Yuma Settler, 1982
Lewis, Ray	Former Neighbor of Charles Meadows. Yuma, Arizona, 1982
Meadows, George	Charlie's Nephew. Yuma, Arizona, 1980-1986
Moorish, John	Former Rancher—Neighbor of Charlie's. Yuma, Arizona, 1986
Pennington, Florence	Niece of Mae Meadows. Yuma, Arizona, 1982

NOTES AND MANUSCRIPTS

Beach, Thomas, Jr.	Notes—Jean Beach King Collection *Circa* 1960
Croxen, Fred	*History of Grazing on Tonto*. Tonto Grazing Conference, 1926. Sharlot Hall Historical Society, Prescott, Arizona
Fitzhugh, Dr. Lee	Notes taken on interview with Louie Pyle, Pioneer, Payson, Arizona. July 26, 1968
Gregory, Ida Meadows	Notes taken from Mr. George Edwards, Yuma Pioneer and friend of Charles Meadows 1965
	Notes taken from Thomas Beach, Jr., regarding Charles Meadows, N. D.
	Notes taken from Mr. Henry Levy, Former Chief of Police, Yuma, Arizona, February, 1965
	Notes taken from Florence Pennington, Yuma, Arizona, 1965
Hazelton, Drusilla	Typescript. *Tonto Basin's Early Settlers*. Arizona Historical Society. Tucson, Arizona N. D.
	Typescript. *George P. Hazelton, Sr.* March 27, 1982
Horton, L. J.	Typescript. Sharlot Hall Historical Society. Prescott, Arizona, N. D.
Keiser, Wm. O.	Manuscript. *King of Arizona Mine*. 1898. Arizona Historical Society, Tucson, Arizona
Meadows, Charles	Manuscript. Century House Museum, Yuma, Arizona, N. D.
Ropp, Minnie Katie	Typescript. *Among the Early Pioneers of Visalia.*
Wills, Tom	Typescript. *Lives of Pioneers*. Jose de Castillo, Pima County, Arizona Historical Society, Tucson, Arizona, N. D.

MAPS

Harmston Circus	Route Maps, Courtesy Victoria College, Burwood Campus, Victoria, Australia

MISCELLANEOUS

Arizona Charlie's Summer Attractions. Program and Itinery, Source Unknown, N. D.

Buffalo Bill's Wild West and Congress of Rough Riders, Historical Sketches and Programme. Rand McNalley. World's Columbian Exposition. Chicago, Illinois, 1893

Charles Meadows Brand. October 10, 1883. Sharlot Hall Historical Society. Prescott, Arizona

Charles Meadows—Last Will and Testament. Dawson City, Yukon, July 4, 1901

Charles Meadows Membership Certificate in Arizona Pioneer's Association #733, dated April 14, 1926

Charles Meadows Scrapbook—Property of the Author, Jean Beach King

Charles Meadows Wild West Show—Checks and Envelopes

Charles Meadows—Journal of Notes of Australia, New Zealand, India, Burma, China, and Japan, N. D.

Countess of Meherenc of St. Pierre, St. Brienc, France. Correspondence to Mr. and Mrs. Charles Meadows, N. D.

Family Notes—Property of the Author, Jean Beach King

Gold ShipmentVoucher Dawson City to Whitehorse on ship, "Nora," White Pass R. R. to Skagway. October 21, 1901

Great Mexican Bull Fight Fiesta and Equestriennce Carnival Poster. Cripple Creek, Colo. August 1895

Log of Southeast Asia Tour. Century House Museum. Arizona Historical Society. November 7, 1891.

Meadows, Marion—Baptism Certificate, 1892 and Death Certificate, March 26, 1944

Palace Grand Theatre—Program for All-Star Sapho Company Performance, N. D.

Palace Grand Theatre—Program Opening Night, N. D.

Program of Charles Meadows Wild West Show, Fiesta Tribunes, Agricultural Park, Los Angeles, California, April, 1897

Tulare County Census, 1870

Valley Hornet, November 3, 1906; September 11, 1916. Yuma Territorial Museum, Arizona

Wirth Brothers Circus and Wild West Programme (Milam Collection.), N. D.

Yavapai County Recorder. Deed, George Ohman to John V. Meadows. Book 18, page 284, 1883.

Deed, from J. M. Clark to John V. Meadows. Book 18, page 286. Concerning Augusta and Atlantic Mining Claims. (Correspondence only.)

Arizona Charlie's Hotel and Casino *by Jani Mae Photographers, Las Vegas, Nevada*

INDEX

ISBN #